3D Graphics and Animation:

From Starting Up to Standing Out

Mark Giambruno

New Riders Publishing, Indianapolis, Indiana

3D Graphics and Animation:
From Starting Up to Standing Out

By Mark Giambruno

Published by:
New Riders Publishing
201 West 103rd Street
Indianapolis, IN 46290 USA

Printed in the United States of America   4 5 6 7 8 9 0

Library of Congress Cataloging-in-Publication Data

```
Giambruno, Mark, 1957-
    3D graphics and animation : from starting up to
standing out /Mark Giambruno.
        p.    cm.
    Includes index.
    ISBN 1-56205-698-0
    1. computer graphics.  2. Three-dimensional
    display systems. 3. computer animation.
    I. Title.
    T385.G5213  1997
    006.6'93—dc21
                                            96-46693
                                               CIP
```

Warning and Disclaimer

Publisher	Don Fowley
Publishing Director	David Dwyer
Marketing Manager	Mary Foote
Managing Editor	Carla Hall

Product Development Specialist
John Kane

Software Specialist
Steve Flatt

Senior Editor
Sarah Kearns

Project Director
Jennifer Eberhardt

Development Editor
Linda Laflamme

Project Editor
Howard Jones

Technical Editor
Simon Knights

Acquisitions Coordinator
Stacey Beheler

Administrative Coordinator
Karen Opal

Book & Cover Designer
Anne Jones

Cover Production
Aren Howell

Production Manager
Kelly Dobbs

Production Team Supervisors
Laurie Casey
Joe Millay

Graphics Image Specialists
Steve Adams
Sadie Crawford
Wil Cruz

Illustrations
Casey Price
Bryan Towes
Marvin VanTiem

Production Analysts
Jason Hand
Erich J. Richter

Production Team
Kim Cofer
Mary Hunt
William Huys Jr.
Daniela Raderstorf

Indexer
Chris Wilcox

About the Author

Mark Giambruno was born in 1957 in the small California foothills town of Placerville. He grew up in Sacramento, where he enjoyed annoying his teachers with epic space battles drawn (during class) in the margins of his schoolwork. In High School and college he pursued classes in art and electronics, but found the displayless computers of the time utterly boring.

In 1982, he used his younger brother's need for computer access at home as an excuse to buy his first microcomputer (an Atari 800) and has been heavily involved with computing ever since. He started his own computer graphics firm in 1990, and took on San Francisco-based Mondo Media as one of his main clients. When he was free to relocate, Mondo offered him a full-time position, and he became one of their lead artists and project directors. He conceptualized, managed, and created graphics for many of the company's projects, including those for such clients as Microsoft, Sierra Semiconductor, and Compaq.

After a few years of doing business-oriented multimedia, he went on to head up Mechadeus' first two CD-ROM games, Critical Path and The Daedalus Encounter (featuring Tia Carerre of *Wayne's World* fame). His responsibilities on Daedalus included design, co-writing the script, art direction, and editing. He also wrote *The Official Guide to The Daedalus Encounter* for BradyGAMES, which chronicles the project as well as provides hints and tips for completing the game.

Currently, he is an independent contractor providing 3D modeling, design, and animation services through his Binary Arts company. He is also a member of CyberDog Studios, a partnership of former Mechadeus employees that is currently working on the development of an online game. In addition, he is working on a sci-fi graphic novel concept and regularly contributes articles and reviews to InterActivity magazine.

Trademark Acknowledgments

All terms mentioned in this book that are known to be trademarks or service marks have been appropriately capitalized. New Riders Publishing cannot attest to the accuracy of this information. Use of a term in this book should not be regarded as affecting the validity of any trademark or service mark.

Dedication

For Chandler, Kelsey, Nicholas, and Marco.

Acknowledgments

I'd like to take this opportunity to thank everyone at New Riders Publishing who put forth their time and efforts right through the holiday season to see this book through to completion:

John Kane, the Acquisitions Editor and Trail Boss for the project, for originating the concept for this book, setting the schedules, negotiating the contracts, and putting the whole team together (not to mention managing much of the development by himself) while remaining supportive and upbeat throughout.

Simon Knights, Technical Editor and good friend, for providing the tower model, direction on the tutorials, and other suggestions based on his years of teaching 3D graphics, and for making sure I had my facts straight.

Linda Laflamme, Development Editor, for managing the book's overall development, and ensuring that all the necessary information was there and presented in an appropriate manner.

Howard Jones, Project Editor, for managing all the editing processes, wordsmithing my grammatical lapses, and ensuring consistency throughout the book.

Jennifer Eberhardt, Project Director, for catching and helping to correct some problems with my unique figure resolution and aspect ratio selections, as well as arranging for the processing of all figures for the book throughout the design and layout process.

Stacey Beheler, Acquisitions Coordinator, for handling document distribution and getting my all-important paychecks processed.

All the Designers, Artists, Specialists, Coordinators, Managers, Proofreaders, and Technicians who I never knew that brought their skills and experience to the development and production process.

In addition, I'd like to thank some other companies and individuals who helped to widen the scope of this project and make it go more smoothly:

Dominic Milano, Editor of *InterActivity* magazine, and Miller Freeman Publishing for allowing me to use excerpts from the 3D Tools and Animata articles.

Lea Anne Bantsari, Managing Editor of *InterActivity* magazine, for letting me take a hiatus from my Animata column to concentrate on this project.

Melisa Bell of Kinetix for providing me with copies of their excellent 3D Studio MAX and Character Studio products, which I used throughout the book for creating the tutorials and sample figures.

Mondo Media/Mechadeus for providing info for the interview portion of the book and allowing me to use images from their portfolio as examples of top-quality 3D work.

Kevin Clark and Mohave, along with Marco Patrito and the Virtual Views team (Fabio Patrito, Tullio Rolandi, Francesco Chirico, and Flavio Chirico) for providing images from the multimedia graphic novel Sinkha, including the cover image for this book.

Ruieta and Deanan Da Silva of Digital Illusion, for providing contact information and doing a 3D scan of yours truly for the book.

Stephanie Pellegrine and my brother Jim Giambruno, for helping out with research and data entry for the appendices.

All the other companies and individual contributors that sent in images, comments, and suggestions for the book, too numerous to mention here (they are grouped and credited in Appendix E).

Laura Hainke and Drew Vinciguerra, CyberDog Studios partners and friends, who continued the development and marketing of our online gaming concept, CLASH!, while I was occupied with this project.

My family and friends for moral support, and understanding when I had to forego gatherings (including one Christmas) to make my deadlines.

Last but far from least, my Mom for her part in making my existence possible, her support and concern, and those delicious home-cooked CARE packages that ensured that not everything I ate came from a box or a drive-through window.

Once again, thank you all for your help, advice, inspiration, and support in this book.

New Riders gives special thanks to Dan Ablan, author of the *LightWave Power Guide*. Dan created all the 3D text icons that accompany this book's sidebars. Thanks, Dan!

Contents at a Glance

Table of Contents

Introduction

When John Kane of New Riders Publishing first contacted me about writing a book, he told me that there were two titles they had in mind. One was a non-product-specific "essential guide to 3D," and the other, also non-product-specific, was a beginner's guide. The latter seemed like the best choice for me, because I've always tried to help others who were interested in getting into the field. There were people who helped me out when I first got started, and I like to carry on that tradition.

I was somewhat concerned about the fact that the book would not focus on any particular program, however. After all, how could I explain a procedure or write a tutorial when every product on the market does things differently, and may even use different terminology for a given operation? On the other hand, even if the book were written specifically for the product I had the most experience with, the DOS version of 3D Studio, what could I cover that hadn't already been detailed in more thorough tomes like *Inside 3D Studio*? After quite a bit of consideration, I came up with some ways to help 3D field newcomers through this book, and those reasons helped me to decide to undertake the four month project.

First of all, I wanted to cover all aspects of getting into 3D graphics, from understanding what it was all about to advice on getting a job. I felt that my experiences as both an employee and contractor in the field for a number of years would be helpful to the newcomer, as would my knowledge gained from my time as both a staff artist and art/creative director.

Besides covering 3D theory and common tools and techniques, I also wanted to point out the things that help to set your work apart from the pack. In other words, the solid design, the mapping, the small details, and the other things that catch an art director's eye. I also wanted to explore the creative process as a whole, getting into the design, storyboarding, and script writing aspects of modeling and animation. I felt that most 3D books and very few manuals touch on the important aspects of creating a reel, such as telling a story, directing the action, editing, and adding music and sound to finish it off.

In addition, I noted that most software manuals take a very piecemeal approach to their tutorials, giving the reader some basic task to perform to demonstrate an idea, then discarding that work when they move on to the next tool. The result is a collection of unusable micro-projects, leaving the newcomer to start from scratch in order to make something presentable.

With this book, the tutorials are inter-related and build on each other to help produce a finished portfolio piece.

Finally, I wanted to explore all these subjects in a comfortable, casual tone that would make reading the book seem less like a college lecture and more like a conversation about a mutual interest. I also decided to inject some of what I try to pass off as humor to ease the reader into the subject matter and occasionally provide relief from the monotony of highly technical information.

The result of my efforts, and the efforts of many others, now rests in your hands. I hope you will find this book to be a useful resource in answering your questions, teaching you new techniques, and achieving your goals.

Getting the Most from 3DGA

There are several different ways to use this book. If you read it prior to ever seeing 3D software in action, it provides a valuable overview of the 3D field, theory, tools, and filmmaking techniques that would aid you in any program you end up using. An alternative is to use it in conjunction with the manuals that come with your 3D package, as a second reference and real-world guide. You can do the tutorials as an alternative to some of the ones in your manuals, or as a way to confirm that you've learned the material thoroughly.

In either case, your best bet is to read through each chapter in a comfortable chair, then move to your computer to do any tutorials. The tutorials have been organized into the final sections of key chapters so that you don't have to read at your workstation (something many people find uncomfortable).

Using Your Manuals with the Book

Since this book is not product-specific, it can't give detailed lists of the steps you must take to accomplish things with your particular 3D software. Therefore, you need to work with your 3D software's manuals to learn how a given tool or operation is used in your package. However, the principles presented here remain the same throughout most programs, and alternative methods can be found for tools or techniques your package may not offer. In addition, this book offers alternative viewpoints and explanations of 3D theory and tools, along with a lot of tips and practical advice.

The best way to use the tutorials is as an addendum to any tutorials provided in your manuals, or as an alternative tutorial once you understand the necessary commands for your software. In other words, consider it a self-test to make sure you have learned the principles, not just a bunch of steps.

For those who are new to 3D, it's a good idea to start from the beginning and work your way through your software's User Guide. If you have read the earlier chapters of this book, you may find some of the introductory information about 3D applications and theory redundant, so feel free to skim through it. It never hurts to read a second resource, however, and you may find some uncertainties cleared up by reading a different presentation of the material.

Users with at least one other 3D package under their belts will probably just scan through the manuals to get a sense of how the program operates, then launch into a couple of the tutorials. Because the 3D principles are similar across most packages, the Quick Reference card and Reference Manual portions of the documentation will probably be their tools of choice.

Overview of Chapters

The book has been arranged in a fairly straightforward manner, from "what is 3D?" to modeling and animation techniques, to developing a reel and landing a job. The ends of Chapters 4–10 contain the tutorial sections for the topics covered. The appendices provide additional information and resources, such as a glossary, lists of schools, organizations and publications, software reviews, and a list of image contributors.

A brief look at the contents of each chapter and appendix follows:

Chapter 1: The Virtual Path gives a quick introduction to 3D graphics and examines the broad range of applications that utilize 3D. It also looks at the kinds of jobs that are available in the field, and has suggestions about how to learn more about computer graphics.

Chapter 2: Nuts and Bolts examines technical issues like hardware platforms, processors, peripherals, and options to help you select the right system, along with advice on optimizing your new or existing gear for best performance. It includes some general advice about picking software packages and getting them at a discount.

Chapter 3: Delving Into Cyberspace provides tips on making the transition from 2D to 3D graphics and explores the principles of 3D graphics in depth. Topics include coordinate systems, polylines, polygons, objects, viewpoints, and axes, to name a few.

Chapter 4: 3D Modeling looks at the different kinds of modelers available and discusses good work habits. It covers the creation of 2D shapes and different methods of turning them into 3D objects, as well as 3D primitives and transforms. This chapter is the starting point for a series of tutorials that build on each other throughout the book.

Chapter 5: Modeling: Beyond the Basics gets into some of the tips and techniques that will help set your work apart from the crowd. It includes information on bevels, deform modifiers, vertice-level editing, face extrusion, and other techniques for accurate and advanced modeling. It also looks at some alternatives to modeling, cool tricks, and more.

Chapter 6: Texture Mapping demonstrates how mapping can be used to enhance the realism of mesh objects by giving them color and texture. The topics examined include the following: how mapping can be used in place of mesh for creating the illusion of detail, the basics of material creation, mapping coordinate systems, and various techniques for obtaining and creating custom maps.

Chapter 7: Lighting explores the principles of light in the real world and how they apply to the 3D environment, along with the basics of photographic lighting techniques and how they can be used to add drama and interesting effects to your 3D objects and scenes. This chapter also covers the kinds of light sources and controls available in the virtual world, and discusses the special capabilities and options available with 3D lighting tools.

Chapter 8: The Camera contains a look at camera terminology, comparing virtual cameras to their real world counterparts, and shows how the position and focal length settings of the camera can increase the drama in a 3D scene. It also examines the use of the camera for storytelling purposes, based on the principles developed by filmmakers over several decades.

Chapter 9: Animation delves into animation terms and techniques, including timelines, motion paths, forward and inverse kinematics, and so forth. It looks at the tools and techniques of character animation, and shows how the storytelling process is advanced by turning objects into performers.

Chapter 10: Rendering and Output explores render time issues like resolution, aspect ratios, color depth, palettes, and atmosphere. The chapter covers the uses and creation of post-production effects like glows and lens flares, and includes an overview of the different types of output, from slides to videotape.

Chapter 11: The Reel begins with a look at the creative process and examines ways to generate and develop ideas. It discusses the value of adding story elements to a reel, and goes through the pre-production processes of script writing, designing, and storyboarding a piece, along with other aspects of doing a reel, including post-production, editing, visual effects, and audio.

Chapter 12: Getting the Job covers the challenges of starting a career in 3D graphics, including researching companies, preparing a resume and portfolio, and securing an interview. It looks at the differences between being an employee or a contractor, what art directors are looking for, the interview process, salaries, benefits, and ways to further your career.

Appendix A: Glossary of Terms is a compilation of 3D terminology used throughout the book and covers related (and a few unrelated) topics, along with concise definitions.

Appendix B: Recommended Reference contains suggested reading, image collections, and reference material to help you find answers to your questions, get your creative juices flowing, or just plain entertain you.

Appendix C: Resources has information about schools, organizations, and companies that can help you learn more about 3D animation and/or provide valuable services for artists and companies in the field.

Appendix D: Software Products and Publisher List consists of mini-reviews of Mac and PC software that I've used, along with other hardware and software of interest and contact information for the companies that produce it.

Appendix E: Image Contributors is a full list of the companies and individuals who have contributed images to this book and/or CD-ROM. Those individuals who are available for contract 3D work have additional contact information listed for use by recruiters or producers looking for outside talent.

Using the 3DGA CD-ROM

Included with the book is a companion CD-ROM usable on both PC and Mac systems. The CD-ROM contains the tutorial files, demo versions of some popular 3D software, sample mesh and textures, and portfolio images from companies and individuals around the world.

Using the Tutorial Files

The tutorial design of the book has the user working from start to finish on a single project, a *Blade Runner*-style advertising blimp. While this approach has the benefit of moving the user toward a completed portfolio piece, the nature of the tutorials makes it difficult to jump in at a later point, because each depends on work done in earlier chapters.

In order to make it easier for users to get around problems or skip over tutorials they aren't interested in, two versions of the model in various stages of completion have been included. One version is in the native 3D Studio MAX (.MAX) format, which contains all the mapping and animation work done to the model. The other version is .DXF, the standard interchange format readable by nearly every 3D program. Unfortunately, .DXF doesn't support animation, mapping coordinates, or textures, so you would have to re-apply these if you use the .DXF files instead of building your own.

The tutorial model files have been saved as the major sub-assemblies, such as the thrusters, gondola, and so forth, as well as in completed project form in the following directories.

> TUT_DXF Contains the model files in .DXF format
>
> TUT_IMG Contains images of the blimp and tower
>
> TUT_MAPS Contains the map files for the blimp and tower
>
> TUT_MAX Contains the model files in 3D Studio MAX format

Viewing the Images and Animation

The IMAGES directory on the CD-ROM contains work created by artists from all over the world. They are here for you to use as study examples and inspiration, but you may NOT redistribute or reproduce them without the express written consent of the artists or companies that hold the copyright.

The images are stored by artist or company name, in the JPEG (.JPG) format. Virtually all of the still image formats can be read directly off the disc by Photoshop or any good image utility, such as Paint Shop Pro. In addition, the BEALS directory contains some 3D Studio R4 (.3DS) and LightWave (.LWO) model files.

The Virtual Path

A virtual dragon flaps its wings amidst a computer-generated background. Image ©1996 Vadim Pietrzynski.

The student watched from the shadows as the Master muttered strange incantations over a glowing pool of light. Slowly, mist-like tendrils rose from the pool and flowed into place, forming the outline of a dragon. The Master paused for a moment, considering the result, then played his gnarled hands across its surface, replacing the ethereal outline with thick, textured scales awash in iridescent colors. Pleased, the Master smiled a toothless grin and waved his arms in a swirling motion.

"Go forth!" he cried, "Take to the skies!" With that, the dragon shuddered, spread its leathern wings, and leapt into the air. The creature hovered for a moment, then began soaring around the room. Awestruck, the student lost his footing and stumbled into the chamber, collapsing in a heap on the stone floor. He looked up at the wondrous dragon just in time to see it advance toward him, belching jets of flame. The student tried to move, but it was too late! The blaze struck him full on, then...

Nothing.

A moment later, the dragon itself dissolved into a shower of tiny sparks, and was gone. Stunned, the student gazed up at the Master, who chuckled.

"An illusion," he proclaimed, "existing only to your eyes. I conjure them to illustrate and entertain." He turned and walked back toward the glowing pool, taking a seat nearby. "Now, what brings you here?"

"Forgive my intrusion, Master," the student replied, "but I came seeking The Virtual Path."

"Indeed? Well, I should say you have found it." The Master laughed. "That creature was but one of a universe of possibilities, limited only by one's skills and imagination as a conjurer. But tell me, why do you seek this path? It's not an easy one, and will require much time and effort. It may also isolate you from others, as the glowing pool will require your undivided attention for hours at a time."

"Because," the student replied with a smile, "it's sooo rad!"

What Is 3D, Anyway?

As with the uncertain but excited student, there are many of you who may know that they want to create computer graphics, but don't fully understand what they are. Well, my notes for this section say "explain 3D graphics in a simple manner," so here goes...

As you probably know, 3D stands for *three-dimensional*. That means that things have three...uh...dimensions, namely width, height, and depth. If you look around the room, everything you see is three-dimensional—the chair, the desk, the building, the yard, your dog, everything.

"Now, wait a minute," you say. "If everything in the room, like this rather heavy book in my hands, is three-dimensional, then how come the 3D graphics I've seen on computer screens are *flat*?"

Well, that's because the term 3D graphics is a LIE. A falsehood. A distortion of the truth. In actuality, 3D graphics should be called "Two-dimensional *representations* of three-dimensional objects. "2D," of course, means two-dimensional, or having only width and height, but no depth. In other words, *flat*.

"Okay, I sort of get it," you say, "but give me an example."

Fair enough. Go grab a camcorder and I'll show you. Don't worry, I'll wait.

Oh, prefer to use your imagination, huh? Very well. Imagine that you're now videotaping the room. You get up from your comfortable seat and wander around, taping things from all angles. You stub your toe on a chair, a painful reminder that you're moving through a three-dimensional world.

Now imagine that you pop the tape into your VCR and play it back on the TV. Yes, there's your three-dimensional room, but now it's *flat*. Pause the tape (no, you don't have to imagine the noise lines rolling through the picture). Anyway, pause the tape and look at the scene. The objects seem realistic enough, and have light and color and shadow. You can see the sides of some objects, but no matter how you move your head around, you can't see behind anything. To put it *flatly*, you are looking at a "two-dimensional *representation* of three-dimensional objects."

In computer graphics, objects exist only in the memory of the computer. They have no physical form—they're just mathematical formulas and little electrons running around. Because the objects don't exist outside the computer, the only way to record them is to add more formulas to represent lights and cameras. The software takes care of most of this nasty math stuff, enabling the user to view the non-existent scene on the computer monitor and manipulate it with mouse and keyboard commands (see figure 1.1).

FIGURE 1.1

Using 3D software, the user interacts with two-dimensional representations of virtual 3D objects, lights, and cameras to compose a scene.

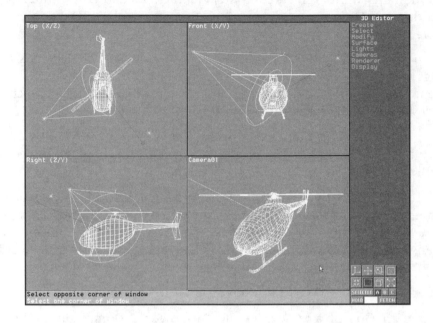

3D Graphics

So, in many ways, using 3D modeling and animation software is something like videotaping a room full of objects that you construct. The software enables you to design the room and its contents using a variety of basic 3D objects like cubes, spheres, cylinders, and cones that you can select and add to the scene. The program also gives you the tools needed to define custom objects by drawing cross-sections and turning them into 3D objects, or by sculpting and transforming the basic ones.

definition

virtual Not real; a computer representation of something.

Once all of the objects have been created and positioned, you can choose from a library of pre-defined materials, such as plastic, stone, wood, or glass and apply them to your objects. You also can create your own materials by adjusting controls such as color, shininess, and transparency, and even use painted or scanned images to make the surface of your objects appear any way you like.

Lighting is another aspect of creating a 3D scene, and software enables you to choose from several different kinds of lights, as well as define their color, brightness, and so forth. By positioning the lights in the virtual space, you can control how the objects are illuminated.

Next, you set up the virtual cameras to record the scene. By adjusting the settings on the camera, you can get wide-angle effects or zoom in on a small detail. Positioning the cameras in interesting ways also adds to the drama of the scene.

The scene is brought to life by moving the objects themselves, as well as the lights and cameras. You can make the objects move mechanically, or appear to take on human characteristics. You can use filmmaking techniques to tell a story with your animation, or simply create something that looks cool.

Finally, you can render the animation to videotape or a computer animation file, enabling you to view the finished results and share it with others. Using 3D graphics, you can create just about anything you can imagine, then use the result as a portfolio piece, a portion of a computer game, a scene from a science fiction epic, or any number of other possibilities.

How Are 3D Graphics Used?

3D graphics have a surprisingly broad range of uses in all sorts of different businesses and fields of study. Some, such as the multimedia, film, broadcast, and game businesses, have more need of 3D modelers and animators than some of the research fields. Still, it's good to be aware that the opportunities are so numerous and varied.

Film

The film industry has traditionally used hand-built, miniature models and full-sized props for most of its special effects (SFX) work. The myriad of spacecraft in the *Star Wars* trilogy and the incredibly atmospheric cityscapes of *Blade Runner* were painstakingly constructed from wood, metal, and Fiberglass, decorated with plastic model parts, and outfitted with tiny lights. Likewise, fantastic creatures were usually portrayed by people in foam rubber suits, by stop-motion models, or even puppets (perhaps the most famous being the gnarled, green-skinned Jedi Master Yoda, from *The Empire Strikes Back*).

Although 3D animation made its big screen debut in *TRON*, it was not until the monster success of *Jurassic Park* that it became recognized as the modern way to do effects work. Since then, the use of 3D animation in films has increased to its logical conclusion; the entirely computer-generated feature *Toy Story*. This feature was partially inspired by *Tin Toy*, an earlier work from the same director, John Lasseter of PIXAR (see figure 1.2).

3D animation is used in many Disney features as reference for the traditional hand-drawn work. An example of this is the carriage from *The Little Mermaid*, which was created as a 3D model, then animated to make the complex motions of rolling along a winding country road. The resulting 3D animation was then redrawn by hand so that it matched the look of the characters and backgrounds.

In addition to 3D, there are other applications of computer graphics in films as well, but these often go unrecognized. For example, *digital retouching* is a process that uses *2D paint* programs (software, such as Photoshop, for drawing, painting, and manipulating images) to modify photographic stills and movies. This method is often used to remove wires from suspended actors, or television antennas from pre-1950's cityscapes. Probably one of the most dramatic and unique uses of this technology was the removal of Gary Sinese's legs for *Forrest Gump*.

> **definition**
>
> **morph** Animated 2D or 3D effect that makes one image or form smoothly transform into another. Heavily used in Michael Jackson's *Black & White* video.

During post-production work on *Terminator 2*, director James Cameron decided that he preferred the semi truck plunging into the drainage canal from right to left instead of the way it was originally filmed. Digital artists complied by flipping the scene, then reversing the street signs and vehicle license plates frame-by-frame. Because there are 24 frames for every second of film, these digital retouching efforts are a lot of work!

Other examples of 2D digital effects include the submarine wakes (water disturbances) in *The Hunt for Red October* and Woody Harrelson's demonic *morph* in *Natural Born Killers*. Digital retouching isn't limited to 2D graphics, however. For the film *Primal Fear*, a church was constructed with 3D graphics and superimposed over an existing structure (see figure 1.3).

FIGURE 1.3

3D graphics and image compositing software allow filmmakers to change the look of a location shot to suit their needs. Here, a church is superimposed over an existing structure. Image created with Composer for *Primal Fear* courtesy of Dream Quest Images. ©1996 Paramount Pictures.

There is a unique showcasing of computer graphics in the *Star Wars* trilogy re-release, which marked the 20th anniversary of the first film. First, portions of the films had to be restored and digitally remastered from numerous copies, including foreign ones, because the negatives had deteriorated in storage. Next, 3D animation was used to add new elements to the film, such as more air and ground traffic around Mos Eisley spaceport. In addition, some scenes that were cut from the original film due to timing, budget, or other concerns were restored, including one featuring Han Solo chatting with Jabba the Hut. In the original footage, Jabba is played by a human actor, which naturally doesn't jive with his appearance as a giant slug in *Return of the Jedi*. For the restored scene, then, a 3D version of Jabba was animated and composited together with the decades-old footage of Harrison Ford.

While film special effects remain one of the most prestigious forms that 3D graphics can take, it is by no means the only application for CG in the entertainment field. In fact, for sheer volume and range of effects, television shows and advertisements probably win out.

Broadcast Television

A few seasons back, the popular science fiction series *Babylon 5* set the standard for broadcast 3D animation effects with its impressive ships and alien vistas. It also raised some eyebrows, because the production house, Foundation Imaging, was using personal computers and relatively low-cost LightWave 3D software for creating the work (see figure 1.4). Indeed, the show became a prime example of what could be accomplished without resorting to Silicon Graphics, Inc. (SGI) workstations and $60,000 software. Of course, the high-end systems and software are well represented in other shows, including the breathtaking opening animation for *Star Trek: Voyager*.

Hypernauts © 1996, ABC and Foundation Imaging

One of the most interesting trends in television series has been the appearance of 3D animated cartoons among the usual Saturday morning lineup. Shows such as *Reboot*, and the one-shot *Crash Test Dummies* are refreshing not only because of their modern look, but because they offer something most of the other contemporary animated shows don't: *movement.*

Commercials are another fertile ground for the eye-catching visuals made possible with CG. Morphs appear to be particularly popular, sucking kids into soda bottles or turning a car into a running tiger. In addition, character animation ranging from dancing automobiles and gas pumps to wisecracking M&Ms has become a commonplace addition to (and welcome relief from) the hordes of human product pushers.

Less apparent to the casual observer is the use of 3D models for product shots in commercials. Using CG instead of traditional (and possibly more expensive) studio photography, even a mundane bottle of dishwashing liquid achieves perfection, with nary a plastic seam, creased label, or air bubble out of place.

While not as glamorous as some the other applications just discussed, station IDs and news graphics also are popular uses for CG in broadcast television (see figure 1.5). These are usually updated every season to keep the look fresh and to try and outdo the competition.

FIGURE 1.5

3D graphics are often used to create station IDs, news graphics, and opening sequences for broadcast television. Image courtesy of Turner Production Effects.

definition

real time The immediate processing of input data and graphics, so that any changes result in near-instantaneous adjustments to the image.

Although the flashiest 3D animation is usually reserved for network and station identification, the idea of having virtual sets for news and talk shows is starting to catch on. The idea is that because the sets can be generated with 3D programs, they can be frequently and cost-effectively upgraded to keep the look of the show fresh. This method also enables effects that would be impossible in a real studio environment.

In this kind of application, the news people or show hosts and guests are videotaped on a *bluescreen* set, which is a mostly empty stage painted a particular shade of blue. The blue areas of the image are then electronically removed and replaced with the 3D background. With some systems, the sets are generated in *real time*, enabling the camera to follow the live performers as they walk around.

Multimedia

Some of my first paying 3D work came as point-of-sale (POS) and trade show demos for high-tech companies. Much of this work is produced by the multimedia companies that are concentrated in San Francisco's SOMA (South of MArket) district, which is also known as *Multimedia Gulch*.

Point-of-sale demos are intended to run on kiosks or computer systems in a retail store environment, attracting the customer's attention and providing information about the product. Often these demos are for advertising the system itself, and virtually every hardware manufacturer uses them to espouse the features, capabilities, and user-friendliness of *their* PC clone over the clearly inferior PC clone on the shelf next to them.

Trade show demos tend to be much flashier than POS demos and cover a much broader variety of products and services. If you've ever been to a big trade show, you know how every booth tries to scream for your attention, using everything from free doodads, to celebrities, to 30' tall video walls equipped with deafening sound systems. Here, the idea is not so much to talk about features (which would be lost on the typical harried show goer) but to make an impression in the viewer's mind about the product and company. Usually, the impressions the demos try to sear into your brain are as follows:

◆ THIS is a HOT company

◆ THIS is a COOL product

◆ THIS is more IMPORTANT than breathing

To this end, trade show demos pull out all the stops, combining video of performers, special effects, (and, of course, 3D animation) into MTV-style eye candy tuned for a three-second attention span. In other words, working on these projects can be a lot of fun!

Far more staid and evenly paced are the presentations and speaker support projects that make up much of the corporate work created in-house or by multimedia companies. These include the typical bullet-pointed slides and graphs, along with 2D and 3D animation to jazz things up. Presentations are usually made one-on-one or to a small group with a laptop system, while speaker support jobs are often big-time affairs where the presentation is made to hundreds of people using big-screen projection systems.

Note

> On the subject of speaker support presentations, there are many times when a company wants the multimedia firm to provide someone to run the computer during the speaker's talk, just in case of a software glitch. I handled this task for the first time at a big National Semiconductor presentation, and can be pretty scary, let me tell you. Just before the presentation started, somebody ran around to all the speaker support stations and dumped an intercom headset on the desk. I put mine on, and the presentation started. After a couple of minutes, I started to hear static, and people began asking where it was coming from. I suddenly realized that it was MY intercom that was causing the problem, and I couldn't figure out how to get the transmitter to work, so that I could respond to the screaming director! One of those "character-building" situations, for sure. Thankfully, it all worked out fine, my intercom was replaced, and every cue was hit.

Web and VRML

The World Wide Web (WWW) is another spot where 3D graphics are often used. In this environment, 3D graphics may range from simple buttons or other graphical elements on the page to integrated VRML (Virtual Reality Modeling Language) applications. *VRML* is a Web browser technology that enables the user to explore simple 3D environments online (see figure 1.6), and is used for such things as graphical chat rooms or evaluating the location of some concert seats before you buy them.

FIGURE 1.6

OnLive! Technologies turns MTV Online, or any World Wide Web site, into a community by enabling groups of people to use their voices to talk online. MTV Tikkiland is the OnLive!-enabled 3D site accessed via MTV's web site at www.mtv .com. Modeled after the Tikki God theme featured in the television show *The Beach House*, a variety of MTV Tikkiland 3D settings let users bask in the warm glow of a virtual sunset by the beach, explore an exotic Tikki God cyber-temple, or lounge by the pool with a tropical mountain backdrop.

Games

To my mind, doing game graphics is one of the most enjoyable applications of 3D. Depending on the type of game, you may end up working with near-broadcast quality images and animation, and probably with more freedom than an individual artist would have when working on a film or broadcast project.

definition

sprite A graphic object (often a character or cursor) that can be moved around on a background image.

3D seems to run rampant in today's games, used for everything from generating the prehistoric fighter *sprites* in Primal Rage to the dozens of video *cut scenes* in Rebel Assault II that show your spacecraft exploding against cliff walls or being vaporized by Tie Fighters (see figure 1.7).

The recent crop of multi-CD motion video games such as The 11th Hour, Zork: Nemesis, and The Daedalus Encounter make heavy use of 3D graphics as a way to provide backgrounds for the live actors. In addition, Zork and the Star Trek Technical Manual provide virtual environments to explore by making use of 360-degree high-resolution surround nodes (see figure 1.8). This technology, called QuickTime VR on the Macintosh, uses a specially rendered still image that enables the player to look all around a particular area before moving on to another explorable node.

Despite the quality and richness of the animation in motion video games, the biggest impact 3D has made in gaming is the real-time play afforded by the DOOM-style engines. Here, resolution and detail are sacrificed in order to achieve the speed and responsiveness that a first-person shooting game requires. As systems continue to increase in power, and more sophisticated software appears, the quality of these games will someday improve to the point where they will be nearly indistinguishable from pre-rendered animation. This trend is evident in the high-res implementation of id Software's Quake, Scavenger's Into the Shadows, and 3D Realms' Duke Nukem 3D (see figure 1.9).

FIGURE 1.9

Although a low-res image is shown here, real-time 3D shooters like Duke Nukem 3D are capable of 800 × 600 or higher resolution output that begins to resemble pre-rendered animation. Image used with permission of 3D Realms/Apogee Software.

Illustration and Fine Art

Taking a break from animation for a moment, the illustration and fine art fields have seen a slow but steady influence coming from the 3D world (see figure 1.10). Still, most 3D illustration work is restricted to technology magazines, despite the fact that Photoshop and other 2D paint tools are well-accepted and widely used.

FIGURE 1.10

A fine art image
created with a process
that alternates between
3D modeling and 2D
paint program
enhancement. Image
©1996 James Mahan.

As far as fine art goes, some avant garde types have been doing CG work for years. Unfortunately, as with photography at the end of the 19th century, a lot of people are having trouble accepting 3D as a valid form of art. Eventually, of course, this will change and 3D modeling software will be seen as just another tool for the artist, not the source of the work itself.

In the comics and graphic novels arena, 3D is starting to show up more and more. Pepe Moreno's *Batman: Digital Justice* broke new ground for 3D in graphic novels, and today, Rival Comics' *Eye of the Storm* uses 3D backgrounds for every issue. In addition, a multimedia graphic novel called *Sinkha* (reviewed in the October '96 issue of *InterActivity* magazine) recently appeared, featuring some of the most stunning 3D work ever seen (see figure 1.11). Even games are crossing over into the graphic novel realm, with a coffee table book featuring imagery from the Japanese CD-ROM adventure Gadget.

Research, Forensics, and Training

Business and marketing people have recognized the value of graphics to represent complex data for a long time, and this holds true for those in the scientific research fields as well. However, whereas a static bar chart is often adequate to communicate a page full of sales figures, it doesn't always work in with research data. It may take the most sophisticated systems, gigabytes of data, and cutting edge programming to create a 3D animation representing a mathematical principle, natural phenomenon, or biological structure. One such application of CG in a research environment is the modeling of weather systems. Here, 3D graphics represent high and low pressure areas, air currents, precipitation, and other factors to accurately model a storm.

definition

digitize The process of transforming images, objects, or sounds into a digital form that a computer can manipulate.

Medical research and techniques also benefit from new applications of 3D technology. One of the most impressive efforts of late has been the development of an amazingly accurate 3D model of the human body, with a level of detail never before imagined (see figure 1.12). The process involved freezing a cadaver, then cutting it into extremely thin 1mm cross-sectional slices. The next step was to *digitize* the cross-sections, then use custom software to reassemble the sections into a completed model.

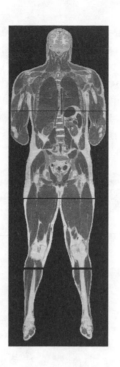

FIGURE 1.12

Body cross-section from the Visible Human™ Project, a digital database of volumetric data representing a complete adult male and female. Produced by the University of Colorado Center for Human Simulation. Image courtesy of the National Center for Atmospheric Research.

Forensic animation, which is usually a re-creation of an automobile accident or plane crash, has become very popular for demonstrating a complex series of events in courtroom situations. This type of animation uses evidence from a scene, eyewitness reports, and real-world physics to generate a simple (but accurate as possible) representation of what happened. Forensic animation is also becoming popular for murder cases as well, but concern is being raised about this. Despite the fact that this type of animation is very plain, and that there are sometimes assumptions made about the actions in the scene, the visual impact of the result can be very compelling.

definition

virtual reality A computer system that can immerse the user in the illusion of a computer-generated world and permit the user to navigate through this world at will. Typically, the user wears a head-mounted display (HMD) that displays a stereoscopic image, and dons a sensor glove, which enables the user to manipulate "objects" in the virtual environment.

Flight simulators make use of the latest real-time 3D technologies in order to accurately re-create the experience of piloting an aircraft. These systems are invaluable for training, particularly because dangerous conditions or mechanical failures can be programmed to occur. This enables the pilots to have an opportunity to experience an emergency situation that they may someday face in real life.

In keeping with the high-tech trend in weaponry, military training is also being done in simulators. For example, tank crews can maneuver on realistic battlefields that simulate conditions and enemy tactics half a world away.

Finally, no discussion of 3D research would be complete without mentioning *virtual reality* (*VR*) (see figure 1.13). The possibilities for this technology are truly immense, ranging from remote control brain surgery to the most awesome movies and games imaginable. Unfortunately, the hype that VR received early in its development cycle has left it looking like a fever dream. Still, there is no insurmountable problem to prevent its full implementation someday, and in the mean time, it remains an interesting field with vast potential.

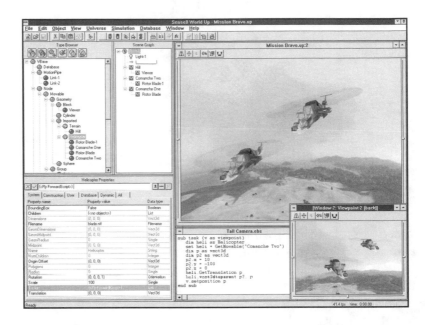

One of the most interesting novels about the potential of VR is Neal Stephenson's cyberpunk classic, *Snow Crash*. It's excellent reading for anyone interested in virtual reality and the future of online VR communities, or for anyone just hungry for some great science fiction.

Design and Engineering

Architecture is another field in which 3D modeling and animation use are on the rise. Much of the drawing work is still done with pencil or 2D drafting software, but some projects are realized in 3D as well. The resulting stills or animation are used as presentation materials and walkthroughs for clients, investors, and planning departments (see figure 1.14). In some cases, 3D models are combined with background photos of the actual site, creating a very realistic rendering of how the building would look in its planned environment.

FIGURE 1.14

Architectural rendering is a popular application of 3D graphics. Buildings can be accurately visualized with the program, and the renderings composited with photographs of the site. Image courtesy of Guillermo M. Leal Llaguno, created in Kinetix 3D Studio MAX.

3D modeling is very popular in product design companies, because it's possible to easily revise the models to meet a client's ever-changing tastes in color, style, and detail. Automobile designers frequently use 3D software because it enables them to evaluate the complex interactions of light and shadow on the contours of the vehicle.

Solid Modeling is a special form of 3D for engineering applications. It adds information about the weight, density, tensile strength, and other real-world facts about the material to the model's *dataset*. By having all of the physical information on the "real" materials available, the bridge, ship hull, or machine part being modeled can be subjected to computer-simulated stresses. This enables engineers to evaluate the design and see if it will perform as desired without having to build a physical prototype.

definitions

dataset A collection of information that describes a 3D object. A dataset may contain 3D coordinates, material attributes, textures, and even animation.

CAD/CAM CAD (Computer Aided Design) is the use of the computer and a drawing program to design a wide range of industrial products, ranging from machine parts to homes. CAM (Computer Aided Manufacturing) uses CAD drawings to control the equipment that manufactures the final object.

Also extensively used in the engineering field are CAD/CAM (Computer Aided Design/Computer Aided Manufacturing) programs, which allow the designer's drawings to be programmed directly into the machines that manufacture the parts. In addition, through the use of a method called *Laser Stereo Lithography*, prototypes of complex physical objects, are quickly formed out of a tank full of plastic goo. Who says *Star Trek*'s replicators are science fiction?

What Kinds of Jobs Are Available?

There are a lot of different job positions in the 3D field, and not all of them are artist positions. This can actually work for you if you're trying to break into the business. You may have the skills to get one of the other positions right away, then get more CG experience working with the people and systems at hand. The following sections discuss the various available roles, starting with management.

Producer/Director

The titles and responsibilities of those working in the project management aspect of 3D vary widely, but in general, they break down as follows:

The *producer* is responsible for project schedules, budget, and communicating with the client. Producers may have been artists at one time, or they may come from project management positions in other fields, then got up to speed on the basics of 3D graphics.

The *director* is responsible for the creative vision behind the project and often manages the artists. Directors are usually experienced senior artists who are familiar with all aspects of graphics production.

Note that these positions are sometimes combined, or that certain responsibilities may fall onto others. For example, there may be a *Creative Director* who's in change of the overall look and feel of the project, while an *Art Director* handles the day-to-day management of the artists. Depending on the situation, producers and directors may or may not actually do some of the artwork themselves.

Designer

Sometimes, the producer or director may designate a *designer* who will be responsible for developing the visual look of the project. The designer may conceptualize the user interface, character designs, environments, mechanical devices, and so forth. Usually, the designer makes sketches that other artists use as a guide for constructing them in 3D form, then may go on to execute some of the modeling work as well (see figure 1.15).

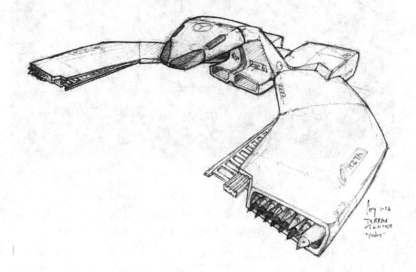

FIGURE 1.15

Design sketch for the Terran Alliance fighters from the CD-ROM game The Daedalus Encounter. Drawing by Cody Chancellor, ©1995 Mechadeus.

Modeler

The next three positions, Modeler, Mapper, and Animator, are usually combined into Modeler/Animator or simply 3D Artist. Still, they require different skill sets, and most artists will be better at one aspect than the others. Also, they may be entirely different positions on some projects or in some companies, so they are presented separately here.

The *modeler* can be thought of as the sculptor (or construction worker) of the group, building 3D models according to the designer's sketches, or based on his or her own ideas (see figure 1.16). Modelers have to be able to think in 3D terms, envisioning how to construct the desired object with the tools and techniques at hand. Some high school math and trigonometry is useful, but don't let that scare you. Having an artist's sense of proportion and composition is far more important than knowing what a cosine is.

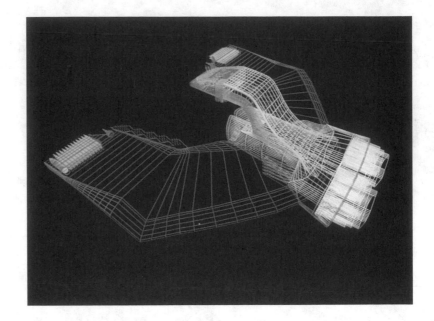

Mapper

Painting skills are the key to being a successful *mapper*, because the job requires the creation of textures (also called maps) in a 2D paint program such as Photoshop, their proper application to 3D objects, and the evaluation of the results (see figure 1.17). Good mapping skills are highly sought for low polygon count games of the DOOM or Virtua Fighter variety, because the models have to be extremely simple, leaving it to the mapper to make them look more interesting and detailed.

Note that even in situations where mapping is handled by a separate artist, the modeler is often responsible for doing preliminary texture work to define the materials, and to confirm that the model is properly prepared for mapping.

FIGURE 1.17

Mappers use products such as Photoshop and Fractal Painter to create the surface textures that give 3D models a realistic appearance. Image by Andy Murdock, ©1995 Mechadeus.

Animator

While animation is almost always part of the modeler's job, it's probably one of the hardest skills to develop. On the surface, it can be said that the *animator* defines the motion of the models, cameras, and lighting according to storyboards and experience. But in fact, the animator must

◆ Understand the structure and intricacies of the model

◆ Be familiar with the principles and practice of photography, lighting, and film direction

◆ Have the ability to breathe life into the scene through realistic, fluid motion

To this end, the animator often becomes something of a performer, lumbering around his desk to get the feel for a giant's gait, or contorting her face in a mirror to find just the right expression for a character.

These skills are so important that companies will often choose people with traditional *cel animation* experience over those with computer graphics training, preferring to teach experienced animators about using 3D tools instead of the other way around.

> **definition**
>
> *cel animation* The process of drawing and painting images on individual sheets of transparent celluloid that are later combined with background art and filmed.

Production Assistant

As with any business endeavor, there are always unglamorous jobs such as managing documents and files, running errands, and making calls. In the CG industry, these tasks often fall into the hands of the *production assistant*.

Now, you're probably wondering, "Why is he talking about this job? I want to do animation, not go pick up somebody's lunch!" Well, the fact is, there are some companies out there that get their pick of top applicants with lots of experience, and it's almost impossible to get a job there unless you have an "in." Becoming a production assistant, or even an unpaid intern, can get your foot in the door and your hands on some high-end gear. In a crunch (and *if* you know the tools), you may even find yourself doing some modeling or animation work to help the staff meet a deadline. This can lead to your name popping up when a new position appears. Hey, it happens!

Programmer

While *programmers* obviously have very different training and tasks from artists, there is a surprising amount of overlap in some fields of computer graphics. In games, for example, artists have to work with programmers to ensure that the graphics meet the proper specifications. In other cases, the programmers may create custom tools for the artists to use, either as stand-alone software or as *plug-ins* that give commercial 3D software new features and effects. Come to think of it, where would 3D artists be if programmers hadn't developed the modeling and animation software in the first place?

What's It Like to be a 3D Artist?

Now that you've been introduced to some of the different jobs in the CG field, let's take a look at what life as a 3D artist is all about. My employment experience is mostly in the multimedia and game development arena, so keep in mind that the conditions in other fields are likely to be very different.

There are all kinds of people in the world, and you'll find a representative sample in the graphics industry as well. Yes, everything from Neo-Morlocks who never emerge from their darkened offices unless their systems go down, to iron-fisted, whip-cracking tyrants (not me, of course). Mutants aside, however, 3D artists tend to be a fairly homogenous group, usually ranging from their early 20s to late 30s, and many have similar interests (these may include computer gaming, comics, action figures, Tim Burton films, motorcycles, rock bands, and eating ethnic foods, to name a few).

As far as workplaces go, it depends on the company, but art departments tend to be mostly weird, fun environments. Desks and systems are cluttered with action figures, generally non-lethal projectile weapons, and stacks of manuals, magazines, and unread memos (see figure 1.18). Music plays, bizarre newspaper clippings, posters and photos adorn the walls, and leftover pizza lurks atop the microwave. But, enough about my house...

FIGURE 1.18

3D artist and comics entrepreneur "Goose" Ramirez ponders a project at his toy-laden Mondo Media workstation.

One of the best things about this environment is that artists can learn from each other and get answers to questions much more easily than searching through a manual. On the other hand, there may be times when you need to work in a quiet or solitary office, and a good workplace provides for this as well. With this in mind, some companies will enable you to work at home on occasion, so you can work uninterrupted and spend that extra hour or two with your nose pressed against the monitor.

In any business that has deadlines, the hours tend to be long from time to time, with 40–50 hour weeks being typical. During a serious end-of-project crunch, that figure can rise to 90 hours or more, and I can recall at least one occasion where I put in a 36-hour day. Still, if you're determined and stay productive all day, it's possible to work on a normal schedule.

For those with nasty commutes, children, or other responsibilities, companies may make flexible schedules available. At times, this can even be a very desirable thing for the company itself, because those working a late shift can make use of equipment that might otherwise be dormant.

Finally, the sordid topic of coin. Pay runs the gamut, but artists can expect to make between $30–60K or more depending on experience. In some cases, art directors, producers, and other art management types can pull down as much as $80–120K (circa 1997).

How Do I Learn More About the Field?

Thankfully, 3D graphics is still a field where what you can do is more important than where you went to school or who you worked for in the past. This makes options like learning on your own possible and practical, although professional training can open some doors for you, as you'll see in the following sections.

Learning on Your Own

The fact that you're reading this book indicates that you're planning to learn at least some of the aspects of 3D on your own, so let me tell you about my own experience with this method.

I started out in computer graphics by purchasing some low-cost hardware and software and just playing with it. My system of choice was the Atari 800, a graphics powerhouse featuring four on-screen colors from a palette of sixteen, and a whopping 48K of RAM. I spent the first weekend learning BASIC, then wrote a little program that made an animated UFO zap a plane. Later, my younger brother reworked my code for the final project in his programming class, resulting in the seminal *Nuclear Destruction of Elko, Nevada*, wherein my UFO obliterated a sleepy desert town. The effort netted the admiration of his teacher and classmates, not to mention an A.

By the way, *my* contribution to the project was never mentioned, teaching me an early and valuable lesson about copyrights and intellectual property. To be fair, he did make up for it later by springing for half of a cassette data recorder (floppy drives were over $400 at the time). After that, we didn't have to write down our code and manually re-enter it every time the machine was rebooted.

At any rate, working with the Atari 800, and later with an Atari 512 ST and an Apple Macintosh IIcx, helped me to learn the principles of computer graphics and 3D animation. Having the machines at hand also enabled me to create some portfolio pieces as well, and all of that gave me a good head start when I decided to enter CG as a career.

Internships

Sometimes, students or others with knowledge but little practical experience opt for an *internship* with a company. These are positions that offer either little or no pay, and mix production assistant-type jobs with graphics work. This situation can be a good way to get started if you can get along for a while without much money. Still, take advantage of every opportunity to develop your skills and portfolio so that you can move into a paid position as quickly as possible.

Schools

These days, there are a number of private and public schools that offer computer graphics and 3D modeling classes (see figure 1.19). While the equipment isn't always state of the art, schools do offer the advantages of having professionals available to answer questions, and access to a number of different software packages. They also offer training in related subjects such as Storyboarding, Design for Multimedia, and Videographics, which help to round out your knowledge of the field.

FIGURE 1.19

A student at the Computer Arts Institute in San Francisco works on a 3D image. Schools like this are an excellant way to learn 3D and can help you get into the business faster.

Public schools, such as community colleges, tend to be less expensive and more accessible to most, with the downside being prerequisites that they may require. It also may take longer to work through the curriculum due to the semester-based system. Private schools, while more expensive and remote than community colleges, usually offer more intensive, shorter-term classes.

In some cases, the schools act like a pipeline to businesses that look for new talent. While I was attending the Computer Arts Institute (CAI) in San Francisco, the staff at the school recommended me to a local multimedia company who was looking for more artists. As a result of portfolio work I had done on my own and at the school, I secured Mondo Media as one of my first clients, and they later hired me full-time.

For a list of public and private schools offering 3D training, see Appendix C, "Resources."

Seminars, Shows, and Organizations

For the fledgling 3D artist, going to a trade show or seminar is *de rigueur*. Seminars are usually very expensive, running hundreds or even thousands of dollars, but they can be an excellent source for the most current information and training. If you can't manage the bucks for the seminars, getting a pass to the trade show floor usually costs less than a hundred dollars (and you may even get free or discount passes if you subscribe to some of the better CG magazines). Visiting the show floor can provide a wealth of interesting presentations, contact information, four-color brochures, and kitchy souvenirs.

Many of the shows and seminars are sponsored by organizations involved in or related to the computer graphics field. Membership in these organizations may provide you with free publications, discounts on the shows and travel, and other benefits. They also may guarantee you a lifetime of CG-related direct mail offers.

There are a lot of different shows and seminars, so the following lists some of my suggestions:

◆ **SIGGRAPH**: Everyone should try to attend this computer graphics Mecca, which is sponsored twice a year by the ACM (Association for Computing Machinery). Here, you will see the latest in hardware, software, and animation from all over the world.

◆ **CGDC**: The Computer Game Developers Conference is a must-see for those in the gaming field. It's pretty expensive to attend, but well worth the money.

◆ **E3**: Infotainment World (associated with *PC Games* magazine) sponsors the Electronic Entertainment Expo, which is another great show to attend if you're in the video game biz. It doesn't offer the conferences or contacts that the CGDC does, and is mostly a massive, noisy trade show for showcasing new games and platforms.

◆ **NAB**: For those interested in the television industry, the National Association of Broadcasters show pays a fair amount of attention to computer graphics.

In addition to these shows, platform-specific events such as MacWorld, PCWorld, and others have a lot to offer as well, and are worth attending for getting an overview of what's out there. They also are a good place to pick up hardware and software bargains.

Finally, local user groups are a good source of information and contacts in your area. These groups often meet at public auditoriums or at local software stores. If you happen to live near large hardware or software firms, you also may find corporate user groups that meet at the facility. Frequently, these groups get the opportunity to see and hear about the company's latest offerings.

Books and Periodicals

When it comes to getting concentrated, current information at an economical price, it's tough to beat books and magazines. In addition to the broadly scoped 3D book you hold in your hands, you may want to get a meaty product-specific reference once you have settled on a software package. For those who plan to work as freelance artists and contractors, there are small business guides that deal with the art field specifically. In addition, there are collections of CG artwork available to provide ideas and inspiration.

As far as magazines go, everyone should get *Computer Graphics World* (*CGW*), which provides excellent coverage of the field. I also recommend *InterActivity* (which I write for), *Next Generation*, *Animation*, *New Media*, and *Wired*.

If you're interested in special effects for film, game, or broadcast applications, then *Cinefantastique*, *Starlog*, and *Cinescape* are worth looking into. If you want the real nuts-and-bolts of the SFX field, however, the best choice is *Cinefex*.

See Appendix B, "Recommended Reference," for a list of suggested books and magazines.

Summary

So far you have gotten a look behind the computer screen at what 3D graphics are and examined the broad range of applications that use 3D. You've also learned about the kinds of jobs that are available in the field, and some different ways to learn more about computer graphics. The overview provided in this chapter gives you a good foundation from which to explore the more specific issues of 3D in forthcoming chapters.

The next chapter delves into the gritty nuts-and-bolts of 3D, from selecting hardware to picking the best software package. You'll also get under the hood of your system, optimizing it for best 3D performance. Are you ready to get your hands dirty?

Nuts and Bolts

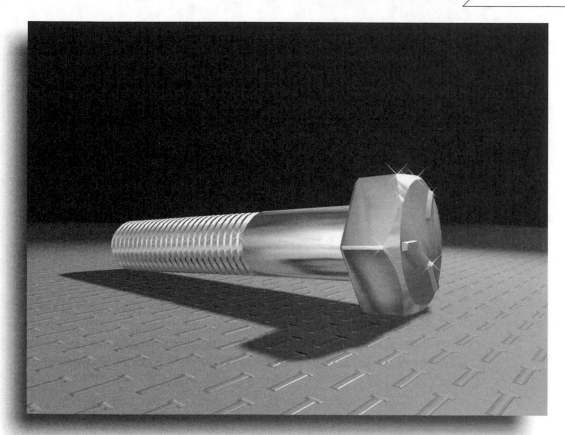

The infamous Lackluster 2-½" x ½" Grade 5 Machine Bolt from the June 1996, "Animata" column in *InterActivity* magazine. Image © 1996 Mark Giambruno.

"*W*ell, here we are at last," sighed the Master as he and the student stood before the door to the odd little shop. The sign that creaked above their heads featured a stylized dragon and the word "Majiks." As he entered the shop, the student's eyes immediately fell upon a large, glittering conjuring crystal, just like the one that powered the Master's glowing pool. Peering into its mysterious depths, the lad caught sight of the price tag on the opposite side.

"Thirty thousand drells!" The student turned his crestfallen face toward the Master. "Not in a hundred years could I afford such a sum!"

"Lad," said the Master, putting a hand on the young man's shoulder, "my first crystal was but the size of a pebble. It was years before even I could manage one such as this. Come, let us look at some others."

"Here's one." The student indicated a more modestly sized orb. "It's twenty-nine hundred drells, but I think I can manage, if..."

"Good day, gentlemen," the shopkeeper called as she emerged from the storeroom. She smiled warmly at the student, then turned her attention to the Master. "Looking for a conjuring crystal, then?"

"Indeed, my lady," replied the old man, "one that will meet my student's potential, but within his limited means."

"Just starting up? Well, young man, you've chosen a fine crystal there." The shopkeeper nodded toward the shimmering stone. "So now you'll need a pool, some majik powders, and a spell book or two, right?"

The student swallowed hard and lowered his gaze. "I...forgot about all that." He sighed. "I don't have enough drells..."

"Oh, now then," said the shopkeeper, "let's see what we can come up with." "Here, I have just the thing for you." She led them around to another table, which displayed an array of small crystal fragments. "This is one of our newest items," she said with pride. "One of these fragments is enough to power a glowing pool, although it will be a bit slow. However, as your skills grow, and you acquire the means, you can add more fragments to increase the power."

"Hmmm. That sounds like a wise course," observed the Master. The student smiled and nodded in agreement.

"Splendid!" replied the shopkeeper. *"Now that we have that settled, I can tell you about our extended warranty programs..."*

Evaluating Your Requirements

The preceding tale is probably a familiar one if you've ever shopped for a computer system. Despite the fact that computers are unusual in that they continue to increase in power and capability while decreasing in price, the system requirements on software packages just keep getting more demanding. This is particularly true of 3D software, which always seems to require just a little more oomph than even the newest processors can provide. As a result, when selecting a computer system, you should keep easy upgradability in mind, particularly if you aren't able to afford top-of-the-line systems. This chapter provides you with some basic information about selecting or upgrading a system, choosing a software package and then optimizing your system for best performance. It starts by helping you figure out your requirements.

There's an old adage in the computer sales business that really applies to 3D applications. *Software sells hardware.* In other words, people buy the necessary hardware to support their chosen software solutions. Therefore, the logical place to start when evaluating your needs is to decide what you want to do, and then select a package that delivers.

Most of you probably fall into one of two categories: either you're learning 3D for the first time, or you're presently working in the field and want to improve your skills. The latter group also may be (or plan to be) self-employed, running businesses that provide 3D services.

3D novices who plan on getting a job in an animation studio may want to consider a fairly basic system with reasonably priced software. After all, once you're employed, you will probably find yourself working with better gear, and with a different software package as well. Of course, learning production-quality packages, like Kinetix 3D Studio R4, Kinetix 3D Studio MAX, NewTek LightWave, Microsoft SoftImage, or Alias/Wavefront Power Animator will make you more readily employable, but the prices of these packages put them out of reach for most beginners.

Those who plan to start their own businesses, however, will want to invest in a system and software that will enable them to be productive and competitive. They also are more likely to need a full range of peripherals, such as scanners and graphics tablets, that the student could get by without.

What kind of 3D work do you expect to do in this new career or hobby? If it is 3D illustrations that involve a limited number of objects, you may be able to get by with a minimal configuration. If you're planning to create high-res 3D environments, you'll need plenty of horsepower and lots of RAM. With this in mind, the following section examines some of the practical considerations in acquiring your software and gear.

Selecting 3D Software

The number and features of 3D products on the market can be bewildering, with packages ranging from a few hundred dollars to the tens of thousands. Likewise, the feature sets and capabilities of these products cover the gamut—so how do you narrow down the choices?

The first filter to apply is financial: Are you willing to spend the price of a good used car to build things that don't exist outside your computer's RAM? Speaking of RAM, don't forget to factor in the price of upgrading or replacing your system's memory to get the optimum level of performance your chosen software requires.

Prices are included throughout this chapter for general comparison only, and are current as of January 1997, when this book went to press. However, prices are very volatile in the computer industry in general, and there are substantial discounts through mail order, so it's likely that many of the items mentioned are available for much less.

3D software can be had for the price of a download in the case of the freeware package POV Ray, or can set you back $60,000 dollars for a full complement of Alias/Wavefront tools. Commercial packages for 3D illustration, light animation, and learning can be had for $200–$1,000, but most of them aren't used in production-level graphics work. In the mid-range, LightWave is a popular and moderately priced program available for $1,000–$1,500 (see figure 2.1).

Portions of the material in this section dealing with 3D software information and reviews originally appeared in an article I wrote for InterActivity *magazine (© 1996 Miller Freeman, Inc.), and is used with permission.*

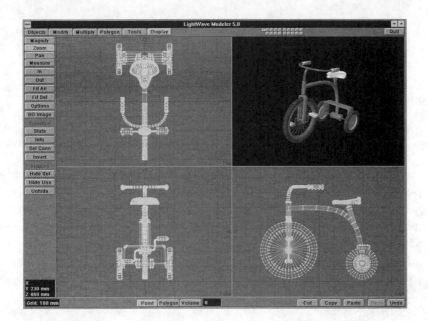

FIGURE 2.1

NewTek's LightWave is a popular mid-priced cross-platform 3D package well-known for its use in creating the graphics on *Babylon 5* and other television shows.

Higher up the scale are the Kinetix 3D Studio packages, which are by far the most popular production packages. They retail for between $2,495 and $3,495, but Kinetix offers major deals ($995 and $1,295 respectively) to students enrolled full time in a degree-seeking program. Contact Kinetix for restrictions and more information. At the extreme end of the PC-based 3D software scale is Microsoft SoftImage, at $8,000.

After you've settled on a software budget, you'll want to research what these tools have to offer. 3D software buyer's guides and in-depth reviews in magazines help illustrate the pros and cons of different software packages, and give you insights about what they're like to use. However, because product features are always changing (and magazines have 3–4 month lead times), you should get the most current information from the companies' Web sites. For a list of popular applications and capsule reviews, see Appendix D, "Software Products and Publisher List."

While reviews are a great place to start, talking with people who use the products will reward you with a wealth of information and advice. You may even be able to see and try out the software. After you narrow your choices down to one or two prime contenders, get hold of the latest demo versions of the products and spend a few days working with them. Try out all the features and look for confusing or clumsy tools and other weak spots. Remember that you're going to be married to that package for a while, so take your time and make the right choice...for you.

Remember too that no product does *everything* perfectly. They all have pros and cons, strengths and weaknesses. Focus on what your primary needs are and where your strengths or interests as an artist lie. If building 3D models is your primary focus, for example, make sure the product's tool set and modeling features are going to live up to your demands.

The Plug-In Trend

Not so long ago, if you wanted a new feature in your 3D software, you had to cajole the publisher and programmers into adding it into the next release—or perhaps the next version, which was due out *someday*. Fortunately, some programs now have the ability to accept *plug-in* features, which are mini-applications that integrate with and extend the capabilities of the main product. These plug-ins can be modeling tools and utilities, particle systems, image processing filters, motion capture interfaces, and so forth. The result is software that is much better at keeping up with the rapid pace of 3D animation technology.

The User Interface

Learning and working with a new 3D program is a big undertaking, so remember that once you have chosen a program, you're likely to be looking at the same interface, good or bad, for a couple of years at least. Make sure that the tools you will be dealing with the most inspire creativity instead of cursing.

Look for tool sets and menus that are clear and well-organized, have flexible viewports, and fast feedback. Pay particular attention to the features that you use all the time, because 90 percent of the work tends to be done with 10 percent of the tools. If there is a particular tool or feature you can't live without, make sure it's available and implemented to your satisfaction.

Customizable features can go a long way toward making you comfortable and efficient with the product, so look for features like user-definable hot keys and menus. Another good feature to watch for is automatic prompting for object names such as 3D Studio R4 offers (see figure 2.2). Working with your models (and the models of other artists) is a lot easier if everything doesn't have default labels, which is often the case if you aren't forced into naming things.

Finally, you also should be aware of a usage issue that isn't a part of the software interface, but does affect the way you use the package—many of the high-end products use copy protection *"dongles" (hardware keys)*. These are physical devices that plug into the parallel port of your computer or attach inline with the keyboard. The software periodically checks to see if the hardware key is in place, and refuses to operate if it isn't. That's fine, but if the dongle is lost, stolen or damaged, you can't use your software.

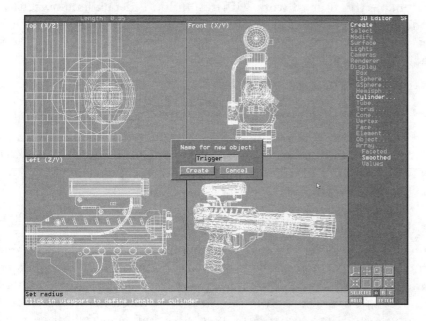

Be warned that damage can occur to these keys if certain peripherals aren't connected according to the hardware key's instructions. Also, if the key is lost or stolen, you may have to buy another full copy of the program, because the publisher will only replace damaged keys that are returned.

Modeling

> This section is designed to be an overview of key feature considerations when selecting software, so much of the following information discusses issues that will be unfamiliar to 3D newcomers. Rather than try to reiterate concepts that are covered in much more detail elsewhere, this section is recommended only for those who are comfortable with basic 3D theory and have some knowledge of the software issues already. Others are encouraged to skip over this section if they aren't planning to buy software right away, or to read the chapters containing information you are unclear about to get a better handle on modeling theory before proceeding.

There are four basic types of modeling systems: Polygonal, Spline, Patch, and Parametric. Many packages combine these systems, because each has its strengths and weaknesses. Polygonal is the most basic, and deals with 3D objects as groups of polygons only. Spline modelers are more sophisticated, and enable the user to work with resolution-independent objects. Patch modelers are well-suited to sculpting organic objects, and parametric modelers allow the parameters of an object to be changed later in the process for maximum flexibility.

In anticipation of the overall increases in processor and display speed, products have been migrating from polygon-based to spline-based modeling. Interestingly, though, the demand for better polygon editing tools has increased dramatically of late, and even the spline modeling giants are paying more attention to polygons. This is due to the needs and incredible popularity of real-time 3D games like Virtua Fighter, Descent, and the DOOM-style POV shooters.

Polygonal is the oldest type of 3D modeling, harkening back to the days when you defined points in space by entering X, Y, and Z coordinates from the keyboard. When three or more of these points are connected by edges, they form a polygon, which can have color and texture. When you put a bunch of these polygons together, you can fashion a representation of just about any object. The downside to polygons is that everything is made up of these tiny, flat surfaces and they need to be fairly small or your object will appear faceted. This means that if you will be zooming in on an object in a scene, you have to model it at a high polygon resolution, even though most of the polys will be unnecessary when you move further from the object.

If you have ever used a drawing program like Illustrator or CorelDRAW!, you're familiar with *splines*, one of the main tools that these programs use. Technically speaking, a spline is a (usually curved) line that is defined by control points (called nodes or knots). One of the main advantages of spline-based modeling over polygonal modeling is that it's resolution-independent, meaning you can get as close as you want to an object and never see any faceting. Spline modelers also are better suited to creating complex organic shapes such as human faces, Tyrannosaurs, and alien spacecraft. Splines are better for applications like this because their method of building forms uses smooth and natural curves instead of jagged and artificial polygonal shapes. There are several different types of splines: B-Splines, Béziers, and NURBS.

B-Splines and *Béziers* have control points called weights (or *Bézier handles*) extending out from the knots, one at each end knot and two on the center control point knot. By adjusting the length and position of these weights, a portion of the spline's shape can be varied (in some cases leaving other portions unaffected), even though the knots remain in fixed positions.

However, no matter how much the curve is altered, it must still pass through the control point knots.

NURBS (Non-Uniform Rational B-Spline) have knots and weights as well, but they reside away from the spline itself. NURBS modeling is often espoused as being the best method for creating sculptural, organic forms.

A patch modeler uses a network of control vertices (CVs) to define and modify the shape of patches, which are usually lattices of either splines or polygons. Patches can be "stitched" together to form large, complex surfaces.

Parametric modeling means that you're working with objects that retain their base geometry information, such as their default shape, their current size, and how many segments their forms consist of. Because this information can still be accessed and changed even after the objects are modified, it enables the user to change or undo alterations to the object later on, and even increase or decrease their resolution (see figure 2.3). Deformations applied to parametric objects can be adjusted at any time, even those applied many operations ago. Contrast this to polygonal modeling, where (tessellation and optimizers aside) after an object is created, its resolution is fixed. Likewise, deforming a polygonal object permanently modifies it, so if you want to reduce that bend significantly, you have to start over with an unbent version of the object.

Parametric Object with Bend Transform

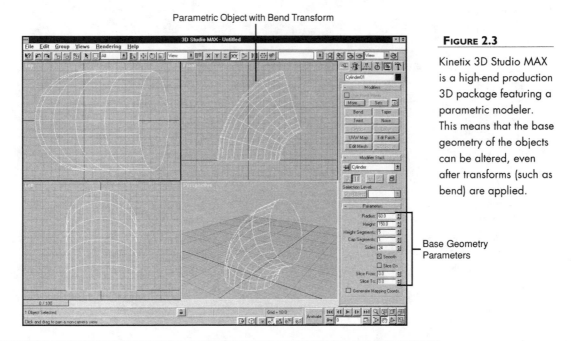

FIGURE 2.3

Kinetix 3D Studio MAX is a high-end production 3D package featuring a parametric modeler. This means that the base geometry of the objects can be altered, even after transforms (such as bend) are applied.

Base Geometry Parameters

Animation

Motion in film, television, and 3D animation is based on the concept of frames, which are still images played at a fast rate so that the images on them appear to move. Video and most animation use 24–30 frames to create one second of motion.

To control animation, most programs use a method called *keyframing*, in which you pose your objects in key positions at specific frames (*keyframes*). Using a process called *tweening*, the computer then interpolates the object's positions in the intermediate frames, resulting in smooth motion from one position to the next.

For example, to bounce a ball from the top-left corner to the middle of the screen to the top-right corner, you would specify frame 0 and place the ball in the top-left corner, setting a keyframe (see figure 2.4). Next, you would change to say, frame 30, and move the ball to the bottom-center of the screen, thereby setting another keyframe at that point. Finally, you would advance the animation again, to frame 60, for example, and move the ball to the upper-right corner, setting the final keyframe.

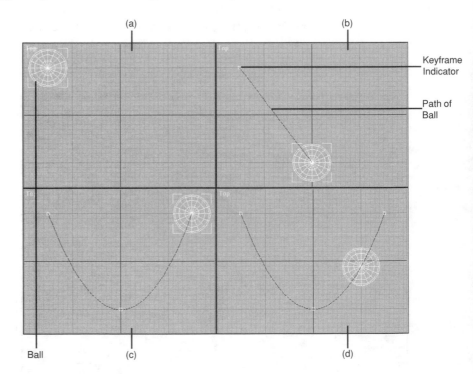

FIGURE 2.4

Keyframing sequence: (a) At frame 0, the ball is positioned in the upper-left corner. (b) At frame 30, the ball is moved to the bottom center of the screen. Note the line showing the path of the object. (c) At frame 60, the ball is moved again, and the path changes to smooth out the movement. (d) Between keyframes, the computer positions the ball according to the path it has calculated.

When the animation is played, the computer makes sure the ball is displayed exactly where you placed it on frames 0, 30, and 60, and figures out how to transition the ball between those frames based on controls for the keyframe called *weighting*. This weighting controls the object's path, allowing the object to make a smooth transition into and out of the keyframe.

As you can with the paths themselves, you can alter the keyframe weighting to affect how the object behaves as it moves through the keyframe. Often this is limited to TCB (Tension/Continuity/Bias) adjustments, but some programs offer a variety of different keyframe weighting schemes, from point-to-point linear to Bézier spline. These provide you with more options, and can save you a lot of time in the animation process.

To manage all this information, most programs have adopted a timeline-style animation interface (see figure 2.5). The horizontal axis is broken down into time units or frame numbers, and the vertical axis consists of a hierarchical list of objects, lights, and animatible parameters. Keyframes are indicated by a marker placed on the line that extends out from the object's name, and positioned on the appropriate frame number as indicated by the timeline below it.

Look for programs with clear and easy-to-use timelines that provide you with the information you need and offer as much feedback as possible. If the timeline offers motion graphs as an alternate method of viewing the animation data, so much the better.

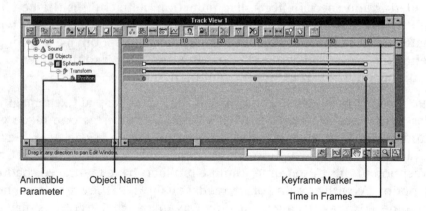

Animatible Parameter **Object Name** **Keyframe Marker** **Time in Frames**

FIGURE 2.5

The animation timeline shows the animatible parameters for each object, with keyframes indicated by a marker placed according to the time (frame number) at which the keyframe was created.

Keyframe weighting is often represented in separate dialogs when the user clicks on a keyframe, but the best feedback and control is provided by those systems that enable you to see and edit both the keyframe position and weight on a Bézier function curve, or on the path itself in the 3D space.

Nearly all of today's 3D animation products feature IK (Inverse Kinematics), which is a method of controlling linked objects in a more natural manner. Before IK, if you were animating an arm and wanted to touch the finger to an object, you started by adjusting the root object (the upper arm), then the forearm, the wrist, and finally, the finger. This was very laborious and inaccurate. IK enables you to move the finger directly to the object, and the wrist and arms adjust smoothly and automatically to make it work. Consider IK support a must for doing any character animation work.

Another way of creating animation that doesn't use keyframing or kinematics is the use of behaviors, such as Look At, Bounce, Spin, and so on. You assign a behavior to a given object, and it performs that motion automatically, freeing you to build on that action to make a more complex movement. For example, if you were animating a scene where an eye was watching a rolling ball, you could assign a Look At or Point Toward behavior to the eye and make the ball the target object. From then on, no matter how you move the eye or the ball, the eye always looks in the right direction. Clearly, this is a timesaving feature that is worth looking for.

Rendering

There are two main kinds of renderers that are used by most 3D products: scanline renderers, and ray tracers.

Speed-wise, *ray tracers* are generally slow to very slow, but offer more precise rendering and special effects, like refraction. Refraction is the bending of light waves that occurs when light waves move through different types of materials, and can be demonstrated by looking at a spoon in a glass of water. Refraction causes the light waves passing from the air to the water to bend, so the spoon looks like Uri Geller got hold of it.

In a ray tracing renderer, a transparent 3D object shaped like a magnifying glass lens actually magnifies what's behind it, whereas one made with a scanline renderer does not (see figure 2.6). Software packages that offer refraction mapping, which simulates this effect in a scanline renderer, are an exception to this. Also, some scanline products have ray-traced shadows as an option. As with any kind of art, render quality is in the eye of the beholder. To some, crisp ray tracing is the only way to go, whereas others may prefer the softer look of the scanline renderers.

If you plan to use these products in a production environment, you should conduct some render speed tests by setting up similar scenes on different software packages and timing them. A few minutes difference in frame rendering time can add up to hundreds of hours on a big animation job. Also, look for network rendering and batch processing capabilities.

FIGURE 2.6

Ray tracing renderers can create refraction effects, so that translucent objects (such as the glass sphere on the left) can magnify and invert light rays just as they would in reality.

If you plan to output to video, watch for field rendering and perhaps the ability to interface with a framestore or single-frame recording VCR directly. You also may want a feature that guarantees NTSC-safe color output.

Miscellaneous Considerations

Most 3D products have three kinds of lights to choose from: omni (or point), distant, and spot. *Omni* or *point* sources are like bare bulbs, illuminating things in all directions. Some programs don't have omni lights that can cast shadows, which may force you to simulate shadow-casting point sources by using multiple spotlights. Distant lights are directional, and simulate infinitely distant light sources like the sun, and cast parallel shadows. Spotlights also are directional, and may offer features like adjustable shape, hotspot, and falloff adjustments, visible cones, and so forth. Some also may enable you to use still or animated images as filters or gels.

There is actually a fourth light source, ambient light, that is offered in 3D software as well. It illuminates all objects evenly, which simulates the light that is reflected from the objects in the scene. It isn't represented by a light source object like the others, but is usually set as a global value that is rarely changed.

One of the current trends in 3D software is animatible properties, especially for materials. *Animatible properties* enable you to vary the material settings over time to create a variety of transformational effects, such as turning a red object into a blue one, or a flesh texture into stone. Some products enable you to animate virtually anything that accepts a range of values, from mesh transformations to post-production glow settings.

3D Software Recommendations

The following are my suggestions for the best software packages, arranged by price and quality.

For PC or Mac modeling on a budget, look at Extreme 3D and trueSpace2, and you might consider Animation Master as well. If you're an illustrator who is more interested in simpler, designer images, a package with more shader options and nicer rendering may be in order. Artists needing a moderately priced tool for Mac or PC 3D illustration work should weigh trueSpace2 alongside others at or below its price point. For students, hobbyists, or those with light 3D needs, Ray Dream has a lot to offer (especially for the price), but the modeler is fairly lightweight.

In the mid-range, LightWave is available for several different platforms, including Amiga, PC, and SGI, and offers an excellent price-performance ratio deserving of strong consideration. The moderately priced Mac package Strata StudioPro is a good choice, and is being ported to the PC as well.

For high-end PC work, it's tough to go wrong with SoftImage, 3D Studio R4, or 3D Studio MAX. Top-of-the-line Mac products include form-Z (dedicated modeler), and Electric Image. On the SGI or Unix platforms, Alias/Wavefront and SoftImage rule.

Choosing a Hardware Platform

Now that you know some of the things to look for in a software package, it's time to think about hardware options. In some cases, your choice of software will dictate the platform and processor required, so check the software's recommendations first. Another key factor is which operating system (OS) the software requires. In most cases, these are linked directly to the hardware, but some 3D software runs under Windows NT, which is available for both PCs and Unix workstations.

There are three major platforms for 3D graphics, namely PC, Mac, and Unix-type workstations. Each offers a range of different manufacturers, models, features, and prices. As with software purchases, you should consult magazine reviews, company literature and Web sites, and most importantly, people who own the system that you're interested in.

Besides shopping for a particular manufacturer and model of system, you also should investigate the peripherals and cards provided. What works for the average purchaser of a computer is not necessarily the best choice for those doing 3D work. For more information, see the section "Choosing Peripherals" later in this chapter.

In the Belly of the Beast

The heart of any computer system is the printed circuit card called the *motherboard*, which contains numerous electronic components (see figure 2.7). One of these is the *Central Processing Unit (CPU)*, or *processor*, which is the brains of the system. This is the component that executes the software commands and makes the whole system work. Processors come in many different configurations, but the two main considerations are architecture and speed.

Memory (SIMMs)

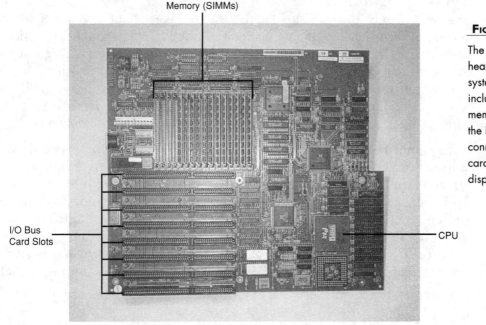

I/O Bus
Card Slots

CPU

FIGURE 2.7

The motherboard is the heart of any computer system. Key components include the CPU, the memory (SIMMs) and the I/O slots for connecting peripheral cards, such as video display adapters.

Chip architecture refers to the internal design of the processor, and that is what separates one manufacturer from another, as well as 486s from Pentiums, or 68040s from PowerPCs and *RISC (Reduced Instruction Set Computer)* processors. The newest architecture is nearly always the fastest, because design and manufacturing know-how increase constantly in the electronics field. Therefore, regardless of which system you choose, try to get the latest generation of processor that is offered for that platform. For PCs, that would be the Pentium Pro (P6); for Macs, the PowerPC, while the desktop SGIs use multiple MIPS R10000 RISC processors. Some other Unix boxes use MIPS processors as well, although the DEC Alpha is a speed demon with a lot of supporters.

The second consideration is *clock speed*, which is basically how fast a processor executes instructions. Clock speed is measured in millions of cycles per second, or megahertz (MHz), and is usually given as a number following the processor architecture, such as 486/33 or P5/166. Clock speed is a very general indicator of processor performance (within an architecture family) because a processor with a clock speed of 100 is 50–100 percent faster than one with a clock speed of 50. For 3D graphics, get the fastest clock speed on the newest processor you can afford, with 100 being the minimum to consider. Make sure that it meets or exceeds (preferably *greatly* exceeds) your program's recommendations.

Processor upgradability is another concern, because sooner or later your system is going to seem slow. This usually takes about two years when working with 3D, but it can happen sooner if you change to a more demanding software package. For PCs, processor upgrades usually come in the form of Overdrive-type processors from Intel or other manufacturers. These consist of processors with clock speeds two to three times faster than your original, with modifications to interface properly with your system. Upgrading is easy—just pull out the old chip and pop in the new one.

For systems that don't offer upgradable processors, accelerator boards are another option. These are CPUs mounted on peripheral cards that plug into a slot on the motherboard and replace or supplement the built-in processor. However, because these tend to circumvent the original processor, these enhancements aren't always completely compatible with the software that runs on the system. Before considering accelerator cards to upgrade a system, look for an in-depth test of the product in a magazine. You also may want to purchase it from someone who offers a 30-day money back guarantee, so that you can try it out on the target system yourself.

My only experience with accelerator cards was a mixed one. When my 68030/16-based Mac IIcx was no longer able to keep up with the demands of the software, I shelled out $1,200 (a deal at the time) for a Radius Rocket accelerator, which had a next-generation 68040/33 processor. As it turned out, the card worked pretty well for most tasks, but usually failed whenever sound was required. The occasional software upgrades from Radius improved the situation, but it never really worked right for most multimedia applications. Ultimately, I ended up buying a Quadra 650 with the same processor speed, and the Rocket resides in my Vault of Obsolete Hardware. No more third-party accelerators for me, pal.

In addition to the processor, there are other *chipsets* (a group of components that supports the CPU) on PC motherboards that can affect performance. When I bought my most recent system, Intel motherboards with Neptune chipsets were the hot item, but this is no longer the case. Check the buyers' guides in PC magazines for sidebars that talk about the latest and greatest motherboards and chipsets. Once you know what the best combinations are, check with the PC manufacturer you're considering to see who makes their motherboard and which chipset it uses.

Another factor that varies among motherboards is the *bus architecture*. This is the size, speed, and connector style of the internal data highway that connects the processor with the video card, hard drives, and so forth. Older PCs use the ISA bus, while Macs use the NuBus. Over the last couple of years, however, the faster PCI bus has come into favor for both platforms, and it's a good way to go.

Remember to take into account your current and future needs as far as internal expansion for additional drives, tape backup systems, and peripheral or interface cards. Desktop and mini-tower systems may run out of space when you add things like SCSI cards, internal modems, extra drives, and the like. Therefore, if you plan to add additional devices in the future, consider full-size tower systems with lots of drive bays and slots. As a minimum, you will want a 2GB hard drive, a CD-ROM drive, a modem, and some kind of backup system, either a removable media type or a tape drive. The backup system also may require a SCSI card, which is a good thing to have for expandability and flexibility anyway.

A final consideration is tech support, no matter which system you buy. 3D artists rarely work from 9–5, so it's critical to be able to resolve problems no matter what time of the day or night it is. Therefore, give due consideration to the tech support offered when choosing between those last couple of systems. You may even try calling the tech support numbers at different times of the day to see how long you have to wait.

Purchase Excuses

When you investigate systems to buy, don't fall into the timing trap. Many people delay buying a system for months or years at a time, because they are waiting for:

A. "...that new processor/CD-ROM/video technology to come out."

B. "...prices to drop on the older stuff once the new processor/CD-ROM/video technology is out."

C. "...a computer that only costs $500."

Excuse A has some validity for those who need the biggest and baddest system available (which includes a lot of 3D artists), but must be weighed against two factors. First, new technology is often buggy technology, so that a 20 percent increase in performance might seem lost among the hours spent troubleshooting and praying for new drivers. Second, the newest stuff is usually the most expensive.

Excuse B is not a bad one, as prices do tend to drop on existing products when new technology is introduced. Of course, they'll drop even more when the next round of high-tech shows up, and so forth. Therefore, weigh this one against the loss of productivity, potential income and experience by not having gear for the next two to six months.

Finally, Excuse C is no excuse at all, since the $500 computer already exists: it's called a used 486. It's not quick, but it does get the job done.

The point is, when you need a system, *go for it*. The benefits of having the tools at your disposal will probably outweigh the potential cost savings or performance increases of waiting. As to the question of *which* system, consider the pros and cons of the different platforms hand-in-hand with your software needs and budget.

SGI/Unix

Silicon Graphics (SGI) workstations have long been considered the ultimate platform for creating computer graphics. The systems feature fast RISC processors, high-speed architectures, 21" monitors, and mind-boggling price tags, running into the hundreds of thousands of dollars. SGI workstations hold the top position in computer graphics due to their speed and advanced scaleable 3D acceleration hardware (which allows objects to be viewed with full shading in real-time). They also are in demand due to the powerful, cutting edge 3D software packages that are available for this platform alone.

The SGI systems the typical 3D user is most likely to encounter are the small business-level Indigo 2 systems (see figure 2.8) and the entry level Indy and O_2 series, which start around $7,500. Note that the entry level systems are sometimes available in a bundle with heavily discounted 3D programs. For those users with Indigo or other SGI systems costing $20,000 or more, however, the software is much more expensive than similar Mac and PC packages, with some of the popular programs running $15–$60K.

FIGURE 2.8

A Silicon Graphics Indigo 2 Extreme, used at Mondo Media/ Mechadeus for creating complex organic models. Image by Cody Chancellor.

Besides SGI, there are other high-powered Unix workstations as well, including the Sun SparcStation, DEC Alpha, IBM RS6000, and others. Despite competition and substantial cost reductions, however, most of these systems are still out of reach of nearly all contract artists and even most small production houses.

PC

Without a doubt, the PC is the overwhelming winner in the desktop computer wars of the late '80s and throughout the '90s. They are relatively inexpensive, going for less than $1,000 for a decent P5/133 to about $6,000 or so for a twin processor Pentium Pro system (circa early 1997). There are many different manufacturers and models to choose from, and mountains of software available, with new titles appearing daily. There also are several different operating systems to choose from, including DOS, OS/2, Windows 3.1, Windows 95, and Windows NT. That said, they also are a pain to configure (especially when adding hardware) due to design oversights in the basic architecture and operating system.

Windows 95 and the recent plug-and-play systems and cards aim to ease the configuration nightmare, but PCs are still trying to catch up to Macintosh when it comes to easy installation and user friendliness. However, PCs still have three significant advantages over Macs: power, price, and software selection.

Although Intel dominates the PC processor market, there is enough consumer demand and pressure from competing chip manufacturers to keep the CPU power curve increasing at an astonishing rate. In fact, the desktop systems of today have more computing power than mini-computers of a few years ago, and this has made a big impact in the 3D graphics world.

For some time, both Mac and PC 3D products have tried to approach the power and user feedback achieved by workstation-level products like Alias/ Wavefront and SoftImage. Until recently, however, the limitations of the hardware could not allow that level of real-time interaction with shaded objects. As a result, the power-starved, spline-based products moved sluggishly, and polygon-based wireframe interfaces continued to be the norm.

Over the past few years, however, the Pentium and Pentium Pro processors (often coupled with the multitasking capabilities of Windows NT) have started to make PC products look and feel much more like their RISC-powered siblings. Of course, the gap remains significant even with state-of-the-art P6 multiprocessor systems and OpenGL cards, but there is no doubt that the PC power curve (and price point) is cause for concern at SGI headquarters.

Most 3D software for the PC requires some version of Windows, with the extremely popular DOS-based 3D Studio R4 being the exception. The features and general move toward Windows 95 would seem to make it the OS of choice unless your software requires something different. Windows NT is another good choice, although it still lacks the broad driver support that Windows 3.1 enjoys and the plug-and-play features of Windows 95, which can mean that some of your hardware may not work under it.

If you plan to work in the Windows NT environment with a product like 3D Studio MAX, you should strongly consider a multiprocessor system. Even if you buy a system with only one CPU installed, it will delay obsolesence to be able to add a second CPU in the future, not to mention overdrive versions of the processors.

Macintosh

Like the PC, the Macintosh (see figure 2.9) has seen a substantial rise in computing power, especially since Apple finally started licensing its architecture and OS to third parties. The new, high-speed PowerPC processors are a real boon to 3D users, because the Mac has always been under-powered when it came to modeling and ray tracing tasks.

FIGURE 2.9

My Apple Macintosh Quadra 650 system, which uses a 68040/ 33 processor. Although adequate for many tasks, the power and speed of a faster PowerPC-equipped system is much more appropriate for 3D graphics.

Pressures from the PC marketplace as well as the new range of Mac manufacturers (Power Computing and Radius) have driven prices on these systems down from their lofty heights of a few years ago. Macs are now much more competitive with similarly equipped PCs, putting them in the $1,000–$5,000 range. However, the Mac power curve is not on quite the same level with the PCs, so even the fastest Mac is likely to be slower than the fastest PC.

Many of the Mac's innovative features, such as its user-friendly interface, plug-and-play hardware configuration, graphic orientation, and unique applications, have made their way to the PC. This has weakened the reasons to choose Mac over PC, although it still has the edge in user-friendliness. Another problem is that it also has never held a particularly big market share, making it less attractive for new software development. Still, it has been an underdog so long that it's legendary, and it is definitely capable of producing some excellent 3D graphics. You need only look at the CD-ROM title *Sinkha* to see that.

Platform Recommendations

As mentioned earlier, software sells hardware, so the right platform for you to buy is the one that runs the software you want. If you're not so sure about the package you want, or it runs on different platforms, here are my thoughts:

I like the Mac and hope it sticks around, but I find it hard to recommend for 3D graphics outside of illustration work. While production rendering for animation is possible, the product of choice is the very expensive Electric Image, the full version of which costs as much as SoftImage for the PC. This, coupled with the uncertain future of the system and weakening software support, puts it at a serious disadvantage.

The PC is the most popular platform, and the intense competition among manufacturers keeps driving the price/performance ratios at a breakneck pace. In addition, the most popular 3D software around is 3DS R4, which runs only on the PC (not too badly on a fast 486, I might add), and there also are lots of other 3D packages in all kinds of price ranges to choose from. These factors make the PC the best choice for most users.

If you have the bucks, the SGI remains the top of the heap, with Alias/Wavefront and SoftImage at the cutting edge of 3D software. While this is likely to remain the case for a while, the performance advantages of these systems are being eroded by high-end PCs. Although recently reduced, the still flamboyant prices make these systems suitable for only those who need (and can afford) the absolute best.

Choosing Peripherals

Nearly every computer system needs some peripheral devices to be truly usable, be it a monitor, hard drive, or other mass storage device, printer or modem. In addition, artists often need other devices as well, including scanners, video and audio cards, digitizers, and graphics tablets.

Some peripherals, such as cartridge hard drives and modems, are available in either internal or external configurations, meaning that you either install them inside your CPU case or they reside in their own enclosure nearby. Internal devices keep your workspace tidier, but external versions can be moved to different locations and even from platform to platform. This can save a lot of money if you have more than one system, or need to use devices on both your home and office systems.

As with any hardware or software purchase, consult magazine reviews instead of relying on manufacturer's claims. That said, the following sections look at some of the common peripherals that the 3D artist is likely to require.

Storage

The first law of computing states that "files expand to overflow your storage capacity." An excellent example is *desktop video*, which enables digital video editing and special effects on a relatively inexpensive system (compared to dedicated video editing systems). On the other hand, video files consume hard drive space at a phenomenal rate. Because animation is often output as digital video files, this situation applies to animators as well as video editors. In addition, 3D software often requires substantial amounts of hard drive space for temporary files on top of the room required for the renders.

Hard Drive Basics

When I first got into computing, hard drives (also called fixed drives) were a bulky, expensive rarity, and practically unheard of for desktop systems (see figure 2.10). Now, operating without them is inconceivable.

By the way, hard drives are sealed units containing a motor that spins a set of metal disks called magnetic *platters*. A *read/write head*, a tiny electromagnet mounted on an arm, moves back and forth over these rotating disks, reading and writing data with a set of electromagnetic pulses that are stored in the magnetic material coating the platter.

FIGURE 2.10

Hard drives have shrunk dramatically in size and price, while increasing in capacity. (a) Photo of a 1980s-vintage 330MB drive, which probably cost several thousand dollars. (b) A new 2.1GB drive, which goes for less than $300.

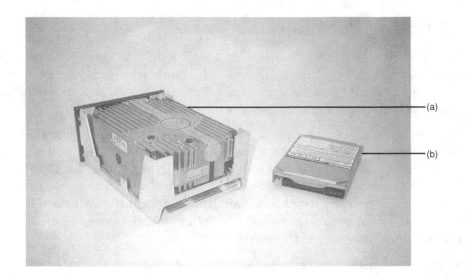

For working with 3D graphics, you should consider 2GB (gigabytes) to be a minimum amount of drive space if buying a new system. It's certainly possible to get by with less than that, but the meager amount of savings over going with a smaller drive just doesn't make sense. If you want more space, be aware that higher capacity drives are still pretty expensive, running around $900 for a 4GB model at the moment.

The speed of your drive also can make a significant difference in the overall performance of your system, especially when you're rendering large 3D models that use the hard drive for virtual memory. This occurs when the 3D software or operating system needs more space than the computer's RAM can provide. The software writes temporary files to the hard drive, saving chunks of data to free up RAM space, then loading them back in when needed again. Because of the amount of time it takes to save and load these files, virtual memory is very slow, and can take a heavy toll on the performance of the software. Therefore, you want fast drives that will reduce the delays as much as possible.

definition

virtual memory The use of hard drive space as temporary storage when the system runs low on RAM.

There are five specifications that will help you gauge drive performance:

1. *Seek time:* The maximum time (in milliseconds) it takes to move the read/write head to a specified location on the disk. Low seek times (10 ms or less) are preferred.

2. *Track-to-track seek time:* The time (in milliseconds) it takes to move the read/write head from one track to another.

3. *Data transfer rate:* The maximum rate (in kilobytes/sec) at which information is delivered from the drive to the computer under ideal conditions. The higher the transfer rate, the more smoothly animation or video is likely to play back from the drive.

4. *RPM (Revolutions Per Minute):* This is related to the data transfer rate, because the faster the drive spins, the faster the data can be transferred. Still, give priority to the data transfer rate figure.

5. *Interface:* There are many different ways that drives can be connected to computers, and the interface on the drive must match the one in the system. Macs and SGIs use SCSI interfaces, while PCs usually have IDE or EIDE interfaces (but some may use SCSI). Currently, SCSI-3 or Ultra-Wide SCSI is the fastest and highest capacity standard interface, but new technology is always being introduced.

Along with these standard specifications, some drives have special characteristics that make them more suitable for desktop video applications. *AV drives* have high throughput rates and avoid thermal calibration during access. *Thermal calibration* is an adjustment made by the drive to compensate for heat expansion, but means that while the drive is sending or receiving data, it won't pause to perform the periodic accuracy adjustments that typical drives perform, because these cause the animation to stutter. These drives are a good choice for 3D applications because they're great for playing back animation as well. You can usually spot these drives easily, because the AV designation is often part of the model number, such as R1272AV.

If you have any experience with SCSI, you're probably aware that it has an annoying habit of not working if you change something, such as adding or removing a device. Sometimes, users find themselves rearranging gear and swapping cables for hours to get a "*SCSI chain*" (the whole assembly of peripherals and cables) working properly. This is known in the trade as SCSI Voodoo, and often results from using cheap or mismatched cables and *passive terminators* (devices that "cap off" the end of a SCSI chain). The best solution I've found for it is an active terminator, like the APS SCSI Sentry, which automatically monitors and adjusts the chain to reduce errors.

There are specialty drive configurations that are worth noting, although it's unlikely that the 3D artist will require them unless extensive desktop video or animation editing is part of his or her needs. A *RAID (Redundant Array of Inexpensive Disks)* is a series of matched hard drives interfaced together to increase data capacity and throughput or provide backup in case of drive failure. These drive arrays can be configured in a number of different ways, and are referred by designations such as RAID 0 or RAID 2.

Manufacturer warranties and exchange policies are another important thing to consider when selecting a drive. See the "Hard Drive Crashes" section later in this chapter for more details.

When considering storage, you should avoid the trap of looking at fixed hard drive space alone, and instead take a broader view by considering all forms of storage. In this way, you can arrive at a proper balance of storage systems that not only provide all the space you need, but ensure that you can archive files as well. A good example of alternate methods of storage is cartridge media.

Cartridge Media

Cartridge hard drives are a storage system that uses removable media to store data. The cartridges have magnetic platters in them just like regular hard drives, but they're sealed to prevent dust from getting in, and are durable enough to be handled and shipped. The current capacities of each cartridge range from 44MB to 1GB. Depending on the type and capacity, drive prices range from $200–$500, and the cartridges run between $12 and $125.

Any kind of removable media, from floppies to video cassettes, usually ends up getting labeled at some point. The problem is that the labels rarely come off easily, if at all. The solution is to get some Magic brand Goo Gone, a natural solvent that is available at most stores. Apply ONE drop to a soft cloth and rub the liquid into the label just until the label darkens slightly. Use *only* one drop so you won't saturate the label, because the liquid might get inside the case and mess up your media (and then your drive). Wait 15 minutes and do it again. After another 15 minutes, slowly pull the label off.

High-capacity cartridge hard drives are an excellent way to expand your storage capacity while making the data portable as well. Fill up your hard drive? No problem, just buy a new cartridge. Need to send a huge file to someone? Pack the cartridge in a bubble wrap container and fire it off.

While it's possible to use these drives as your primary work disk, I don't recommend it. If you forget your cartridge or it gets damaged, your system is dead. They also tend to be slower than the typical fixed hard drive. However, I would definitely suggest adding one of these instead of a second fixed drive when you need more capacity. Cartridge drives also make good short-term backup devices, although using one can be significantly more expensive then using a tape backup system.

Two of the best known manufacturers of cartridge drives are Iomega and SyQuest. Both make a range of products and media designed for the needs of most users, and at very affordable prices. Other manufacturers also are jumping in, licensing the technology or coming up with their own, so capacities should continue to rise dramatically even as the prices drop into the cellar.

I have Iomega ZIP drives ($199) for both my PC and Mac, and love the cross-platform portability they provide. I also like the fact that my parallel port-style ZIP drive will hook up to virtually any PC, because it doesn't require a SCSI connection. Recently, I added a 1GB Iomega JAZ drive ($499) to my system, giving me unlimited storage potential.

One caveat, however—plan to buy another cable or adapter if your SCSI chain uses the common Centronics-style 50 pin connectors. The SCSI versions of the Iomega products come with cables for SCSI-2 (50 pin High Density) and Mac CPU (DB-25) connections only.

Optical Media

Magneto-Optical (MO) drives are another form of cartridge-based storage that offered comparatively high storage capabilities (650MB–1.2GB) at a time when most cartridges handled less than 100MB. However, their high cost, lack of a single standard, and generally slow operation (particularly during writes) have prevented them from becoming a mass-market solution. While the newest crop of MO drives boast capacities of 2.6GB or more and high data transfer rates, they are seeing increased competition from low-cost Iomega JAZ drives and the new affordable, *recordable* CD-ROMs. My advice is to pass on MO drives in favor of one of these alternatives.

CD-ROM Recordable (CD-R) drives have finally dropped in price to mass-market levels, and are bound to have a big impact on the way you archive programs and files. After all, if you can just pop in a CD-ROM that contains all of those seldom-used programs clogging your hard drive, it's likely that you'll trade the CD drive's slower access time for the additional free space. In addition, CD-R is great for doing prototype runs of CD-ROM products, sending large files to people who don't have compatible cartridge hard drives, and for making your own custom music CDs.

However, lest CD-R seem like the ultimate back-up media, there are a few caveats. First, the media is about $5–$10 a disc at the moment, and "only" holds about 650MB of data. That means that it would cost you $15–$30 every time you wanted to back up your 2GB hard drive. Ouch! Second, the media is susceptible to damage, so you really need to have at least two copies or use another backup system for safety.

No system, however, should be without a standard (nonrecordable) CD-ROM drive at least. In fact, they have probably become more necessary than floppy drives for installing commercial software. There are two key considerations when it comes to selecting CD-ROM drives. First is the data transfer rate, which is based on a single-speed drive level of 150 KB/s. Prices being what they are, there's no point in getting anything slower than a 6X drive, which means it has a transfer rate of 900Kb/s (still glacial by hard drive standards, but sufficient for most applications). The other thing to think about is a multi-disc drive, one that holds three or more discs. This is great if you have a texture or mesh library CD-ROM that you use a lot (because it always remains available), but still enables you to pop in a reference disc, music CD, or the latest game.

Finally, the new kid on the block is *Digital Versatile Disc (DVD)*, which is an optical disc format for both video and computer files. The video people are excited about it because it offers near-broadcast quality video in a highly compressed MPEG2 format. The computer people are excited about it because a single DVD disc can replace several CD-ROMs full of video, and will eventually provide very high-density (4.7–8.7GB per disc) writable storage for all kinds of files. Of course, this will be a boon to storage-hungry computer animators, once they become widely available and reasonably priced.

Tape Media

Tape backup systems are often an afterthought, but they should be part of any 3D artist's system. Graphics files tend to be large and numerous, and tape offers an economical way to back up your system as well as to safely archive old work.

There are several different types of tape backup formats and systems available, including Colorado, Travan, QIC (Quarter Inch Tape), DLT (Digital Linear Tape), and DAT (Digital Audio Tape). The main considerations for selecting one system over another are capacity and cost. Most users should consider a reasonably priced ($100–$400) 800MB-4GB QIC-based tape backup system. If you're into production animation, desktop video, or other work that requires a lot of storage capacity, however, a DAT drive may be more practical. These drives range from $700 2GB DAT models up to monster 280GB autoloader systems.

When choosing which way to go, try to get a tape system that's able to back up all of your hard drives onto a single cassette. Otherwise, you'll have to back up across multiple cassettes, which is inconvenient. Note that the printed capacities of drives are somewhat misleading, because they anticipate a 50 percent reduction in file size due to compression that they perform while backing up. If many of your files are already in a compressed format, you may need a higher capacity tape system.

In addition to the price of the drive, pay particular attention to media costs, as the cassettes may well end up setting you back more than the drive in the long run. Try to estimate your total storage needs over the space of a few years, then break down the cost of the tape system and media into a "cost-per-megabyte" form. That should help determine the most economical route in the long run. Remember that you should always have at least two backups of a given file in case the media is lost or corrupted. It's also a good idea to keep one of your backup sets off-site.

Not only is making a backup important, but you also should watch where you put those tapes. Years ago, someone at work put a box of DAT backups on the floor. Later, people started to complain that they were having trouble restoring files from those tapes. As it turns out, the janitors had large magnets on the front of their vacuum cleaners, and these were erasing the tapes!

Video Display Cards

The *video display card* ($100–$400) is responsible for converting the text and graphics data in the computer into a form that the computer monitor can display. There are several things to think about when you're selecting a video card for your system. One is how fast the card can move graphics data, because this is key to smooth playback of desktop video or animation. Speed is often indicated by two things: The type of bus (interface) that the card uses, and how many bits of data it can move internally in a single operation. Other factors include the resolution of the card (how many pixels it can display) and the refresh rates.

Speed Factors

One of the biggest speed factors in video display cards is which bus the card (supported by the motherboard, of course) uses. Currently, the PCI bus is one of the fastest for video applications and is used in both PCs and PowerMacs. Older PCs use the slower ISA bus, EISA or VESA, while older Macs use the NuBus interface.

The internal data specification can be rather confusing, because it uses the same nomenclature as the color depth specification, even though they are unrelated. For example, the ATI ProTurbo card I mentioned earlier has a 64-bit data path. That means that it can move a fairly large chunk of graphics data with each operation. In other words, the fact that it's a 64-bit card means that it moves four times as much graphics data at a time as my old video adapter, a 16-bit Orchid Fahrenheit card.

The fastest set of video adapters generally available today are the new 128-bit cards, with 256-bit cards in development. Where will it end? It probably won't, at least until the cards are fast enough to change the color and position of every pixel on the screen in $\frac{1}{30}$th of a second.

> In case you're wondering how 8 bits equals 256 colors, it's because computers use binary numbers, also called Base 2. A single binary number (called a bit in computerese) can only be one of two things: either 0 or 1. Therefore, to represent larger numbers, a series of bits are strung together, like 1011. The position of each binary number within the series (from right to left) becomes an exponent of 2, and then they are added together. In this way, 8 bits = binary 11111111 = $2^7+2^6+2^5+2^4+2^3+2^2+2^1+2^0$ = 128+64+32+16+8+4+2+1 = 255. Because zero counts as a number, a total of 256 numbers can be represented.

Now, contrast the data path figure with the bit depth of the card, which specifies how many colors the card can display. The old Fahrenheit card had a maximum color depth of 8 bits, which means it was limited to 256 colors. The ProTurbo, on the other hand, has a color depth of 24 bits, which allows it to display 16,777,216 colors, which is nearly the full range of colors that are visible to humans. Cards with 24-bit color depth are desirable, because they enable you to work with smooth, accurate color images.

Resolution and Refresh

The next factor to consider is the *resolution* of the card, which means how many vertical and horizontal *pixels* it can display. Resolution is defined by a set of two numbers, such as 640 × 480. This means that the card can display 640 horizontal pixels, and 480 vertical ones. 640 × 480 is considered the minimum resolution for most applications (except games), with 1024 × 768 or higher being popular among graphics professionals.

Refresh rate is the number of times per second that the screen image is repainted on the monitor, and is measured in cycles per second, or Hertz (Hz). Refresh rates of less than 72Hz tend to cause the screen to flicker, and this is known to cause eye fatigue in many individuals. This flickering is particularly apparent at refresh rates of 60Hz or less. As a rule of thumb, 72Hz should be considered the minimum, with higher rates being desirable.

Because graphics adapters enable the user to define refresh rates without regard to the capabilities of the video monitor, it may be possible to input a refresh rate that could cause physical damage to the monitor. Therefore, make sure you have your monitor's spec sheet available when you're setting up the graphics adapter, and only use values that the manual specifies.

Note that there's a close interrelationship between bit depth, resolution, and refresh rates due to the amount of video memory on the graphics adapter. For example, increasing the resolution on a card to 1024 × 768 may force its bit depth to drop to 65,536 colors or less, and its refresh rate to drop below the 72Hz level. Because graphics users want high resolution, bit depth, and refresh rates, the solution is to buy the card with additional video memory installed. Usually, this means buying a card with 4MB of VRAM. If you need to trim back and plan to upgrade the card's VRAM later, make sure the card you purchase will enable you to do so.

Another nasty surprise to watch out for is that some of the bit depth/ resolution/refresh listings may be for *interlaced* output. Interlaced means that when the screen is being redrawn, every other horizontal scan line is skipped. For example, first all the odd numbered lines are redrawn, then all the even numbered ones. This is appropriate when the card is connected to a television-style (NTSC) monitor for a video output application, but is bad for most computer monitors, which will flicker like crazy. Make sure the setting you are looking for is going to produce *non-interlaced (NI)* output. All of this stuff is easy to overlook when selecting a card, so check the card's specifications *very* carefully.

Acceleration

Acceleration is a hardware enhancement to the video card that handles certain tasks much more quickly than if the CPU did them, such as moving blocks of video memory around. Many PC graphics adapter cards offer Windows acceleration, which speeds up graphics and video when running in that environment, but some manufacturers (like Matrox) seem to have abandoned DOS speed considerations in the same breath. This could be trouble if you use the DOS-based 3D Studio or are a serious game player.

The increasing popularity of video in games and applications has led to some cards adding accelerated QuickTime, Video for Windows, or MPEG support, allowing full-screen, full-motion (30 frames per second) playback.

In addition, some cards offer *video capture* capabilities, which means that they can digitize video stills or movies coming from a camera, VCR, laserdisc, or other source and save them as files on the hard drive. Users can then use programs such as Adobe Premiere to edit the video, composite them with 3D graphics and 2D special effects, and then output the result to tape. In some cases, you can buy a video card that enables you to add the additional capture hardware later on.

Driven by the demands of 3D graphics in modeling and real-time games, some of the newest cards now offer hardware *3D acceleration*. This can dramatically speed up the display of 3D objects *if the software is written to take advantage of this capability*. Therefore, the decision to purchase a card like this will depend on the software you plan to use. There are several different 3D acceleration schemes, including OpenGL and Heidi, and card performance claims vary widely, so do your homework if you plan to go this route.

Video Card Recommendations

Your choice of graphics card will depend on your motherboard, because you will want to use the fastest bus available. For PC or Mac users with newer systems, PCI is the way to go.

For users doing 3D illustration work or light animation, an unaccelerated video card with at least 16-bit color graphics at 800×600 is the minimum. Users doing production animation should have 24-bit color at 1024×768, in an 64-bit package at least. Power users should get a card featuring at least the same resolution, as well as accelerated 3D graphics with support for their software in a 128-bit package.

Display

It's ironic, but the computer display, or monitor, is often the most overlooked component in the system. Part of this extends from the fact that many systems come bundled with a monitor, and unless you examine several monitors side-by-side, it's difficult to see much of a difference. Regardless, the differences are definitely there, affecting the brightness, clarity, and color of the image in a big way.

For 3D and graphic arts, a 15" monitor ($300–$450) should be considered the minimum size, with 17" or larger ($550–$900) desirable (see figure 2.11). Workstation-class systems generally offer spacious 21" monitors, but then you're talking a display costing you over $1,600.

FIGURE 2.11

My 17" Nokia Multigraph 447X monitor. As is typical of monitor size specifications, the actual viewable image size is only 15.5".

On the subject of size, the figures given for monitors are deceiving. When a monitor is claimed to have a 15" diagonal picture, this actually refers to the size of the picture tube (a.k.a. Cathode Ray Tube or CRT). Now, because part of this tube is contained within the display's case, the actual viewable size of a 15" monitor is usually around 13.5"! Likewise, 17" monitors are about 15.5", and so forth. Thankfully, many manufacturers now list "maximum viewable size" figures in their advertising.

The difference between listed and viewable size varies by model and manufacturer, so you may want to take a cloth measuring tape along to the store when you shop for a display. Don't use a metal tape measure, or you may find yourself the owner of a floor model with a scratched tube.

As you may recall from the discussion of display adapters, the resolution and refresh rates available from your video card may not be supported by a given monitor, and the wrong settings may damage your display. Therefore, make a careful comparison of the specifications for your video card and your monitor to make sure you can get the combinations of color depth, resolution, and refresh rates that you desire.

Multiplatform connectivity is desirable for anyone who uses both Macs and PCs or other platforms. Those doing video work may want to look for displays that offer direct RGB connections as well. A good monitor is an expensive investment, so you might as well get the maximum amount of flexibility from it.

On the safety front, there is a great deal of concern over the long-term effects of monitors and other electrical devices on our bodies. As a result, a number of standards and recommendations have been established, and it's advisable to get a monitor that meets the low emission (TCO92) or even micro emission (MPR90) standards. The proper position and distance for the monitor also are outlined in most video display manuals.

Input Devices

Virtually every computer comes with a mouse these days, so you might wonder why you would want to buy something that you're already getting with your system anyway. Comfort and ergonomics aside, some software may require a certain kind of mouse (such as a three-button model) or may work better with a different sort of input device. There are all kinds of different mice out there, with one, two, three or more buttons, reversed for left-handers, wireless, programmable...you name it.

One popular mouse alternative is the *trackball*. A trackball is sort of an upside-down mouse, and the user rolls his or her hand around on a large ball to move the cursor, while the base remains motionless. The buttons are large and easy to reach without removing your hand from the ball.

For 3D artists, there are three unusual input devices that may be of interest: flying mice, spaceballs, and dial boxes. *Flying mice* are meant to be picked up off the desk and moved around in the air, which probably looks kind of stupid but makes sense if you're working in a 3D environment. *Spaceballs* and other three-axis input devices remain on the table, but you can push and pull them to affect the Z-axis as well as move them around along the X- and Y-axis. *Dial boxes* consist of a set of knobs that you turn to adjust the size and position of 3D objects along the selected axes.

Graphics tablets (see figure 2.12) also are popular among 2D and 3D artists. Because tablets use a pen-like stylus for input, they feel comfortable and familiar, like using a pad and paper. Some find it difficult to make accurate menu selections when using a stylus, however, so many of the tablets enable you to alternate between mouse and stylus input, providing the best of both worlds. In addition, the tablet may have a *puck,* which is a mouse-like input device with built-in cross-hairs for precision positioning. This device is good for tracing a sketch, allowing precision input of a shape without measuring or scanning the image.

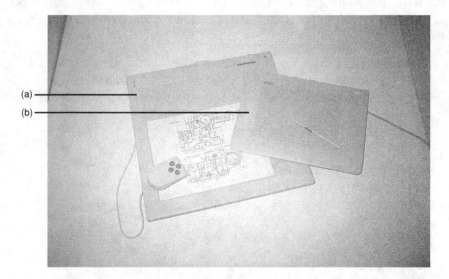

(a)

(b)

FIGURE 2.12

Two types of graphics tablets. (a) A non-pressure-sensitive tablet with a wired stylus and puck, which is adequate for 3D work. (b) A pressure-sensitive tablet with a wireless stylus is great for 3D work and 2D painting.

There are several different kinds of tablets, but one of the key differences is whether the tablet is pressure sensitive or not. Standard tablets provide X and Y position data only, which is fine for 3D. *Pressure-sensitive* tablets, on the other hand, read the amount of force that you place on the point of the stylus, and send this information along to the software. This is desirable if you also do 2D paint work, because the software uses the information to vary the density or color of the paint, the size of the brush, and so forth. The result is better control and images that can look more like they were created with traditional materials.

Many tablets these days are cordless, which means that the stylus is unattached to the tablet. However, less expensive models that have a wire running from the stylus to the tablet are still available. While these don't allow quite as much freedom as the cordless units, they're worth considering if you can't afford the others. Because these input devices all have very different feels and behaviors, it's a personal choice as to which is the best for you. Be sure to try them out for a while on an operational system before choosing one, and check to make sure that your system and software will support it.

Scanners, Cameras, and Digitizers

Scanners can be a terrific asset to the 3D artist, because they enable you to digitize photographs, fabric, tiles, and other flat materials for use as textures. Along with providing mapping assistance, some 3D packages enable you to load a background image into your modeling workspace. This enables you to scan in drawings or photos of objects and then build 3D objects right on top of the reference material.

Scanners come in many sizes and configurations, but there are three main types for desktop use: handheld, flatbed, and slide scanners (see figure 2.13). In addition, scanners also are available in either grayscale or color versions.

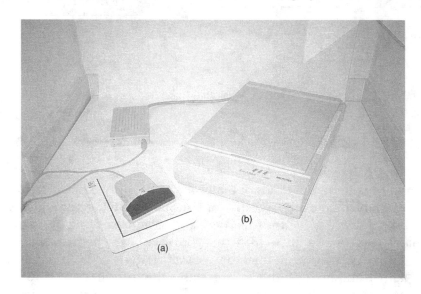

Document Scanners

The *handheld scanner* ($90–$180) is a mouse-like affair that you drag over the top of an image. They are compact and inexpensive, but limited in terms of the width of the image that they can scan as well as their accuracy.

Flatbed scanners ($300–$1,400) are the most popular type, and consist of a case with a glass top and cover. Images are placed onto the glass and held in place by the cover while the scanner's in operation. There are three major factors to take into account with these scanners: document size, number of passes for color, and resolution.

The first consideration in selecting a flatbed scanner is the maximum document size. Many scanners have a maximum document size of 8.5" × 11.7", which may not be big enough to scan images from oversized art books in a single pass. If you often work with big images, then get an 8.5" × 14" or larger model.

The next consideration is whether the scanner is a *one-pass* or *three-pass* model. This refers to how many times the scanning head has to move across the document to digitize it in full color. The three-pass models tend to be less expensive, but single-pass scanners are three times as fast and generally more accurate.

Finally, resolution is less of an issue for 3D artists than it is for those in the print profession, so a minimum of 300dpi (dots per inch) is probably more than adequate. If you desire a higher resolution model, be forewarned that sometimes the dpi figures are inflated by pixel doubling tricks, and may not truthfully reflect the resolution of the scanner.

Slide Scanners

The last type of optical scanner is the *slide scanner* ($700–$1,200). These are moderately-sized devices used for scanning 35mm (or larger) slides and negatives. They have the advantage of being able to scan a photo directly without having to make a print of it first, and provide more accurate color reproduction because of that.

If you plan to do a lot of scans from your photos, you may want to have the film processed directly onto PhotoCDs, which provide computer-ready images in several resolutions. Be warned, however, that quality varies widely among PhotoCD processors, so ask around at a good photography store to find out who does the best job. Despite this, you may still find yourself doing color correction and other adjustments in a paint program to achieve satisfactory results.

Another alternative to slide scanners and PhotoCDs are the newest digital cameras, which provide respectable resolution at moderate prices. *Digital cameras* ($200–$1,200+) record images onto built-in memory or tiny diskettes that can be downloaded directly into your system through a serial cable or PCMCIA card. These cameras are convenient for quick grab shots and for shiny or three-dimensional objects that can't be scanned on a flatbed unit.

3D Scanners/Digitizers

3D scanners and 3D digitizers are powerful tools for modelers, but they're still very expensive. *3D scanners* use optical and/or laser technology to scan a physical object, then generate a wireframe mesh (and sometimes a full-color map) of the object. This technology is often used to create highly accurate models of complex objects or people.

Much less expensive than the 3D scanners are *3D digitizers*, which use a mechanical arm with sensors inside to determine the position of key points on the physical object. 3D digitizers are much slower to use because each point has to be registered one at a time, but they have the added advantage of enabling the user to determine the density of the key points. This allows the modeler to input more detail where it is needed, and leave the mesh simpler in other areas.

Printers

While printers aren't a necessity for doing 3D work, they are a convenient means of showing off your work when a computer is unavailable. Obviously, they also are needed for the myriad of non-graphics work you probably do anyway, such as word processing.

Printers for home and small business work fall into two main categories: laser and inkjet. Laser printers ($300–$1,200+) produce a very sharp, professional image, but nearly all of them are limited to black-and-white printing. Inkjets ($150–$300) aren't quite as sharp, but are often less expensive, sometimes more portable, and are available in reasonably priced color versions ($200–$500) as well.

Laser printers show off their greatest differences when printing a full page of black or halftone graphics, so you may want to take an image or two along to test print when shopping. Another consideration is how well the printer handles heavy stock, labels, transparencies, envelopes, and other oddball tasks.

If you opt for a color inkjet, go to a well-stocked store and compare the quality of the full-color printouts. Note that some inkjet printers may not have as large a printable area as laser printers do. You'll probably need to use special paper recommended by the manufacturer to get the best results, and this can be expensive. Consider the cost of the paper and replacement ink cartridges if you plan to do a lot of printing.

Finally, keep in mind that service bureaus may be your best bet if you rarely plan to do color prints, or when you want higher quality printing for your portfolio pieces. You'll find more information on this in Chapter 10, "Rendering and Output."

Audio

You may wonder what the heck audio has to do with 3D graphics, but the ability to work with sound within a 3D application is on the rise, and it can be a tremendous time saver. For example, some programs enable you to tie animation to an audio file, which makes it easier to have objects moving to the beat of the intended soundtrack. In other cases, a voice track may be used to drive the mouth movements of a 3D character. Imagine how much time and trouble that could save!

Sound cards come in a plethora of different quality levels, ranging from screechy no-name cheapos to top-of-the-line professional gear with external patch panels. Price ($80–$300+) is a pretty good indicator of quality, but consult reviews and listen to the cards themselves to help you decide what suits your needs. Note that compatibility is more important than sound quality, for most users, so for PCs that usually means getting a SoundBlaster card (see the section "Buying a PC: A Case Study," later in the chapter for more information).

In nearly all cases, sound cards are able to handle two types of audio data— digital audio and music. Depending on the card and the way it's configured, the music is either produced directly by a chip on the board, or the data is routed to external musical instruments that use the *MIDI* (Musical Instrument Device Interface) communications standard. MIDI allows for music to be recorded and played back using relatively compact codes that basically tell an instrument which note to play and for how long, as well as a great deal of other specifics. While the synthesized music produced by most sound cards is only acceptable for games, the results can be excellent if the card features *wavetable synthesis*. Cards with this feature use digitized samples of real instruments to produce much more realistic sounds.

The other type of sound that the card can reproduce is digital audio, like you get from an audio CD player. *Digital audio* works by converting sounds into a form a computer can deal with, namely a binary file. CD-quality audio, for example, is digitized at a 16-bit, 44.1KHz rate, but 8-bit or 16-bit sound at a 22KHz rate is much more common for computer applications.

To get the most out of your audio card, don't skimp on the speakers ($15–$300). Tinny little speakers will make even an expensive audio card sound bad, while a decent set (with a subwoofer, if you can manage it) will make even a cheap audio card sound pretty good. Well, *loud* anyway.

Modems

Rounding out this discussion of peripherals you can't live without is modems ($50–$300). A *modem* (MODulator/DEModulator) is a device that allows your computer to communicate with others over phone lines, enabling you to access online services, the Internet, and (perhaps most importantly) play online games. For 3D artists, modems provide the opportunity to download mesh, images, and software updates from companies and individuals. They may enable you to work from home, using FTP or e-mail to get your files to and from work. Modems also mean access to online services and newsgroups where you can get answers to your software and hardware questions.

Modems vary chiefly by communications speed, measured in bits per second (bps), which is also often referred to as the baud rate, although this isn't technically correct. Today, the popularity of the Net and the World Wide Web (WWW) make 28.8Kb/s modems practically a must-have item.

For users who want even faster access than 28.8Kb/s modems can offer, the next step is to get ISDN (Integrated Systems Digital Network), which provides speeds of 64Kb/s to 256Kb/s or more. While ISDN installations are becoming affordable, they can still cost a great deal more than standard telephone service and require special modems and interfaces. They also don't necessarily speed up all Web operations, because you're still at the mercy of the remote server's capacity and the conditions of the network between it and your service provider. ISDN installations are most appropriate for users working from home or another remote location who need to access large amounts of data from the office. Still, it's likely that nearly all serious computer users will end up with ISDN or some other type of high-speed Internet access in the not-so-distant future.

Buying a Computer: A Case Study

At this point, it might be useful to hear about my own experiences when buying my current PC (see figure 2.14). I believe it will give you some valuable insights into some of the unexpected surprises that await the computer buyer.

FIGURE 2.14

My Gateway 2000 P5/90 system. While top-of-the-line just two years ago, it is now too slow for some of the large 3D projects I am doing with 3D Studio MAX.

I started shopping for my current system back in August of 1994, about the time that I decided to start working from home whenever possible to avoid the hellish commute into San Francisco. My old system, a Northgate 486/25, was definitely not up to the extensive 3D Studio work I was expecting to do, however.

My first step was to pick up several magazines that contained roundups of the new Pentium systems, which were 60–90MHz models at the time. I also looked for articles that focused on the new motherboard chipsets, video cards, and monitors. After reading the reviews, I narrowed the choices down to a few different systems, including Dell, Zeos, Micron, and Gateway 2000 (G2K).

At this point, I started asking around for people who had recently bought similar systems from these companies, and got their opinions. That helped to eliminate a couple of the options.

I ultimately selected a Gateway P5/90, partially because most of the systems we had been buying for Mondo Media/Mechadeus were G2K, so I was very familiar with them. I also liked the fact that the system had an Intel motherboard with a new chipset that was highly regarded in the trade magazines. Note that this is not to say that I think Gateway makes the best systems, it's just that I knew the ups and downs of them better than the other brands.

Naturally, I wanted full 24-bit color at high resolutions, so I asked G2K sales if I could get the ATI ProTurbo video card with a full 4MB of VRAM. I was surprised to find that the card was not upgradable, which was at odds with the article on true color video cards I had read. Further investigation turned up that Gateway often has manufacturers make cards according to G2K's specifications, and even though the card may have the same name as the commercial product, it isn't necessarily the same. It's likely that many of the other PC companies do the same thing, so be aware and ask about these peripherals. Because the ATI ProTurbo that Gateway sold wouldn't provide the features I wanted, I had it deleted from the order, and instead bought the fully equipped model from another vendor.

After I received the system, which took about a month, I very quickly regretted not deleting the Ensoniq SoundScape audio card that shipped with the system. The card was supposed to be Sound Blaster compatible, but because software authors sometimes make use of hardware-specific tricks, it really wasn't. It took a couple of frustrating months before new drivers and patches came out that allowed it to work with popular games like DOOM II. Frankly, despite some of the desirable features that other sound card manufacturers work in, I plan to stick with Sound Blaster from now on to avoid such compatibility problems.

Next stop on this PC configuration extravaganza was Modem Hell, which came in the form of a nice, low-cost Supra 28.8K Plug and Play (PnP) modem card. My system had a Plug and Play BIOS, and because the card was PnP also, I expected the installation to be effortless. *Wrong*. The auto-configuring software, which is supposed to locate safe places in memory to install drivers, cheerfully installed the modem software right on top of my mouse driver, locking up the system. Many frustrating hours and calls to tech support later, I ended up using Intel's ICU (appropriate name, huh?) software to manually configure the modem driver location. Now I know why some people call this technology "plug and pray."

So, you may be thinking that I really hate this system, right? No, not at all. I'd probably buy another Gateway, because I know this kind of stuff happens to everyone, no matter what brand of PC they have. The point is, PCs (make that ALL computers) can be a real chore to configure and maintain. If you aren't up to doing it yourself, make sure you either have a *really* good friend who can, or buy from someone close by who will provide good service and tech support. The other thing to remember is that you can't always trust the literature, so make sure you're getting the brandname motherboard and peripherals you think you are, not an OEM version with hidden restrictions.

Choosing RAM Wisely

Although most users will purchase their system with RAM installed, it's a good idea to know something about the type of RAM you're using and how it's configured. This can have a big impact when the time comes to increase your system's RAM, or you upgrade to a new system and want to transfer your old RAM to it.

Unless you're dealing with an early 486 or older system, the RAM in your machine consists of a strip of memory chips on a circuit card, called a *SIMM* (Single Inline Memory Module) or Macintosh *DIMM* (Dual Inline Memory Module). For purposes of simplicity, this section refers to both versions as SIMMs, however.

SIMM Sizes

SIMMs come in two bus sizes, 30-pin and 72-pin, which aren't interchangeable, although there are some adapters available. 72-pin SIMMs are the new standard, because they support the 32-bit operating systems such as Windows 95, NT, and System 7. Another difference is *parity*, which means that the SIMM has an additional chip that helps check for memory errors. Lately, however, there has been a move toward non-parity SIMMs (which are cheaper), because RAM is more reliable now, and the systems double-check memory at startup.

RAM comes in a range of memory sizes, from 256K to 64MB or more. This is a critical thing to consider when you're selecting your SIMMs, because 3D programs are very memory-intensive, and additional RAM can make a big difference in performance, especially at render time. While some programs will get by okay with 16MB, others may require at least 32 or 64MB to function efficiently. Check the *recommended* memory (as opposed to minimum memory) in the system requirements for your 3D software before deciding.

Motherboard Considerations

Speaking of RAM sizes, the motherboard plays a big part in deciding what size SIMMs to buy. Obviously, the fact that the motherboard requires 72-pin SIMMs instead of 30-pin is the major factor, but almost as important is the number of SIMM slots available. Back when SIMMs were running in the 256K–4MB range, motherboards tended to have eight or more slots available. Now, with high-density RAM running in the tens of megabytes, only four slots may be provided, so, you must carefully consider your future needs. For example, say you have four slots, and you decide to start out with 16MB of RAM. If you put 4MB SIMMs in every slot, you get 16MB, but you've also used up all your expansion space. Using slightly more expensive 8MB or 16MB SIMMs leaves room for expansion without having to remove some of the existing RAM to make room.

One other motherboard-related issue is the position of the SIMMs in relation to the peripheral card slots. Some boards have a problem: you can't use a full-size peripheral card in a certain slot or slots with them because it runs smack dab into the SIMMs. The only way to know if this is a problem is to look at the motherboard yourself, or read an in-depth review of it.

Access speed (measured in nanoseconds) is another factor, and you must use RAM that's at least as fast as the motherboard manufacturer specifies. In other words, if the system requires 70ns RAM, you can use 60ns RAM (lower number equals faster), but you can't use 80ns RAM. Bear this in mind if you plan to keep your RAM when you upgrade, because your new system may demand faster access speeds. Note as well that your system may not enable you to mix different speeds of RAM, even if they're faster than the minimum.

Price

Of all the components and peripherals in computerdom, RAM is the most volatile in terms of price. One megabyte of memory seems to range anywhere from $6–$50, depending on what's going on in the operating system market (notice how high prices were during the Windows 95 rollout?) and the manufacturing sector (prices dropped dramatically after many manufacturers jumped into the fray). Therefore, you may want to upgrade your RAM if the prices are low, rather than waiting until you really need it, which is probably when prices are at a peak. Also, note that the best memory deals are usually available mail-order through companies that specialize in RAM sales.

One final consideration when selecting SIMMs—there's a new type of memory called EDO RAM, which is appearing on some of the high-end Pentium systems. It's supposedly faster and less expensive than standard RAM and may turn out to be the new standard. Because it's incompatible with older systems, you may find yourself having to sell off your old RAM anyway if you move up to one of these systems. Isn't it funny how that works out?

Getting Started on a Budget

After you decide what you need, you're faced with two more decisions: How do you pay for it and where do you get it. Don't lose heart if you get sticker shock when shopping for systems and software. Others have started with little or no equipment and a small budget, and you can as well.

Beg, Borrow, or Buy

Assuming you don't have a winning lottery ticket gathering dust in your pocket, you're going to have to raise a healthy sum to finance the hardware and software you need. Even with a basic system, costs add up quickly. Begging your parents for the money is always an option, but there are other creative ways to cut costs.

For example, recycle someone else's unwanted equipment. People who have been into computing for a while tend to have some old equipment lying around. Sometimes they hold onto it to use as a back-up, or as a second machine to play network Duke with, or just because they can't bear to sell it for pennies on the dollar. Friends with an old system may actually be very pleased that you want to use it, because it puts the system to good use while helping out a pal.

If a full system isn't available, ask around for components. One person may have an old motherboard but no video card, while another may have a spare video card and monitor. In any case, tap this source first if you have the opportunity. They might sell it to you cheap, or just lend it to you for as long as you need it. In the worst case scenario, try renting it from them for $20 a month.

If borrowing a system isn't possible, you can stay on budget by purchasing used gear. Like new cars, computer systems tend to have a nasty depreciation once the polywrap is off them, so consider taking advantage of that. If you find one that's fairly new, it may even have a manufacturer's warranty still in effect.

The first option is getting used gear from the classified ads, thrift stores, or a swap meet. Generally you can find anything from the latest hardware to some near-antiques, with prices ranging from $50 to thousands. As with almost anything purchased as-is from a private individual, there is some risk here. The gear may not work at all, or could have intermittent problems that don't show up until later. Obviously, you get no warranty other than what might remain on the manufacturer's. Another source is computer stores that stock used gear. Some may offer a limited warranty or technical support, which is some comfort. The prices tend to be substantially higher than buying from a private individual, however.

If you have your heart set on unsullied, pristine new equipment, there are still a lot of opportunities to save money. Prices can vary significantly among stores, and the mail-order market can offer some excellent bargains—more on this later.

The do-it-yourself (DIY) option is another good way to go if you want to save a few extra bucks and have the time, knowledge, and patience to assemble your own system. The benefits include getting the exact case, motherboard, keyboard, cards, and peripherals you want, which results in a highly customized package. The downside is that because system manufactures buy components in massive volume, the difference in price between a DIY computer and an already assembled name brand can be surprisingly small. Also, you may have to deal with several different companies if software doesn't work properly, and each may finger the other guy's product as the source of the trouble. In other words, there's no system manufacturer to hold responsible for your computer as a whole.

Retail versus Mail Order

Where you buy your system and software can be almost as important as what you buy. One of the first steps in choosing a vendor is to decide whether you want to buy from a store, or purchase your gear by mail order.

Buying from a store has several positive aspects. First, it's probably a local facility, with real people there to answer your questions and make suggestions. You can compare different products head to head, immediately see what's in the box you're buying, and probably return it within 30 days if you're not happy. In addition, some retail store vendors, particularly those who call themselves *VARs (Value Added Resellers)*, may offer training and technical support as part of the package or system that you buy.

The downside of *retail stores* is primarily the *retail store* prices, which tend to be significantly higher than mail order. Another disadvantage in all but the superstores is selection and availability. Finally, you probably have to pay sales tax, which can amount to several hundred dollars on a system purchase.

Mail-order outlets offer a larger array of product brands and models, significantly to dramatically lower prices, and the convenience of shopping by phone. In my opinion, the systems also seem to be more up-to-date in the mail-order market, probably because they're often manufactured to your order and the components are always being updated. Some vendors also may offer 10–30 day money back guarantees on systems or software. If you're going the DIY route or selecting your own mix of peripherals, mail order is a convenient way to get the best price on each component. If you order from an out-of-state vendor, you also may avoid paying sales tax, although this is no longer guaranteed.

Computer Shopper is a thick newsprint magazine packed with advertising. It's one of the best resources for mail-order shopping, and features an index that helps you locate products of interest quickly. It's highly recommended for those who are looking for either full systems or components at the best prices.

On the other hand, mail order has some well-known drawbacks, the worst of which is not getting what you ordered. You also have to wait at least a day to get whatever it is you're buying, and in the case of full systems, it may take several weeks to receive your hardware. Returning things can also be a pain, requiring you to get an RMA (Return Merchandise Authorization) number from the vendor and then paying for the shipping to return it. Finally, you can't look at any of the merchandise (or it's box specs) before you buy it, so you may also need to shop at a retail store first, or rely solely on literature, reviews, and advice to make your choices.

When I'm in a relative hurry to get some computer thingy, I tend to order from places that are well-established, such as the Mac/PCZone, Mac/

PCWarehouse, or Mac/PC Connection that offer overnight delivery. If I have the time or want a better deal, I'll leaf through *Computer Shopper,* looking for companies that have been in business for a number of years, and have at least a one-page advertisement (unless it's a specialty item, like RAM).

Overall, I've had pretty good luck ordering from mail-order companies, with only a couple bad experiences so far (knock on wood). One was an NEC XV17 monitor that I was very unhappy with, and it cost me $50 to ship back. After that, I bought a Nokia Multigraph 447X monitor at the local CompUSA store so it would be easy (and cheap) to return if it didn't pan out. With most other components, I wouldn't worry about this, however.

Raiding the Bargain Bin

When it comes to finding software deals, the bargain bin at your local software store, electronics shop, surplus outlet, or warehouse chain can be a gold mine. You may come across a pretty old version of some product you're looking for, then be able to save hundreds of dollars by buying an upgrade to the newest release from the developer.

Upgrade policies vary by company and sometimes change over time as well. For example, Macromedia used to charge different amounts for Director upgrades, depending on which version you were upgrading from. Later, they settled on a single amount regardless of how old the version was. Obviously, this can be a great deal if you get hold of a version 1.0 cheap.

Now, suppose you find LamePaint 1.0 in the bin for $20, but you really don't want LamePaint 3.5, regardless of how much you can save. In that case, look for competitive upgrade offers from the publisher of the product that you *do* want. Competitive upgrades give you a discount on Product A if you send in a disk, proof or purchase, or page from the manual of Product B. In other words, the publisher of AwesomePaint 4.1 may offer a substantial discount if you "upgrade" from any version of the competing product, LamePaint.

Shareware, Samples, and Demos

If you're really working on a shoestring budget, start looking for shareware 3D programs, as well as commercial samples and demos.

Distributed online and through CD-ROM compilations, *shareware* is software that you're expected to pay for if you use. To help encourage contributions, the authors may include tiresome reminders, remove certain features, or limit the amount of time or number of occasions the software can be used before it shuts itself off. Examples of 3D shareware include ClayWorks, Image-3D, and ProtoCAD 3D. POV-Ray is a *freeware* (no money expected) ray tracing renderer available online for a number of different platforms and operating systems. Check in the libraries of your commercial online service (AOL, CompuServe, and so on) or use a Web search engine or Gopher to locate the files on the Internet. You can often find discussion groups for these packages and other software through your online service or in the Usenet newsgroups as well.

On the commercial side, demo versions of 3D packages are available from most publishers, enabling you to try the product before buying it. Generally, these demo versions are either "timed" fully functional versions that stop working after 30 days, or they're disabled in some way, such as not allowing you to save your work. You'll find some demo versions of 3D software on the companion CD-ROM in the back of this book.

Also included on the CD-ROM are samples of 3D mesh and textures, and more are available from other companies, either by request or through their Web sites. In addition, many 3D packages now come with collections of mesh and textures. In some cases, these collections may have additional locked images on them, which can be purchased and unlocked with a phone call to the company.

System Optimization Tips

Even if you assembled the most powerful system available, 3D graphics is a time-consuming, computer-intensive occupation, and sometimes even small improvements can make a big difference in your productivity (and disposition) over the long haul. This is where system optimization comes in. Not only can some small alterations to the startup parameters and routine hard drive optimization and maintenance speed things along, but customizing your system makes it more efficient and fun to use.

That said, before you start cheerfully editing your PC's .SYS files or adding more Control Panel goodies to your Mac, a few caveats. First, any changes to your system should be performed only if you have a current, easily restorable backup of your hard drive. Second, the road to improvement is often fraught with experimentation and delays, so the day before your deadline is not the time to go messing with OS upgrades.

If your improvements involve installing or replacing hardware, be sure to yank the power cord out of the back before you open the case, and always wear an anti-static grounding strap to avoid zapping any components. Also, check for loose doodads or other contamination before closing the case by tipping the system back and forth. A little screw wedged on a circuit board can cost you hours of troubleshooting or even a new motherboard.

Finally, think twice about installing warranty-voiding hardware add-ons, like clock doublers and the like. If you do decide to go for it, think about having the store do the installation. It might cost you an extra $30, but then the onus is on them if something goes wrong.

Memory and Bootup Optimization

Optimizing your SIMM selection was discussed in the section on Memory, so this section deals with software-related issues, namely memory managers, virtual memory, boot menus, and hard drive partitioning.

Memory managers for the PC were devised to help the machines deal with a nearsighted flaw in the machine's basic design that has plagued them to this day. Simply put, they have a hard time dealing with more than 640K of RAM. To overcome this problem, DOS uses programs such as EMM386 to separate and manage memory. The trouble is, different applications like different memory configurations, or no memory management at all.

The new 32-bit operating systems such as Windows 95 and NT overcome many of these kinds of problems, but as long as there are still DOS applications around (3DS R4 for example), these issues will still be with us.

One solution to the problem of differing memory configurations is called the *boot menu*. This is a modification to the CONFIG.SYS and AUTOEXEC.BAT files that bring a menu up on the screen when the machine is started. You can then select from different combinations of memory manager configurations (which you have previously defined). You can find information about how to make a boot menu in your DOS manual or online help.

Hard Drive Customizing and Troubleshooting

Another option for creating an operating system configuration tuned to your application is to partition your hard drive into multiple boot drives. *Partitioning* is a low-level formatting procedure that takes one drive and divides it into smaller sections, each of which is assigned its own drive letter or volume name. One advantage of partitioning is that each partition can have its own operating system software or even a totally different file system without interfering with the other drives. Then, you can use a custom menu to boot from the desired operating system for a given session.

Another advantage of creating custom-sized partitions is that you can limit the amount of data that one of them holds to the same capacity as a cartridge hard drive or recordable CD-ROM. This prevents you from running out of space when doing backups onto removable media because the total size of the files turned out to be larger than you expected.

Optimizing your hard drive involves running a utility such as Norton to defragment files and consolidate free space on the drive into contiguous chunks. This can really speed things up when you're working with large files and doing rendering, because both may use virtual memory (VM). Most operating systems use virtual memory, and performance can be significantly affected depending on how that VM is configured and arranged. There are two main ways to configure virtual memory—temporary and permanent.

Permanent virtual memory writes a file onto your drive that it later uses as needed. It is usually faster than temporary VM, provided the drive was optimized before the file was created. The downside is that this file is always there, taking up space even if you aren't running that operating system at the time. Temporary VM, on the other hand, doesn't take up hard drive space when it isn't in use, but may slow the system down if your hard drive is seriously fragmented.

One other thing—whenever your system crashes, it's a good idea to run Norton Utilities, SCANDISK, or another disk diagnosis program to check for damage to the FAT or files. Crashes that occur in Windows often leave damaged files behind that eat up hard drive space. A disk utility will locate and offer to delete these useless files.

Hard Drive Crashes

As noted earlier, hard drives have a nasty reputation for failing, either due to software errors or physical damage. In either case, the crash can mangle some files or render the entire drive contents inaccessible. The latter is known to cause some individuals to start pounding on their systems while screaming, *"Give me back my data, you hardwired demon from hell!"* Ahem.

Soft crashes are caused by any number of software glitches, and usually result from an error that occurs while the hard drive is updating its table of contents file, called the *File Allocation Table (FAT)*. In this case, the drive becomes confused about what's located where, and even minor errors can grow into full-scale failures. Luckily, utilities provided with the system, or third-party software such as Norton or MacTools, can fix many soft crashes. Some of these products also come with startup utilities that automatically make backup copies of the FAT elsewhere on the drive, increasing the probability of being able to recover your data.

The other type of drive failure results from *hard crashes* that occur if the tiny read/write heads inside the drive come in contact with the rapidly spinning magnetic platters that hold the data. A sudden jolt to the drive can cause this sort of crash, which is why you should never move your system while it's operating. Hard crashes are often fatal for the data that's under the head where it touches the platter, because the head may damage the magnetic coating, obliterating the data and creating a bad sector. In other cases, the read/write head itself becomes detached from the arm that positions it, which ruins the entire drive.

definition

bad sector A damaged or defective portion of a hard disk where data can't be reliably stored.

In the case of a serious hard crash where the drive is making nasty screeching noises or refuses to retrieve data or be reformatted, you have only two options. The first is to send it to a data recovery center, where they *may* be able to rescue some of the data. This can be extremely expensive, however, costing hundreds or thousands of dollars. Clearly, you would only take this course of action if you absolutely need the data on that drive, and no backups exist.

The second option is to write off the data and replace the drive. This is when a good warranty can be a real money saver, so be sure to investigate the manufacturer's policies when selecting your drive. Be aware that these policies may differ depending on which *model* you buy, so read the literature carefully. I recommend getting a drive that has at least a two-year replacement warranty.

In addition to the length of the warranty, look at the service policy as well. Some manufacturers require you to send the drive back to them and wait weeks or months for repairs. This is often a major annoyance (even if you have extra drives), and is totally unacceptable if you have only one. Others may offer an exchange upon receipt, or even send you a replacement drive first, which has the added benefit of providing you with approved packing materials for returning the bad unit.

Regardless of whom you buy your drive from, you should deal directly with the manufacturer when seeking service. Your turnaround time will be faster (unless the dealer has their own "hot swap" policy) and you run less of a risk of your drive getting lost in the shuffle.

> I have personal experience with the pitfalls of returning a drive to the dealer instead of the manufacturer. It happened when I sent back a defective Hewlett Packard 330MB SCSI drive to the mail-order company it was purchased from, ProDirect. They said they would return it to HP for repair, but that it would probably take a couple of months to get back. A couple of *years* later, and despite numerous calls and letters, I still haven't seen that drive again.

Note

Miscellaneous Utilities and Tips

There are all kinds of handy utilities out there to help you manage your time, track your hours, and make your lists. Others enhance your system software and make programs more accessible. Below are a few of my favorites.

For the Mac, NOW Utilities provides a great selection of system enhancements, including menus of commonly used programs, and a little item that should be standard on every operating system called Super Boomerang. This utility keeps track of the most recent files and folders you've accessed, enabling you to jump quickly from one drive and folder to another without digging down through the file hierarchy.

Another great enhancement for the Mac is DOS Mounter, which enables you to work with DOS formatted media such as floppies, cartridge hard drives, ZIP disks, and so forth. This is a must-have for the cross-platform user. Macs come with AccessPC, a similar product, but it only works for floppies.

On the PC side (when working in Windows 3.x) there's Microsoft Office Manager, a little floating program launcher that comes with MS Office. It's customizable, and once you start using it, you'll rarely find yourself digging around in Program Manager again. Another hot item is WinZip, a utility for compressing and decompressing files that's integrated into File Manager.

Customization applies to your 3D software as well. Many programs enable you to define startup viewport settings, define your own hot keys for commonly used commands, create links to other utilities, and so forth. Taking the time to set up your software in a way that is customized to your needs and habits makes your work more efficient and enjoyable.

Customizing Your Workspace

Finally, the arrangement of your gear can make a big difference in your comfort and productivity. Whenever possible, you should use ergonomically-designed furniture intended for computer applications. The three most important ergonomic concerns are the position and height of the keyboard, the chair, and the monitor.

Accessibility is another important concern, especially if you move your gear or some of your peripherals from time to time. Try to find a location for your system that makes it easy to get at all the cables and open the case if need be without resorting to contortionism. Cable extensions can be a big help in positioning your system comfortably, but beware of monitor extension cables, which can often cause rolling or sparkling interference on your screen.

If space is tight, many systems and peripherals are designed to be placed in a vertical position. Monitor arms also are available to lift the monitor off your desk and make it easier to position properly. For the ultimate close-quarters situations, consider a roll-around system cabinet that holds all the gear and can be moved into a closet or out of the way when not in use.

Speaking of the closet, consider removing the doors completely or replacing them with bifold doors, taking out the closet pole, then putting a desk or cabinet inside. Placing a bunch of stacking letter trays on the shelf will create a great place to file away printer paper, envelopes, and other supplies while keeping them easily accessible.

Summary

By now, you probably know more than you ever cared to about shopping for 3D software, hardware platforms, processors, peripherals, and off-the-wall mice. Remember to check Appendix D, "Software Products and Publisher List," for capsule reviews of popular 3D software packages and contact information to help you make your selection.

The next chapter discusses making the transition from 2D graphics, explores the principles of 3D graphics, and offers tips on how to learn your particular package in an efficient and effective manner.

Delving Into Cyberspace

The Lesson, a 3D image created especially for this chapter by AniMagicians. Image by Aaron Shi, Ken Lee, and William Bobos, © 1996 AniMagicians.

"*Now then, lad—as I was saying, the navigational references along The Virtual Path are akin to the cardinal points of the compass. Here, you can see that the Northern direction is not unlike the…*"

The student's mind wandered as the Master continued with his tutelage, drawing diagrams and formulae on the large slate at the front of the chamber. The student was eager to get back to working with his glowing pool, where he had conjured some simple forms this morning.

The Master was still facing the slate, so the student turned to watch the pool as the primitive forms floated gently above it. Simply experimenting with the pool had taught him much, and he was ready to try making a more complex object, perhaps a castle turret…

Suddenly, a large amber globe struck the table in front of him, jarring the student out of his reverie. His eyes followed the gnarled wooden staff attached to the globe until he saw the even more gnarled hand of the Master holding it. The old man scowled at him, obviously displeased.

"So, eager to return to the practical, are we?" the Master lifted the end of the staff from the table and absent-mindedly examined the translucent globe for scratches. "No need of all this boring theory and background, have you?"

The student swallowed hard and tried to blurt out an apology, but the Master interrupted him.

"No, no…perhaps you're right," the old man said, walking slowly toward the student's glowing pool. "Here, why not show me your skills. Conjure something for me." With that, the Master settled heavily in a chair near the pool and gazed, unblinking, at the student.

The lad got up and hurried to the glowing pool. "Uh, how about a…castle turret?" he asked. The Master nodded with an oddly crooked smile and waited.

Beads of sweat began forming on the student's forehead as he erased the basic forms he had built before. Forcing himself to be calm, he began to summon a cylinder that would form the walls of the turret. Wisps of light emerged from the pool, weaving a gossamer tube that towered above their heads. Pleased, the student stole at glance at the Master, who only grunted. His confidence building, the student started to summon a roof for the structure.

"Wha…" gasped the student as the roof appeared, but tipped on its side, as though it had fallen from the turret. He tried to rotate it into an upright position, but it only spun around like a top. The beads of sweat turned into rivulets as the student attempted numerous adjustments, then gave up and tried to move the roof into position instead. He commanded it to rise up, but instead it skidded sideways, ending up a few inches from the Master's nose. He tried to pull it back toward the tower, but this time it flew up to the ceiling. Adjustment after adjustment sent the wayward roof zigzagging around the room. Finally, the student accidentally sent it hurtling back into the glowing pool, where it shattered into a spray of brilliant lights.

The Master turned toward the student and raised a solitary eyebrow.

"I…" stammered the lad, "I…believe you were talking about cardinal points, Master?"

Expanding from 2D to 3D

As our unfortunate student found out, working with 3D graphics can be frustrating if you don't have a solid handle on the principles and theory involved. True, it's nowhere near as interesting as playing around with the software, but understanding it now will save you a lot of time and trouble later on.

The easiest way to start is with a look at how 2D and 3D skills overlap. If you have experience with Illustrator or another drawing program, you can make good use of what you already know about working with 2D shapes. As you recall from Chapter 1, "The Virtual Path," the main difference between 2D and 3D is depth. 2D drawings have only height and width; no depth whatsoever. While objects can be drawn so that they look like they're 3D, if you want to change the perspective or viewpoint in any way, you have to redraw the object from scratch (see figure 3.1).

Because 3D objects have depth (at least inside your computer), you only have to "draw" them once, then you can view them from any angle or perspective without starting from scratch. Also, 3D programs automatically calculate the proper highlight and shadow information for a scene based on how you arrange the objects and lighting (see figure 3.2).

FIGURE 3.1

2D drawing programs can be used to create images that look 3D, but if you want to view the object from a different perspective, you have to draw it over again.

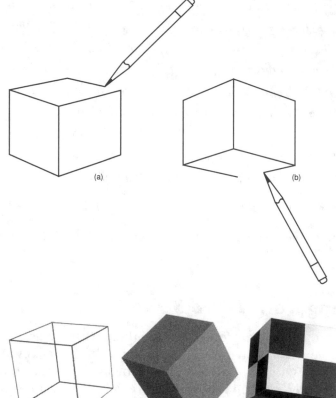

FIGURE 3.2

Once an object has been constructed in a 3D program, it can be given color and texture, lit, and then rendered from any angle.

In a sense, then, 3D programs not only redraw your subject from any angle you choose, they also create a painting of it based on the colors, textures, and lighting that you decided on when you built the model. With all of those benefits, it's no wonder many artists rarely go back to traditional drawing and painting once they've gotten into 3D.

Now, while there are some major differences between 2D and 3D, many of the 2D drawing tools you may be familiar with are implemented in 3D programs as well. Tools like the freehand pencil, Bézier pen, circles, arcs, polylines, polygons, lassos, and so forth are usually available, and work in much the same way as their 2D counterparts. The difference is that instead of being used to create a finished shape in a 2D environment, these tools are used as a starting point for creating a 3D object. Some of the most common 3D forms that start with a 2D shape are lofts, sweeps, lathes, and extrudes. Exactly what they are and how they are constructed is discussed in Chapter 4, "3D Modeling Basics," but the important thing to remember for now is that they rely heavily on 2D drawing techniques.

Another similarity between 2D and 3D software is the concept of layers. A *layer* in the 2D world is like a clear acetate sheet that you draw or paint on. By adding other layers (or sheets of acetate), to a 2D image, you can add additional elements in front of or behind the initial layer (see figure 3.3).

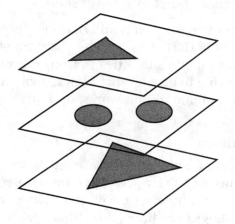

FIGURE 3.3

2D programs enable drawings to be created in layers, which is not unlike drawing on sheets of acetate. Elements can then be edited individually, without the visual clutter of unnecessary layers.

Because the layers are all separate, you also can change things on one layer without affecting any of the others. You also can place reference images in the background layer and trace over them in the foreground. One of the biggest advantages to working with layers is that you can turn them on or off to reduce clutter on the screen. You can also *gray out* (screen back by 50%) a layer to keep it visible for reference but make it less obtrusive.

Although some 3D programs (LightWave, for example) implement layers for 3D objects in a very similar manner, by allowing objects to be separated into layers, most limit this layering to a basic foreground/background arrangement. In many cases, the background is further limited to being an image of some sort.

As with their 2D cousins, 3D programs use *groups* to define a collection of objects that can be dealt with as a whole. Grouping enables the user to choose a related collection of objects, then temporarily combine them into a single unit. This makes it much easier to move, scale, or do other operations to the group, because you don't have to choose each element individually every time you want to do something to them. Also, the user can add, remove, and reassign objects to or from a particular group as desired.

Principles of 3D Graphics

In Chapter 1, an imaginary camcorder was used to record the video of a room full of objects as an analogy for how 3D graphics are presented on a 2D screen. You should remember that 3D was defined as a "two-dimensional *representation* of three-dimensional objects." If you're a little hazy on this point, go back and reread that section. Don't worry—it's short.

The important thing to remember is this: In computer graphics, objects exist only in the memory of the computer. They have no physical form; they're just mathematical formulas and little electrons running around. Because I know you're just dying to dust off that high school geometry book and get into the nitty-gritty of how all this works, read on.

3D Space Defined

Basically, 3D space is a mathematically defined cube of cyberspace inside your computer's memory. *Cyberspace* differs from real physical space because it only exists inside the computer (movies and science fiction novels notwith-

standing). In addition, this virtual space can be manipulated by the system's software and used to simulate just about anything imaginable.

Like real space, however, 3D space is *vast*. Even with modern 3D software, it's easy to get disoriented or to "lose" an object out in some cyber-backwater. So, if it's so big, how do you get around? Luckily, 3D space comes with its own sort of built-in Global Positioning System (GPS), called coordinates.

Coordinates

In 3D space, the smallest area that it is possible to "occupy" is called a *point*. Each of these points is defined by a unique set of three numbers, called *coordinates* (see figure 3.4). An example would be the coordinates 0, 0, 0, which define the center point of the cyberspace universe, also called the *origin point*. Other examples of coordinates include: 12, 31, 57 or 359, –2315, 143.

You can consider coordinates an address for each position in cyberspace. 3D software makes use of these addresses to define objects and their locations.

So, have you figured out why there are *three* sets of numbers, instead of two or four? Right, because they're related to the three dimensions: width, height, and depth. However, in cyberspace terms, these are referred to as *axes*.

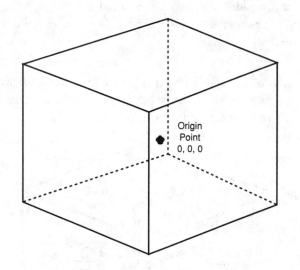

FIGURE 3.4

Every point in 3D space is defined by a set of three coordinates. At the very center of this "cyberspace" is the origin point, coordinates 0, 0, 0.

Axes

An axis is an imaginary line in cyberspace that defines a direction. There are three standard axes in 3D programs, which are referred to as X, Y, and Z (see figure 3.5). For reasons discussed later, terms like *up*, *left*, and *in* are difficult to apply to 3D space. However, they can be used to explain the X, Y, and Z axis if you remember that this description is only applicable from a particular perspective. The "width" axis, X, runs horizontally (left to right and vice-versa). The "height" axis, Y, is vertical, going from top to bottom and bottom to top. The Z-axis is related to "depth." It travels from the front to the back of cyberspace and vice-versa.

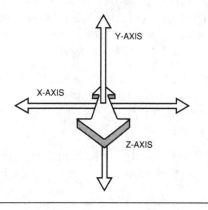

FIGURE 3.5

An axis is an imaginary line in 3D space that defines a direction. The standard axes used in 3D programs are called X, Y, and Z.

Now that you know what axes and coordinates are, how do they work together for navigating in cyberspace? Let's start by combining the two systems into a single diagram (see figure 3.6).

FIGURE 3.6

Coordinates and axes are interrelated. Coordinates on the positive side of a main axis are greater than 0. Those on the negative side are less than 0.

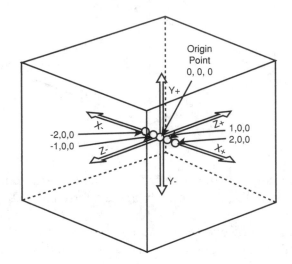

As you can see, if you center the X, Y, and Z axes within 3D space, the coordinate at the intersection of all three axes is the origin point, 0, 0, 0. If you plot (diagram) the point immediately adjacent to the origin along the "right" side of the X-axis, the point would be identified as 1, 0, 0. The next point in the same direction would be 2, 0, 0 and so forth. On the other hand, if you had moved toward the "left" side of the X-axis, the numbers would be negative—in other words –1, 0, 0 followed by –2, 0, 0, and so on.

The same holds true for the other axes as well, with numbers going positive when traveling "up" the Y-axis, and negative when going "down." Therefore, plotting the point immediately "above" the origin would yield 0, 1, 0, while the one below it would be 0, –1, 0.

Likewise, the Z-axis has positive and negative directions too. Positive is toward the viewer (in this example), while negative is away, toward the "back" of cyberspace. So, the point in "front" of the origin would be 0, 0, 1, and the point "behind" it would be 0, 0, –1.

Therefore, if you were trying to determine where coordinate 128, –16, 25 was, you would find it 128 points to the "right" of the origin, 16 points "below" it, and 25 points closer to you.

Lines, Polylines, and Polygons

Okay, so you've got this vast virtual space with zillions of points, each with its own set of coordinates, but right now, it's just a huge virtual box full of nothing. To make it useful, some shapes and objects need to be defined. Let's start with a simple line.

Suppose you played connect-the-dots with some of those cyberspace points by drawing a line between 0, 0, 0 and 5, 5, 0 (see figure 3.7). If you continue the line to 9, 3, 0, you have what is called a *polyline*, which is a continuous line that consists of multiple segments. Finally, draw the last line right back to the origin point, 0, 0, 0. The result is a *closed shape*, which means the shape has an "inside" and "outside." This also is a simple three-sided *polygon*, and is the basis of objects created in the 3D environment.

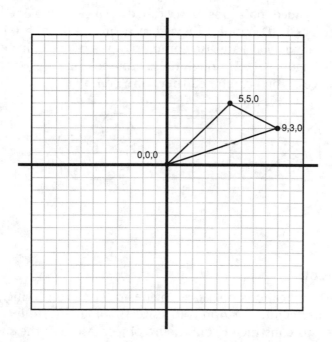

FIGURE 3.7

When a connection is made between two points, a line is formed. If that line is extended to additional points, it is a polyline. If the line is further extended to the starting point, it forms a polygon.

As with many commands in 3D graphics, your software may use different or conflicting terms to describe some of the following components.

Let's dissect our polygon, breaking it down into the basic components that 3D programs can manipulate, namely vertices, edges, and faces (see figure 3.8). A *vertex* is a point where any number of lines come together and connect to each other. In the previous example, each one of the points you drew became one of the vertices in the polygon. Similarly, each one of the lines you drew formed a boundary, or *edge*, of the polygon. Finally, when the shape was closed, it created an "inside" and an "outside" to the form. The area enclosed by the edges of the polygon, the "inside," is called a *face*.

FIGURE 3.8

Polygons are composed of vertices, edges, and faces.

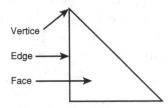

While three-sided polygons (also called *triangles*) are one of the most common types in 3D graphics, they are by no means the only type. Four-sided polygons (called *quads*) are also common, but a poly can have any number of sides (see figure 3.9). Although these dull-looking polygons are not much by themselves, when combined they form complex objects.

FIGURE 3.9

Most polygons in 3D programs are either (a) triangles, or (b) quads. However, there is no limit to the number of sides a polygon can have (c).

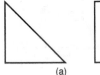

3D Objects

In most 3D applications, objects are made up of polygons, which are arranged by the computer into the form you desire. In some cases, only a few polygons are needed to construct a convincing object. Most of the time, however, hundreds or thousands are needed, creating a massive amount of data to keep track of. Thankfully, because the computer is so good at handling reams of complex numbers, it's able to keep track of all the polygons, points, edges, and faces in the scene.

For example, in the case of a simple cube, the software has to keep track of eight vertices, six faces, and twelve edges, assuming the cube is made up of quads (see figure 3.10). If it's constructed from triangles, the number of edges and faces doubles. For more complex objects, the number of polygon elements can soar into the tens of thousands.

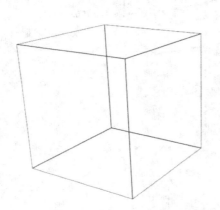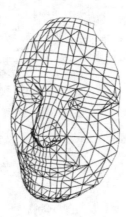

FIGURE 3.10

A simple cube has eight vertices. Complex objects can have hundreds or thousands of vertices.

Because these objects are made up of polygons, which are in turn defined by coordinates in cyberspace, the objects themselves take up space in our mathematical universe. For example, a cube may have one corner resting at the origin point 0, 0, 0, and be 101 points wide in each direction (see figure 3.11). That would mean that the corner of the cube immediately "above" the origin point would reside at coordinates 0, 100, 0, which should be considered the "upper-left front" of the cube. Since the cube is on the positive ("right") side of the X-axis (the horizontal one), the next set of corners is at 100, 0, 0 (lower-right front), and 100, 100, 0 (upper-right front). Finally, because the cube is positioned "behind" the origin point along the Z-axis (depth), the final sets of corners would be at 0, 0, –100 (lower-left rear), 0, 100, –100 (upper-left rear), 100, 0, –100 (lower-right rear), and 100, 100, –100 (upper-right rear).

Viewpoints

Just as it would be rather challenging to drive your car if it didn't have windows, manipulating the objects in 3D space is much easier when you can define a viewpoint (see figure 3.12). A *viewpoint* is a position in or around cyberspace that represents the user's location. Most programs use a default viewpoint that has the X-axis running horizontally, the Y-axis vertical, and the Z-axis indicating depth as discussed. Usually, the viewpoint is located at the extreme positive Z-axis (the "front") of cyberspace, and is focused on the origin point.

FIGURE 3.11

The construction of a cube in cyberspace demonstrates how linking coordinates can form a 3D object out of polygons.

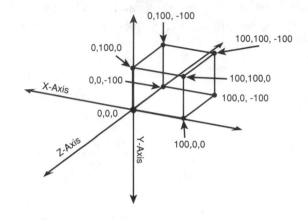

FIGURE 3.12

The viewpoint represents the current vantage point of the user. The viewing plane indicates the limits of the user's view, because only objects in front of that plane are visible.

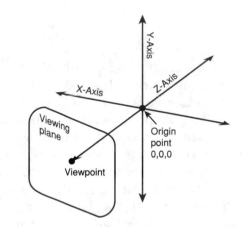

Surrounding the viewpoint at a perpendicular angle is the *viewing plane*, which is an imaginary flat panel that defines the limits of the user's "sight." In other words, the user can only see things that are in front of the viewing plane, and everything else is "clipped off." In fact, another name for the viewing plane is the *clipping plane*.

In order to see anything "behind" the viewing plane, the user's viewpoint must change. In a sense, the viewing plane is like the limits of your peripheral vision. If you want to see something that's in back of you, you either have to turn your head (in other words, rotate the viewing plane) or step backward until the object is in front of you (move the viewing plane).

> At this point, perhaps you've realized why the earlier references to "up, left, and behind" were used with caution. It is because whether something is left or right depends on the viewer's perspective. In the 3D universe, the viewer can be virtually anywhere, so what is "left" from one viewpoint may be "up" or "right" from another.

In 3D software, the windows that look into the 3D space are often called *viewports*. The monitor screen itself is akin to the viewing plane, because the user can only see what is "beyond" the monitor in cyberspace. This perspective is bound on the sides by the size of the viewport. Default 3D viewports typically show objects as *orthographic projections*, which may sound familiar if you ever took any mechanical drawing classes. Orthographic means that the viewer's location is infinitely distant from the object, so that all lines along the same axis are parallel. So far, all the diagrams in this chapter have been drawn in the orthographic style.

Display Modes

So, just what *do* you see when peering into cyberspace from your chosen perspective? It depends on the capabilities of your software, and its current settings. Because it takes time to convert all those polygons and data into a form that you can see, there are several different ways of viewing 3D objects to keep things moving along at a reasonable pace (see figure 3.13).

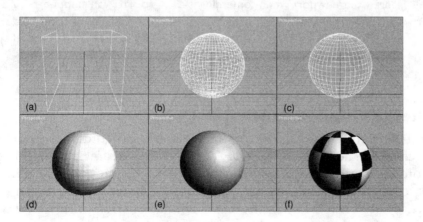

FIGURE 3.13

Typical 3D program display modes.
(a) Bounding Box,
(b) Wireframe, (c)
Hidden Line, (d) Flat
Shaded, (e) Smooth
Shaded, (f) Smooth
Textured.

The fastest and simplest display format is the *bounding box*, which is a box that has the same overall dimensions as the object. This is a very fast way to indicate an object's position and rough shape, and is frequently used by the software when the user is moving an object around in the scene.

Wireframe mode draws the object using lines to represent the edges of the polygons, which makes it resemble a sculpture made of wire mesh. This enables the user to see the true form of the object and have access to individual vertices for editing and modification. Unfortunately, because every edge is visible (even the ones on the far side of the object), wireframe mode can sometimes be confusing. The remedy is to use *hidden line* mode, which draws the edges as in a wireframe display, but only the ones that would be visible to the user if the object were opaque. The result is much less confusing to the eye.

For a higher level of realism, opt for a shaded or textured display mode. *Flat shaded* mode shows off the surface and color of the object in a coarse manner. The objects appear faceted, but the effects of lighting can be seen for the first time. *Smooth shaded* mode (which shows the surface of the object with color and smoothing) has become very popular now that the hardware is able to support it. It is still very computationally intensive, however, and may only be appropriate for objects that you're currently editing. *Smooth textured* mode starts to look like a finished rendering. This mode is only supported by a few products right now, and requires lots of CPU horsepower and memory to be of practical use.

The more accurate or detailed the display mode, the longer it takes to redraw the viewport when something is changed. This can amount to quite a bit of time over the course of a project, especially with complex models or a scene with a lot of objects. If you find things bogging down, hide unneeded objects or switch to a simpler display mode.

Alternate Coordinate Systems

Until now, the focus has been on the fundamental coordinate system of 3D space, also called the *world coordinate system* (see figure 3.14). While world coordinates are always used by the software to keep track of everything in 3D space, you may want to switch to different coordinate systems for convenience and control. Two of the most common alternatives are view coordinates and local coordinates.

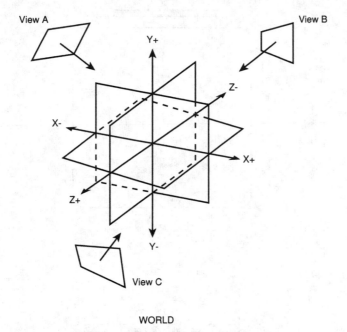

WORLD

FIGURE 3.14

The fundamental coordinate system of 3D space is world coordinates. They remain the same regardless of the viewpoint.

View coordinates use the viewport as the basis for the X, Y, and Z axis, and remain the same no matter how your viewpoint on the 3D scene changes (see figure 3.15). This can be convenient for repositioning objects. For example, to move an object to the right in your scene, you always know that you have to move it positively along the X-axis when using view coordinates.

Local coordinates use the object itself as the basis for the axes, and each object can have its own coordinate system (see figure 3.16). This is very desirable when you're rotating the object, because using other coordinate systems may produce unexpected results. To see why, look at how rotation works in cyberspace.

Coordinate Systems and Rotation

When you rotate an object, there are three factors that influence the way it turns:

- ◆ Which coordinate system (world, view, local, or user) is currently active
- ◆ The location of the rotational center point
- ◆ Which axis you choose to rotate the object around

FIGURE 3.15

View coordinates are tied to the viewport, and are always oriented in the same manner.

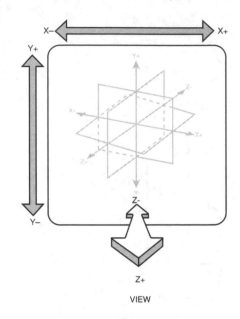

FIGURE 3.16

Local coordinates are assigned on an object-by-object basis. They make it easier to rotate objects predictably.

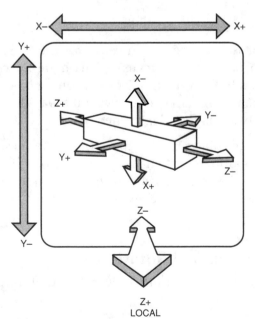

As you know, the current coordinate system setting can have a big impact on how the axes are oriented, so this is the first thing that should be decided. In general, you will want to use the local coordinate system when rotating objects around one of its own axes.

When local coordinates are selected, the center point is usually in the center of the object because the three local axis usually meet there. In this way, it is something like the origin point of the world coordinate system—as a default, it resides at the center of the X, Y, and Z-axes. However, it is possible to relocate the center point anywhere in 3D space.

The final factor, the selected axis, determines which of the three axis to spin the object around, subject to the position of the center point.

In order to illustrate why you must often switch to using the local coordinate system for rotation, imagine that you have just created an elongated box shape in your 3D program (see figure 3.17).

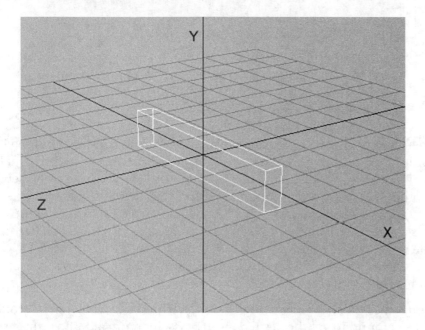

FIGURE 3.17

When an object is in alignment with the world coordinates, coordinates can be used to manipulate it predictably.

By default, the box is created in alignment with the world coordinate system. At this point, then, you could rotate the object using the world coordinates without any problems. After rotating the box at something other than a 90, 180, or 270 degree angle, however, the object's local axis are no longer aligned to the world coordinates (see figure 3.18). Therefore, if you were to use anything except the local coordinates to try rotating the object along its

X-axis, you would be out of luck, because the object's local X-axis and the world X-axis are not the same anymore. Indeed, the object would rotate at some oddball angle, and it would take some effort to get it rotated in the proper manner.

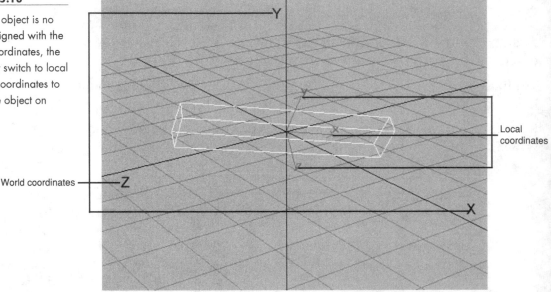

World coordinates

Local coordinates

There are some ways to accomplish a controlled rotation without relying on the local axis, however. One is to carefully position the viewpoint to make the view and local axes align, then rotate the object using the viewpoint coordinate system axes. Another method is to define a user axis (see figure 3.19). A *user axis* is just what it sounds like—an axis that you define. A user axis can be at any angle, or it can be aligned to an existing axis. In this case, you could define your user axis along the same line as the object's local X-axis. Then, you could rotate the object around the user axis to accomplish the same result.

Sometimes it can be confusing to decide which axis you want to rotate an object around to get the desired results. As a memory aid, the terms used for flying a plane (pitch, yaw, and roll) are often applied to axes rotation (see figure 3.20).

Imagine a plane flying toward you. In order for it to climb or dive, it must *pitch*, or rotate around the X-axis (see figure 3.21). To change course to the left or right, the rudder causes it to *yaw*, which is like rotating it around the Y-axis.

Finally, to make it through a narrow mountain chasm, the pilot must *roll* the plane, which rotates it around the Z-axis. The pitch, yaw, and roll mnemonic is so effective that some 3D software uses these terms instead of X, Y, and Z rotation.

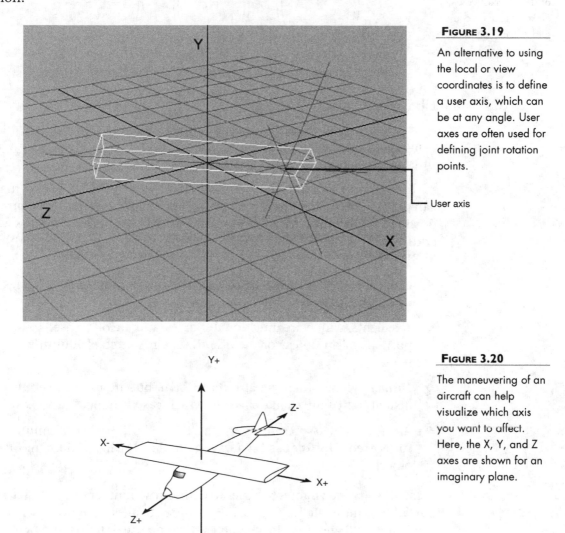

FIGURE 3.19

An alternative to using the local or view coordinates is to define a user axis, which can be at any angle. User axes are often used for defining joint rotation points.

User axis

FIGURE 3.20

The maneuvering of an aircraft can help visualize which axis you want to affect. Here, the X, Y, and Z axes are shown for an imaginary plane.

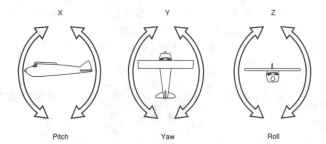

X   Y   Z

Pitch   Yaw   Roll

FIGURE 3.21

X-axis (pitch) rotation makes the plane climb or dive. Y-axis (yaw) makes it change course, and Z-axis (roll) rotation makes it bank.

Lights

So far, you've been wandering around the 3D universe in the dark. You need some lights to illuminate these rotating objects so you can see them in the finished render.

3D lights work very much like real photography studio lights, except that you can position them anywhere (including inside the object) and they don't fall down if objects bump into them. Also, most lights can cast shadows, which adds a great deal of realism to a scene. There are four main kinds of lights used in 3D software:

◆ *Omni* or *point* lights, which are like bare bulbs, illuminating things in all directions.

◆ *Spot* lights, which are directional sources, and are often used to highlight portions of an object or provide the main source of illumination for a scene.

◆ *Distant* lights, which are also directional, but are used to simulate very distant light sources like the sun, which casts parallel shadows.

◆ *Ambient* light is present everywhere in the 3D space, illuminating all surfaces equally. It's used as a way to simulate the light bouncing off other objects.

Most 3D software enables the user to define any number of lights in a scene, but adding more lights increases the time it takes to render. Chapter 7, "Lighting," will get into the characteristics and use of lights in much greater detail.

Cameras

Cameras are non-rendering objects that you can position in the 3D scene. They work like real cameras in that they provide a viewpoint on the scene that can be adjusted and animated. This camera viewpoint is different from most of the ones users employ for modeling, because it enables the scene to be viewed in more realistic and natural perspective modes. Just like real cameras, the 3D kind often have different lens settings, formats (film sizes), and the like.

3D cameras may also have *targets*, which are positioning aids that enable you to see where a camera is pointed from a non-camera viewport. You can usually define and position as many cameras as you need, although some programs may only enable you to have one. These issues and more are discussed in depth in Chapter 8, "The Camera."

Animation

Modern 3D software enables you to animate just about everything: You can move and change objects and pieces of objects, lights, cameras, and even textures. While computer animation can be a very involved process when working with complicated objects such as 3D people, most of the time it is fairly straightforward. You choose how long you want a particular movement to take, then simply reposition the object, light, or camera to the new location. The computer takes care of moving the object smoothly at render time, subject to your controls. Chapter 9, "Animation," deals with the techniques of computer animation.

Rendering

Rendering is the process wherein the computer interprets all the object and light data and creates a finished image from the viewport you have selected. The resulting image may be either a still, or a frame in an animation sequence.

To understand how the computer takes a bunch of polygons and turns them into a finished rendering, you have to examine how the computer interprets polygon surfaces. First of all, to be "seen" by the computer as a surface, a polygon face must have a normal. A *normal,* usually represented by a little arrow sticking out of a face, indicates which side of the polygon is visible, and what direction it's facing (see figure 3.22). When the 3D software begins rendering, it calculates how much (and from which direction) light is striking a particular polygon face, based on the orientation of this normal.

Most of the time in 3D graphics applications, only one side of a polygon face has a normal, making it a *single-sided polygon.* Single-sided polygons can only be "seen" from the side with the normal, which can cause problems in some rendering situations (such as when a camera is moved to the inside of an object). Therefore, the software also can be instructed to make a polygon *double-sided*, so that it can be viewed from either side (see figure 3.23).

FIGURE 3.22

Normals are imaginary lines extending from polygon faces. They are used by the software to calculate the intensity and direction of light striking the face.

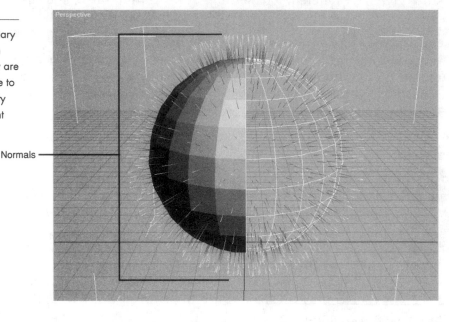

FIGURE 3.23

Single-sided polygons have only one visible face, whereas double-sided polys are visible from either side.

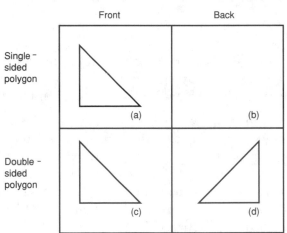

Rendering troubles such as "invisible" polygons also can arise if a polygon is non-planar. Using a four-sided polygon (a quad) as an example, imagine that it's resting on a flat plane (see figure 3.24a). If you take the right front vertex and pull it up away from the rest, the polygon becomes "bent," or *non-planar*

(see figure 3.24b). While it is still an acceptable polygon (remember, polygons can have any number of sides), part of it may not render properly, because the normal won't be in the right position. One solution to this kind of problem is to convert all the objects to triangular polygons (see figure 3.24). Because they have only three vertices, it is impossible for them to be "bent" or become non-planar.

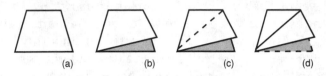

(a) (b) (c) (d)

FIGURE 3.24

Polygons with more than three vertices can become non-planar if one of the vertices is out of alignment with the others. This can result in rendering errors.

In addition to taking into account the position of normals, when the computer renders a scene, it considers any color or texture that has been applied to that polygon, the light positions, intensity, and color, and many other factors. Then, the computer "paints" the results of these calculations on the screen as an image. Most packages support several different rendering modes, and each produces a different look for the finished image (see figure 3.25).

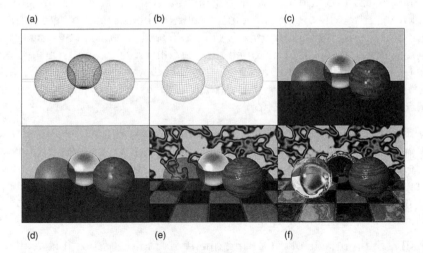

(a) (b) (c)

(d) (e) (f)

FIGURE 3.25

Common Rendering types: (a) Wireframe, (b) Hidden Line, (c) Flat shaded, (d) Gouraud Shaded, (e) Phong Shaded, and (f) Ray Traced.

The most basic, and fastest, rendering mode is wireframe, which is similar to the wireframe display mode discussed earlier. It is rarely used except for animation tests or when a "computery" look is desired for the image.

For a *flat render*, the computer calculates the color and value of a polygon face based on a single normal in the center of the face. The resulting image is a collection of sharply defined polygon surfaces, each with one solid color. Texture information is ignored, and the image has a faceted appearance. This is a very quick way to render a scene, and is often used for making test renders of animation sequences.

The next level of quality is called *Gouraud* or *smooth render*. The software calculates the color and value at each vertex of the face and then interpolates the result across the polygon face. The effect is smoothly blended object surfaces that are much more realistic than a flat rendering's surfaces. Smooth shading also incorporates textures that may have been applied to the objects. Many of the newer real-time 3D games and flight simulators use Gouraud shading.

Phong rendering retains the smoothness of Gouraud shading and adds specular highlights for even more realism. *Specular highlights* are the bright reflections of light seen on glossy objects. In Phong renders, the computer calculates the surface normal for every pixel on the screen that is representing an object. Phong rendering is probably the most common mode used for finished images and animation.

The highest level of rendering quality available from most desktop 3D packages is called ray tracing. *Ray tracing* is a method where the color and value of each pixel on the screen is calculated by casting an imaginary ray backward from the viewer's perspective into the model, to determine what light and surface factors are influencing it. The difference between ray tracing and the other methods mentioned earlier (collectively called scanline rendering techniques) is that the ray can be bounced off surfaces and bent, just like real light. The result is very realistic, with extremely accurate shadows, reflections and even refraction.

Refraction is the bending of light waves that occurs when they move through different types of materials, and is noticeable in things such as eyeglasses and water. In a ray-traced render, a transparent 3D object shaped like a magnifying glass lens actually magnifies what's behind it, whereas a similar lens in a scanline render would not. The packages that offer refraction mapping are an exception to this, simulating this effect in a scanline render.

Finally, the pinnacle of rendering quality is radiosity, but it is available on only a few packages and is extremely time-consuming. Even a relatively simple scene may take hours or days to render on a desktop system. *Radiosity* rendering takes into account the color and shape of all surfaces in the scene when calculating illumination levels, and produces images of near-photographic realism.

The differences between some of these rendering modes, are explored more fully in Chapter 10, "Rendering and Output."

Summary

Congratulations! You've successfully made it through the worst of the 3D theory. You can now hold the rapt attention of others at parties by telling them all about the principles of 3D graphics, from coordinate systems to user axes, to rendering modes. In any case, this chapter has prepared you for the practical application of all this theory—building some models!

The next chapter finally gets into the thick of it, showing you a software package while embarking on a series of basic modeling tutorials. Ultimately, these tutorials will lead toward a finished portfolio piece.

CHAPTER 4

3D Modeling

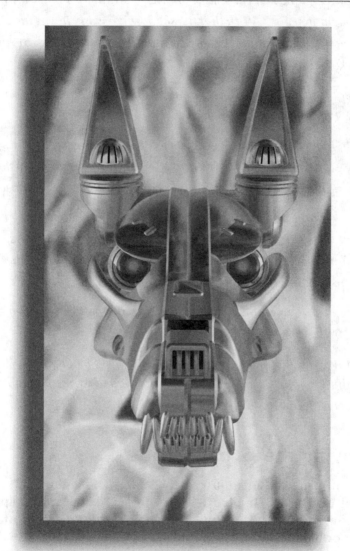

This CyberDog model was created in 3D Studio R4 using basic lofts and modified 3D primitives. Image © 1996 Mark Giambruno.

"*A*t last!" *The student sighed as he finished the day's spell book studies. "Now I can add some more detail to my castle project." He got up from his chair and stretched, then wandered over to the glowing pool to admire his work. Before him floated an impressive castle tower, its walls dotted with windows. He smiled at the fine roof, finally perched properly atop the turret.*

"Not bad," the student said to himself. "I think I'll build an inner gate next...a wrought iron one." With that, he sat down to work. It was nigh on two hours later when the Master returned from his errands and approached to examine his student's work.

"Very good, lad," the Master remarked. "But aren't those iron bars usually twisted? Say, here and there?"

"Oh, I forgot about that. I guess I should have looked at the ones downstairs first." The student frowned thoughtfully. "Well, I can fix them easily enough." A few incantations later, the vertical iron bars were endowed with decorative twists.

"Now for the arches." The student turned his attention to the bent iron bars that formed a decorative bridge between the vertical pieces. He spoke the Words of Deformation, but something went terribly wrong. The arches wrapped around themselves like Olde Gold pretzels!

"Aargh!" groaned the student, realizing the problem. "I can't twist them after they're bent. The axis..."

"Quite so," interrupted the Master. "Seems you forgot one of the key principles of conjuring, lad," he sighed, tapping on a large wooden sign on the wall. It read simply, "P L A N A H EAd."

Laying the Groundwork

As our hapless student just discovered, it isn't enough to know how to use a tool. You have to be able to see the project as a whole and plan a strategy for accomplishing it. Therefore, through theory and then tutorials, this chapter not only introduces you to the basic modeling tools, but also offers suggestions for planning, good work habits, and using your 3D tools in novel ways.

The first step in planning any project is to sit down and think it through. Identify the hard parts, note the things you're uncertain about, and so forth. Remember that there's always more than one way to solve a problem, so if there seems to be an aspect of the project that's particularly daunting, try to find a creative alternative.

Modeling Approaches

Whenever possible, take the simplest path to success when figuring out how a model will be constructed. The KISS (Keep It Simple, Stupid) principle applies very nicely to 3D work, because complicated models and operations tend to bog down the system and are more likely to cause trouble later on.

Bump and diffusion mapping (discussed in Chapter 6, "Texture Mapping") uses surface images and normals manipulation to give the impression that there are additional mesh details on an object. Because of this, mapping can often substitute for lots of detailed mesh, particularly with objects that aren't the focus of attention or are distant in the scene. So, think about whether a texture could be used on a simpler object (or even a flat polygon) and still achieve the same results.

If you're uncertain about whether a given modeling approach will work, do a test run with a quickly defined version of the object to find out. Experimenting in this way will often turn up alternatives that you wouldn't have thought of otherwise.

Object Naming

Developing good work habits early on will save you a mountain of time and frustration. 3D scenes can become very complex, particularly in a production environment, and good organization is vital. After all, when you're dealing with multiple versions of scenes, with dozens of objects created by different artists, you don't want to deal with unnecessary problems—like what Object126 is.

One of your most important organizational tasks is naming objects properly. It's extremely helpful throughout the project if all objects follow a consistent naming convention, and it's practically vital if the model will be passed on to others for mapping or animation work. Naming conventions are a matter of personal taste, and are influenced by the size of the name that the program enables you to use, as well as the complexity of the project. For example, if you're planning an animation of a single jet fighter, it might be okay to use names such as Nose, Right Wing, and Left Wing. If you're planning to do a dogfight, however, you'll need to mark all the parts to identify to which aircraft they belong.

One convention that I suggest uses 1-, 2-, or 3-letter codes and *intercaps* (the use of capital letters at the beginning of each word, but no spaces in between). These keep the names compact but legible, and work well with programs that don't allow long names. Using the dogfight example, the two jets might be labeled as the following:

> J1Nos
>
> J1WngLt
>
> J1WngRt
>
> J2Nos
>
> J2WngLt
>
> J2WngRt

Here, J1 is Jet 1, J2 is Jet 2, Fus is fuselage, Wng is wing, Lt is left and Rt is right. Putting the L and R after the part they describe keeps things organized in a neater way. If you used the direction designation first, the list would end up being alphabetized like this instead:

> J1LtWng
>
> J1Nos
>
> J1RtWng
>
> J2LtWng
>
> J2Nos
>
> J2RtWng

As you can see, the wings for a given jet are now separated by other parts in the list, which makes it more difficult to find things quickly.

Assuming your program supports long object names, this hierarchical approach also can have advantages when you get into small details, because the location of the object is built into the name. For example, say that you had two clusters of two missiles to add to each wing on the plane. If you build onto the existing name, it identifies their general locations:

> J1WngRtClsInMisLt
>
> J2WngLtClsOtMisRt

The first example would identify the object in question as being on Jet 1, right wing, inboard cluster, left missile. Likewise, the second object is on Jet 2, left wing, outboard cluster, right missile. Obviously, when a model starts to get this complex, you'll need to keep a list of what your abbreviations stand for.

File Naming

Following conventions for filenames is as important as following them for object names, but until recently has been more problematic. While Mac and Unix users have enjoyed 32-character filenames for years, the PC's limit of eight characters plus an extension forced users to use cryptic, non-descriptive names. Now that Windows NT and Windows 95 is becoming commonplace among PC artists, however, you can finally start to cast off over a decade of filename oppression. With Windows NT and Windows 95, you can use STAR BATTLE V2.01 as your filename instead of STRB2_01.XXX. Note, however, that you can only use such long filenames if you don't plan to share your files with someone running under an older operating system. For example, MS-DOS-based 3D Studio R4 still follows the old eight-plus-three rule, so any filenames would be truncated to eleven characters. Whatever naming abbreviations and conventions you choose, they should explain what's in the file so you don't have to open it.

As with the object naming convention, the size of the project helps determine how the file should be named. If it's a single isolated model or scene you're doing, then simply using a descriptive name plus a number (to record the version) is ample. Remember to always use a two-digit number (01 instead of just 1) if you expect the model to take a while to construct. Otherwise, your directory listing will end up looking like this:

    MODEL1.DXF

    MODEL10.DXF

    MODEL2.DXF

    MODEL3.DXF

See how version 10 follows version 1? If you use 01, 02, 03, and so on, you will keep the files in proper order. This goes for assigning output filenames for rendering as well, although you may have to start with 001 or 0001 instead if the animation sequence is more than 100 frames long.

If your project is fairly complex, and consists of numerous scenes, you may want to consider a filename code. This is what was done with *The Daedalus Encounter*, which had about two hours of video and animation (see figure 4.1).

There are two key items to designing a good filename convention—first, that it makes sense (at least if you have a legend with the codes), and second, that it's flexible and extensible, enabling you to add new categories of files without discarding the conventions.

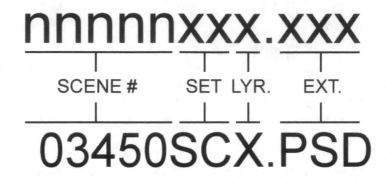

In The Daedalus Encounter file naming convention, the first five characters referenced the scene number that was noted in the screenplay, in this case, scene 03450. A scene number remained valid until the camera position was changed, at which time the scene number was incremented by 10. This allowed up to an additional nine scenes to be inserted without fouling up the scene number sequence.

Following the scene number was a two-character code that indicated the name of the virtual set, or location where the action in the scene took place. In the sample, SC stands for "Salvage Cockpit," which was the bridge of the salvage vessel *Artemis*. The final code was normally an X, and was there for situations when the scene imagery was made up of multiple layers. For example, in the cockpit scenes, the starfield, hull, control panels, and foreground console were all rendered separately with alpha channels. The X character became a B for the Background (starfield) layer, and an F for the Foreground (console) layer. The other components in the scene took up the designations C (hull), and D (control panel), moving from background to foreground. This made it easy to identify (in a directory full of filenames) which files belonged to the same scene and, to a degree, what portion of the scene they made up.

Saving and Backing Up

Carefully named files and objects won't help you if you lose your data, but frequent saves and backups can save your uh...neck when something goes wrong. How often is frequent? Save anytime you do a significant amount of work and always before doing a tricky operation or anything else that might alter things in an undesirable way if something screws up. You also should save whenever you leave your computer for any reason, particularly if you work in an office or studio. You also should save your file as a new version at any critical points, like when you're doing an operation that permanently changes the characteristics of an object and can't be undone later (a Boolean operation may be one example). In this way, you can always go back to the file with the old version of the object in it, make any needed modifications, and perform the operation again. Saving as a new version several times a day also protects you against accidents, or unnoticed errors in the file that get saved on top of your working backups.

Speaking of accidents, a common problem I've heard many times from 3DS R4 novices is; "I opened my file (with the model I worked all day yesterday) and it was empty!" The problem here is that after starting up the program, the user accidentally clicked Save Project instead of Load Project (which is easy to do) and then selected the file with the project in it. The result is that they saved the empty scene over the top of their project file.

While saving frequently (and in different versions) will go a long way toward preventing the most common file overwrite problems, it offers no protection against the dreaded hard drive crash. Therefore, you should save to multiple drives at least twice a day or whenever you do a substantial amount of work on the project.

The basic rule of backups is that you should always have three copies on three separate pieces of media. Of course, one copy should be kept off-site, in case of fire, theft, natural disasters or janitors with big magnets on their vacuum cleaners. For the ultimate off-site storage, you could e-mail the file to yourself (at a seldom-used address, if available)—that way, it's stored off-site (on your ISP or online service's computers) and accessible at work or elsewhere if your system meets with any misfortune.

Modeler Concepts

Now that we've nipped any potential bad habits in the bud, it's time to move on to the software itself. As you know, modeling is the process of creating objects with a 3D software program. The term *modeler* was defined in Chapter 1 as the person who performs this work, but it also is used to describe that portion of the 3D package that deals with object creation as well.

Types of Modelers

There are four basic types of modeling systems: Polygonal, Spline, Patch, and Parametric. Many packages combine these systems, because each has its strengths and weaknesses. Polygonal is the most basic, and deals with 3D objects as groups of polygons only. Spline modelers are more sophisticated, and enable the user to work with resolution-independent objects. Patch modelers are well-suited to sculpting organic objects, and parametric modelers allow the parameters of an object to be changed later in the process for maximum flexibility. While each program takes a different approach, many of them incorporate two or more of these different modelers for flexibility.

Polygonal Modelers

Polygonal modeling is the oldest type of 3D modeling, harkening back to the days when you defined points in space by entering X, Y, and Z coordinates from the keyboard. As you know, when three or more of these points are connected by edges, they form a polygon, which can have color and texture. When you put a bunch of these polygons together, you can fashion a representation of just about any object. A downside to polygonal modeling is that everything is made up of these tiny, flat surfaces, and they need to be fairly small or your object may look faceted along the edges (see figure 4.2). This means that if you will be zooming in on an object in a scene, you have to model it at a high *polygon resolution* (density), even though most of the polys will be unnecessary when you move further from the object.

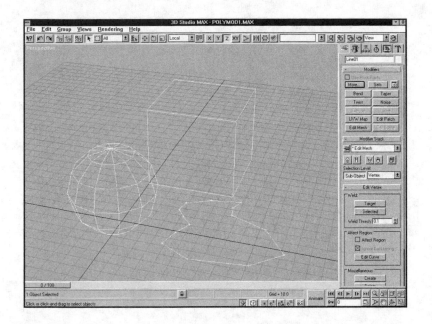

FIGURE 4.2

With polygonal modelers, objects are constructed with polylines, or splines that are converted to polylines. Once an object is created in this type of modeler, it generally can't be increased in resolution.

For consistency, all of the interface screen grabs in this section are from Kinetix 3D Studio MAX. Like many 3D software offerings, MAX has several different modelers integrated into the package.

In anticipation of the overall increases in processor and display speed, products have been migrating from polygon-based to spline-based modeling. Interestingly, though, the demand for better polygon editing tools has increased dramatically of late, and even the spline modeling giants are paying more attention to polygons. This is due to the needs and incredible popularity of real-time 3D games like Virtua Fighter, Descent, and the DOOM-style POV shooters.

Spline Modelers

If you've ever used a 2D drawing program such as Illustrator or CorelDRAW!, you're familiar with splines, one of the main tools that these programs use. Technically speaking, a *spline* is a (usually curved) line that is defined by control points. One of the main advantages of spline-based modeling over polygonal modeling is that it's resolution-independent, meaning that (in theory) you can get as close as you want to an object and never see any faceting (see figure 4.3).

Figure 4.3

Spline modelers use resolution-independent splines to define objects. This makes for smoother vertice-level object editing and allows the final resolution of the object to be adjusted after creation.

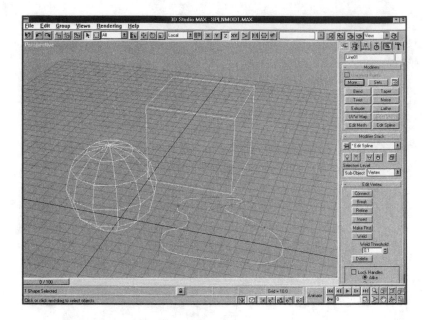

Spline modelers also are better suited to creating complex organic shapes like human faces, tyrannosaurs, and alien spacecraft. Splines are better for applications like this because their method of building forms uses smooth and natural curves, instead of jagged and artificial polygonal shapes. There are several different types of splines, with modelers commonly using the B-Spline, the Bézier, and NURBS. Spline types and the differences between them are discussed later in the chapter.

Patch Modelers

Patch modelers use a network of control points to define and modify the shape of the *patch*, which is usually a lattice of either splines or polygons (see figure 4.4). These control points, called *control vertices* (*CVs*), exert a magnet-like influence on the flexible surface of the patch, stretching and tugging it in one direction or another. In addition, patches can be subdivided to allow for more detail and can be "stitched" together to form large, complex surfaces.

Parametric Modelers

Parametric modeling means that you're working with objects that retain their base geometry information, such as their default shape, their current size, and how many segments their forms consist of. Because this information can still be accessed and changed even after the objects are modified, it enables the user to change or undo alterations to the object later on, and even increase or decrease their resolution (see figure 4.5). While parametric modeling is usually spline-based, not all spline modelers are parametric.

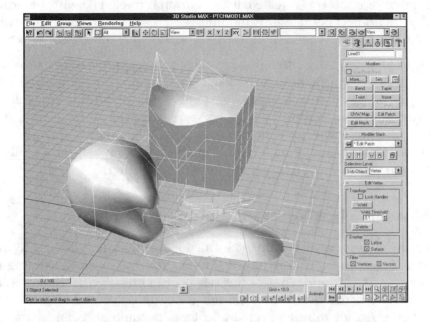

FIGURE 4.4

Patch modelers use magnet-like Control Vertices to affect the surface of an object. They are particularly useful for organic modeling.

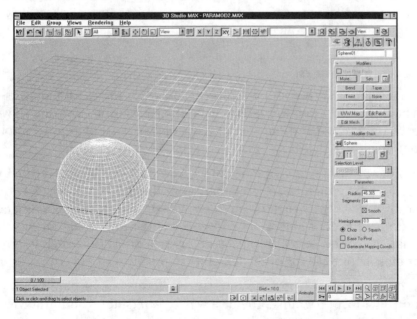

FIGURE 4.5

Parametric modelers are spline-based, but allow operations to be adjusted or undone even after several modifications have been done to an object. Among other things, this enables the resolution of objects to be adjusted after creation and modification. The controls on the right show the present settings for the sphere object.

Deformations applied to parametric objects can often be adjusted at any time, even though they may have been applied several operations ago. Contrast this to polygonal modeling, where (tessellation and optimizers aside) once an object is created, its resolution is fixed. Likewise, deforming a polygonal object permanently modifies it, so if you bend an object, then later want to reduce that bend significantly, you probably have to start over again.

The fact that so many different types of modeling approaches exist is another reason that it's difficult to give specific instructions for the tutorials. While a spline or parametric modeler will work best for the rounded organic forms in the tutorial, such as the helium bag, you can use polygonal as well, making sure that you set the mesh density to a reasonable level when you create the objects. Regardless of which type of modeler you have, however, all of the tutorials can be accomplished in one way or another.

Working in the 3D World

Because each program is individual and does things a little differently, it's up to you to get up to speed on the user interface for your product, learning about how to move around, change the viewports, and so forth. However, all of them have some things in common. They have viewports onto the 3D universe, sets of mouse-selected and type-in commands and parameters, dialogs, text files where you can set options, and so forth. Take a look at some of the things to be concerned with.

Getting Around

You will probably be using a mouse to construct and modify objects, as well as navigate your way through the 3D universe. Familiarize yourself with any special functions the mouse performs through the use of mouse button or key combinations.

In order to modify a shape or object, you have to select it, which usually highlights it somehow to set it apart from the rest. You can select things in the normal ways, by clicking on them with the cursor or dragging a marquee around a cluster of objects. In addition, many products enable you to open a dialog box and select objects by name, type or color, which is very useful for picking out groups of related objects quickly.

You'll spend a lot of time peering at viewports, so get familiar with their controls. Most programs provide a way to *pan* (slide around the viewpoint) so that you can see things that are off to one side. You also can *zoom* in for detail work or zoom out to see more of the scene. There is also a *zoom all* control that will automatically zoom out to show you everything in the scene. This is very helpful when trying to locate and move wayward pieces that were imported or created somewhere away from the rest of the model.

Programs also enable you to customize your viewports, selecting where you want the top view, the left view, the perspective view, and so on located. You also can change the size of the window in many cases. To save time, learn the hot keys for changing views without resorting to the menu.

Grids and Snaps

Grids are cross-hatched lines that can be seen in the viewport and used like graph paper for determining scale when creating objects (see figure 4.6). When you build objects, they generally appear near the origin point, in the center of the 3D universe. This can be changed through the use of *construction planes* or *construction grids*, which are settings that move the default location to other parts of the model. These are useful when you have a large scene and are working in a particular section only, or if you want objects to appear already aligned to a particular plane.

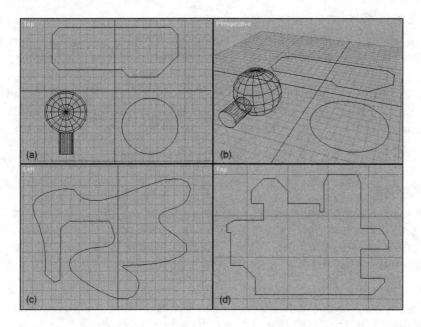

FIGURE 4.6

Using grids and snaps: (a) Grids and snaps make the creation and alignment of shapes and objects easier. (b) Because both are active regardless of viewpoint, you can align objects from any perspective. (c) For creating free-form shapes or objects, turn snap off. (d) Snaps can be set independently of the grid, making it easier to create sub-grid refinements.

The *snap* feature is usually employed in conjunction with a grid, and causes the cursor to snap from one position to another, often at the intersection of two grid lines. Depending on the program, you may be able to snap to the vertices or faces on objects as well. Note that the snap setting can be different from the grid setting, which is convenient for creating or moving objects precisely without having to alter the grid setting.

It's a good idea to use grids and snaps whenever possible, because it will make your shapes and alignments more exact, and you will probably find that it makes the modeling process go faster.

Hide and Unhide

Hide enables you to make a shape or object disappear from the scene; use *Unhide* to make it reappear later. This pair of commands is great for clearing out mesh that you don't need to see at the present time (and preventing it from being accidentally modified), and it makes the scene render faster as well. Sometimes, however, you want to see the object, but don't want it to be accidentally modified. That's where Freeze or Ghost come in.

Freeze/Ghost

When you apply *Freeze* or *Ghost* to a shape or object, it still appears in the scene, but you cannot select (and therefore change) it while it's frozen. This is a very useful feature, because 3D scenes tend to get quite complex, and it's easy to pick and transform the wrong object. Frozen objects usually change color, letting you know the object is frozen so you don't get frustrated trying to figure out why you can't select it. When you want to modify the object, you can *Unfreeze* or *Unghost* it.

Groups

Grouping is a convenient way to attach a number of different shapes or objects together temporarily. This enables you to deal with them as a whole for transforms, mapping, and other operations, but still tweak them on an individual basis if need be.

Creating a group is easy—just select the objects you want, Group them, and give the group a name. In addition, some programs enable you to manipulate individual objects within a group without using *Ungroup* first.

2D Shapes

Because many of the upcoming 3D operations use 2D shapes as a starting point, a good understanding of how to create and manipulate them is fundamental.

You probably had your fill of 2D polygon *theory* in the last chapter, so I'll keep this recap brief. 2D shapes can consist of lines, polylines, polygons, or splines. As you recall, a polyline is a type of line with more than one segment (in other words, containing three or more vertices). A polygon is an enclosed shape with three or more edges. Polygons have faces that show up when rendered in a 3D program, while lines and polylines do not.

Why Use 2D Shapes?

2D shapes are an excellent way to begin creating a complex 3D object. By creating 2D outlines of some of the forms, it's possible to use the software tools to convert them into 3D objects.

Working in 2D first makes it possible to visualize and define cross-sections, and to establish the proper composition and scale of the components. In addition, 2D polygons serve as *cheap mesh,* which is a slang term for an object that has a low polygon count or is very efficient and quick to render. An example would be constructing the walls of a room scene out of flat polygons, rather than using several 3D boxes, which contain six times as much mesh.

A good example of this is the "Gizmo" model I constructed for Mplayer Interactive, an Internet gaming company. The Gizmo is a device that looks like a high-tech portable TV and serves as the user interface for the Mplayer service (see figure 4.7).

As a starting point, I imported the 2D Illustrator drawing of the Gizmo into 3D Studio. Next, I broke down the complex, flowing design into a few key cross-sections, which I drew as 2D shapes (see figure 4.8). A modified version of the original Illustrator drawing (by Tom Gooden of Good Dog Design), in conjunction with the additional cross-sections, formed the skeleton of the object. These 2D forms were then "skinned" (covered later in the chapter) to create the finished object.

The 2D cross-sections in this case weren't polylines, as have been discussed so far. They were splines, which are much more appropriate for the required curved shapes.

FIGURE 4.7

This 3D model of the Mplayer "Gizmo" was constructed with 3D Studio MAX. Image by Mark Giambruno and Laura Hainke, ©1996 Mplayer.

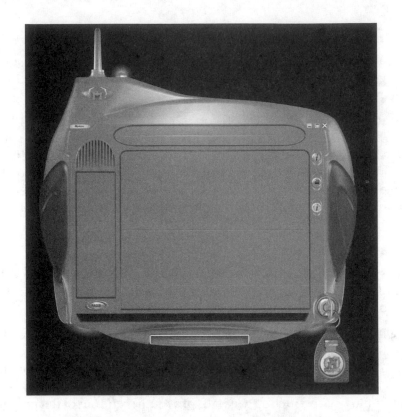

FIGURE 4.8

The Gizmo's basic form was developed out of spline-based cross-sections. The initial shape was imported from an Illustrator presentation drawing, then additional cross-sections were defined to outline the shape at various depths. Mplayer Gizmo ©1996 Mplayer.

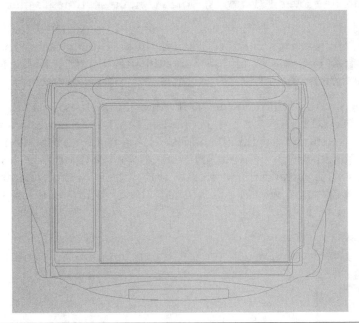

Splines

As discussed earlier, a spline is a (usually curved) line that is defined by control points. There are several different types of splines. Modelers commonly use the B-spline, the Bézier, and NURBS (see figure 4.9).

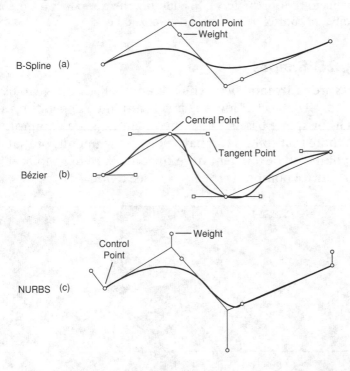

B-Spline (a)

Control Point
Weight

Bézier (b)

Central Point
Tangent Point

NURBS (c)

Weight
Control Point

FIGURE 4.9

Three types of splines commonly used in 3D programs: (a) B-spline, (b) Bézier spline, and (c) NURBS (Non-Uniform Rational B-Spline).

All splines are similar in that they consist of a line or shape that's controlled by a polyline or polygon. The poly itself (also called a *control line, control polygon,* or *hull*) isn't seen—it merely serves to define the curvature of the resulting spline. Depending on the type of spline, there are *control points* or *control vertices* that mark key positions along the control lines, and *tangent points* or *weights* that act like little magnets to attract the spline in their direction. By manipulating these points, the user modifies the shape of the spline.

B-splines use control points with equal weights to adjust the shape of the spline. Control points rarely reside on the resulting curve in this type of spline.

Bézier splines have control points that always reside on the resulting curve. Extending out from the control points are tangent points or handles, which enable the curve to be modified without moving the control points. These tangent points also can be operated independently of each other, which makes the curve less smooth but allows for a great deal of control.

NURBS (Non-Uniform Rational B-Splines) also have control points that reside away from the resulting curve, but instead of tangent points, they have weights to control the curve. In addition, there are *knots* that define the number of control points on a given portion of the curve.

Editing 2D Shapes

2D shapes are easily modified, which is another advantage to using them as the basis for 3D objects. How a shape is modified depends on whether it's polygonal- or spline-based, but some operations are common to both. In addition, note that splines can have polyline segments, or that some of the control points can be different from the others. Here's a look at some of the different control point or vertice types (see figure 4.10).

FIGURE 4.10

Control point types:
(a) Standard Bézier
(b) Bézier Corner
(c) Smooth (d) Corner.

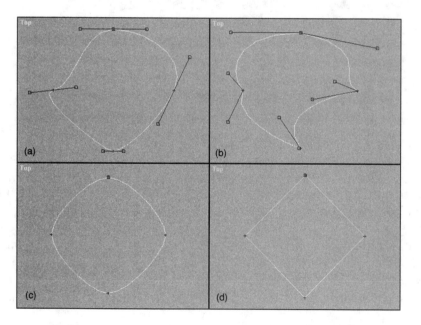

Standard Bézier control points have handles that are tangent from the curve, and move as a unit when they're rotated or their lengths adjusted. This tends to keep the curves fairly smooth.

Bézier corner control points have handles that can be adjusted independently of each other, enabling you to define much sharper and more angular curves.

Smooth control points don't have handles at all, and use a pre-determined formula to calculate how the spline curves between control points.

Corner control points apply no curvature to the spline, making segments between them straight lines.

By mixing these different control point types, you can make virtually any 2D shape. These control points and vertices can be adjusted further with editing operations.

The basic line and polyline editing operations include moving, adding or deleting lines, vertices, or edges (see figure 4.11). Note that there may not be specific commands for these operations, because they're usually selected through the use of the mouse buttons or modifier keys like SHIFT, CTRL, and ALT.

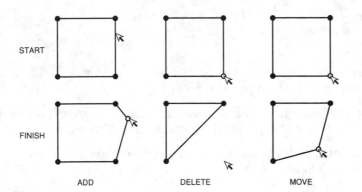

START

FINISH

ADD   DELETE   MOVE

FIGURE 4.11

Basic line and polyline or polygon vertice editing operations. Move and Delete directly affect existing vertices, while Add creates a new one.

Add Vertice creates a new vertice, either along an existing edge or as an extension of the last point of a line or polyline.

Delete Vertice removes a vertice and its adjacent edges, and causes a new edge to be formed between any vertices to which it was connected.

Move Vertice enables you to reposition the selected vertice and the edges to which it's connected.

Note that many programs may indicate the *first vertice* (the one that was created first) by surrounding it with a box or making it a different color when editing. This isn't important for most operations, but it does affect skinning, which is discussed later in the chapter. For now, remember that any vertice can be reassigned as the first vertice by using the appropriate poly or spline editing tool, which may be called First or First Vertice.

Although much less common than basic line and vertice editing commands, some programs offer useful 2D trimming and rounding (filleting) operations (see figure 4.12).

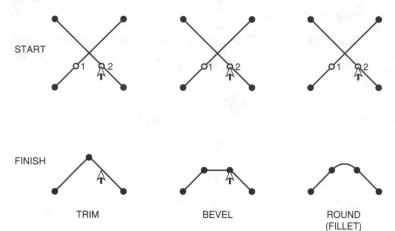

Trim Lines connects overlapping lines at their intersection, and deletes portions that extend past that point.

Bevel Lines creates a new segment to bridge the gap between selected points. It also deletes portions that extend past the selections.

Round or *Fillet Lines* creates a new segment like Bevel Lines, but in this case, it's a smooth curve.

The basic modifications for splines include moving, adding or deleting control points, and adjusting tangent controls or weights (see figure 4.13). As with the line, polyline and polygon modifications, there may not be specific commands for these operations. They are usually done through the use of the mouse buttons or modifier keys like SHIFT, CTRL, or ALT.

Add Control Point creates a new vertice, either along an existing curve or as an extension of the last point on the curve.

Delete Control Point removes a vertice and its adjacent curves, and causes a new curve to be formed between any vertices to which it was connected.

Move Control Point enables you to reposition the selected vertice and the curves to which it is connected.

On standard Bézier curves, the tangent points are locked together most of the time. If you move one, the other moves in a mirror fashion. Through the use of modifier keys or by changing the control point type, it becomes possible to adjust them independently, varying the distance (and sometimes the angle) of one side while leaving the other side undisturbed.

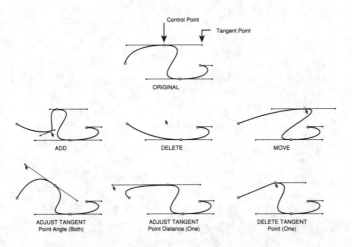

FIGURE 4.13

Common Bézier spline modifications. (upper row) Control point adjustments. (lower row) Tangent point adjustments.

In addition to these common modifications, many programs enable you to convert polygonal lines or objects to splines, and vice versa. Drawing an outline with a polyline and then converting the shape to a spline can make it easier to create a smooth, complex object, because many people find it easier to work with polylines (see figure 4.14).

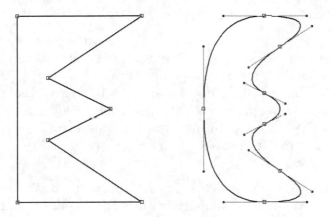

FIGURE 4.14

Some programs enable you to convert a poly into a smoothed spline. This can make it quicker and easier to create complex organic shapes.

Shape Resolution

Related to the disposition of control points and vertices on a shape is its resolution. As you know, image resolution relates to the number of pixels on a screen or image, allowing for more or less detail. Similarly, polygon resolution specifies the density of line segments and polygons for mesh, and therefore defines the amount of detail and smoothness in the object (see figure 4.15).

FIGURE 4.15

Effects of resolution on objects and open splines: (a) High resolution (b) Medium resolution (c) Low resolution.

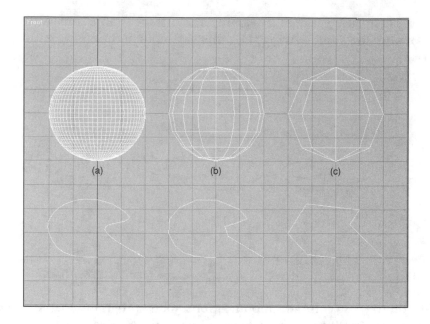

While the resolution of a polyline or polygon is usually set at the time you create it, it's sometimes possible to increase or decrease the resolution later on. Splines, on the other hand, must go through a conversion process when they're used in a polygonal modeler, and the resolution setting has a major effect on how smooth the curves remain.

A common term for indicating a shape or object's resolution is how many steps it contains. *Steps* refers to the number of additional vertices generated between control points on a spline or vertices on a poly. For example, a setting of 1 step would mean no subdividing vertices would be added, because the line travels between the original control points or vertices in a single step. If the object had a step setting of 3, however, there would be two additional vertices added, making the line between the original points break into three segments, or steps.

It's important to note that resolution settings affect the shape or object as a whole, so if you increase the number of steps to smooth out a curve, the program will also subdivide the straight portions of the object as well, creating unnecessary vertices. Some programs will give you an option to delete these extra vertices automatically, however.

2D Attach/Detach

Often, it's useful to attach 2D shapes together to join separately drawn elements, or to form a composite shape. *Attach* is a common command for 3D programs that enables you to join separate elements into one object (see figure 4.16). Implementation varies, with some programs prompting to see if you want to attach whenever 2D vertices are moved within range of each other. Other programs require you to select the elements and specifically command the software to attach them.

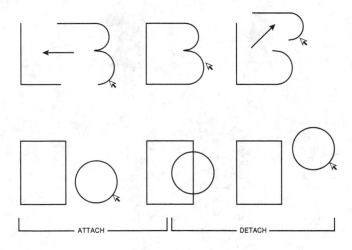

ATTACH ———— DETACH

FIGURE 4.16

Attach and Detach: (upper row) Attaching and detaching line segments makes it easier to create complex 2D shapes or to use portions of one shape elsewhere. (lower row) Attaching objects together is similar to grouping them. They can be detached at a later point.

Attaching two polylines together doesn't necessarily mean that they form a single *closed shape*. In some cases, you may have to *weld* (combine) the endpoints of the shapes together in a separate operation.

Likewise, you may want to *detach* part of a shape that divides the original object into two elements for use elsewhere, essentially the opposite of attach. Doing this usually requires you to select the elements you want, then use the command detach or something similar.

2D Booleans

Boolean operations enable you to build onto or carve away at shapes by combining or subtracting the shapes from each other. Booleans are very powerful and useful tools, because they enable you to make some changes to a shape that would take much longer if you made the changes by manipulating the vertices.

Shapes selected for Boolean operations are called *operands*, and the order in which you choose them will affect the outcome in some operations, like Subtract. Other Boolean types include Add, Intersection and Split (see figure 4.17). Note that programs tend to use different terms for Booleans, but the range of operations is similar.

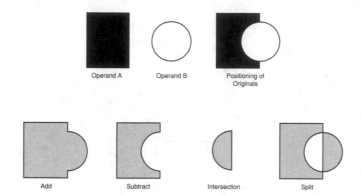

FIGURE 4.17

The 2D Boolean operations Add, Subtract, Intersection, and Split. When using Subtract, the second object selected is subtracted from the first.

Add combines the shapes into one, adding their volumes together and deleting any overlaps.

Subtract removes from the first shape any portions of the second shape that overlap it.

Intersection deletes any portion of either shape that isn't overlapping.

Split deletes any portion of both shapes that overlaps.

Importing/Exporting Shapes

Another advantage of working with 2D shapes is that they're readily transportable from 2D drawing programs to 3D modelers, and vice versa. This means you can *export* (save in a compatible format) existing work created in Illustrator or CorelDRAW!, for example, and *import* it into your 3D program.

Most 3D programs support at least one 2D import/export format. DXF (Drawing eXchange Format) is a common one, along with AI (Adobe Illustrator) and IGES (Initial Graphics Exchange Specification). See Chapter 10, "Rendering and Output," for more information.

Turning 2D Shapes into 3D Objects

You've seen how to create and edit 2D shapes, but how are they turned into 3D objects? Actually, you can apply several different operations to one or more shapes, with a surprisingly broad range of results. The most commonly used operations are extrudes, lathes, sweeps, and skins. Shape resolution plays a part in these operations as well, because the software usually enables you to define how many increments (steps or segments) are used when converting an shape from 2D to 3D. Also, bear in mind that even a simple flat polygon should be considered part of your 3D toolbox, in that it can be used in modeling to great effect.

Most 3D programs make heavy use of the mouse for defining and moving shapes and objects, but most offer numerical entry as well, enabling you to enter precise coordinates, distances, or transformation percentages.

Extrusions

The most straightforward way of making a 2D shape into a 3D object is by extruding it. An *extrusion* is simply pushing the 2D shape into the third dimension by giving it a Z-axis depth (see figure 4.18). The result of an extrusion is a 3D object with width, height, and now, depth.

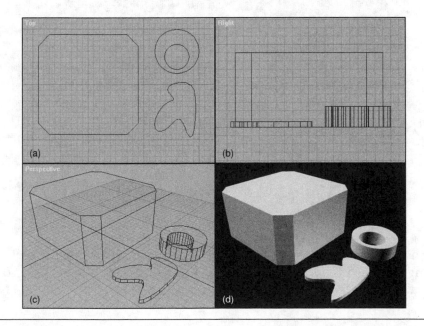

FIGURE 4.18

Extrude process: (a) 2D shapes are defined using polylines or splines. (b–d) Extrude is applied to the 2D shapes, giving them whatever depth is desired.

Extrusions are very useful for creating block-like shapes, columns, panels, and the like, but the sharp-edged result definitely has a computer graphics look to it. In Chapter 5, "Modeling: Beyond the Basics," you'll learn how to modify the extrude operation to make this less obvious.

To create an extruded object, first define the 2D shapes with polylines or splines. Note that if you create shapes within shapes, such as the two circles in the figure, the inner ones will leave holes in the object. Next, select the desired shapes and apply an Extrude operation to them, setting the depth of the object with mouse movement or numerical entry.

Lathing

The next method of forming a 3D object is lathing. In woodworking, a lathe is a device that rotates a block of wood at high speed, enabling you to trim away and form the wood with a sharp gouge. Lathes are used to create intricately carved cylindrical objects like chair legs and bed posts. In 3D modeling, a *Lathe* command spins a 2D shape around an axis, extruding it in small steps as it rotates (see figure 4.19).

FIGURE 4.19

Lathe process: (a) A 2D cross-section is created, and the lathe axis selected. (b–d) The Lathe operation spins the cross-section around the axis, extruding it in small steps.

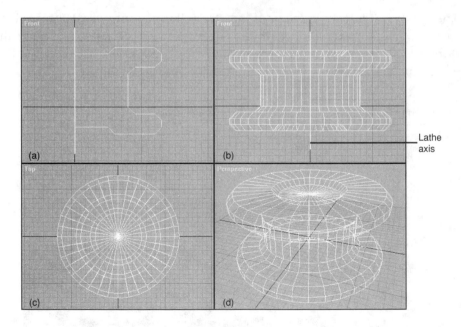

Lathe axis

Lathe is ideal for creating any kind of radial object, like pulleys, reels, pipe flanges, and of course, *wine glasses*. Along with extrude, it's one of the fundamental operations in 3D graphics.

To create a lathed object, define a 2D object or objects with polylines or splines to use as a cross-section. Selecting the Lathe command will enable you to define the axis around which the cross-section will be spun. The result is a radially symmetrical 3D object.

One of the nice things about Lathe is that the results can be dramatically different depending on how you set your axis. If the axis is adjacent to or inside of the cross-section, it results in a *closed lathe*, while an *open lathe* is the result if the axis is moved away from the cross-section (see figure 4.20).

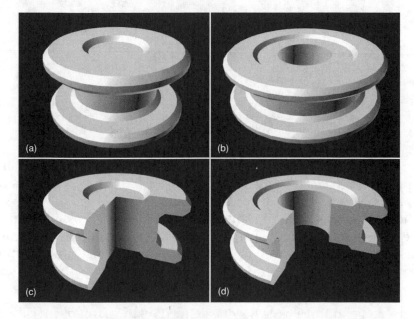

FIGURE 4.20

Lathe types: (a) Closed lathe (b) Open lathe (c) Closed partial lathe (d) Open partial lathe.

Lathes don't have to be a full 360 degrees—they could just as easily be 90, 180, or 272 degrees, resulting in a *partial lathe*. Partial lathes are useful for creating cutaway views of objects, or for eliminating unnecessary portions of the form, such as when part of the lathed object will be inside of another object.

Sweeping

Although common, the next two 2D to 3D operations have different (and sometimes contradictory) terms applied to them depending on the software being used. For example, 3D Studio refers to these operations as lofts, but many other products refer to them as sweeps, and that's what they'll be called here. A *sweep* is a single 2D cross-section that is extruded along a path (see figure 4.21).

FIGURE 4.21

Sweep process:
(a) Define a 2D cross-section. (b) Create a path using polylines or splines. (c) Assign the cross-section to the path or vice-versa, adjusting its orientation. (d) Sweep the cross-section along the path to create a 3D object.

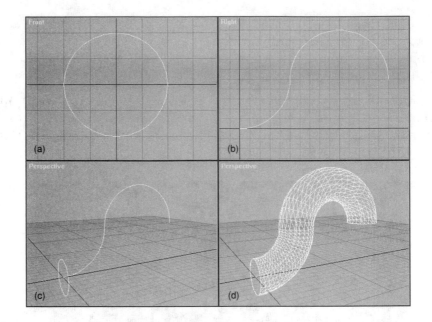

To create a swept object, start by defining a 2D cross-section with polylines or splines. Next, create a path for the cross-section to follow using polylines or splines. Note that this path can be open or closed. Assign the cross-section to the path or vice-versa, adjusting its orientation. The cross-section doesn't have to be centered on the path, nor does it need to be perpendicular. Of course, the orientation will affect the final result. Finally, performing the Sweep operation extrudes the cross-section along the path to create a 3D object.

Sweeps come in three basic flavors, defined by the path: open, closed, and helical (see figure 4.22). While helical could just be considered another open sweep, it is used so often that it deserves special mention.

Open sweeps are created with paths that have two ends, and are ideal for creating a curved extrusion, which the standard Extrude command can't do. Obvious uses are creating wires, rope and tubing, plant stalks, snakes, or any sort of bent stock used in manufactured items.

Helical sweeps are a form of open sweep in which the path coils around like a spring, which happens to be the most common use for this type. It's also useful for creating screw threads, such as the ones in the opening figure for this chapter. Most programs offer controls for generating the helical path for this sweep easily.

Closed sweeps are created by closing the path, so that the cross-section meets up with itself as it is swept along. Closed sweeps are good for creating fan belts, trim, or bumpers around other objects and so forth.

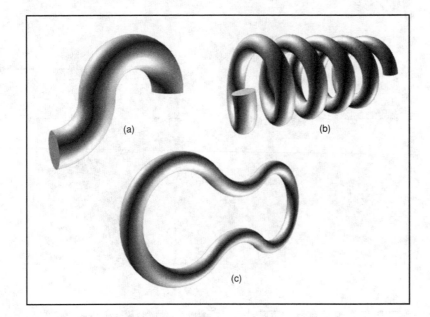

FIGURE 4.22

Sweep types: (a) Open sweep (b) Helical sweep (c) Closed sweep.

Skinning

The final means of converting 2D shapes into 3D objects is by *skinning,* which is similar to an open sweep, except that you can use different cross-sectional shapes along the path (see figure 4.23). In essence, the program creates a "skin" to wrap over this framework, something like the way an umbrella's tines hold the fabric in place.

Depending on your program, skinning operations may require some extra preparation. For example, your program may demand that each cross-section (CS) have the same number of vertices. If this is the case, you will need to add vertices to some objects so all of them have the same quantity.

In many cases, skinning operations are sensitive to the orientation of the first vertices (discussed earlier) on each cross-section, because the program starts the skin by connecting them. In general, you want the first vertice of each CS to be more or less in line with the others. Otherwise, the object may appear to be twisted (see figure 4.24). This will require some planning on your part to arrive at a good combination of vertice quantity and placement.

FIGURE 4.23

Skinning process:
(a) Define the 2D cross-sectional shapes.
(b–c) Create a path and determine where the cross-sections will be located. (d) Perform the Skin operation, which creates a surface to bridge the cross-sections.

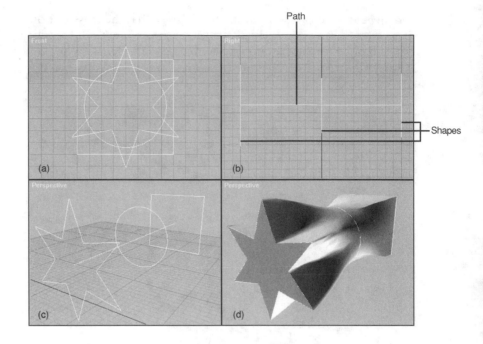

(a)   (b)

FIGURE 4.24

Skinning gone awry:
(a) Problem: the 3D object appears twisted.
(b) Examining the cross-sections shows that the first vertices are not aligned. (c) Rotating the cross-sections creates a better alignment.
(d) The skin on the adjusted object is now much less twisted.

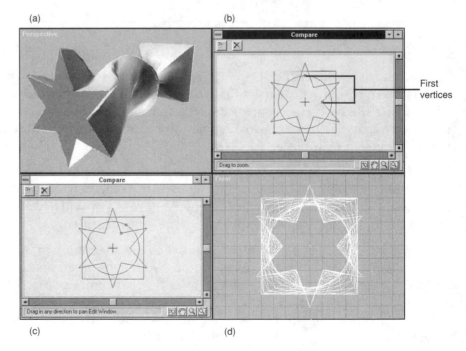

(c)   (d)

Once the cross-sections are ready, you create a path (straight or curved) to define the depth of the final skinned object. The last step is to assign the cross-sections to the path, which may be done in different ways, depending on the software. Some products require you to position the cross-sections at their appropriate depths, then do the Sweep operation by selecting each CS in order. Other programs enable you to leave the cross-sections in their original location, then assign them by distance or percentage to the path. In either case, the process is an excellent way to create models of people, automobiles, or other complex objects.

3D Primitives

Primitives are the building blocks of 3D—basic geometric forms that you can use as is or modify with transforms and Booleans (see figure 4.25). Although it's possible to create most of these objects by lathing or extruding 2D shapes, most software packages build them in for speed and convenience.

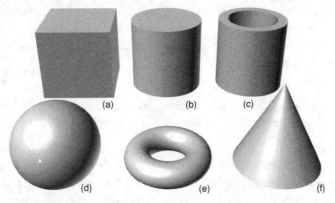

(a)   (b)   (c)

(d)   (e)   (f)

FIGURE 4.25

Common 3D Primitives:
(a) Cube (b) Cylinder
(c) Tube (d) Sphere
(e) Torus (f) Cone.

The most common 3D primitives are cubes, pyramids, cones, spheres, and toruses. Like 2D shapes, these primitives can have a resolution level assigned to them, making them look smoother by boosting the number of sides and steps used to define them.

Inappropriate use of unmodified primitives is probably one of the most common novice mistakes. By their very nature, primitives have a mathematically perfect appearance that screams, "I am a 3D object!" As you will learn in Chapter 5, "Modeling: Beyond the Basics," you're generally better off using less perfect 2D shapes as the basis for your 3D objects. Primitives are best suited for your scene's background, where any extra detail will be lost anyway. They also make good Boolean operands for modifying each other or more complex objects. Finally, primitives can be very useful as foreground objects when they're altered through the use of transforms and modifiers (more on this in Chapter 5).

Transforms

In general, *transforms* are operations that alter the position, size, or orientation of an object. Such basic transforms as Move, Scale, and Rotate are essential to any modeling task, because you have to be able to adjust the position and orientation of the separate objects to make a scene.

Transforms may be affected by *axis locks* or *axis constraints*, which are controls in the software that enable you to turn off movement along the X, Y, or Z-axis, or any combination of them. Axis constraints enable you to transform objects along the desired axis only, preventing accidental movement in unwanted directions.

> Because so many things affect axis orientation, what the correct axis is one minute may be wrong the next, so if your object stubbornly refuses to move, rotate, or do any other transform in the desired direction, check to see if axis constraints or some other type of locks are active.

The current coordinate system (view, world, local) in operation often has a big impact on transforms. See the Rotation section for more details.

Transforms also may be affected by the pivot point location, because they use it as the center of the transform operation. The pivot point may be centered in the object or offset into the boonies somewhere. Usually there's an indicator of some kind showing you whether the program is set to use the object's pivot point, or is using one that the software sets in the center of the object.

Move

It comes as no surprise that *Move* relocates objects, enabling you to place shapes and objects anywhere in the 3D universe. In most cases, this is done with the mouse, but some programs enable numeric entry for precise adjustments.

Move may be affected by the current coordinate system and axis constraints only, unless Inverse Kinematics (see Chapter 9, "Animation") are in effect.

Rotate

Rotate turns an object around an axis. The tricky part about Rotate is making sure you know which axis you want to rotate around. Do you want to use X, Y, or Z in the Screen, World, or Local coordinate system? Is the pivot point centered in the object or offset somewhere? Are axis constraints set properly? To help clear up confusion (and avoid lots of trials and Undos), make sure the visual axis indicator is turned on, if your software has one. This will tell you where and which way the axes are located before you do the rotation. As you can see, the axis you choose to rotate the object around has a dramatic effect on the results (see figure 4.26).

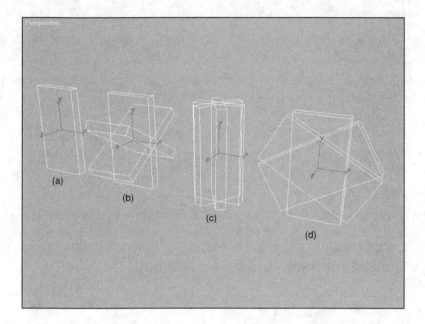

(a)

(b)

(c)

(d)

FIGURE 4.26

Rotate revolves objects around the desired axis. (a) The base object. (b) Rotation around the X-axis. (c) Rotation around the Y-axis. (d) Rotation around the Z-axis.

Scale

Use *Scale* to adjust the overall size of an object. Like other transforms, the results of a scale operation may vary according to the coordinate system, axis constraint settings, and pivot point. For example, if the X-axis is the only one active, a scale stretches the object horizontally only. If all three axes are active, scale re-sizes the object in all directions (see figure 4.27).

Figure 4.27

The Scale command re-sizes objects along the desired axes (a) The base object (b) Scaling the X-axis (c) Scaling the Y-axis (d) Scaling the Z-axis (e) Scaling all axes simultaneously.

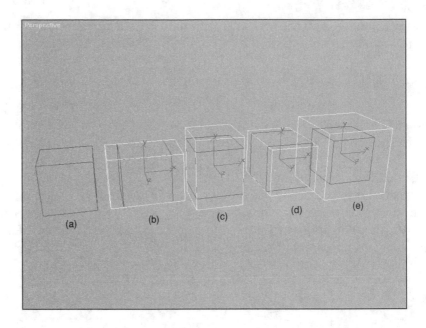

If the scale operation is set to use the object's non-centered pivot point, the scale will transform the object toward or away from that point. For example, if the pivot point is located on the left face of a cube, a scale operation will leave the left face in the same position while scaling all of the other faces away from it.

Mirror

The transform command *Mirror* either reverses an object or copies a reversed version of it along the selected axis (see figure 4.28). Some programs enable you to select multiple axes to mirror around as well. Mirror may be affected by the coordinate system and axis constraints.

Figure 4.28

Effects of mirror: (a) The object is selected, and a mirror axis defined. (b) If the user elects to Mirror-copy the object, a second reversed version is created.

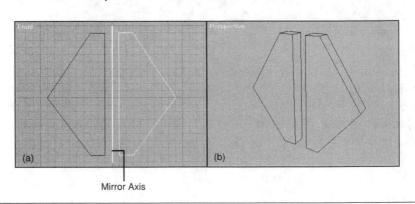

Mirror Axis

Align

Align enables you to bring object surfaces flush with each other or center multiple objects along one or more axes. Align is great for getting objects lined up the way you want them without tedious zooming and repositioning. Align is also useful for quickly bringing an object into the appropriate area of a scene if it has been accidentally created or imported into some obscure corner of 3D space. Align may be affected by the axis constraints.

There are quite a few different Align settings, depending on your software. The basic ones are *Align Center*, *Align Left*, and *Align Right,* which do exactly what they say (see figure 4.29). The alignment can take place on one or more axes, and some products enable you to align to any object, face, edge, or vertex to another.

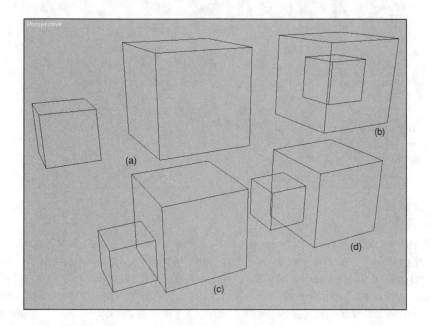

FIGURE 4.29

Typical Align types: (a) The base objects— the small square will be aligned to the larger one. (b) Align Center, on both the X- and Y-axes. (c) Align Left on the X-axis. (d) Align Left on the X-axis, plus Align Center on the Y-axis.

Deforms

You have learned how to move, scale, and rotate things, now it's time to apply some torque to them. *Deforms* like Bend, Twist, Skew, and so forth enable you to easily alter primitives and other objects in subtle or dramatic ways.

Like transforms, deforms may be affected by axis constraints, the current coordinate system, and the pivot point settings. In addition, deforms are affected by resolution. If the object on which you're performing a deform doesn't have enough steps or segments, the result won't be satisfactory (see figure 4.30). This means you have to think about how you will be modifying an object at the time you create it to ensure that you will be happy with the results after the deform. Clearly, this is one of the reasons why spline and parametric modeling is so popular, because they enable you to adjust the resolution of an object at just about any point.

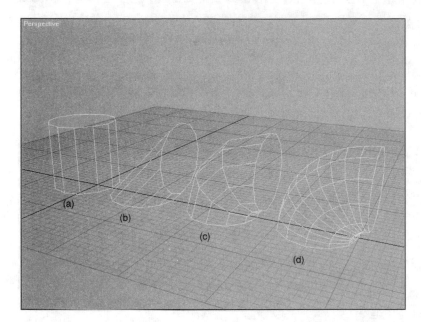

Bend

The *Bend* deform distorts an object evenly around the selected axis. As the student in this chapter's opening story discovered, Bend requires some planning if you expect to do other deforms on the same object. This is because once you bend an object, it no longer conforms to one or more of the axes you may need for a later deform, such as a Twist. Therefore, Bend is often one of the last deforms you do to an object to distort it into the finished form. Also, Bend may be affected by the coordinate system, the axes constraints, and the position of the object's pivot point (see figure 4.31).

Taper

The *Taper* command compresses and expands an object along the selected axis. Taper may be sensitive to coordinate setting and axis constraints, as well as the position of the object's pivot point, because it uses it as a sort of fulcrum for the operation (see figure 4.32).

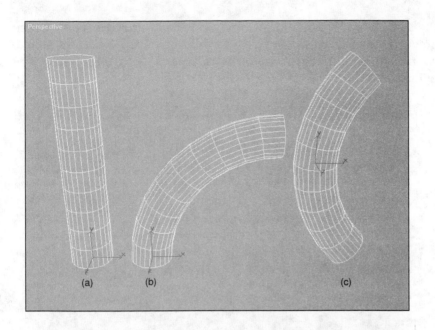

FIGURE 4.31

Bend distorts an object around an axis. (a) The base object. (b) 90 degree bend with pivot point at base of object. (c) 90 degree bend with pivot point in center of object.

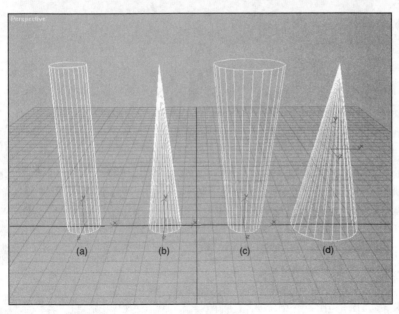

FIGURE 4.32

Effects of pivot point location on Taper: (a) The base object. (b–c) If the pivot is at one end of the object, that end is unaffected. (d) If the pivot is centered in the object, both ends are affected in opposite ways.

Skew

Skew forces one side of the object in one direction along the selected axis, and the other side in the opposite direction. This is akin to putting your hands on the sides of your face and pushing up with your right hand while pulling down with your left. Like the other deforms, Skew may be affected by the coordinate system, the axis you have selected and the pivot position (see figure 4.33).

Figure 4.33

The effects of Skew: (a) Skewing on the X-axis. (b) Skewing on the Y-axis. (c) Skewing on the Z-axis.

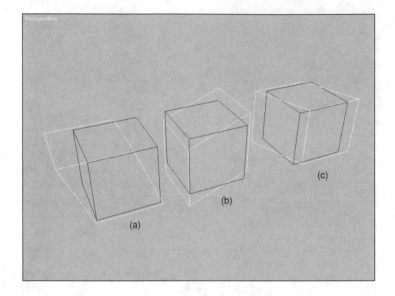

To be sure, Skew probably isn't going to be one of your most commonly used operations. It does have its uses, though the results are often attainable using other tools instead.

Twist

Twist winds an object around an axis like the stripes on a barber's pole (see figure 4.34). Twist may be affected by coordinates, axes constraints, and the pivot point. Twist makes heavy demands on the affected faces of the object, so setting the proper mesh resolution is important.

Squash and Stretch

The transforms *Squash* and *Stretch* are modified scale operations that treat the object as though it had volume. Instead of merely expanding or collapsing an object to any degree, they make it act like it was made of bubble gum. Squashing the object makes it spread out around the edges, while stretching it makes the object get thin in the middle (see figure 4.35). Squash and stretch may be affected by coordinate settings, axes constraints, and the pivot point.

FIGURE 4.34

Twist winds an object around the selected axis. It requires a fairly high-resolution object, or the effect may be very coarse.

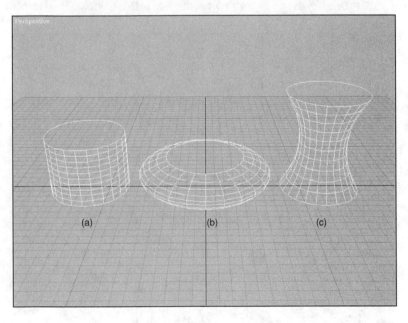

FIGURE 4.35

Squash and stretch in action: (a) The base object. (b) Squash makes the object spread out around the edges. (c) Stretch makes the object thinner in the middle, as if you were pulling gum apart.

Duplicating Mesh

Shapes and objects often have to be duplicated in the process of modeling, and there are several ways to do this. Many programs enable you to duplicate shapes and objects easily when doing a transform operation by holding down a modifier key like SHIFT as you move, scale, or rotate the object. This generates a copy that you continue to transform while leaving the original intact. As with the transform and deform operations, the current coordinate system, axis constraints, and pivot point may have an effect on the outcome.

Copying and Instancing

Most of the time, you'll use a *clone* or *copy* operation similar to the method just outlined to create an identical duplicate of the selected object. There are a couple of variations on the cloning theme, however. Straightforward clones are simply copies of the original, and become objects in their own right, just as if you had made them from scratch. Each of them can be modified completely independently of its mesh brethren (see figure 4.36). Naturally, this is desirable if you're trying to create variation between the objects.

FIGURE 4.36

Cloning and instancing:
(a) The original object.
(b) Duplicate made by Move-copy or some other operation.
(c) With regular copies, each duplicate can be modified independently.
(d) With instanced copies, modifications made to any of the copies affect them all.

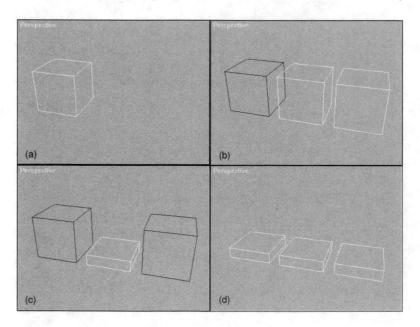

On the other hand, there will be times when you want to be able to affect a large number of objects in the same fashion, without working on them one by one. In these cases, you can opt to create *instanced objects*, which appear to be copies, but are actually the same object seen at different points in space. It's sort of like going into a house of mirrors—there's only one *you*, but there seem to be a small army of clones about.

Instanced objects are a real time-saver when dealing with scenes that use lots of identical objects, like a structure made up of identical columns. If you decide to make them wider or taller, you need adjust only one and the rest will change automatically. As a bonus, instanced objects consume very little memory, so your system tends to operate and render faster than if the copies were straight clones.

Arrays

A convenient way to create a series of clones, instanced or otherwise, is to use the array command. *Array* creates a matrix or pattern of objects based on the one you have selected.

A *linear array* is a series of copies made in a line along a selected axis (see figure 4.37). To create a linear array, you select an object, then define an axis, distance, and number of duplicates desired. The duplicates can either be identical to the original, but simply offset, or they can have additional transforms done to them, such as Rotate or Scale.

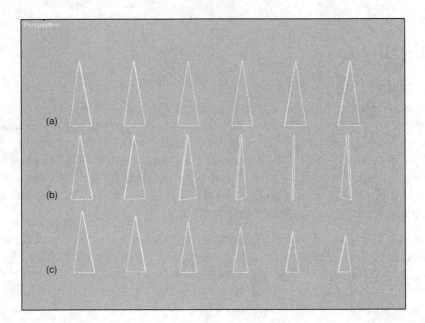

FIGURE 4.37

Examples of linear Arrays: (a) A basic linear array. (b) A linear array with rotation applied. (c) A linear array with scaling applied.

Arrays don't have to be linear, however. They also can be rotation-based, resulting in a *radial array* (see figure 4.38). The process here is very similar, except that you select a rotation axis and specify the number of copies along with the angle in degrees that you want them offset from each other.

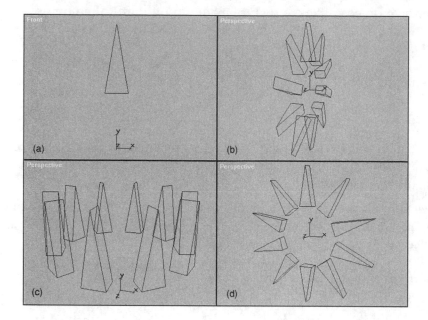

Digging In

Enough theory! It's time to think about *building something.*

Because this book doesn't focus on a single product, the tutorials provide general instructions instead of details about the specific tools you must use for each step. For example, they will tell you to "make a rectangle and extrude it" rather than "press CTRL-R to make a rectangle and CTRL-E to extrude it." I've made every effort to ensure that the operations presented are available in most programs or that you will be able to use alternative methods for tools or techniques your package doesn't offer.

If you've already spent some time with 3D programs, you may be able to plunge right in, then use the reference guide section of your manuals to get over any rough spots. If you're totally new to this or are using a brand-new package, you'll need to learn how a given tool or operation is implemented in your software. In this case, you may be better off going though sections of the user's guide in your manuals, and perhaps do the basic tutorials as well.

After doing the software manual's tutorials and learning the necessary commands, try the ones later in this chapter. Think of them as an addendum to your manual or as tests to make sure you have learned the principle, not just a bunch of steps.

> For marking important pages or chapters in your manual, try Post-It™ Tape Flags, which are little self-adhesive colored tags available at office supply stores. You can label them, then apply them to the top or right edge of a page. They're pretty durable, so if you stick them to the back side of a page, you can actually pull on them to open the book right where you want it. Because the adhesive is of the Post-It™ variety, it won't leave any residue if you remove it later.

Tip

Note that most manuals take a very piecemeal approach to their tutorials, giving you a basic task to perform to demonstrate an idea, then discarding that work when you move on to the next tool. The result is a collection of unusable micro-projects, leaving you to start from scratch in order to make something presentable. With this book, the tutorials are interrelated and build on each other towards producing a finished portfolio piece.

The tutorial subject is an advertising blimp, inspired by Ridley Scott's *film noir* masterpiece, *Blade Runner* (see figure 4.39). Due to copyright restrictions, I couldn't use the film's exact blimp design, but this version offers more opportunity to try out the tools in more or less the order in which you learned them. In addition, this project should be challenging enough for most of you just starting out, and you are encouraged to enhance it anyway.

The blimp is ideal for a tutorial of this type because it's a subject that encompasses just about every tool and technique presented, from basic 3D shapes to deform modifiers. More importantly, it can be customized easily, so you can modify it to your own taste and showcase your creative strengths and style, not to mention your newfound 3D skills. For example, you could give it a 1950's or Victorian look, or make it totally *Alien*. You could incorporate it into your demo reel and plaster the sides with "billboards" of your contact information or the reel's credits. (If you decide to alter the blimp, you may want to first read the section on concept and design in Chapter 11, "The Reel.")

FIGURE 4.39

The *Blade Runner*-esque advertising blimp, which you can construct with the help of the tutorials. By customizing and adding addition details and mapping, you can turn it into a real portfolio piece.

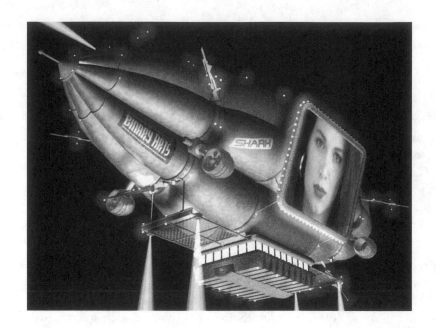

3D Modeling Tutorials

Topics covered:

> **Using Extrude**
>
> **Using Lathe (Closed, Open and Partial)**
>
> **Using Sweep (Closed, Open)**
>
> **Using Skinning**
>
> **Using Transforms (Move, Scale, Rotate, Taper, Twist, Align)**
>
> **Using Duplication and Instancing (Mirror, Array)**

About the Tutorials

In the following tutorials, you will begin to construct portions of the blimp model. At this point, you should either have tried out the following techniques, or be working with your software manuals to see how your package accomplishes each one of these operations.

If you run into difficulties, review the section of the book that deals with the problem operation, paying particular attention to tips that may help you figure out the problem. The life of a modeler/animator is fraught with problems to solve, so consider this as part of your training and try to find a creative way around the problem. As a last resort, there are mesh files from the tutorial project on the CD-ROM saved at various points in the process.

At the start of the chapter, the strategies of planning out a 3D project were presented. For the blimp, the logical overall strategy would be to construct the gasbag first, then add the large video screens. Next would come the other major sub-assemblies, like the engines and spires. The logos and other details would come last. Unfortunately, that doesn't work out well for the tutorial flow, so you'll be doing the monitor screens and engines first. The individual object strategies will become apparent when you do the tutorials.

There will probably be several occasions during the course of these tutorials where objects don't come into the world exactly where you expect them. Read up on construction grids and planes in your manual to aid in building objects where you want them. To help locate and move wayward pieces, use the Zoom All command, which adjusts the viewpoint to show all the mesh in the 3D universe. Most of the time, you'll find "missing" mesh off in the virtual backwater somewhere. You'll probably use Zoom continuously to make the objects large enough to work with.

Using Extrude

Most programs enable you to work in various kinds of units and scales, including English, Metric, generic, or custom, subdivided into fractions or decimals. These are covered in detail in Chapter 5, "Modeling: Beyond the Basics," so the important thing to note for the tutorial work is that the units are generic. Set your software to use whole numbers for measurements if possible, as opposed to decimals or fractions.

Start the tutorials by creating the monitor screen for the side of the blimp using a simple extrusion. The following steps show the procedure:

1. Turn on Grids and Snaps. In the right viewport, create the 2D monitor shape 575 units wide × 460 units high using lines and arcs (see figure 4.40a). If your software requires it, Attach the shapes together and/or Weld their vertices to create a single closed shape. Name it MonSHP01.

2. If your software doesn't leave the original shape intact when doing an Extrude, copy the shape and move the copy out of the way. You'll need it later on for another operation.

3. Select the first shape and Extrude it 15 units deep into a thin 3D panel, with one step or segment (see figure 4.40b). Name the object MonScn01.

4. Save your file as B_MON01 and close it.

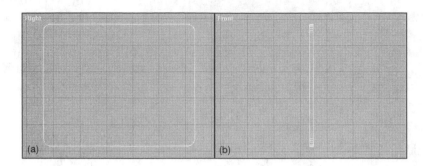

Using Lathe (Closed, Open, and Partial)

To try out the different lathe operations, switch over to working on the engines of the blimp, which are called thrusters (see figure 4.41). The thrusters are enclosed, electrically-powered propellers that move the blimp around.

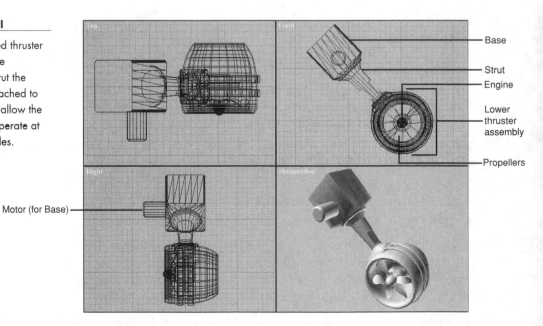

Creating a Closed Lathe

Here are the steps for creating the nose cone in the center of the prop. Note that this shape could also be created by scaling a 3D hemisphere primitive, but where's the fun in that?

1. Create a new document. In the front viewport, draw three circles (with radii of 10, 45, and 56 units) to use as a reference in setting the scale of the thruster shroud and nose cone (see figure 4.42a). These lines won't be used to create the 3D objects, but are useful for "roughing out" a shape before modeling. If your software doesn't support the creation of 2D shapes in the 3D environment like this, ignore these references.

2. In the right viewport, offset the circles from each other by 10 units so that you can see them from this view, then Freeze or Ghost them so that they stay put (see figure 4.42b).

3. In the right viewport, create an arc that is the same radius as the small reference circle you drew in the last step, 10 units (thickened here for clarity). Add a polyline that connects to the endpoints of the arc. If your software requires it, Attach the shapes together or Weld their vertices to create a single shape (see figure 4.42c).

4. Scale the shape 150% along the X-axis (horizontally) to give it a more graceful appearance (see figure 4.42d).

5. Save your work as B_THR02.

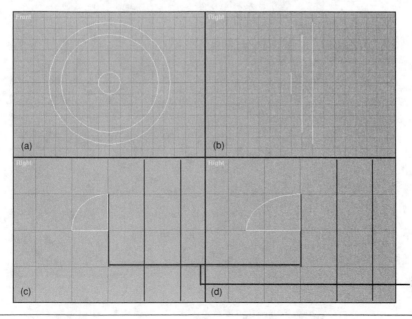

(a)   (b)   (c)   (d)

Small reference circle
(line thickened for clarity)

FIGURE 4.42

Steps for creating the
nose cone shape:
(a) Rough out the
thruster with circles to
establish scale.
(b) Offset the circles to
see them from the side.
(c) Draw 1/2 of the
cross-section. (d) Scale
the cross-section 150%
along the horizontal
axis.

In most programs, choosing the Lathe command will enable you to define the axis that you want to serve as the centerline of the lathing operation. In some products, however, you may need to define the object's axis in advance.

6. Choose Lathe and set the axis along the lower edge of the shape (see figure 4.43a). This will determine the centerline around which the shape will be spun. This is a closed lathe, because the axis touches the shape, creating a "solid" result.

7. Complete the Lathe operation, spinning the shape 360 degrees into a 3D object with 16 segments (see figure 4.43b).

8. Examine the results in a Camera or Perspective viewport (see figure 4.43c). Does the object appear to have the right shape and proportions? If you were experimenting, this would be the point to Undo the operation and adjust the shape before Lathing it again.

9. Render a close-up of the nose cone (see figure 4.43d). Some programs have trouble with Lathes like this, and may create odd artifacts near the centerline. Your software may offer a Weld Core command to correct this—if not, doing a Smooth operation (discussed in Chapter 5, "Modeling: Beyond the Basics") should take care of any problems.

10. Name the object ThrNos01 and save your work as B_THR03.

FIGURE 4.43

Steps for lathing the nose cone object:
(a) Set the axis for the lathe. (b) Spin the shape 360 degrees around the axis.
(c–d) Examine the resulting object for proper appearance.

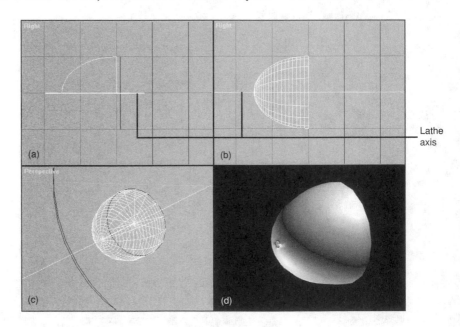

Creating an Open Lathe

To create the propeller shroud, use another lathe operation, this time with the axis some distance from the shape. The following are the steps you need to use:

1. Using the reference circles as a guide, create a closed spline cross-section of the shroud 102.5 units long (see figure 4.44). Use five control points to define the spline. You may find it easier to create the rough shape with straight lines first, then use the Bézier control points to adjust the curves.

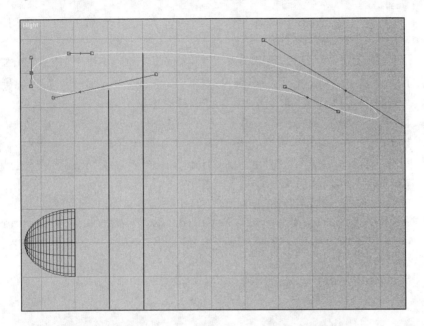

FIGURE 4.44

Use a Bézier spline to create a cross-section of the thruster's engine shroud. Use polylines if your software doesn't support splines.

2. Choose Lathe (set to 16 steps or segments) and set the axis along the centerline of the nose cone. This will spin the shroud around the same axis as the cone. Complete the Lathe operation, spinning the shape 360 degrees into a 3D object (see figure 4.45a).

3. Render the results in a Camera or Perspective viewport (see figure 4.45b). Name the object ThrShr01.

4. Save your work as B_THR04.

FIGURE 4.45

Steps for lathing the engine shroud object. (a) Set the axis for the lathe in the center of the thruster and spin the shape 360 degrees around it. (b) Examine the resulting object for proper appearance.

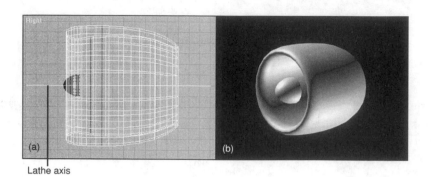

Lathe axis

Creating a Partial Lathe

Next, create the reinforcing bands that partially surround the shroud.

1. In the right viewport, draw a polyline cross-section of the band 11 units wide × 3.25 units high (see figure 4.46a).

2. Position the cross-section as shown and set the axis to the same place as the previous lathes, the center of the thruster (see figure 4.46b).

3. Lathe the object around the axis, but limit it to 300 degrees instead of the full 360 (see figure 4.46c).

4. The result is a partial lathe with a 60 degree gap starting at the top of the engine. If your software puts the gap on the opposite side, rotate the band around so that it matches the figure. Name the object ThrBnd01 (see figure 4.46d).

5. Save your work as B_THR05 and close the file.

FIGURE 4.46

Doing a partial lathe of the support band: (a) Create a polyline cross-section. (b) Position the cross-section and set the axis. (c) Spin the shape 300 degrees around the axis. (d) Make sure the gap is in the position shown.

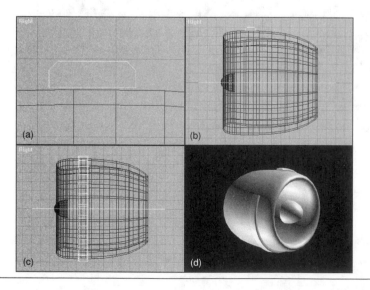

Using Sweep (Closed, Open)

This is an opportunity to get experience with two kinds of sweeps: open and closed.

Closed Sweep

To try out a closed sweep, go back to the blimp monitor project and add a frame around it.

1. Open the file B_MON01.

2. Draw a polyline cross-section of the monitor frame 26 units wide × 32 units high (see figure 4.47a).

3. If necessary, position the cross-section along the spline MonSHP01 (or its duplicate) that you made earlier. Note that some programs may be sensitive to where the object is positioned for an operation like this, while others will enable you to position it independently when doing the sweep (see figure 4.47b).

4. Perform the Sweep operation, using the spline MonSHP01 as the path. Set shape segments to 0 and path segments to 1. The resulting sweep object should be centered around the screen. Name it MonFrm01 (see figure 4.47c).

5. Render the monitor from a perspective view and check for proper appearance (see figure 4.47d).

6. Save your file as B_MON02.

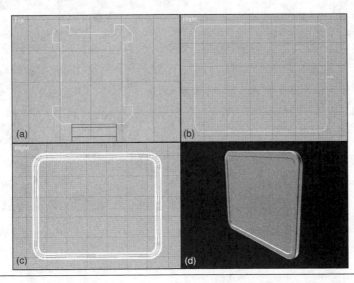

FIGURE 4.47

Create a closed sweep for the monitor frame:
(a) Draw a polyline cross-section.
(b) Position the cross-section up against the screen edge. (c) Sweep the object using the monitor shape as the path. (d) Check your results.

Open Sweep

Next, an open sweep is used to create a cable coming off the edge of the screen and connecting to a control box.

1. Create a box 200 units wide × 70 units high × 40 units deep and position it on the far side of the object MonScr01. This will be an electrical box for the monitor. Name it MonBox01 (see figure 4.48a).

2. To make a cable running from the electrical box to the monitor frame, draw a spline coming out the end of the box, dropping down then curving back up toward the MonFrm01 object. Create a circular cross-section nearby, with a radius of 5 units (see figure 4.48b). Make sure the shapes are centered on the box depth-wise by checking the Front viewport.

3. Create a swept object with the circle, using the spline as a path. Name it MonCab01 (see figure 4.48c).

4. Render a perspective view of the box and cable. Note that the end of the cable is hanging out in space right now. It will get fixed later on (see figure 4.48d).

5. Save your file as B_MON03.

FIGURE 4.48

Creating an electrical box and cable:
(a) Create and position the box. (b) Create an open spline path and circular cross-section.
(c) Sweep the circle along the path.
(d) Check your work.

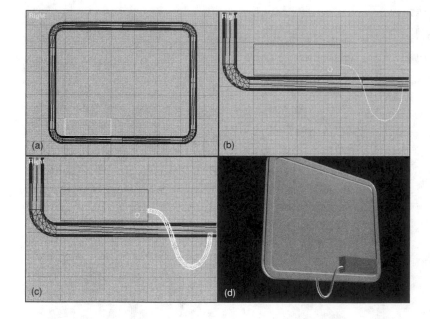

Tip

Using Skinning

This is a tricky spot, so make sure you understand how your program deals with skinning before you do the tutorial. When you're ready, use skinning to create the bracket where the thruster attaches to the strut:

1. Open the file B_THR05.

2. In the Right view, create a closed polyline (50 units square) and two circles (radii 20 and 16 units) that will form the shape of the mounting bracket (see figure 4.49a).

3. If your program requires that you use the same number of vertices for each cross-section, add an additional four vertices to each of the circles. Align the first vertices of each of the shapes as closely as possible, using rotate (see figure 4.49b).

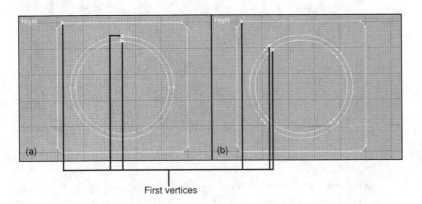

(a)   (b)

First vertices

FIGURE 4.49

Create a skin object by drawing cross-sections: (a) Make sure that the first vertices are aligned now or during the skinning process. (b) If your program requires an equal number of vertices in each cross-section, add additional ones to the circles.

4. In the Front view, create a straight path 15 units long to define the depth of the skinned object. Position it in the center of the other shapes (see figure 4.50a).

5. Using the method outlined by your program, assign the cross-sections to the path. The outermost shape should be used twice, once at the back (the point where the cross-sections reside) of the object and again at the 50%

point on the path. The larger circle is used at the 75% and 90% points, and the smaller circle at 100% (see figure 4.50b).

6. If the first vertices were properly aligned, the polygons in the object should not appear to be overly twisted (see figure 4.50c).

7. Render the object to check for proper appearance. The shape or path step settings may have to be adjusted for a smooth result. Name the object ThrMnt01 (see figure 4.50d).

8. Save the file as B_THR06.

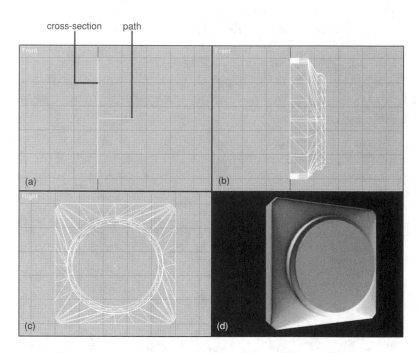

FIGURE 4.50

Creating the mounting bracket: (a) Draw a straight path defining the depth of the skinned object. (b) Skin the object by assigning the cross-sections to the appropriate points along the path.
(c) Check for overly twisted cross-sections.
(d) Check your work.

Move

Here, use Move to reposition the mounting bracket you made in the last tutorial into position on the side of the thruster:

1. In the Front viewport, select the mounting bracket and Move it to a point midway between the ends of the partially lathed band (see figure 4.51a).

2. In the Right view, move the mounting bracket horizontally until it is positioned as shown (see figure 4.51b).

3. Save the file as B_THR07.

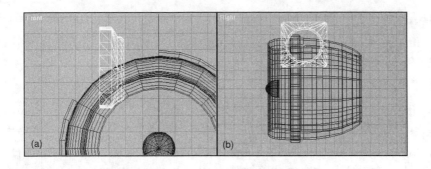

FIGURE 4.51

Moving the mounting
bracket: (a) Move the
bracket midway
between the ends of the
partially lathed band
created earlier.
(b) Adjust the
horizontal position of
the bracket as shown.

Rotate

Now, use Rotate to orient the mounting bracket:

1. In the Front viewport, Rotate the object 120 degrees counter-clockwise around its center until both ends are intersecting the engine shroud evenly, (see figure 4.52). In the figure, the rotation is made on the Z-axis, but this may be different in your software.

2. Save the file as B_THR08.

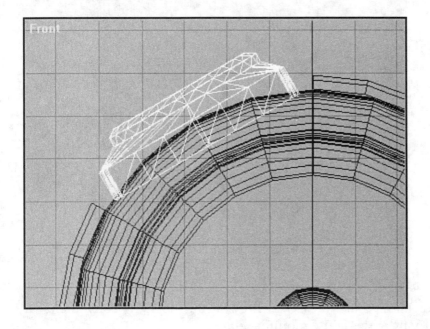

FIGURE 4.52

Rotate the bracket
(around the Z-axis in
this example) until both
ends intersect the
engine shroud equally.

Bend

Returning to the monitor project for a moment, you can take care of that loose cable with a Bend.

1. Open the file B_MON03.

2. From the Top view, select the cable object MonCab01 and examine the axis indicator, which is probably centered in the object (see figure 4.53a).

3. Use Axis Move or the appropriate command for your software to relocate the axis to the point where the cable meets the box. Because the bend occurs around the axis, it needs to be relocated or both ends of the cable would be affected (see figure 4.53b).

4. Apply a Bend to the object until the end of the cable is centered in the monitor frame (see figure 4.53c–d).

5. Save the file as B_MON04.

FIGURE 4.53

Bending the monitor cable: (a) The default position of the axis is the center of the object. (b) Relocate the axis to the end of the cable. (c–d) Apply Bend until the end of the cable is centered in the frame.

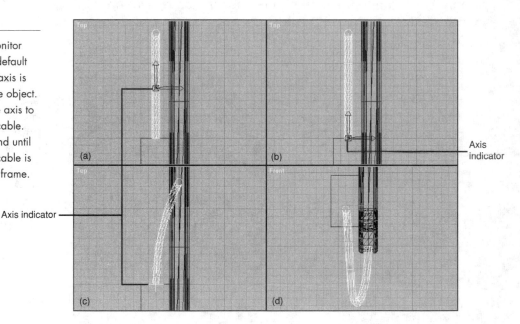

Scale

You know, that cable looks a little too big (how very convenient). Give Scale a try by re-sizing the monitor cable:

1. Make sure your software is set to scale along all three axes at once.

2. Check to make sure the axis of the object MonCab01 is centered along all three axes at the point where the cable meets the box. Scale the object MonCab01 down to 75% of its original size, noting that because the axis was at the end of the cable, it is scaled in that direction instead of toward the center of the object (see figure 4.54a).

3. From the Front view, Move the cable horizontally until it's centered in the monitor frame again (see figure 4.54b).

4. Save the file as B_MON05 and close it.

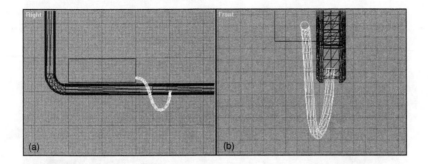

FIGURE 4.54

Scaling the monitor cable: (a) Scale the cable down by 25%. (b) Move it so that the cable is centered in the monitor frame.

Taper

Next, use Taper to create a connector between the mounting base and the reinforcing band:

1. Open the file B_THR08.

2. Working near the top of the thruster, draw a polyline slightly larger than the cross-section of the band created earlier (see figure 4.55a).

3. Extrude the connector outline until it bridges the gap between the mounting bracket and the band (see figure 4.55b).

4. With the object's axis set at the band end of the connector, Taper the opposite end out about 30 degrees along both available axes (see figure 4.56a–c).

5. Render the model to check for proper appearance (see figure 4.56d). Name the object ThrCon01.

6. Save the file as B_THR09.

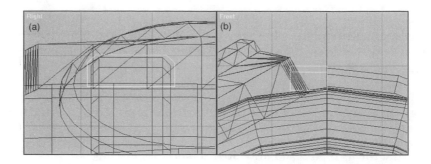

FIGURE 4.55

Creating the connector:
(a) Draw a polyline
around the band cross-
section. (b) Extrude the
polyline to bridge the
gap between the
bracket and band.

FIGURE 4.56

Tapering the connector:
(a–c) Set the pivot point
flush with the band end
of the connector. Taper
the object along both
available axes.
(d) Compare your result
to this image.

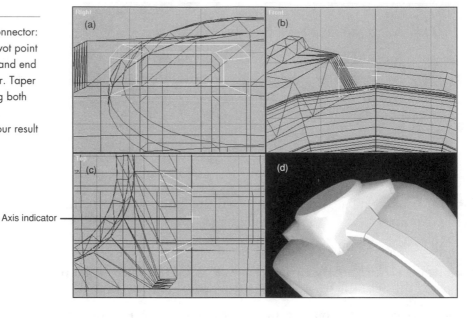

Axis indicator

Twist

Twist makes heavy demands on the affected faces of the object, so setting the proper mesh resolution is important here. If trouble shows up, you also may want to increase the number of polygons on the object by increasing the number of steps in the propeller object prior to extruding it.

Note

Some odd things may show up in the tutorial figures when twist is applied. This is due to low mesh resolution, but is unavoidable in this case because the figures would be too confusing and unclear if the mesh were made denser.

To demonstrate Twist, go ahead and make some propellers for the thruster.

1. In the front view create a cylinder (radius 7.5 units, 10 units deep) in the center of the thruster, behind the nose cone (check your placement in the right view). Name the object ThrPrp01 (see figure 4.57).

2. Create a spline outline of a propeller blade (45 units wide × 17 units high) with a total of 4 vertices.

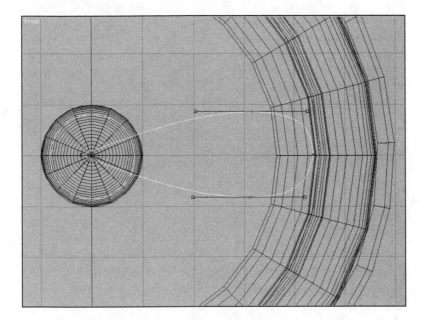

FIGURE 4.57

Creating the propeller objects: First, make a cylindrical hub for the propeller. Then, create a spline outline of one of the propeller blades.

3. Move the propeller blade spline out in front of the thruster so it's easier to see and work with (see figure 4.58a).

4. Extrude the spline 1 unit to make a thin blade (see figure 4.58b).

5. Twist the blade about 30 degrees around the long axis (see figure 4.58c).

6. Render the blade and look for smoothing problems. Subdividing or tessellating the object before applying the twist may help. (See figure 4.58d.) Save the object as ThrBdA01.

7. Save the file as B_THR10.

FIGURE 4.58

Twisting the propeller
blade: (a) Move the
spline away from the
thruster. (b) Extrude it
to create a thin blade.
(c) Twist it 30 degrees
around the long axis.
(d) Examine the result
for flaws.

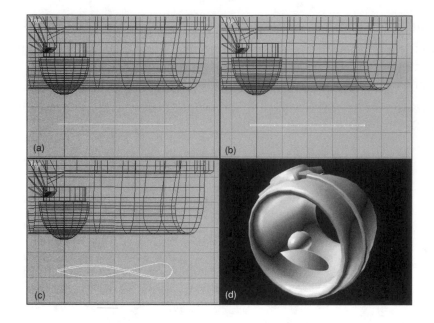

Mirror

Normally, it's a good idea to apply mapping coordinates and texture to a single object before duplicating it, because it saves you time later on. Unfortunately, it would be disruptive to the tutorial to get into mapping issues at this point. You may, however, wish to look over the mapping coordinate section of Chapter 6, "Texture Mapping," and do the work at this point.

For this tutorial, use Mirror to generate a reversed copy of the connector built earlier:

1. Select the connector (object ThrCon01) and Mirror copy it along the appropriate axis so that a reversed version appears (see figure 4.59a). You may need to use a SHIFT key or other modifier to make Mirror create a copy instead of just reversing the original.

2. Set the connector copy to use the center of the thruster as the rotation axis. Rotate the copy counterclockwise about 55 degrees into position on the opposite side of the mounting bracket (see figure 4.59b).

3. Save the file as B_THR11.

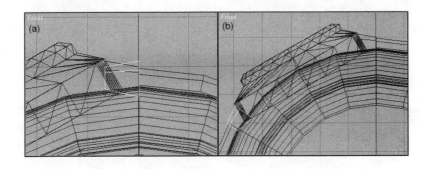

FIGURE 4.59

Mirroring the connector: (a) Mirror copy the connector. (b) Rotate it into position on the opposite side of the mounting bracket.

Copy

At this point, balance things out by copying the band and connectors:

1. Select the band and connectors (see figure 4.60a).

2. Use the modifier key (usually SHIFT) for your software in order to do a Move-Copy operation. Drag the copy about 20 units into the position shown (see figure 4.60b). Name the new object ThrBdA01 (ThrusterBandAssembly01), if a name is required.

3. Save the file as B_THR12.

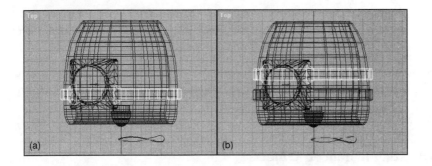

FIGURE 4.60

Copying the band and connectors: (a) Select all three objects. (b) Use a Move command with the correct modifier key (check your manual) to create a copy and position it as shown.

Align

Getting back to the propeller blades, use Align to position the first blade on the thruster model:

1. In the Top viewport, select the blade, ThrBld01. Choose Align, then select the prop object ThrPrp01 (see figure 4.61a).

2. Choose the appropriate Align options to center the blade on the hub along the thruster's central axis (see figure 4.61b).

3. Save the file as B_THR13.

FIGURE 4.61

Aligning the blade:
(a) Choose the blade,
then Align. Select the
prop hub object as the
destination (b) Set the
Align options to center
the blade as shown.

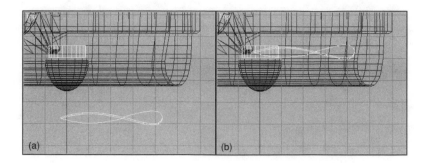

Arrays

Next, use a radial array to make the rest of the propeller blades:

1. From the Front viewport, select the propeller blade ThrBld01, and make sure the pivot point is set to the center of the prop hub, ThrPrp01 (see figure 4.62a).

2. Choose Array and set the rotation angle to 60 degrees, the number of duplicates to 5, and the type of duplicate to "instanced." The result should be a radial array of six blades (see figure 4.62b–c).

> If your software doesn't allow instanced objects, work around this by transforming one blade, then using it as the basis for a new propeller array.

3. Render the model and observe the results. You may notice oddities in the blades now that you are seeing them from different angles (see figure 4.62d).

4. Save the file as B_THR14.

Adjusting Instanced Objects

In the last tutorial, you created a radial array, using instanced objects, so that any adjustments made to any one of the blades are made to all of them. To demonstrate this, adjust the pitch (angle) of the blades in the thruster model:

1. In the Top view, select one of the blades and increase the Twist setting (or apply an additional one), to increase it by another 30 degrees (see figure 4.63a).

2. Render and examine the results. Looks a lot more high-tech now, doesn't it (see figure 4.63b)?

3. Save your work as B_THR15 and close the file.

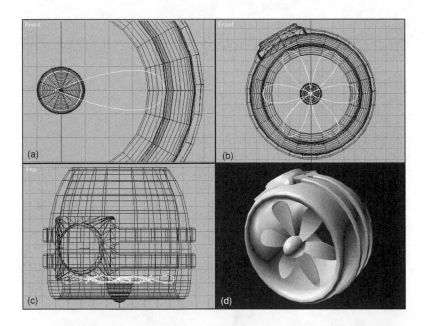

FIGURE 4.62

Using Array to create the rest of the propeller: (a) Choose the blade and check that the pivot is in the center of the hub. (b–c) Use Array to make 5 instance-type duplicates rotated 60 degrees. (d) Check the results to see if any new anomalies have shown up in the blades.

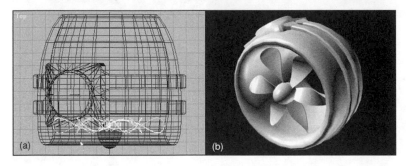

FIGURE 4.63

Adjusting the blade pitch with instanced objects: (a) Select a blade and increase the Twist to a total of 60 degrees. All the blades are twisted by the same amount, because they are instance objects. (b) Render the result.

Summary

The functions you learned about in this chapter—from working with 2D shapes to creating 3D objects to instanced arrays—are the foundation for most of your modeling work. The basic tutorials have helped you to create the beginning of an interesting model, and you can continue to add to it—and learn from it—in the chapters ahead.

Speaking of the next chapter, it will build on the modeling basics from this chapter and move you toward some more advanced operations. You'll also find tips and techniques that will help to set your work apart from the crowd. This is where you'll start to discover the things that few manuals will tell you: the importance of bevels, techniques for accurate and advanced modeling, cool tricks, and more.

5

Modeling: Beyond the Basics

The Sinkha mutlimedia graphic novel features some very impressive 3D work created with Macintosh-based Strata Sudio products. Image by Marco Patrito/Virtual Views © 1995-96 Mohave.

"*Mithrak's bane!*" grumbled the student, "*this still looks terrible.*" He sighed heavily and regarded the form floating above his glowing pool. He had been trying for nigh on the entire day to build a guard, one that could populate the ramparts of his otherwise unoccupied castle model. Unfortunately, the crude objects he had assembled to build the artificial sentry resulted in unrealistic lumps and seams covering the entire surface.

"*It looks like one of those nutcrackers from the Rhinelands,*" he muttered to himself.

"*Problems, lad?*" the Master called from across the chambers. "*I did warn you about such an advanced undertaking…*"

"*Yes, but I wanted to try anyway. That's the only way to learn, right?*" The student rose and walked over to where the old man was working.

"*Rightly so,*" said the Master with a chuckle. "*Say, perhaps if I showed you one of my own human models, you could gain some insights.*"

"*Oh, that would be great!*" The lad plunked himself down in front of the Master's glowing pool.

"*Very well, then,*" the Master replied, closing his eyes and taking a breath. "*Dizkmann Eemayl Kolecktkali.*" The master waved his arms mystically. Suddenly, a human figure appeared, floating in midair before them.

The student was stunned. He expected a disgustingly detailed and precise model, but this…this wasn't much better than his own piecemeal effort. The figure had more details and was better proportioned to be sure, but it still looked like a cross between a jigsaw puzzle and the Frankenstein monster.

"*Well, does this help?*" the Master asked with a toothless grin. "*It was an early effort, but still pleases me.*"

"*Why, yes, Master.*" The lad got up from his seat and prepared to beat a hasty retreat to his own pool. "*I don't feel so bad…I-I mean, I think I understand now,*" he finished, edging away with a smile.

"*Ah, do you indeed?*" The Master raised one of his bushy brows. "*Then why are you leaving before I finish?*

"Huh?"

"Heetlampp Kuizinarte Vaasoleen," the old man whispered, and the seams and bulges on the human figure began to blend together and disappear, resulting in a disgustingly detailed and precise model.

"Dohh!" cried the student, slapping his forehead.

Reference and Accuracy

There are many paths to a destination, and as our student discovered, some may be right in front of us, yet hidden because it may not occur to us to use a tool or technique in a certain way. This chapter looks beyond some of the basic modeling tools and techniques, and finds some different paths to building complex models.

As when hiking real paths, when you're modeling, an accurate reference is very useful. As proof, try an experiment: Close your eyes and imagine you have to model and map an ordinary pen. Try to visualize the overall form, details, and material colors in detail. Now look at a real pen. Chances are, you see details that you forgot about, like subtle chamfers and indentations. The materials probably look different as well, perhaps glossier than you thought, or with interesting reflections and refractions. The point is, you probably don't remember a lot of the details about objects, even ones that you look at every day, and it's these details that make the difference between ordinary 3D work and true professional-quality models.

Using reference materials when designing, building, and mapping your projects can improve the quality of the results immensely. Your reference may consist of the actual object, photographs, drawings, video—any kind of visual record. Of course, you don't have to follow the reference precisely, but seeing the kinds of details that are there can help you to determine how much additional mesh or mapping is required to get a professional result, or give you ideas about how to change the design but still keep it believable.

Reference Materials

The types of reference materials you may require naturally depend on the subject you're trying to model. If it's a building, then architecture books or your own photos of local structures may be used. If it's a product of some sort, you might have the actual item available, or a mock-up or model of it.

Books

For most work, maintaining a good collection of reference books provides you with a ready source of high quality images and information. A highly recommended tome is *The Macmillan Visual Dictionary*, which is just what it sounds like, a dictionary that defines words through images. Art books are also excellent references, especially for science fiction and fantasy imagery. For real-world objects, check out the low-cost Eyewitness Books reference series, which have lots of images and include volumes like *Ancient China*, *Knight*, and *Invention*.

A great source for inexpensive reference books is the bargain bins at stores like Tower Books or Barnes and Noble. You also can find lots of visual material quickly by using one of the World Wide Web search engines, like Yahoo, Alta Vista, or HotBot. For those who prefer time-honored research methods, a trip to the museum, the library, or just thumbing through an encyclopedia will turn up some ideas and materials.

Videos

Videos are another good source of reference (especially for animation), because you can study how an animal moves, for example. Videos also are great for studying natural and man-made effects, like waterfalls or explosions.

Unfortunately, video doesn't offer the clarity of still images, and it's rather inconvenient to use. One way to minimize the clarity problem is to get your reference on Laserdisc whenever possible, because it has higher resolution output than VHS tape. If possible, get the Laserdisc in *CAV (Constant Angular Velocity)* format, which enables you to take advantage of perfect still frames, slow motion, and other effects. Most Laserdiscs are in *CLV (Constant Linear Velocity)* format, which enables a feature-length movie to fit on a single disc, but doesn't even enable you to see a still frame unless you have a high-end Laserdisc player with built-in digital freeze frame capability.

You also can make video sources a lot more convenient to use by using a digital video editing system or video frame capture card on your computer. This enables you to digitize certain frames of the video, and then use them as image files or print them out. *Video printers* also can be used to create color hardcopy directly from a video source.

Photos

If you're doing models of common household items, you may just opt to have the real thing sitting on your desk for reference. Of course, if that household item happens to be a refrigerator, taking photographs may prove slightly more practical.

Photographs are one of the most convenient reference sources to deal with, because they don't take up much space and can be taped onto the border of your monitor. Taking your own reference photos also ensures that you have all the angles covered, and even enables you to use the images as texture maps.

When taking photos that will be used for modeling an object, try to use a 50mm or longer lens in order to minimize distortion, which will throw off your measurements. You also will run into distortion problems when photographing large objects or buildings. You can minimize this by using a parallax-correcting lens on your camera, or by un-distorting the image later with Photoshop. It's also a good idea to measure key distances on the object and to put a ruler or other measurement reference in the photo to help you determine scale later on.

Measurement and Estimation

Once you have your reference material, the next step is to establish the units and scale. Most programs enable you to work in various kinds of *units*, including English, Metric, and generic or custom. They also offer different ways of subdividing the larger units, using either decimal (10ths, 100ths, and so on) or fractional divisions (1/4, 9/16, and so on).

If you're working on an architectural model, you'll probably opt for English, using feet and fractional inches, because most building materials follow that system. On the other hand, if you're dealing with manufactured objects, you will probably find that working with either English using decimal inches or the Metric system to be the easiest.

In the game The Daedalus Encounter, for example, we needed an accurate 3D model of the weapons that were used in the live action portion of the game. The props, which were modified Stingray paintball guns, seemed to conform to the 1/10 inch divisions on an engineering rule nicely, which made it much easier to model them accurately.

You also will need some kind of a ruler to use for measuring distances on your reference materials. The triangular rules made for architects and engineers are best for this, because each features a number of different scales to choose from. For example, the architectural rule has *scales* running from 1/16"=1'-0" up to 1"=1'-0". By choosing a scale that closely matches that of the reference material, you will get more accurate measurements and be less likely to make an error. Measuring in this way enables you to work in the same units when modeling, so building a 3'-0" wide door from an architectural photo or plan will result in a virtual door of the same size.

To help find the proper scale of a reference image, try to locate objects that have known sizes. This is fairly easy when dealing with an architectural model, because doors, lumber, and other building materials usually fall into a standard range of sizes. If the photo includes people, you can estimate the scale by using their heights as a reference.

If the object in the reference has no readily apparent references for scale, consider how it's used or what kind of things it may need to interconnect with in order to help estimate a scale. For example, if the object is held in the hand, the size of the grips will probably be about 4" long, because the palm of your hand is probably 3" 3-1/2".

If you don't need to use architectural scales, using metric units or decimal inches will save you a lot of headaches and errors, because you avoid dealing with fractions. Decimal numbers are much faster and easier to do array calculations with, figure centerpoints, and so forth.

When you begin construction of your model, construct the larger pieces first, then work downward toward the detail items. This helps to prevent scale and positioning errors during the construction, because you can compare the visual relationship between the objects you're building. It also helps you to adjust arrays of objects to fit within the proper boundaries, because even a tiny error in a dimension can become a large one when the object is duplicated a number of times.

Grids

As you know from Chapter 4, "3D Modeling," grids can be used like graph paper for determining scale when creating objects, and the snap feature causes the cursor to jump from one point to another, often at the intersection of two grid lines. Grids and snaps make it a lot easier to create shapes of the proper size and proportions. They also can be used for spacing objects the proper distance apart.

If you're trying to model an organic shape that doesn't easily lend itself to measurement because of freeform or complex curves, you can use a grid drawn or printed onto a sheet of clear acetate and placed over your reference image to help. By setting up a relationship between the grids on the reference material and the grid in the viewport, you can better estimate the right shapes and positions of the curves.

Scanning and Tracing

A good alternative to the measurement or grid methods of ensuring scale is to scan the reference image into digital form and import it into your 3D package. This may enable you to draw shapes or build objects right over the top of the reference image for ease and precision. This method is not without its drawbacks, however.

One common problem is that the resolution and position of the reference image is fixed, which means that much of your initial modeling work has to be accomplished without zooming or panning, or the mesh will become offset from the reference image. A way to deal with this (if you have a program that can display textures during modeling work) is to apply the reference image to a flat polygon as a texture map. This enables you to build on top of the image as before, but now you can zoom and scan at will because the polygon is part of the scene, rather than part of a separate background layer.

Another thing to watch for if you use the mapped polygon route is to be careful that the mapping coordinates or other scaling settings don't cause the image to be stretched in one direction or another. Check for this by comparing the aspect ratios of portions of the mapped polygon to those on the original reference.

> If you're trying to do accurate work with scanned images or by tracing, it's a good idea to calibrate your monitor's horizontal and vertical width settings to ensure that your circles are perfectly round and your squares aren't actually rectangles. The easiest way to do this is by opening a viewport as large as possible, then turning on the grid, or making a perfectly square shape that nearly fills the window. Measure the height and width of the square and adjust your monitor settings until they're equal.

If your software doesn't support either images in the background or real-time shaded views, a low-tech but effective alternative is drawing or photocopying the reference material onto a sheet of clear acetate and taping it over the front of your monitor. Of course, the same restrictions apply as with a background image—you can't zoom or pan without disturbing the relationship between the image and the model.

> If you plan to photocopy onto acetate or use it in your laser printer, make sure that the acetate is approved for that purpose (like 3M CG3300), or it may melt inside the device and result in nasty repair bills. Check your copier or printer manual for other special notes on creating transparencies.

Mesh Optimization

In the quest for accuracy, you may frequently "over-model." While lots of detail definitely adds to a scene and helps to make your work more professional, too much mesh can slow the modeling process, not to mention the rendering, down to a crawl.

Managing mesh resolution at the time you create the object is best, but you have another option—*mesh optimization*, which can reduce the number of vertices and faces on an object substantially without having too much of an impact on the rendered results (see figure 5.1). This feature, either built in or added on to your program as a plug-in, also comes in handy when you have to work at high resolutions, even though the number of polygons seems wasteful. At other times, you may need both high-res and medium- or low-res versions of the same object, but who wants to build two or three different versions from scratch?

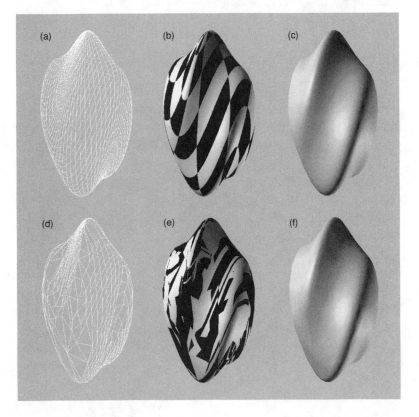

FIGURE 5.1

Effects of mesh optimization:
(a) Original mesh,
(b) original mapping,
(c) original render,
(d) mesh reduced 50% by optimization,
(e) scrambled mapping due to optimization,
(f) optimized render.

Optimizers work by combining faces that fall within a user-defined angle of one another. If these faces have very little variation between them, they can be combined without causing any significant amount of change in the model, yet the overall results (especially on a mesh-intensive scene) can be dramatic.

The downside is that optimization wreaks havoc with the mapping coordinates, so you can't rely on parametric or loft coordinates to remain intact. Of course, if you have applied spherical, cylindrical, cubic, or one of the other post-modeling coordinate methods, you need only reapply them after optimization.

Optimization capabilities saved the day on the *Daedalus* project, because of the polygon-intensive method needed in 3D Studio R4 to create and modify hi-res organic models. By using the Yost Group's Optimize plug-in when the modeling was done, however, scene mesh densities usually dropped 50% or more. This made a dramatic difference in how long it took to render the scenes, because the un-optimized mesh usually caused massive virtual memory consumption at render time.

Radius Edges and Bevels

One of the most fundamental, yet often overlooked, tenets of better modeling is that you should avoid having square edges in your mesh whenever possible, by using bevels or radius edges and corners instead (see figure 5.2).

FIGURE 5.2

Non-squared edges help catch the light and look more realistic. (a) Flat bevel, (b) bevel with smoothed normals, (c) radius edges.

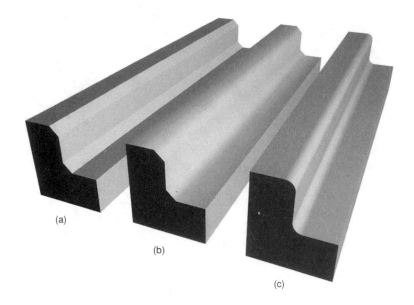

(a)

(b)

(c)

A *bevel* or *chamfer* is a flat transitional plane located between two other planes, usually set at an angle that is half the difference between the two. In other words, if you had a 90 degree corner, the bevel would be 45 degrees.

A *radius edge* uses an arc to transition between the planes, resulting in a smoother transition when the object is seen close-up, or when the transition is very large. A *radius corner* follows the same principle, rounding off a square corner by using an arc.

Why use bevels or radius edges? Well, they're much more realistic, because almost nothing in the real world has a perfectly sharp edge the way 3D objects often do. The extra surfaces also tend to catch the light, making the object more interesting visually. Adding even a few bevels on an object can create the illusion that it's modeled at a much higher resolution, and your results will look more professional (see figure 5.3).

FIGURE 5.3

The use of bevels on the blades and cylindrical trim rings make this mace look as if was created at a higher resolution than it really is. Image by Mark Giambruno/ Mondo Media for Zork:Nemesis ©1996 Activision.

While some programs may have built-in automatic bevel tools or options, many do not, leaving you to generate the bevel as part of a deform modifier (which the next section explains), or to draw two cross-sections, one slightly larger than the other, for skinning. Note that your software may offer an outline tool that can be used to create the second cross-section easily.

Another option for creating bevels is to leave an extra step or segment in the loft or extrusion that you can manually edit by manipulating the faces or vertices. The problem with creating bevels by scaling vertices or faces is that unless the object is symmetrical, the scaling won't be even (see figure 5.4). The only option you will probably have is to do a lot of tweaking to small groups of vertices to even out the bevel.

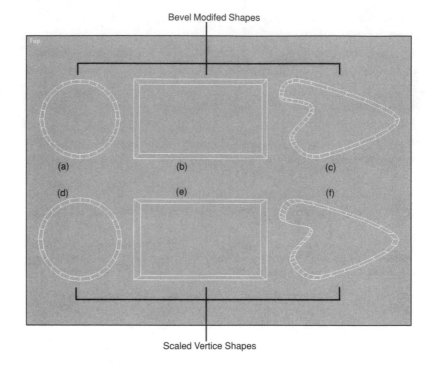

FIGURE 5.4

Using Bevel modifier vs. scaling vertices: (a–c) Bevel modified shapes. (d) Symmetrical shapes work fine for vertice scaling, but (e) oblong or (f) freeform shapes require additional vertice-level tweaking to even the outline.

Deform Modifiers

Deform modifiers are transform settings (like scale, twist, bevel, teeter, and deform/fit) that are applied to cross-sectional shapes as they are swept along a path. In other words, they modify an otherwise straightforward sweep object. This enables you to vary the size and orientation of the cross-sections, as in the bellows of the accordion-like Wertmizer musical instrument from *Zork:Nemesis* (see figure 5.5).

You have already gotten a look at what bevel deform modifiers would be used for from the previous section, so the following are some of the other available deforms.

Scale Deform Modifier

The *scale deform* and other modifier controls usually take the form of a graph, which you adjust to set the amount of deformation desired as a generic value or percentage (see figure 5.6). In this scale deform example, the swept cross-section (in this case, a circle) remains unaffected (in other words at 100% scale) until one-quarter along the path, then the scale of the cross-section is increased to 150% by the mid-way point. The scale is dropped to -50% at three-quarters of the way, then returns to 100% at the end. In addition, the deformations can be either symmetrical, affecting both the X- and Y-axes, or asymmetrical, and affect only one axis.

FIGURE 5.5

The bellows of the accordion-like Wertmizer were created using a scale modifier on the cross-section as it was swept along a curved path. Image by Mark Giambruno/Mondo Media for Zork:Nemesis ©1996 Activision.

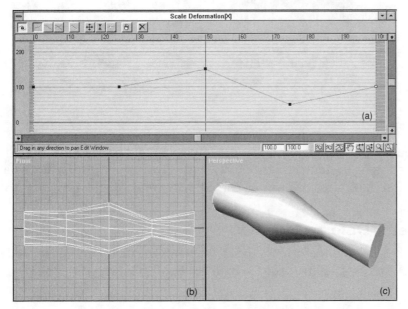

FIGURE 5.6

Scale deformed object: (a) the graph defining the position and scale percentage of the cross-section. (b–c) The resulting object.

As you can see, scale deform modifiers are capable of creating lathe-like variations in size on an object with a circular cross-section. Unlike lathe, however, they can be applied to any cross-sectional shape, and the X and Y scaling values can be set independently. Also, the path can be curved, whereas a lathe axis is always straight.

Twist (Rotate) Deform Modifier

Another deform modifier is twist or rotate, which spins the cross-section around the path as it is extruded (see figure 5.7).

FIGURE 5.7

Rotate or twist deformed object: (a) the graph defining the position and twist or rotate percentage of the cross-section. (b–c)The resulting object.

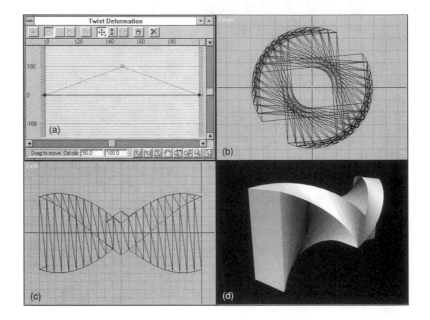

The results of the *twist modifier* are not unlike the twist transform you learned about in the last chapter. The difference is that the amount of twist can be varied along the length of the object, which is difficult to do with the transform version. Also, the path can be curved, whereas a twist axis is always straight.

Teeter Deform Modifier

Teeter is another deform modifier. It rotates the cross-section around its own local axis as it's extruded (see figure 5.8).

The *teeter deform* is an odd one, and it's probably not a deform you're likely to use often. It's useful for creating some odd, asymmetrical variations along the swept object, so you might use it for creating an alien tree trunk or something. Note that if the teeter settings are too high, the cross-sections overlap and result in creases or other mesh troubles.

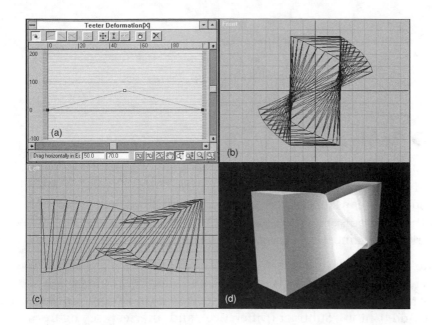

FIGURE 5.8

Teeter deformed object:
(a) The graph defining
the position and teeter
percentage of the cross-
section. (b–c) The
resulting object.

Deform/Fit Modifier

Some programs have a *Deform/Fit modifier* that enables you to define the shape
of an object using an X-axis outline, a Y-axis outline, and one or more cross-
sections. Although this type of modeling may have some constraints depending on your program, it can create some fairly complex forms quite easily, such
as the wooden stock of a musket from *Zork:Nemesis* (see figure 5.9).

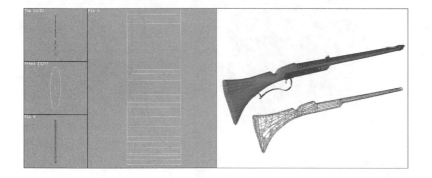

FIGURE 5.9

Using Deform/Fit:
(a) The X- and Y-axis
outlines of the musket
stock are defined, along
with a rounded cross-
section. (b) The cross-
section is swept along
the straight path, but
forced to stay within the
outline boundries,
forming the finished 3D
object. Image by Mark
Giambruno/Mondo
Media for Zork:Nemesis
©1996 Activision.

3D Booleans

Boolean operations are very powerful sculpting tools, enabling you to cut or drill one form with another, among other things. As such, they give the modeler a means for creating objects that are difficult or impossible to make with other tools. You learned about 2D Booleans already, and 3D Booleans work in the same way, except that they deal in three-dimensional volumes.

The objects used in Boolean operations are called *operands*. In most cases, there will be two operands involved, and their positioning and the type of operation perfomed determines the results. The most common Boolean types are Add (Union), Subtract (Difference), and Intersect (see figure 5.10).

FIGURE 5.10

Common 3D Booleans:
(a) The operands, a cube and sphere.
(b) Add combines the volumes together.
(c) Subtract removes one volume from the other. (d) Intersect leaves only the overlapping portion of the two volumes.

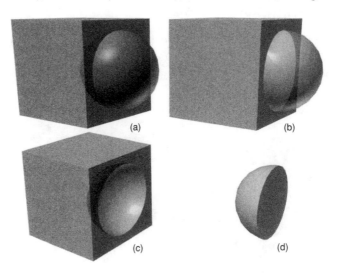

Add combines the operands into one object, adding their volumes together and deleting any overlapping polygons. This is similar to simply attaching two objects together, except that the Boolean deletes any overlapping mesh, leaving only the polygons that form the surface of the combined object.

Subtract removes from the first volume any portions of the second volume that overlap it. This is like using the second object as a drill or scoop to carve away at the first object.

Intersect deletes any portion of either volume that isn't overlapping. In other words, a new object is formed out of those parts of the two objects that are overlapping.

When working with Boolean objects, it's important to remember that they are usually destructive, which means that the original operands are lost in the process. Therefore, it's very important to save a version of your project before attempting a Boolean operation, to make it easy to go back later and adjust the operands if you find the result wasn't to your liking.

Booleans sometimes fail, either because the computer is unable to deal with the complexities of the operation, or because their positions are creating vertice overlaps or other problems. If a Boolean fails, try adjusting the position of the operands slightly. As a last resort, you may need to tessellate the faces on one or both operands.

One last thing about Booleans—they may cause an automatic optimization of the affected faces, meaning that unnecessary faces are removed. While this is often desirable, in some cases it will cause polygons to become non-planar or generate mesh troubles. Test render your Boolean results to look for problems like this, and consider turning off the optimization option and re-trying the Boolean if problems show up.

Editing Mesh

You saw the use of vertice-level editing to adjust 2D shapes back in Chapter 3, "Delving into Cyberspace." Well, vertice and face-level editing also can be used on 3D objects. This process of vertice-level adjustment is often called *pulling points*, and is very useful for sculpting or refining objects, adding small integrated details, and fixing glitches in the mesh.

The tools and techniques used are similar to those used for shape editing: vertice move, rotate, twist, and other standard transforms. As with shape editing, these transforms can be applied to a single vertice or a selected group. Naturally, doing this type of editing work is much more challenging on a 3D object, because you have the added dimension of depth to contend with, and because the greater number of vertices makes it easier to select and manipulate the wrong ones.

Vertice level editing is often used to make small adjustments on isolated sections of an object, or for fixing stray vertices or scrambled faces created by other modeling operations, particularly Booleans. But vertice editing, being very precise, also has applications for doing sculpting on objects. In fact, this is one of the methods suggested for doing organic models such as human heads, the creation of which is discussed later in the chapter.

Some programs provide *magnet* tools designed to make sculpting easier by attracting or repelling vertices when the tool is brought close to the object. These are faster than selecting sets of points and adjusting them a group at a time, and create smoother, more natural projections and depressions as well.

For an example of how vertice-level editing can be employed, consider the method I used to create some crystals for *Zork:Nemesis*. Because we were using 3D Studio R4 for the project, the crystal effect had to be accomplished without relying on refraction effects, because the program isn't a ray tracer.

Starting with a sketch by Cody Chancellor, I created a number of leaf-like spline shapes, then extruded them with a bevel at each end to catch the light. This resulted in a very glassy-looking assembly of blocks, without the "fire" you expect from gems. Gems have internal facets that catch the light, and these were missing from the mesh at this point. However, by using vertice-level editing to pull points on the faces inside the crystal, and by adding some additional internal polygons as well, I was able to make the internal structures (see figure 5.11).

FIGURE 5.11

The reflective surfaces inside these free-form crystals from Zork:Nemesis were created by pulling points and adding additional polygons. Image by Mark Giambruno/ Mechadeus ©1996 Activision.

By the way, to finish off the crystals, an additive, highly translucent bluish material (see Chapter 6, "Texture Mapping") was applied to the object, and I placed an omni light in the center to give the crystals a glowing appearance and increase the intensity of the reflections.

For more conventional gems, the same principle of modeling the internal and external reflective structures still applies, but to do it accurately, you will need a reference book that describes these structures clearly so that you can duplicate them in 3D. See Appendix B, "Recommended Reference," for suggestions. Also, if you're using a ray-tracing program, there are a host of other settings and considerations that can be applied to increase realism even more.

Face Extrusions

Another useful tool for object sculpting is *face extrusion,* a process that takes a selected face (or faces) and extrudes it in or out from its current position (see figure 5.12).

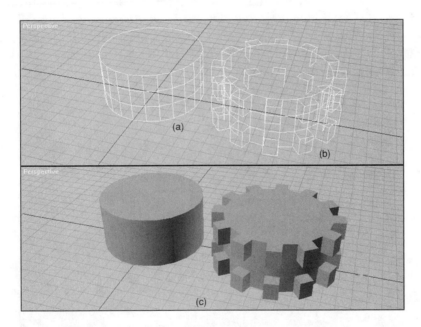

FIGURE 5.12

Effects of face extrusion: (a) Cylinder showing unmodified faces, (b) A group of selected faces extruded outward, (c) The resulting object in shaded view.

The value of face extrusion may not be immediately obvious, but it has a number of uses. First of all, it enables you to create additional surface details using the faces of an existing object, which can quickly result in effects that would take quite a bit of work to generate otherwise. Note that once you've extruded a face, you can extrude it again to create another step, or extrude some of the new faces that were created in the process.

The fact that face extrusion enables you to build up additional mesh out of a single object makes it easier to create projections that are smoothly blended into a single form. For example, you could use repeated face extrusions to create the fins of a shark by drawing the extra needed mesh out of the smoothly swept body.

Face extrusions also are useful for building bevels from a squared-off surface, or for doing sweep-like work on an existing object. As you generate an extruded face, you can make use of the fact that it's already selected in order to scale, rotate, and move it into other positions.

Displacement Mapping

Yet another tool in your arsenal of mesh manipulation weapons is displacement mapping. Unlike bump mapping, which is a material embellishment that affects the surface normals to make an object *appear* to have projections or depressions, *Displacement mapping* or *deformation mapping* actually affects the mesh, extending it outward or inward (see figure 5.13). Depending on the program, black pixels may have no effect, while white ones cause the greatest amount of displacement, or vice-versa.

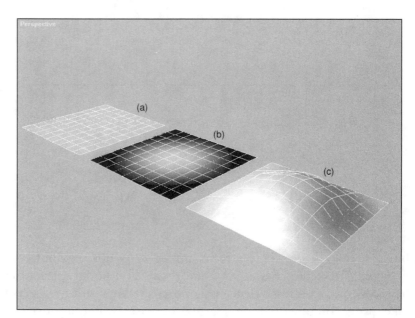

FIGURE 5.13

Displacement mapping:
(a) Grid object
(b) Radial gradient bitmap used to determine relative displacement of vertices, (c) Deformed grid after displacement is performed.

Displacement mapping can be used to solve a host of other modeling problems, from creating *bas-relief* (a style of sculpture where the subject is only slightly projecting out of a flat background) to doing patch modeling-like modifications to existing mesh. It is often used to create *terrain models* based on grayscale imagery (see figure 5.14).

FIGURE 5.14

Terrain models are often created with displacement mapping. For more accurate results, some products, like TruFlite, can generate models directly from geological survey maps. Image©1996 Martin D. Adamiker.

One thing to keep in mind if you're planning to use displacement mapping is that there should be a fairly substantial number of faces on the base object in order to create subtle curves and detail. If you're planning to deform an extruded object, for example, you may have to tessellate the object first in order to provide enough faces, which is wasteful and still may not work out properly. The best way to design objects to be deformed is to build them with grid objects so that they have a uniform pattern of faces and vertices for displacement.

The displacement level or strength setting is the adjustment for how much displacement occurs to the mesh, based on the grayscale range in the bitmap. Another factor that affects a displacement operation is the mapping coordinates. For information on how mapping coordinates work, see Chapter 6, "Texture Mapping."

> **definition**
>
> **grid object** A flat polygon, subdivided into triangular or square faces.

> Using displacement to create terrain-style effects can be useful on a smaller scale as well. For example, displacement mapping can be used at a low strength level to create crumpled sheets of paper from a simple rectangular grid object.

Building Organic Forms

Organic forms have always been a tricky subject for 3D modelers, especially if the form is something well known to the viewer, like the human form. A face, for example, is so complex, with so many curves, hollows and subtleties, that it's difficult to know where to start. It also requires that the user have a great deal of control over small areas, yet the use of a large number of vertices in the model makes editing difficult and confusing.

One of the most tedious but precise methods of building a complex form is to construct it, spline by spline or vertice by vertice. This method was used to create some impressive 3D heads often seen in Animation Master advertising and demo reels, and for the model of Hyleyn from the *Sinkha* CD-ROM (see figure 5.15).

Using a technique like this requires excellent sculptural sensibilities, as well as good reference material showing the subject from several angles. This is a good example of where employing scans of the reference material as a background layer (discussed in the beginning of this chapter) would be invaluable.

Skinning

For those of you without the patience, time, or sculpting talent for the vertice-by-vertice method, most 3D programs offer some software-assisted options. One such method of creating humanoid and sculptural forms is using the skinning technique discussed in Chapter 4, "3D Modeling." By creating a number of cross-sections of the figure, applying a skin results in a smooth, nearly seamless model (see figure 5.16). Of course, designing and adjusting the cross-sections takes a lot of care and experimentation, especially if your program requires that all cross-sections have the same number of vertices.

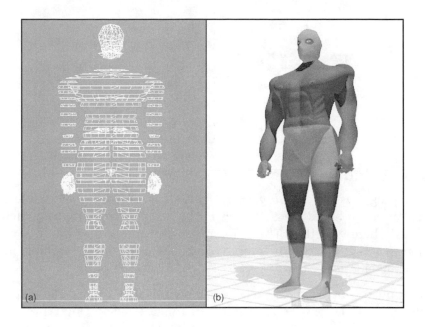

FIGURE 5.16

Example of a skinned figure: (a) The cross-sections defining the figure may be polylines, splines, or 3D objects, depending on the program. (b) The skinning process connects the cross-sections with a surface mesh, which can be virtually seamless depending on the methodology and limits of the software.

Metaballs

Metaballs is a form of modeling in which you build forms out of spheres. The software blends the spheres into a single mass. Metaballs are a popular way to make lots of different organic forms, even complex ones like human heads and animals.

To build a Metaballs form, you scale and arrange spheres to follow the contours of the object you want to create. Different hardness settings can be assigned to the spheres, which tells the software how pliable that particular sphere is when the time comes to blend them together at render time (see figure 5.17). The harder the sphere, the less it will blend into the others.

Although you can build some very impressive objects with Metaballs, it's a tedious job (because you're limited to spheres), and you can't stretch them or do other transforms other than moving and scaling. This means that to make a cylindrical form, for example, you have to line up a bunch of spheres. In some cases, you may have to put a bunch of little spheres around the points where they meet in order to keep the finished mesh from having low spots. Needless to say, there's a lot of trial and error with this technique.

FIGURE 5.17

Metaballs modeling:
(a) Sphere-like
metaballs scaled and
grouped together to
form a rough heart
shape.
(b) With some products,
the resulting metaballs
object may only be
seen when rendered.

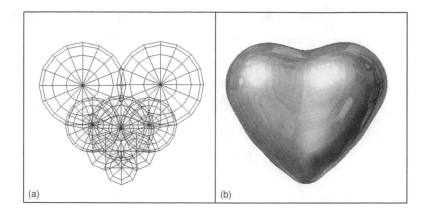

Mesh Blending

Some programs have *mesh blending* features or plug-ins that enable you to smooth out or blend pieces of mesh together, similar to the way Metaballs blends spheres together. The difference is that the objects don't have to be spheres, and you have much more control over the degree and regions that are being blended.

This kind of tool can be a real boon for organic work, especially if you use a polygonal modeler. A good example of this is the Foo Dog Cannon that I constructed in 3D Studio R4 as part of Mondo Media's contract artwork on the CD-ROM game Zork:Nemesis (see figure 5.18).

FIGURE 5.18

Modeling the Foo Dog
Cannon: (a) 3D prim-
itives were stretched
and overlapped to
rough out the form.
(b) Using the Smooth
plug-in, the primitives
were blended together
with near-seamless
results. Image by Mark
Giambruno/Mondo
Media for
Zork:Nemesis ©1996
Activision.

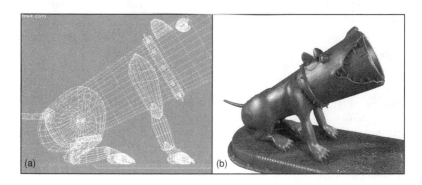

To build the dog-shaped artillery piece, I started with a rounded-off tube for the barrel, then added the dog musculature to it with primitives that were squashed and bent. A leg, for example, consisted of a couple of elongated spheres for the upper and lower spheres, meeting at the elbow. The paw was a set of five or six squashed spheres forming the pads and toes. Bent cones were used to create the claws.

Once a limb was completed, I would save it, Boolean Add the components together, and then use the Smooth plug-in from Bones Pro to smooth the mesh together. It took a fair amount of test runs and experiments, but the results were very fluid, and it was a pleasure to create.

What if you don't use 3DS R4? Well, LightWave offers a feature called Metaform that can do the same sort of things (as well as many more), and there are similar plug-ins available for other programs as well.

A fast way to create human figures is Fractal Design Poser, which contains a library of different body types. Be sure to use the thumbwheel-style fine tuning controls in order to pose the models, or you may end up with human pretzels.

Modeling Alternatives

There may be times when it's just too difficult or impractical to model an object from scratch using only the tools provided by your software program. In this kind of situation, there are some alternatives.

Back in Chapter 2, "Nuts and Bolts," some of the peripherals mentioned were 3D Scanners and Digitizers. As you recall, these were devices capable of creating 3D mesh from physical objects, including people. While these systems (particularly the scanners) are often prohibitively expensive to own, there are service bureaus that will scan people or objects for you at whatever resolution you desire, clean them up, and export them in the proper file format (see Appendix C).

One of these service bureaus is Digital Illusion in Emeryville, CA., and they were kind enough to give me a demonstration of their CyberWare head scanner. The subject (yours truly) was seated on a platform, then remained relatively motionless while being scanned by a rotating laser and video camera. The scanner sent the data to a nearby computer, where the mesh version of the subject could be seen (see figure 5.19). Shiny objects (like eyes) and wispy objects (like what's left of my hair) cause problems for the laser scanner, so these elements were cleaned up or removed in the 3D program. Because the video scan was created in tiny vertical increments as my head was being scanned, it created an interesting wrap-around texture map. The map was then applied to the mesh head, adjusted for scale and position (a time-consuming process) and the resulting 3D CyberMark rendered.

FIGURE 5.19

3D scan example: (a) Medium-density mesh generated by the scanner, after clean-up. (b) The flattering video image capture performed at the same time. (c) Rendering of the mesh head. (d) Rendering of the mesh head with the image map applied. Spooky.

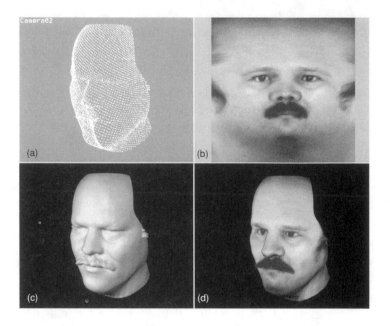

While 3D scanning is clearly a good way to go if you're trying to produce an accurate model of a human head and/or body, it's also advantageous for any complex character. *Maquettes* (small sculptures made of plaster or Super Sculpty) can be created of just about any sort of character, then scanned or digitized. This method was used to create the termites in the Orkin pest control commercials, for example.

Mesh Libraries

A popular alternative to constructing mesh from scratch is to buy a model from one of the *mesh library* providers like Viewpoint, Zygote, or Acuris. These companies provide mapped and unmapped 3D models in a variety of different formats and resolutions (see figure 5.20).

The objects cost hundreds or thousands of dollars each, but in a pinch, or in a situation where a complex and accurate organic model is needed (such as realistic people or animals), they can be a very practical alternative. On top of the price tag, there are some other caveats to be aware of. First, unmapped objects may require quite a bit of work to map properly, because you may have to break them down into small elements to apply mapping coordinates. Second, objects with lots of individual pieces also may have totally incompressible names, or may simply be numbered.

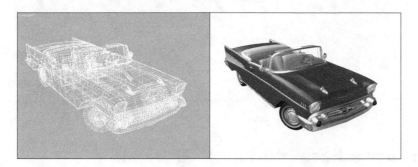

FIGURE 5.20

The classic '57 Chevy model from Viewpoint is a good example of the high-quality models available from mesh libraries. This is actually a sample mesh distributed with 3D Studio R4.

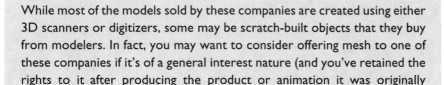

While most of the models sold by these companies are created using either 3D scanners or digitizers, some may be scratch-built objects that they buy from modelers. In fact, you may want to consider offering mesh to one of these companies if it's of a general interest nature (and you've retained the rights to it after producing the product or animation it was originally intended for).

If the mesh library doesn't offer exactly what you want, consider using what's available as a starting point and adding modifications to it. We ran into this situation on *Zork:Nemesis*, because six or seven suits of armor were needed for one of the puzzles. Because the budget was too restrictive to model them all from scratch, we got a basic medieval suit of armor from Viewpoint, mapped it, then applied or removed pieces of mesh to make them more reminiscent of other eras. While the results certainly weren't historically accurate, they did do the trick (see figure 5.21).

Many of the mesh library producers offer free samples online or on their CD-ROMs for you to use and evaluate. Look at their web sites (listed in Appendix C) for more information. In addition, a fair amount of public domain 3D objects of all quality levels are available though the Internet or in online providers' libraries. Try Avalon at http://www.viewpoint.com/avalon.html for lots of free mesh.

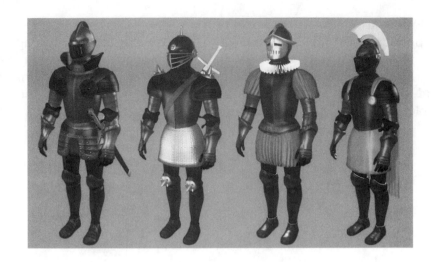

FIGURE 5.21

Using a basic medieval suit of armor, variations were made by adding or subtracting mesh details. Image by Mark Giambruno & Laura Hainke/Mondo Media for Zork:Nemesis ©1996 Activision.

Intermediate Modeling Tutorials

Topics covered:

Using Deform Modifiers

Using Booleans

Using Bevels

Using Face Extrusions

Editing Mesh

Completing the Model

> The tutorials in this section are intermediate in difficulty, and assume that you have developed enough familiarity with the basic tools to enable you to determine the best approach for constructing some of these objects. Therefore, some of the instructions are more general.

Continuing with the blimp construction will give you the opportunity to put some of this chapter's modeling theory and techniques to work. By the end of this set of tutorials, most of the mesh work on the blimp project will be complete. This also is a good time to take the project further and make it into a true portfolio piece by adding your own details and variations.

Using Deform Modifiers

Form the skin of the ship by creating a sweep using the Scale deform modifier to create variations in the diameter of the object.

1. Create a new document or scene.

2. Using the Arc tool, create a cloverleaf-like cross-sectional shape 440 units wide for the helium gas bag, or skin, of the blimp (see figure 5.22a). Make a copy of this shape unless your software's sweep operation will leave it intact.

3. Define a straight path for the sweep 2500 units long, with the axis running through the center of the cloverleaf shape (see figure 5.22b).

4. Sweep the cloverleaf cross-section along the path. The result should look similar to the lower figures (see figure 5.22c–d).

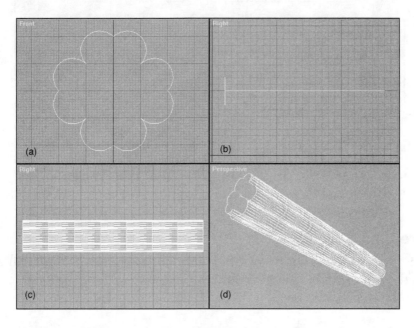

FIGURE 5.22

Creating the helium bag for the blimp:
(a) Use arcs to create a cloverleaf shape for the cross-section. (b) Make a straight path to define the length of the bag. (c–d) Sweep the shape along the path.

5. Using a Scale Deform Modifier, create an "envelope" that defines the diameter of the cross-section using a Bézier spline or whatever control point type your software offers. Use the settings in the graph as a guide. The horizontal scale represents the length of the path, and the vertical scale is the percentage of scaling to apply to the cross-sectional shape (see figure 5.23a).

6. The finished sweep should resemble this figure. You may need to adjust the number of steps and segments to achieve a good balance between smoothness and mesh density (see figure 5.23b).

7. Render the object from a perspective viewpoint and check for problems (see figure 5.23c). Name the object GasBag.

8. Save the file as B_MAIN01.

FIGURE 5.23

Using Scale Deform to shape the helium bag: (a) Set Scale Deform to create an envelope similar to this one. (b) Adjust the steps in the resulting mesh for a good compromise between detail and density. (c) Render and check the results.

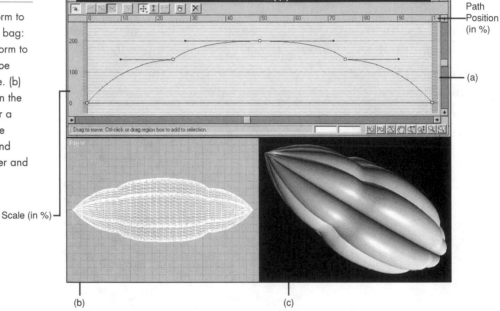

(a)

Scale (in %)

(b)   (c)

Creating Bevels

This tutorial offers a couple of different options for creating supporting rings for the gas bag. Use whichever one is supported by your software or is the most convenient.

If your software doesn't offer either of the following beveling options, you can create the beveled object by sweeping the cloverleaf shape along a path 2 units long. Use the Scale deform modifier to create a roughly beveled sweep object, then use vertice-level editing to slide sections of the front and back faces around to even out the chamfer. Another method is to create two cloverleaf shapes—one slightly larger than the other—and then use the two cross-sections to create a skinned object, much as you did with the thruster mounting bracket.

Some programs offer either Bevel tools that directly manipulate an object according to the parameters, or have a Bevel deform modifier for use on swept objects. If your software offers one of these options, use it to do the following:

1. Hide the GasBag object. Select the clover-like cross-section used for the gas bag or the duplicate you made earlier (see figure 5.24a).

2. If your software doesn't offer a Bevel tool to do the job directly, plan to make it into a sweep object by creating a path 20 units long. Otherwise, go to step 3.

3. Use the Bevel Tool (if available) or Bevel Deform Modifier to create a beveled sweep object. Use the Bevel Deform modifier in the same way as the Scale modifier was used in the last tutorial in order to create this object (see figure 5.24b).

4. Adjust the bevel to get results similar the this side view (see figure 5.24c).

5. Adjust the steps for the shapes and path to control the mesh density. Render the object and check it for problems. Name the object BagRng01 (see figure 5.24d).

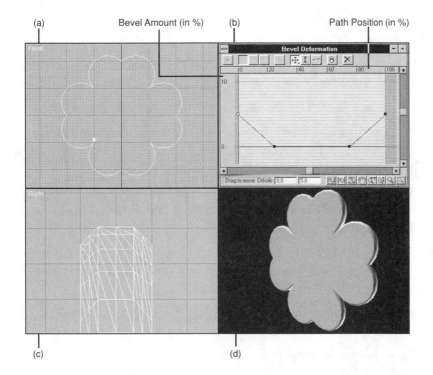

FIGURE 5.24

Beveling a support ring for the blimp: (a) Select the cloverleaf cross-section. (b) Use a Bevel tool, or create a sweep object and use a Bevel Deform Modifier.
(c) Adjust the bevel as shown. (d) Render the result and adjust step settings if necessary.

6. Unhide the GasBag object and use move and scale to position BagRng01 about 975 units from the end of the blimp. The BagRng01 object should extend out from the edges of the GasBag object slightly. Copy, move and scale three duplicates into the positions shown (see figure 5.25a).

7. Render the objects from a perspective view (see figure 5.25b).

8. Save the file as B_MAIN02.

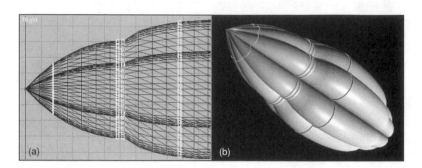

Editing Mesh

Mesh editing can be used instead of scale deformation to create simpler forms, like the strut used to attach the thruster to the ship.

1. Open the file B_THR15. Hide the thruster components.

2. In the Right viewport, create a 16-sided cylinder 75 units long with a 15 unit radius and 3 segments that will be used as the strut. A perspective view is shown here for clarity (see figure 5.26a).

3. In the Front viewport, enter vertice-level editing mode (if applicable) and scale the one set of mid-object vertices to 80% of their original diameter, then move them 20 units to the right (see figure 5.26b).

4. Scale the other set of mid-object vertices to 110% of original diameter and move them 15 units to the left. Scale the leftmost set of vertices 160% (see figure 5.26c).

5. Name the object ThrStr01. Render it from a perspective view to see the results (see figure 5.26d).

6. Save the file as B_THR16.

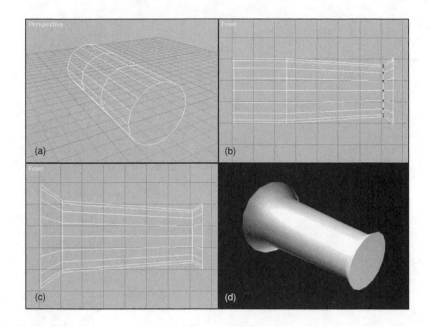

FIGURE 5.26

Using vertice editing to
create the strut:
a) Create a cylinder.
(b) Use vertice editing
to scale and move the
first set of vertices into
position. (c) Complete
the strut by editing
the other vertices.
(d) Render the result.

Using Booleans

This tutorial uses Boolean subtraction to add interest to the strut created in the last exercise.

1. In the Front view, create a box 28 units wide, 10 units high and 32 units deep, and position it as shown (see figure 5.27a).

2. Use Align or move in the Top view to make sure the box extends past the edges of the strut in both directions (see figure 5.27b).

3. In the Front view, rotate the box 5 degrees clockwise (see figure 5.27c).

4. Mirror copy the box and move the duplicate to the opposite side of the strut (see figure 5.27d).

> Because Boolean operations don't always work as expected, always save your work prior to executing one. If the Boolean fails, try repositioning the mesh slightly. You also may need to tessellate one or both objects (as a last resort).

5. Following the methods outlined in your software manual, use Boolean Subtract to remove the first box's volume from the strut (see figure 5.28a).

6. Repeat the use of Boolean Subtract to remove the second box's volume from the strut (see figure 5.28b–c).

FIGURE 5.27

Preparing to Boolean
the strut: (a) Create a
box to use as a cutting
object. (b) Make sure
the box extends past
the edges of the strut.
(c) Rotate the box to
match the strut. (d)
Mirror copy the box
to the opposite side.

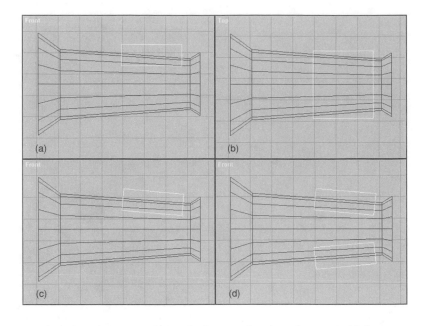

7. Render the object and check the results (see figure 5.28d).

8. Save the file as B_THR17.

FIGURE 5.28

Performing a Boolean
operation on the strut:
(a) Referring to your
manual for the steps,
subtract the first box's
volume from the strut.
(b–c) Repeat the
operation for the
section box. (d) Render
the results.

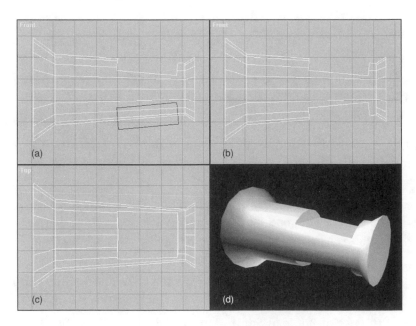

Completing the Model

Using the techniques you've learned in the last two chapters, and the general directions that follow, complete the modeling work on the blimp by constructing and positioning the rest of the components.

> The figures and instructions will become less detailed at this point, and issues like size, position, object naming and so forth are up to you to determine from the figures, unless specifically noted. Becuase many of the remaining items are not critical, experiment and add additional detail, if desired.

Complete the Thruster Assembly

Complete the thruster assembly by rotating the strut into position, and creating the base and other details.

1. From the Front viewport, Unhide the thruster assembly and rotate it counterclockwise 15 degrees, so that the ThrMnt01 object is now at a 45 degree angle. Move and rotate the ThrStr01 strut into position, making sure it is centered over the thruster mount (see figure 5.29a).

2. Create an engine for the thruster (ThrEng01) using a beveled cylinder. Create a support (ThrSup01) to hold the motor in place with a simple cylinder (see figure 5.29b).

3. Copy the mounting bracket ThrMnt01 from the thruster and rotate it 180 degrees, positioning it as shown. Scale the bracket up until the circular face is a bit larger than the end of the strut. Use vertice-level editing to extend the end of the bracket. Name it ThrBas01 (see figure 5.29c).

4. Create a cylinder and bevel one edge, positioning it so that it appears to be a motor mounted to the bracket. Name it ThrMtr01 (see figure 5.29d).

5. Save the file as B_THR18 and close it.

Create the Gondola

> There will no longer be specific "save your work" steps from this point on. Be sure to save your work frequently, incrementing the filename as you go.

FIGURE 5.29

Finishing the thruster
assembly: (a) Rotate
the thruster and strut
into position. (b) Add
an engine and support
to drive the propeller.
(c) Copy and modify
the thruster mount to use
as a base. (d) Add a
motor object on the side
of the base.

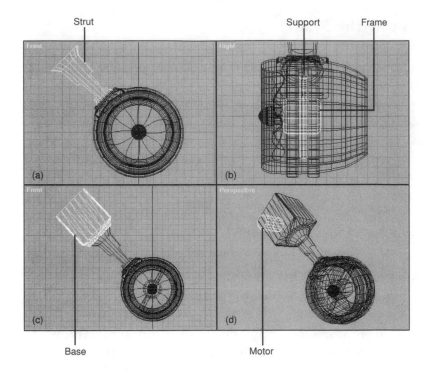

Create the gondola following these basic steps:

1. Open the file B_MAIN01, and use the GasBag mesh and the views in the figures to determine scale and proportion. Overall size of the gondola is about 400 units wide, 160 units high, and 500 units long (see figure 5.30).

2. From the Top view, create a beveled rectangular shape to use as the outline of the gondola.

3. Using sweep and bevel modifier techniques, create the roof of the gondola (35 units high). Use Gon*Xxxnn* as the naming convention.

4. Mirror the roof and position it directly below to form the base (75 units high) of the gondola. Extend the bottom of the floor downward with vertice editing.

5. Create a 4-sided cylinder for use as a window frame component, 50 units high. Use Array to create a row of identically placed window frame objects. Use Array again to create a second set perpendicular to the first. If necessary, center the assembly in the middle of the gondola.

6. Use a single box object to create the window glass, positioning it through the centers of all the window frame objects.

7. Create a thin box object to act as a trim/support piece. Use Array to duplicate it across the bottom of the gondola.

8. In the Front view, create a diamond-like shape and use sweep with a bevel modifier it to form a skid on the bottom of the gondola.

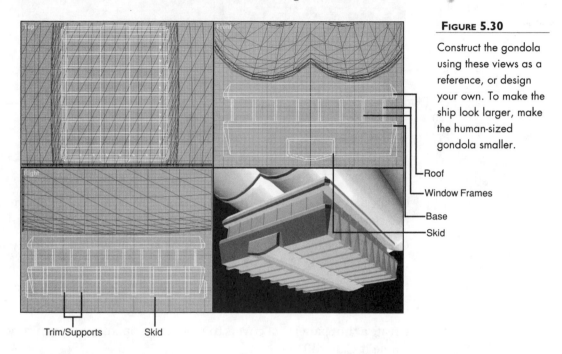

Construct the gondola using these views as a reference, or design your own. To make the ship look larger, make the human-sized gondola smaller.

Roof

Window Frames

Base

Skid

Trim/Supports   Skid

Create the Catwalk Assemblies

Follow these basic steps to create the catwalk area adjacent to the gondola.

1. Use the previously constructed mesh and the views in the figures to determine scale and proportion. Overall size of the catwalk is about 300 units wide, and 400 units long (see figure 5.31).

2. Create an I-beam-like cross-section shape and extrude it to make the beam that hangs from the bottom of the GasBag rings next to the gondola. Use Cat*Xxxnn* for the object naming convention.

3. Create a clamp shape near the end of the beam and extrude it to be wider than the I-beam (see figure 5.32).

FIGURE 5.31

Construct the catwalk area using these views or invent your own layout. Consider adding additional details like railings, electrical conduits and equipment, and so on.

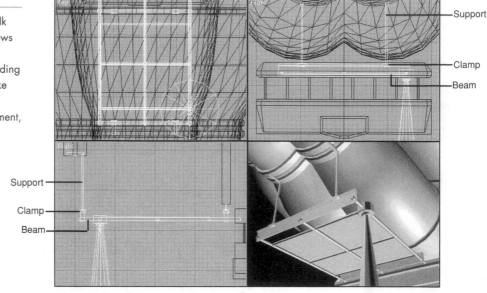

4. Create a 4-sided cylinder to connect the clamp to the ring above. Copy the clamp and support and move it to the opposite end of the I-beam.

5. Copy the I-beam, clamps, and supports and move them directly under the adjacent ring. Adjust the supports to reach.

6. Use 8-sided cylinders to create a framework of six horizontal supports mounted to the I-beams.

7. Create a thin panel that covers the four large openings in the framework. Name it CatGrd01.

The ship has a total of five searchlights with visible beams. We'll presume that your software doesn't offer volumetric lighting, so the visible beams will be created with mesh and material settings.

8. Create a beveled 8-sided cylinder to form the base of the searchlight.

9. Create a hemisphere, then use vertice editing to pull the center portion toward the interior, creating a depression.

10. Create a cone that fits into the depression and extends downward.

11. Move the assembly into position on the catwalk. The assembly will be duplicated after mapping.

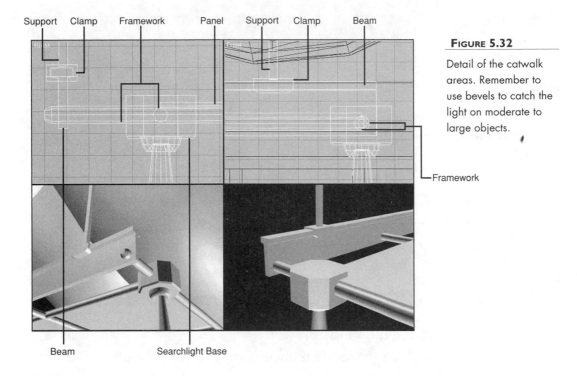

Support   Clamp   Framework   Panel   Support   Clamp   Beam

Framework

Beam   Searchlight Base

FIGURE 5.32

Detail of the catwalk
areas. Remember to
use bevels to catch the
light on moderate to
large objects.

Create the Spires

The spires are antenna-like probes extending outward from the ship, and
have small lights attached to them.

1. Use the previously constructed mesh and the views in the figures to
    determine scale and proportion. Overall length of the spire is about 400
    units (see figure 5.33).

2. Create a side view of the spire and fins as 2D polyline shapes.

3. Extrude or bevel all three shapes. Use Spr*Xxxnn* as the object naming
    convention.

4. Rotate the fins 90 degrees and center them on the main spire.

5. Add a sphere at the thick end of the spire to serve as a base.

6. Add some small low-res spheres to act as "lights." Use SprLit*nn* as the
    convention for the lights.

7. Group the objects together as SprGRP01 and move them into position on
    the ship.

FIGURE 5.33

Create spires to serve as antennae and to add extra interest to the form by extruding or beveling some 2D polyline shapes. Add small spheres to serve as non-illuminating "lights."

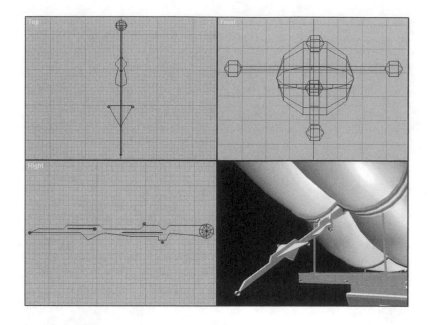

Position the Thrusters

Bring the thruster assembly into the model and position it.

1. Merge the contents of the latest B_THR*nn* file into the B_MAIN*nn* file you've been working with.

2. Move and rotate the thruster assembly as shown. Make sure the ThrMtr01 motor object doesn't go inside the GasBag object (see figure 5.34).

Position the Monitor

Bring the monitor assembly into the model and position it.

1. Merge the contents of the latest B_MON*nn* file into the B_MAIN*nn* file you've been working with.

2. Move and rotate the monitor assembly as shown (see figure 5.35).

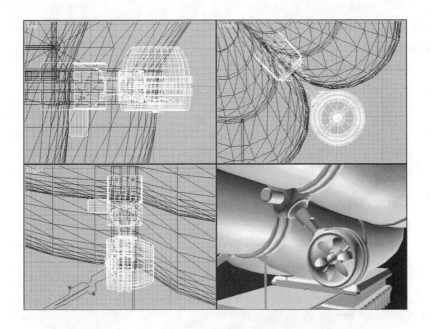

FIGURE 5.34

Merge the thruster
assembly file into the
main model and
position it as shown.

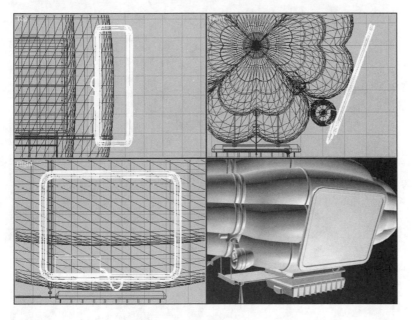

FIGURE 5.35

Merge the monitor
assembly file into the
main model and
position it as shown.

Add the Detail Mesh

At this point, add all the little detail mesh to the model, such as guy wires, supports, the nose cone on the end of the GasBag and so forth.

1. Using the figures as a guide, add small diameter cylinders as guy wires from the monitor to the BagRng01 object (see figure 5.36).

2. Use a cone to cover the end of the GasBag object, and add a cylinder and sphere projecting off the end of it. They will be used in the animation tutorials as part of the docking sequence, so make sure the sphere has a radius of 10 units. Add a tube protruding near the base of the cone to add some interest.

3. Add more low-res spheres as "lights" onto the spires, rings, gondola, and other portions of the ship. Use the name GotLit*nn* for the gondola lights, MonLit*nn* for the monitor frame lights, and RinLit*nn* for the lights on the rest of the ship, so that they can be selected and modified as groups. You also may want to make them instance objects so that their size can be varied *en masse* as well.

4. Add, modify, or fix anything I forgot to mention.

FIGURE 5.36

Adding detail mesh like guy wires and fake lights makes the model more interesting and realistic. Small details also help establish scale, especially when the viewer can relate the objects to their "real life" sizes.

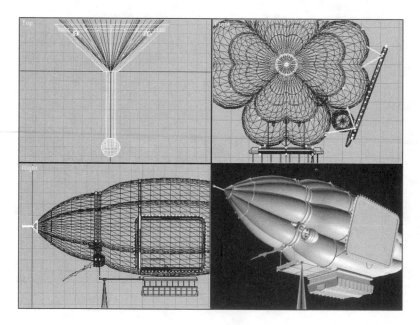

Summary

This chapter has moved beyond the basics of modeling and into some of the more intermediate (and perhaps even advanced) techniques. Despite the fact that it may be a while before you're ready to take on an advanced project like building a character, it's important to understand some of the approaches so you can apply them to simpler objects as well as note possible advanced applications of tools you already use.

The value of reference and how to make the most efficient use of it was discussed. You also looked at the importance of bevels, explored deform modifiers, vertice-level editing, face extrusion, and other techniques. Finally, you saw some alternatives to modeling, as well as tips on doing crystals.

In the next chapter, you will see how mapping can be used to enhance the realism of mesh objects by giving them color and texture. You also will look at how mapping can be used in place of mesh for creating the illusion of detail without bogging things down.

6

Texture Mapping

The texture mapping on this model was created with a 3D paint package, SudioPaint3D. Image by Daniel Hornick, courtesy of Alias/Wavefront.

*T*he student worked carefully, adjusting the stone texture on his castle model until the blocks were neither too large nor too small. At last, the pattern tiled properly.

"Perfect!" The student leaned back to admire his work.

"Perfect indeed," commented the Master, who walked up to examine the scene. "Mayhaps too perfect…"

"Say what?" The lad shot his teacher a confused look.

"Oh, you've done a fine job, lad. The structure is properly proportioned, all your textures are in place…but it's somehow lacking, don't you think?"

The student studied the scene intensely, mulling over the Master's critique. "Too perfect…" he muttered to himself. "I don't get it."

"Here, look at the path that leads to your castle gate," the Master said. "You have made it a brownish gray, like earth, and even given it some grittiness. But it's still too perfect. It looks artificial."

"But, it is artificial!" shot back the student.

"Ah, but it needn't look that way. Come, look out the window." The lad got up and joined the Master, looking down at the path that lead to his own keep. "See there, how the path is rutted with the tracks from wagons? There are patches of grass, hoof prints, and, uh, droppings as well."

"Oh, I see," said the student. "And there are pools of water in the ruts and tracks that reflect the sky. Those would look interesting in the model as well."

"Now you have it," the Master laughed, putting his hand on the lad's shoulder. "Say, perhaps you should go down there and have a closer look. Observe the variations in the stone walls and the grass patterns as well. Oh, and take care of those road apples while you're at it, hmmm?"

Mapping Defined

The key to stunning 3D scenes is practice—practice to be imperfect. Modeling perfectly rectangular and pristine brick is easier than shaping a more realistic, rough-edged one. The same is true of texture mapping. In many ways as important as the modeling, a scene's textures have a major impact on its final appearance. Think of the brick: A wall of slightly irregular rectangles all with flat red surfaces look just as unconvincing as a wall of perfect blocks. This chapter looks at the basics of texture and mapping, and explores tips and techniques to make your texture work stand out from the pack.

Note

Every year, I attend E3 (the Electronic Entertainment Expo) and am always impressed with the sheer number of new games out there, especially with the quantity that rely on 3D graphics. While many of the games tout the fact that they've been produced on pricey Silicon Graphics systems, it's interesting to note that a respectable portion of the nicest work doesn't come from these workstations, but from desktop systems. This follows suit with the old saying, "It's not what you've got, it's how you use it."

Two things that set the best work apart are the detail and quantity of mesh in the scenes, and the quality of the mapping. Even a beautifully sculpted model with a ho-hum map may pale next to a less detailed mesh with an excellent set of texture maps.

Texture mapping is one of many areas in the 3D field that use a lot of confusing and contradictory terms, depending on which software package (or book) you happen to be using. Therefore, this section starts off with a few basic definitions:

Mapping (or *texture mapping*) is the process of developing and assigning material attributes to an object. Before textures are applied, all objects in a 3D package have a default plastic appearance, either gray or some range of colors. Mapping enables the user to give the object a specific color, adjust whether it's shiny or matte, apply a pattern, and so forth.

Material is the encompassing term for all of the different attribute settings that are assigned to an object's surface. A material might be identified by a name, like "Shiny Red Plastic," "Tarnished Silver," or "Rosewood."

Surface attributes refers to the basic material settings, such as Color, Shininess, Transparency, and so on. These affect all parts of an object equally.

Texture is used here as a means of referring to a bitmapped image, either scanned or painted, that gives a material unique qualities that aren't available by simply varying surface attributes. Sample textures might include a scan of a block of wood that captures its grain patterns, a painting of rusty metal, or a 2D logo imported from a drawing program. Textures also can be used to vary the surface roughness, transparency, and color of an object.

Procedural is a type of texture that is mathematically defined. It can simulate wood, marble, and other materials, but usually doesn't look as realistic as scanned textures.

To sum up, then, mapping is the process of making and using materials consisting of surface attributes and/or textures that allow an object to appear as something other than default plastic. For example, the object could be mapped to appear as though it were made of glass, metal, stone, fabric, or wood, to name a few textures (see figure 6.1)

Sample Textures

FIGURE 6.1

Textures make objects appear to be made of different materials. In most 3D programs, objects appear to be made out of a default plastic until a different material is applied.

plastic glass chrome

fabric wood procedural corrosion

Light and Color

When you look at an object rendered in a 3D program at Phong level (discussed in the next section) or better, you see the effects of three potentially different color sources: Ambient, Diffuse, and Specular (see figure 6.2).

Ambient color is the hue an object reflects if it's not directly illuminated by a light source (its color when in shadow). This is rarely black, because the ambient light in the scene usually guarantees at least some illumination on every surface. Generally, the ambient color is a very dark shade of the diffuse color, but it can be set to whatever the user desires.

Diffuse color is the hue assigned to the object. This is the color that's reflected when the object is illuminated by a direct lighting source. Diffuse color is set by the material editing section of your software, where it may simply be referred to as Color.

Specular color is the hue of any highlights that appear on the object (at Phong rendering levels or higher). Specular color is also set by the material editing section of the package.

Note that Ambient, Diffuse and Specular colors are affected by the color of any light sources. See Chapter 7, "Lighting," for more details.

Color Sources

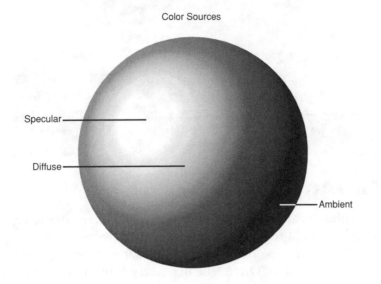

Specular —

Diffuse —

Ambient

FIGURE 6.2

An object's rendered appearance is influenced by three different sources of color and value. Ambient is the color of the object in shadow, Diffuse is the color of the object's material, and Specular is the color of the highlights.

Render Limits

Chapter 3, "Delving into Cyberspace," discussed the effects of rendering at different quality levels: Flat, Gouraud, Phong, Metal, and so forth. Many programs enable you to assign *render limits* to a material as well, so that despite the final output settings, any objects with that material only render to their preset maximum (see figure 6.3).

For example, say you set material A to have no render limit, but you set material B to have a limit of Flat. If you assign them both to objects in the same scene and render the scene at Phong level, the object with material A renders at Phong level, but the object with material B looks as though it was rendered at Flat level.

Render limits are often used when creating a scene in which most objects are rendered normally, but you want some objects to appear in wireframe. They also are useful for speeding things up in certain test render situations in which you need to have multiple objects in the scene, but only some of them need to be rendered at maximum quality levels.

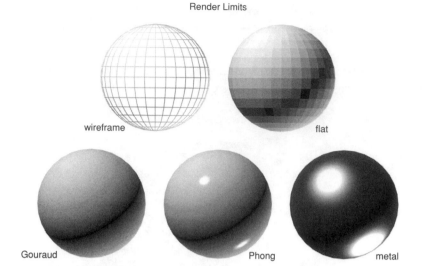

Render Limits

wireframe

flat

Gouraud

Phong

metal

FIGURE 6.3

Materials can have render limits assigned to them that aren't exceeded even if the scene is rendered at a higher quality level. The scene at the right was rendered at Metal level, but most of the materials on the objects were set to lower levels.

Surface Attributes

Surface attributes can be considered the most basic type of material settings, supported by virtually every 3D program. Most of these attributes are set with sliding controls or type-in boxes in the material editing section of the software (see figure 6.4). Often, the material editor offers a preview feature, enabling the user to see what the material will look like before it's applied to the object. There are many different attributes that can be modified to alter an object's appearance, including: Color, Shininess, Specularity, Transparency, Falloff, Index of Refraction, and Luminosity.

Color

Color is the combination of three elements: Hue, Saturation, and Value. The *Hue* (or *Chroma*) of an object is generally what you think of when you hear the term color—it's determined by the frequency of the light coming from the object, be it up in the red range, or down in the violet. *Saturation* (or *Intensity*) is the measure of how concentrated a color is, a way to measure whether a red, for example, is as rich and full as it can be, or is somewhat weak and grayish. Finally, *Value* is the lightness or darkness of a color, and gauges whether a red is a tinted pink pastel or some dark wine-like shade.

Most software offers a full 24-bit range of color choices, or over 16.7 million different colors, including 256 gray values (see figure 6.5). Color is usually set using *RGB* (Red-Green-Blue) or *HSV* (Hue-Saturation-Value) slider-type controls. In general, these controls also allow numeric input, using values ranging from 0 (none) to 255 (maximum) for each of the RGB settings.

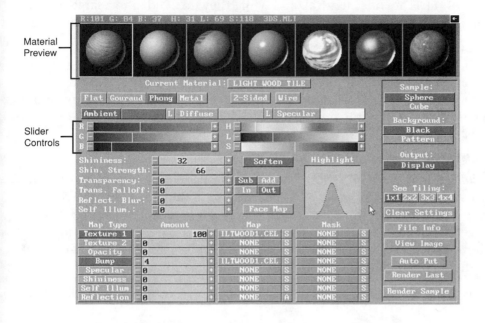

Material Preview

Slider Controls

FIGURE 6.4

The Material Editor module of Kinetix 3D Studio R4 enables the user to set surface attributes, assign image maps, and see a preview of the material before it's applied to the object.

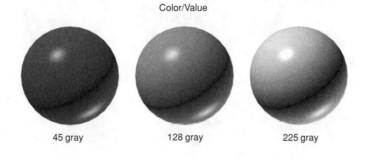

Color/Value

45 gray   128 gray   225 gray

FIGURE 6.5

A material's color (value in this case) can usually be selected from any one of 16.7 million possibilities, including 256 levels of gray. In grayscale, a setting of 0 is black, 128 is neutral gray, and 255 is white.

It's a good thing to remember that not *all* colors can be duplicated by the RGB or HSV models, despite the millions of colors available. This may make it difficult to match the color of a physical object, with strong yellows in particular being hard to achieve. The root of the trouble is that real world objects use the *subtractive color* model in which Red, Yellow, and Blue are the primary colors, and mixing the three together results in a muddy brown. Computer monitors, televisions, and other types of displays use the *additive color* model, in which Red, Green and Blue are the core colors, and mixing them together creates white! As a result, the *gamut* (color ranges) of these two color models are not identical, and while they do overlap to a large degree, certain colors available in one gamut are impossible to achieve in the other.

Another reason that computer colors can be tough to match to real objects is that the color of most physical objects is created by light reflecting off the surface and entering our eyes. With computers, the light is created within the monitor at the proper color frequency for each pixel, so everything on the screen has a self-illuminated appearance, like looking at a 35mm slide.

Shininess

Shininess is the overall reflective nature of the object—in other words, its glossiness. Shininess has an effect on the size of the specular highlight (the bright reflections of light seen on glossy objects), with matte objects having larger highlights and shiny objects having smaller ones (see figure 6.6). Shininess, like most of the other surface attributes, is set by a slider control in the material editing section of the software.

FIGURE 6.6

Shininess is a measure of an object's surface gloss. At 0%, the material is matte, while 100% is maximum glossiness. Note how the specular highlight shrinks as the object is made glossier.

Shininess

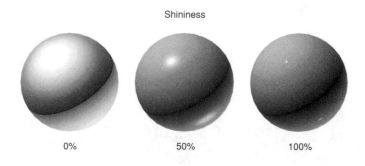

0%   50%   100%

Shininess works together with Specularity to give the viewer information about the surface reflectivity and characteristics of the material, so pay close attention to how the two affect a material's appearance.

Specularity

Specularity adjusts the intensity of the object's highlight, if it has one (see figure 6.7). Specular highlights are the bright reflections of light seen on glossy objects in Phong-level rendering or above. Remember that the size of a specular highlight is related to the Shininess of the object. Specularity is often set with a slider control or type-in percentage.

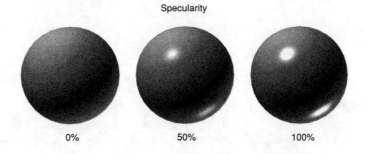

Specularity

0%   50%   100%

FIGURE 6.7

Specularity sets the intensity of a material's highlight. Specularity and Shininess work together to define an object's glossiness. It also plays a major role in simulating metallic materials.

Don't underestimate the value of getting the Shininess and Specularity settings as close as possible to the material you're trying to represent. The behavior of reflections can have a big impact on the believability of an object or scene. Try to avoid completely matte or glossy settings for objects, because most materials are somewhere in-between.

Transparency and Opacity

Transparency and *Opacity* are opposite terms that both have the same results—they control the amount of light that can pass through an object. If Transparency is set to 100% (or Opacity to 0%), the object is virtually invisible. If Transparency is set to 0% (or Opacity to 100%), the object is completely opaque. Any other setting makes the object more or less translucent (see figure 6.8).

Bear in mind that unless your program supports ray tracing, some transparent objects may not look very realistic because the material doesn't refract light the way a real object would. See the following section on Refraction for more information.

There are some additional settings for transparency that have an impact on a material's behavior. First, you can set a material to be filtered, additive, or subtractive (see figure 6.9). Filtered materials multiply the colors behind the translucent surface by the filter color, which the user sets. Depending on the relationship between the filter color and the color of the pixel behind the translucent surface, this setting either has no effect or darkens the background pixel.

FIGURE 6.8

Transparency controls the amount of background imagery that can be seen through an object. A 100% transparent object is nearly invisible, except for any specular highlights.

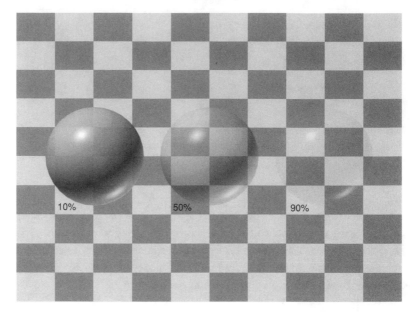

Transparency

FIGURE 6.9

Materials seen through translucent portions of an object are affected by Additive or Subtractive settings. Subtractive darkens the RGB values of the filtered images, while Additive increases them.

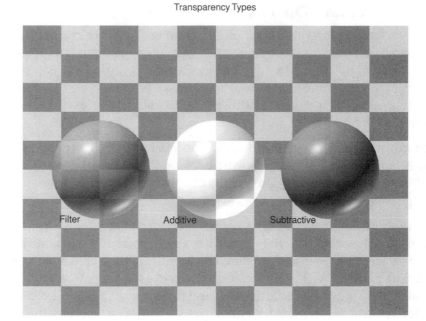

Transparency Types

Additive materials lighten the RGB value of whatever is seen through the object's translucent portions by adding the object's diffuse color to colors behind the translucent surface. Using the additive setting for transparent objects yields a more realistic effect, because the object appears to be picking up light sources.

Subtractive materials darken the values by subtracting the filter color from the colors behind the translucent surface.

Another important setting for translucent objects is *one-sided* or *two-sided*, which tells the renderer whether or not to ignore faces on the opposite side of the object. The default setting is one-sided because it speeds up rendering, and you can't see the backfaces on an opaque object anyway. However, because you can see the opposite side of a translucent object in real life, use the two-sided setting.

Falloff is another setting used in conjunction with transparency to set how much more or less transparent an object is at its edges. Falloff uses the angle of a face's normal to determine the amount of variation from the overall transparency setting to apply. Faces that are perpendicular to the viewer are unaffected, while faces that are edge-on to the viewer have the maximum amount of change applied.

There are two types of falloff settings: Inward and Outward (see figure 6.10). *Inward Falloff* reduces the amount of transparency as the faces become edge-on. This simulates materials that are denser at the edges, like blown glass objects. *Outward falloff* reduces the amount of transparency as the faces become perpendicular to the viewer. This simulates materials that are denser in the center, like a container of murky liquid.

Refraction

Refraction controls how much light is bent when it passes through a translucent object. This simulates the realistic bending of light in nature when it passes through different materials (see figure 6.11). Refraction is supported only in programs that do ray tracing, but it can be simulated in other products by using refraction mapping (see the following section on map channels).

The use of translucent objects and refraction can make for some beautiful ray traced scenes using only simple forms, when they are carefully lit and arranged. Because refraction is based on physical laws, you can make lenses that really magnify and add them to your scene.

Falloff

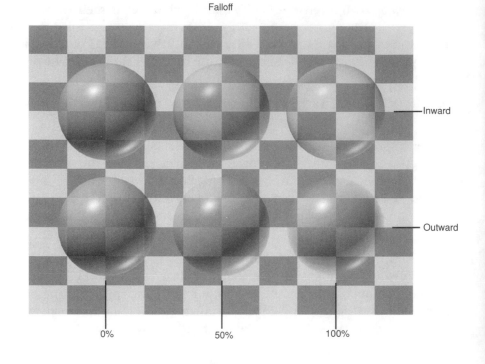

FIGURE 6.10

Falloff controls how much more or less transparent an object is at its center as opposed to its edges. Falloff can be either Inward or Outward.

Inward

Outward

0%   50%   100%

Refraction

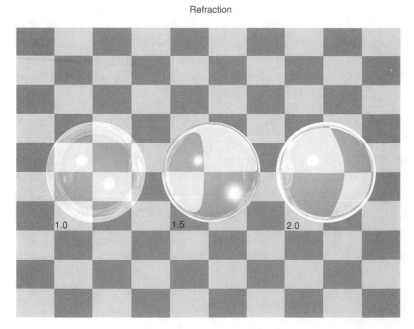

FIGURE 6.11

The Refraction setting adjusts the amount that light is bent when it passes through a translucent object. A setting of 1.0 means that no refraction occurs, while higher numbers increase the amount of bending.

1.0   1.5   2.0

The amount of refraction is set by a scale called the *index of refraction*, in which a setting of 1.0 means that no refraction occurs. The proper index of refraction settings for different materials can be found in reference texts, like CRC's *Handbook of Chemistry and Physics*. The following are some common material examples (rounded off to two decimal places).

Diamond:	2.42
Emerald:	1.57
Glass:	1.5-1.9, depending on composition
Ice:	1.3
Opal:	1.45
Quartz:	1.5
Ruby:	1.77
Water:	1.33

Luminosity

Luminosity (Self-Illumination) adjusts how much an object appears to be lit from within. As the percentage of luminance is increased, it flattens out the effects of the ambient and diffuse light sources, until the object appears to be one solid value (see figure 6.12). Luminosity has no effect on specular highlights, however. Note that self-illumination is not to be confused with glow, which is an effect that extends outward from the object's edges (see Chapter 10, "Rendering and Output").

Luminosity

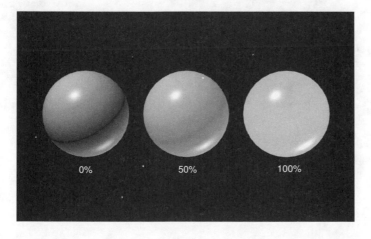

0%   50%   100%

FIGURE 6.12

The Luminosity setting adjusts how much an object appears to be lit from within. 0% is completely unlit, while 100% is totally self-illuminated.

Map Channels

Despite the range of settings that surface attributes provide, objects with materials that use only these settings tend to have an unrealistic, computer-generated look. Textures or procedurals are needed to bring more realism to the scene.

Textures (also called maps) can be derived from scanned images, 2D paint work, mathematical processes, and just about any other method that can be used to generate an image or pattern. Depending on your program, these images can be used to affect different aspects of the material's appearance, giving it a realistic visual pattern (such as wood grain or marble) or varying the roughness of the surface, its reflectiveness, transparency, and so on. The surface attributes of the material that can accept an image are called *map channels*.

Map channels fall into four basic categories: Diffuse, Bump, Reflection, and Opacity. Some programs also offer Shininess, Specularity, Luminosity, and Refraction channels as well (see figure 6.13). Note that some channels only use the grayscale values of an image, regardless of whether it's in color or not.

Map Channels

FIGURE 6.13

A wide array of material characteristics can be altered by using bitmaps in different map channels. Only displacement mapping alters the object's mesh, however.

As with the surface attributes, map channels usually have sliders or percentage values to adjust the amount of effect these maps have on the object. These sliders prevent the map from having any effect when set to 0%, or completely override the base attribute for that channel (or set the channel to its maximum value) when set to 100%. At other percentage levels, the channel's effect is reduced from maximum, or the result is a blend between the map and the base material.

Note that in addition to each of the map channels contributing to the overall look of a material, some programs allow more than one map to be placed in a channel. In fact, some programs allow an unlimited number of maps (subject only to the amount of RAM in the system). This enables the user to blend different maps together without having to composite them in a paint program first. Some software also may allow mathematical or masking operations to be performed on the maps, such as multiplying the images together, subtracting one from another, and so forth. The result is a much greater range of effects and patterns without having to resort to custom paint work.

Diffuse Maps

Diffuse maps are generally in color, and are used to alter the object's color away from that defined by the Color setting into a pattern or image. The amount of change from the base color of the object toward the map is set with a slider or percentage control. This enables the user to create a mixture of base color and map. However, in the case of diffuse maps, the map is usually set to 100%, completely overriding the base color.

To simulate a wood material on an object, for example, the diffuse map would be a scan or painting of wood grain set to 100%.

Bump Maps

Bump maps vary the surface roughness by manipulating the object's normals according to a grayscale image. Note that bump maps don't actually distort the mesh, so the effect may be lost at the edges of a rounded object. These maps use the value (lightness or darkness) of the map to determine whether a given section is protruding, flush, or indented. In some programs, for example, black portions of the image would cause an indentation, while white portions would protrude. The overall effect a bump map has on an object is also determined by the slider or percentage value for this channel.

In the wood material example, the bump map would probably just be a grayscale version of the diffuse map, because grain tends to be darker than the rest of the wood already. This would cause the grain to appear indented.

Reflection Maps

Reflection maps are used to create an environment for a reflective object, and roughly simulate the effects of ray tracing in programs that don't offer it. They do this by overlaying (according to the percentage value or slider) a secondary diffusion map over the existing material, giving the impression that the object is reflecting the scene contained in the image. To simulate chrome trim on an outdoor surface, for example, it's common to apply a reflection map of a cloudy sky. Some programs offer automatic reflection mapping, which generates an image by rendering a panoramic view around the object and using it as the map.

You could use a reflection map on the wood example, in order to make it appear freshly polished. The percentage of reflection mapping used should be kept fairly low, however.

Opacity Maps

Opacity maps are grayscale images that override the transparency settings of the material, and allow the object to vary from opaque to transparent. Like bump and reflection maps, they use grayscale values, and the slider or percentage value of the channel to set transparency. As an example, opacity mapping would be useful in a situation where you're modeling dirty panes of glass that have been wiped clean in the middle. You also can use them as a way to put holes in objects without resorting to mesh changes.

For example, say you wanted to create a chain link fence. One option would be to construct it with lots of thin cylindrical objects in a crisscross pattern, but an easier and more efficient route would be to use an opacity map. The crisscross material would simply be a flat panel with a metallic material and a crisscross opacity map applied. See the tutorials at the end of this chapter for more information on using opacity mapping.

Shininess Maps

Shininess maps adjust the reflectivity of the surface to which they are applied, overriding (depending on the slider or percentage setting) any Shininess settings in the surface attributes with their grayscale values. Shininess maps are useful for accurately portraying materials that have a range of shininess, such as metal with rusty spots, fingerprinted glass, or varnished wood.

Returning to the wood grain example, the same grayscale image used for the bump map could be employed in this channel as well, to vary the shininess of the surface. This makes sense because even when varnished, grain is often less reflective than the surface of the wood.

Specularity Maps

Specularity maps vary the color and intensity of the specular highlights of the surface, depending on the image used and the percentage or slider value for the channel. This can be used to simulate various materials, like metals or metallic paints that reflect light in a spectrum of colors and intensities.

For example, if you wanted to create an object that looked like it was made of tricolor gold, you would create a specularity map that consisted of speckles of the appropriate colors. When applied to the specularity channel, the map would add these colors to the specular highlights, without affecting other parts of the object.

Self-Illumination Maps

Self-Illumination maps are grayscale images that create the impression that some portions of the object are illuminated from within. Like many of the other map channels, self-illumination uses a slider or percentage setting in conjunction with the grayscale values in the image to control the effect.

Self-Illumination mapping would be useful for mapping a stained glass lampshade, for example. The map would be set to make the glass panels appear to be lit, while leaving the lead that holds them together unaffected.

Refraction Maps

Refraction maps are a means of simulating the effects of light refraction in programs that don't offer ray tracing. The amount of simulated refraction is based on the grayscale values in the image, and the slider or percentage control. Some programs may feature automatic refraction mapping that takes the shape of the object into account.

Displacement Maps

Displacement maps aren't surface embellishments like the rest of the material attributes are. In fact, a more appropriate location for this item is the modeling section, because the grayscale values of the displacement map and the percentage of strength applied actually affect the mesh, extending it outward or inward. Displacement mapping is often used to create terrain or organic models based on grayscale imagery. See Chapter 5, "Modeling: Beyond the Basics," for more information about displacement mapping.

> Although texture maps have the capacity to make materials much more realistic, they suffer from two main drawbacks. First, they consume memory, and scenes with numerous or very large maps may slow the rendering process to a crawl unless the system is equipped with a great deal of RAM. Second, they require mapping coordinates on the objects, and as you will see in the Mapping Coordinates section later in this chapter, it may be difficult to apply these properly once the object is built.

Procedural Textures

One way to get around the restrictions of using texture maps, but still retain some of their realism, is to use procedural textures. As was mentioned earlier, procedurals are mathematically defined textures that can be made to simulate such things as wood grain and marble (see figure 6.14). In addition, they are useful for creating randomized or fractal patterns as well, and do a good job of creating realistic snow, rock, and gaseous nebulae.

Procedurals have several advantages over bitmapped textures. The most obvious advantages are that they consume much less memory than bitmapped textures and require no mapping coordinates. Unlike textures that only affect the surface of an object, procedurals go all the way *through* an object, so that Booleans and other cutting operations done to an object will reveal a properly formed interior texture. In addition, procedurals are easily animated, which allows them to change over time. This capability allows them to simulate all kinds of natural effects, such as wind blowing across grass, smoke, mist, or water, plus some interesting special effects as well.

Procedural Textures

Wood Marble Noise

FIGURE 6.14

Procedural textures require no mapping coordinates, and much less memory than bitmapped textures. However, they're generally not very realistic. Procedural noise can be used to add realistic variation to any type of texture, or be applied as a bump map.

A smoke procedural was used to great effect in The Daedalus Encounter to create a weird animated bump map for the alien ship's propulsion system. By applying the animated texture to the translucent intake and exhaust mesh on the ship, the craft seemed to come alive, driven by some unfathomable energy source.

One of the most useful functions available in procedural mapping is *noise*, which is mathematically derived "static." The amount of noise can be varied or calculated in different ways, and can be used to create a natural variation in the coloration of surfaces (or any one of the other map channels) without resorting to a grayscale image. For example, using fractal noise for bump and specularity mapping is a good way to turn a flat surface into a carpeted one.

Animated Textures

Procedurals aren't the only texture that can be animated. *Animated textures* use video or animation files instead of still images, which cause the texture on an object to change over time when the scene is rendered. This could be useful for showing such effects as a landscape changing from spring to fall, or a 3D model of a television with a moving image on the screen. Animated textures are discussed in more detail in the Incorporating Video into Materials section later on.

It's important to note that if the sequence you are rendering is longer than the animation or video file used for a texture, the animation or video will loop, meaning that it starts over again from the first frame. If this isn't a smooth transition, you can either use a longer source animation or video, or use a video editing program to smooth out the differences between the last few frames of the sequence and the first few frames at the beginning.

Tiling

Tiling is a method of repeating one image over a large area, something like using individual floor tiles to cover a large kitchen. Tiled images use less memory because the image is only stored once, but they suffer from some drawbacks. First, they tend to look *too regular*, with tiled stone or grass ending up looking like indoor-outdoor carpeting instead. Also, the tiles have a tendency to show seams or patterns because the images are all lined up in neat rows (see figure 6.15)—like on your kitchen floor.

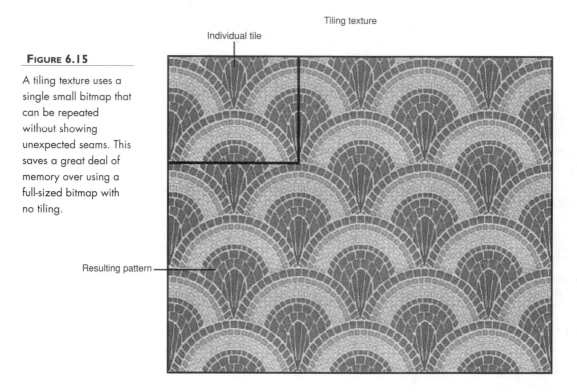

Tiling texture

Individual tile

FIGURE 6.15

A tiling texture uses a single small bitmap that can be repeated without showing unexpected seams. This saves a great deal of memory over using a full-sized bitmap with no tiling.

Resulting pattern

Your software may offer several tiling settings that can help reduce patterns by mirroring pairs of tiles. Also, see the "Mastering Maps" section later in this chapter for more information about creating custom seamless tiling textures.

Face Mapping

Face mapping ignores any mapping coordinates applied to the object and instead tries to conform the image to pairs of faces that share an invisible edge (see figure 6.16). Face mapping is done by selecting the desired faces in the object and applying the material to them. Note that the method by which objects are created or modified may have a dramatic effect on the way the faces are formed, so some planning or face-by-face manipulation of the mesh may be necessary to use this technique.

Face Mapping

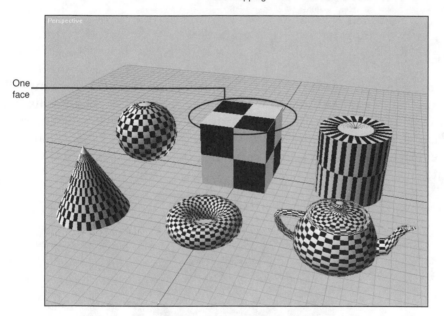

One face

FIGURE 6.16

Face mapping causes the bitmap image to conform to each face on the object individually. No mapping coordinates are required, but the bitmap is deformed depending on the size and shape of the faces.

Face mapping does conform nicely to many objects, especially ones with a fairly even size and distribution of faces. However, as with any tiled material, you may see some problems if you aren't using a texture that can be seamlessly tiled in a range of sizes (see figure 6.17).

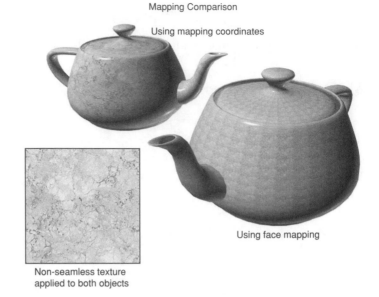

Using mapping coordinates

Using face mapping

Non-seamless texture
applied to both objects

FIGURE 6.17

A comparison of
mapping coordinates to
tiled or face mapping.
With the same (non-
seamless) texture
applied to both objects,
tiling is evident on the
face mapped object,
while the other one
stretches the image over
the whole object.

Decals

Decals are images that can be applied to an object independently of any other
texture mapping. They are great for adding small bitmapped details to an
object that could otherwise make do with a procedural texture. They also can
be used to precisely position image elements on a complex shape that would
otherwise take a lot of trial-and-error image or UV coordinate adjustments to
achieve (see figure 6.18).

Decaling

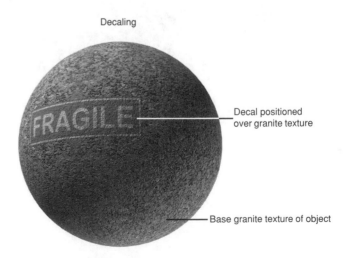

Decal positioned
over granite texture

Base granite texture of object

FIGURE 6.18

Decals are bitmaps that
can be independently
positioned over an
object's base material.
They can sometimes be
set to allow some of the
base material attributes
to show through, as
with the bump map in
this example.

Texture Tools

Before you can use textures in your material development, however, you must get them into your system. You have several options, some of which use the hardware discussed in Chapter 2, "Nuts and Bolts."

Scanners

Scanners provide a way to duplicate a texture or logo easily, and can provide raw material for creating custom maps as well. You can even scan real materials, as long as they have one flat side. Wood or paper samples scan well, but reflective materials tend to cause some undesirable color shifting. If a material is too shiny, too heavy, rounded, or otherwise inappropriate for a scanner, take a photo instead.

If you plan to scan anything abrasive with your scanner, such as a lightweight stone sample, use extreme caution so as not to scratch the glass. Taping down a sheet of clear acetate should help to protect it.

Be wary when scanning printed images, because they can cause problems to pop up in your scans. The most common problem is a *moiré* effect, which is a pattern that appears when the scanning resolution doesn't match the printing resolution perfectly (see figure 6.19). In other words, a 135 dpi image scanned at 135 dpi should not have a *moiré* problem. There are inexpensive "screen finder" tools available at graphics arts supply stores that help determine the number of dpi or lpi (lines per inch) that were used in the printing process, but these are tricky to use and not very accurate.

Frankly, I've never gotten satisfactory results when scanning magazine or book images, so I use a "brute force" method that requires scanning at high resolution:

1. Scan the image into Photoshop at 200% and 135dpi. For an 8.5"× 11.0" image, this makes a large 20+MB file at about 2K resolution.

2. Rotate the image if necessary to straighten it up. Often it only needs to be adjusted about 0.5–1.0 degrees. That sounds small, but can make a big difference, especially on a tiled pattern. To determine the amount of rotation needed, turn on the Info palette, then make a line of width 0 (so it's invisible) along the edge of a portion of the image that you want to be vertical or horizontal. The angle of the line you are drawing will show up in degrees in the Info palette, and help you to estimate how much to rotate the image.

3. Crop the image, removing any unwanted areas.

4. Choose FILTER:DESPECKLE to blend together all of the fine dots of color that make up a printed image. You also may use Median if you need more control over the results.

5. Reduce the image to fit your needs.

6. Use FILTER:SHARPEN or FILTER:UNSHARP MASK to sharpen things up. Typical settings are: Amount 50–100%, Radius 1.0, Threshold 0.

7. If the image seems a bit washed out, try IMAGE:ADJUST:LEVELS and move the B and W pointers in a little to make sure the image has a full range of tones from black to white.

8. Using the printed image as a reference, adjust color and saturation with IMAGE:ADJUST:HUE/SATURATION. Settings will vary by scanner. In some cases, you may have to select one of the color ranges on the left side of the dialog box and adjust it separately.

9. Use the Burn tool to darken any areas where the outside light has bled in and washed out the image. This often happens along the spine edge of a book.

Remember that nearly all material found in books and magazines is protected by copyright, so you're limited by what you can legally use. Because of the difficulty in finding license-free source material, and because the process of scanning it in and making corrections is time consuming, you will probably want to rely on image libraries for most of your common mapping needs.

Photography

Because you own the copyright to your own photographs, this is a safe and popular alternative to scanning book and magazine images. As mentioned in the preceding scanner section, using photography is a good alternative to scanning reflective or awkward objects as well.

For best results, you should use a good 35mm camera, preferably one with a macro lens for doing close-ups of materials. Because textures typically need to be sharp, use a tripod or copy stand when photographing objects. If you plan to shoot indoors, you will either need to use tungsten slide film with incandescent lighting, or use a strobe (flash) or other light that produces a daylight spectrum. If you try to use normal daylight film with incandescent or fluorescent lights, you will get a severe color shift toward blue or yellow. Of course, you could try to correct this later in Photoshop, but it's more work and less accurate.

> If you plan to get some tungsten slide film, don't bother going to your drug store's camera department for it, because the clerk will just give you a blank look. Go to a *real* photography store and ask for Kodak Ektachrome 64T or something similar.

Once you've shot the roll, you have to get it processed. Larger prints are better, of course, because you get more detail when you scan them in. For the best quality, however, consider using a slide scanner (which also works for negatives) or getting the roll processed onto PhotoCD.

PhotoCD processing can be done to undeveloped rolls or existing slides and negatives, and involves taking or sending the images to a film processing outfit that offers the service. They put the images onto a multi-session CD-ROM that can be used with most of the CD-ROM drives built in the last few years. The images are archived in five resolutions, ranging from 128×192 thumbnails to 2048×3072 high-res, and more images can be added to the same disc later. For most textures, 128×128 or a multiple of that is ideal, due to the way that most programs allocate memory for maps or re-scale them to one of these multiples. Few texture maps will exceed 640 x 480, unless extremely high detail is needed over a very large object.

Be aware that PhotoCD processing quality seems to vary widely, so it would pay you to try a company's service with a test roll before you commit all your film into their hands. Otherwise, you may find yourself doing a lot of color and level correction work. Try asking at a good photography store for a recommendation.

Digital photography offers many of the advantages of scanning without the extra step of having the film processed and made into a PhotoCD or color print. The downside is that pro-quality cameras still cost thousands to tens of thousands of dollars, although they're available for rent at reasonable prices. There are some less expensive alternatives that may work for low- to medium-res maps, but in general their quality is still not good enough for use as a high-res texture map. Still, this technology is definitely on the fast track, and will probably change the way we take photos in the near future.

Image Libraries

Image libraries are usually collections of royalty-free images on CD-ROM, professionally photographed and scanned. Some of them feature seamlessly tiling textures in addition to images of rock, wood, metal, tile, and so on. Many 3D packages come with image libraries already, but having too many textures to choose from is seldom a problem. Some of the popular texture libraries include Wraptures, Artbeats, and Imagetects (see figure 6.20).

Another place to locate royalty-free textures is on the Web. For example, try AXEM at http://axem2.simplenet.com/ for a number of tilable wood and stone textures. See Appendix C, "Resources," for other useful Web sites.

Note that while some artists use these images straight off the CD-ROM or as starting points for custom maps, others feel that they're too recognizable (or overused) and prefer to create the textures from scratch. That's where 2D paint software comes in.

FIGURE 6.20

Sample textures from Form and Functions' Wraptures image library CD-ROM. Royalty-free image collections like this make excellent source images for your own materials.

2D Paint Programs

Among paint programs, Adobe Photoshop is legendary, and often regarded as a must-have application for artists. While it lacks some of the texture tools and custom brushes that Fractal Painter offers, it has a solid and easy-to-use interface that can be used with little training (see figure 6.21). For those who want to explore its depths, Photoshop has a long list of powerful editing, compositing, and filter capabilities. In addition, adding Kai's Power Tools, Alien Skin's Black Box, and other plug-in tools is a good way to add even more texture-generation possibilities. See Appendix D, "Software Products and Publisher List," for more information.

Fractal Painter has some excellent brushes and features, and uses what should be an intuitive set of tools for the artist, based on natural media such as chalk, oil paint, watercolors, and so forth. Unfortunately, the product isn't as quick or easy to use as Photoshop, and its oversized tools tend to eat a lot of screen real estate (see figure 6.22). Still, its range when mastered is unequaled, making it a powerful addition to the 3D artist's toolbox. Like Photoshop, it too can be augmented by plug-ins.

FIGURE 6.21

Adobe Photoshop is one of the most popular programs for creating and manipulating object textures. It enables you to rasterize EPS files, create gradients and seamless tiles, and create opacity maps and other multi-channel images.

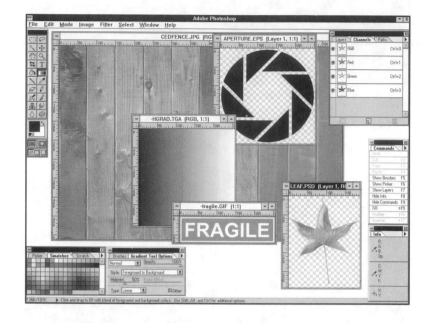

FIGURE 6.22

Fractal Painter uses a traditional media metaphor for its interface, but many artists find it awkward to use at first. Still, it offers an excellent number of unique tools.

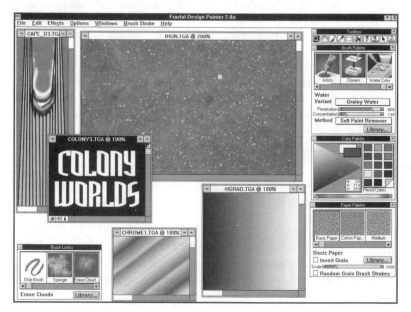

3D Paint Programs

New to the scene are *3D Paint programs*, which enable the user to paint directly on the 3D model. These applications include the *StudioPaint 3D*, *Amazon*, and *Taarna* 3D Paint programs for the SGI, and *Mesh Paint* for 3D Studio, among others. Some 3D software, such as Ray Dream Designer, offers a 3D paint package built in. Overall, 3D paint is a very powerful new application that can solve a number of problems with precise positioning of maps, coordinate application, and most of all, the painful paint-render-repaint cycle that regular mapping with 2D paint images demands.

Beyond even the capability to paint on a 3D object is Taarna's ability to apply displacement mapping, turning a pressure sensitive tablet and stylus into a virtual chisel for chipping away and deforming mesh.

Other Tools

Terrazzo is a Xaos Tools product designed to create tiled textures or backgrounds from portions of other images. It works something like an electronic kaleidoscope, and can produce some surprising effects.

A Wacom pressure-sensitive tablet and stylus seem to be *de rigueur* for texture mapping, enabling the user to work in a natural way while increasing subtlety and control of the virtual paint immensely.

Mapping Coordinates

In order for your masterfully created image maps to appear on an object, you often need to apply mapping coordinates (unless you're doing face mapping). *Mapping coordinates* are a set of coordinates that specify the location, orientation, and scale of any textures applied to an object. Without mapping coordinates, the software doesn't know where to apply any textures in the material.

Before delving into mapping coordinate systems and types, however, it would be good to understand image coordinates, because they also affect the orientation of a map on an object.

Image (XY) Coordinates

When an image is used as a texture map, it's assigned a set of *XY coordinates*. At the top left corner (in some programs at least) is 0,0, which is also called the origin point (see figure 6.23). The other three corners are also assigned coordinates. While the image is generally left in the default position shown, the material editing section of your software may enable you to offset the XY coordinates for each texture image. This enables the image to be shifted in order to line up with elements in the mesh.

Image (XY) Coordinates

0,0   X   1,0

Y

0,1   1,1

For example, say you were applying a tiled map to the floor in a 3D model of a kitchen. You notice that the floor tile pattern looks a little odd because only a sliver of the tiles are seen along one wall (because the rest of the tiles are covered by the wall). By adjusting the XY coordinates, you can shift the tiling pattern to make more of the tiles visible, or shift them so the seam is even with the wall.

Mapping (UVW) Coordinates

The mesh itself also has a coordinate system for mapping, but it is the *UV* or *UVW coordinate system*. UVW coordinates look similar to the XY image system, but they conform to the mesh no matter how it twists or bends (see figure 6.24). Note that the orientation of the UV or UVW coordinates may vary by product.

UVW coordinates can be offset like the XY coordinates, but provide much more accurate positioning. In fact, a particular pixel in the image can be made to line up with a given vertice in the mesh. UVW coordinates are used in pairs, such as UV, UW, or VW, to adjust the orientation of the map.

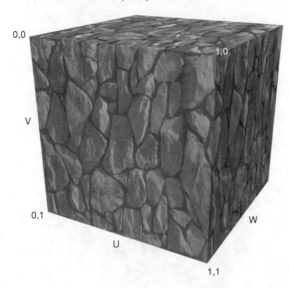

Mesh (UVW) Coordinates

0,0

1,0

V

0,1

W

U

1,1

FIGURE 6.24

UVW coordinates are used for mesh objects, and shifting them allows very precise repositioning of maps on an object.

There are four common mapping coordinate types or *projections*: Planar, Cylindrical, Spherical, and Cubic. In addition, some programs offer Loft or Parametric coordinates as well, which are automatically applied (with differing levels of success) when you create the object.

If you apply a material that contains texture maps to an object, but the texture doesn't show up when you render the scene, you've probably forgotten to apply mapping coordinates. Also, check to make sure that the texture is active and turned up to a visible level in the material editor.

Planar Coordinates

Planar coordinates are flat, like a sheet of paper (see figure 6.25). Planar maps act as though they're pushing the map through the mesh, which may cause streaks along the side of the object. This is a common 3D *faux pas*, and can be avoided by using a different coordinate system or by mapping the affected faces separately (see the preceding Face Mapping section).

Planar coordinates are useful for mapping flat objects, like walls and doors, but you may want to use them in other cases as well, because they're very useful for precise positioning of texture map elements onto a mesh object, and don't distort the texture maps like some of the other coordinate types do.

For example, if you built a 3D model of a book, you would want to use a planar map for applying the cover texture and title.

Planar Mapping

FIGURE 6.25

Planar mapping applies a single, flat set of mapping coordinates to the object. This often results in streaking along the sides of the object, however.

Mapping coordinate representation

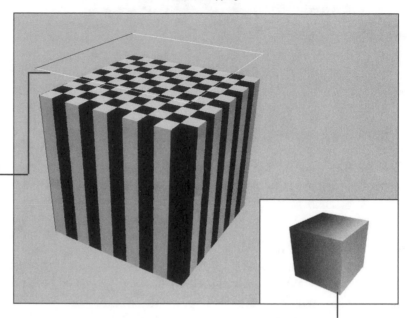

Grad mapped sample render

Cylindrical Coordinates

Cylindrical coordinates wrap the image around one of the object's axes until it meets itself (see figure 6.26). This may result in a seam, so consult the seamless tiling section of this chapter for information about correcting this situation. Also, like planar coordinates, cylindrical projections tend to create streaks across the top and bottom of the cylinder, so the end caps may need to be mapped separately. Some programs offer an option for automatically planar mapping the end caps.

Cylindrical coordinates are obviously ideal for cylindrical object shapes, such as applying a label to a 3D bottle, or to apply a wood texture to a post.

Spherical Coordinates

Spherical coordinates wrap the image around the object in a cylindrical manner, then pinch the top and bottom closed to surround it (see figure 6.27). The pinching often results in a undesirable distortion of the image, so some additional tweaking may be needed on the image. Also, just as with the cylindrical coordinate system, a vertical seam may show up where the two ends of the image meet.

Cylindrical Mapping

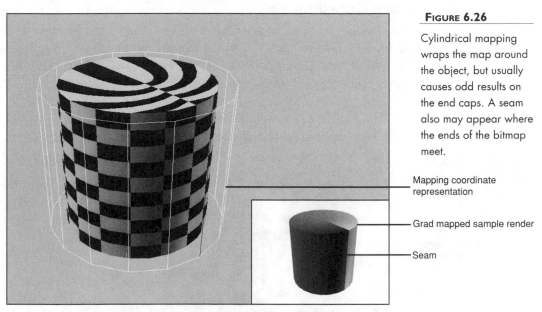

FIGURE 6.26

Cylindrical mapping wraps the map around the object, but usually causes odd results on the end caps. A seam also may appear where the ends of the bitmap meet.

Mapping coordinate representation

Grad mapped sample render

Seam

FIGURE 6.27

Spherical mapping surrounds the object, pinching the top and bottom of the bitmap together to enclose it. This may result in a distorted, streaked appearance to the texture at these points.

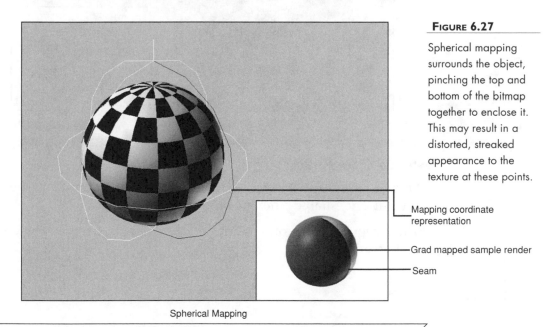

Mapping coordinate representation

Grad mapped sample render

Seam

Spherical Mapping

In addition to being ideal for mapping spherical objects, this coordinate system is useful for just about any irregular form that will be taking a generic sort of texture, like rust or marble.

Cubic Coordinates

Cubic coordinates apply the image from six different directions, and are also known as *box coordinates*. Obviously, they're ideal for mapping box-like objects, because they apply the image in planar form to each side of the object, preventing streaks (see figure 6.28).

Cubic Mapping

FIGURE 6.28

Cubic mapping applies the bitmap to six sides of the object.

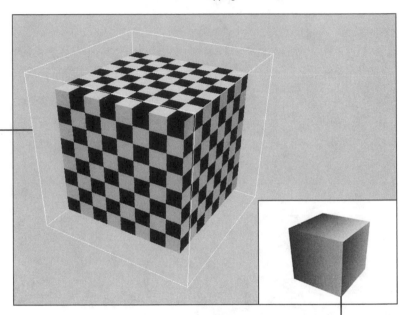

Mapping coordinate representation

Grad mapped sample render

Wrap Coordinates

Wrap or *shrink wrap coordinates* try to smoothly surround an object while reducing undesirable pinching or streaking (see figure 6.29).

When mapping a freeform object, you may want to try wrap coordinates as an alternative to spherical.

Wrap Mapping

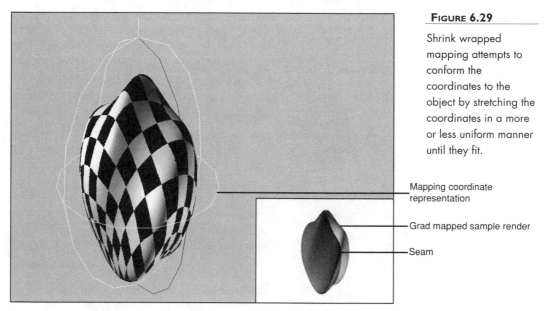

FIGURE 6.29

Shrink wrapped mapping attempts to conform the coordinates to the object by stretching the coordinates in a more or less uniform manner until they fit.

Mapping coordinate representation

Grad mapped sample render

Seam

Lofting Coordinates

Lofting coordinates are applied to objects during the extrusion, sweeping, or skinning process. By applying coordinates during these mesh operations, the coordinates can follow a winding path much more faithfully than if you attempted to apply them later. Therefore, it's highly recommended that you make sure to use this option whenever you're creating a complex, winding form (see figure 6.30).

The construction of a 3D snake would be a perfect opportunity to use lofting coordinates, because the scale texture would be evenly applied along its winding length.

Parametric Coordinates

Parametric coordinates are a form of semi-automatic coordinates that can be applied during the creation of any parametric object (see figure 6.31). While this can be very convenient if they work out, the results are sometimes unpredictable, and you may find yourself applying new coordinates later on.

FIGURE 6.30

Lofting coordinates are applied at the time an object is extruded, or swept, and allow the texture to follow the form of the resulting object closely.

Seam

Grad mapped sample render

Parametric Mapping

FIGURE 6.31

Parametric mapping coordinates are automatically generated by parametric modelers. Like other types of mapping coordinates, they are distorted along with the object when it is transformed.

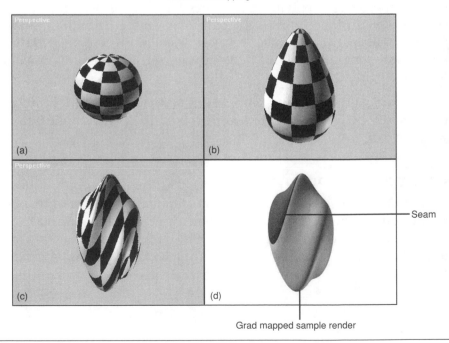

Seam

Grad mapped sample render

Mastering Maps

Mapping is a an art form in and of itself, much more of a painting technique than a 3D modeling one. Although strong 2D paint skills can be incredibly helpful in creating standout texture mapping, you can get along pretty well as long as you can use the tools properly.

This section looks at how to go about the process of creating and applying texture maps that will transform your austere, plastic-looking models into a rich and realistic scene.

Using Maps Effectively

A common piece of advice about modeling is to use maps instead of mesh whenever possible. This often cuts down on rendering time and also makes it easier to work on your scene. However, here's another piece of advice to bear in mind as well:

Don't be stingy with the mesh.

Maps can be very effective, but there are times when just a little more mesh, even if it's just some simple boxes or other primitives tacked on to break up the surface or the outline, will make the difference between being efficient and looking amateur.

The other thing to remember is that bitmapped textures consume memory, and too many maps can really bog down the rendering process unless you have a lot of RAM (64MB or more). Note that mapping a number of different objects with the same image has far less impact on memory consumption than using different images to map each object.

Portions of the following material dealing with mapping techniques and special effects are from my Animata articles "Plenty of Space," "Cry Havoc," and "Treasure Maps" that originally appeared from January to March 1996 in *InterActivity* magazine (Copyright 1996 Miller Freeman, Inc.), and are used with permission.

One Artist's Approach

Sometimes the best way to learn, as our medieval student knows, is to watch a master at work. Take a look at how one artist approaches the task of doing highly detailed map work for 3D environments.

Laura Hainke is a former senior graphic artist with Mondo Media/Mechadeus, now a freelance contractor and one of the partners in our CyberDog Studios online game development venture. She earned her in-house nickname "The Texture Goddess" as result of her impressive 3D mapping work on both *Critical Path* and *The Daedalus Encounter*.

Since the development process at Mondo Media/Mechadeus used to separate modeling and mapping in order to maintain consistency, most of the mesh that Laura received had little or no mapping applied. It often didn't have mapping coordinates either, which meant she had to apply her own. This was often very difficult when complex objects were involved, so in many cases, she would use the Detach Faces feature to break an object down into multiple pieces, mapping each element individually.

Laura applies basic materials to the objects first, then renders the scene to get a feel for the space, the lighting, and what the most important items in the shot will be. This enables her to home in on the key objects and make sure that the time spent on mapping them is budgeted accordingly. It also enables her to determine an overall color scheme and feel for the room to have. She usually starts with either the walls or the most difficult objects first, painting the patterns and textures on one machine while rendering the 3D scene on another. She reuses patterns from key pieces on other objects to save time and unify the design.

When creating textures for walls, she renders an elevation view (no perspective) of the wall and the objects attached to it, using it as the basis for a planar map. If there are pipes coming out of the wall, she paints stains running down beneath them. Oil lamps get smoky smudges above them, and so forth. When she has finished a detail, she applies the map to the object and renders the scene to see how it looks in 3D.

Dirt and wear add a lot of character and realism to your mesh. Laura tries to imagine the way a room would be used by its virtual occupants, then dirties it up accordingly. For example, she might pick out a "favorite spot" on a couch and apply extra stains and fraying to that cushion.

When working with spherical or cylindrical maps, Laura sometimes turns to Mesh Paint, a 3D painting IPAS for 3D Studio, as a way to outline the perimeter of a map and mark key locations on it. She then likes to work on the map with her usual 2D paint programs, because Mesh Paint's tool set is not as fast or powerful. Another way to approach this is to apply a numbered grid to the object, then use a render as reference when painting on top of the grid.

Like other artists, Laura likes using Photoshop for its speed and control, often starting a map in Photoshop, then switching to Fractal Painter to make use of its superior texturing capability. Case in point: to create a brick surface, she would paint the bricks in Photoshop, making sure that the map would tile properly. Switching to Painter, she would create the brick's grittiness by adjusting the image luminance, turning shininess off, setting up a light to reveal the media's grain, then fading it down to about 20%. She often switches back to Photoshop again to apply the finishing touches, then uses the map as the basis for the grayscale bump and specularity maps.

Laura enjoys using Fractal Painter's watercolor tool for staining things. A small spattering brush "dipped" in burnt sienna makes good mold spots on cardboard or paper. After applying the spatters, she grays out the color and enlarges the brush, then squiggles it around the perimeter of the stains to create the fuzzy white mold.

She makes use of specular maps to vary the shininess of a surface, adjusting it where the object has been damaged or stained. For example, a shiny leather briefcase shouldn't be shiny where it is scuffed or scratched, so she modifies the bump map and uses it a specularity map.

Laura also relies on procedural maps, which can be very fast and powerful. They also can be real time savers when dealing with an object that the camera gets very close to in an animation, because they don't become pixellated or "break down" the way bitmapped textures can. They also are convenient because they don't require mapping coordinates to be applied to an object (which can be a real lifesaver with a complex organic object, or one you need to map quickly).

Laser digitized mesh offers some special challenges. For a model of a 3D character named Chavo, a physical sculpture was created by a local artist then scanned by CyberWare in Monterey, CA. The sculpture was scanned in pieces which had to be reassembled once the objects were digitized. The pulling and stretching of the mesh during reassembly caused some loss of information in the joint areas. There were no mapping coordinates, so the model had to be separated into multiple pieces again to work with the planar mapping scheme. Laura used Mesh Paint to apply reference marks to the map, letting her know where details like the facial features were.

Using the Render/Retouch Method

The *render and retouch* approach Laura often uses for creating custom maps is a popular technique that makes a big difference in the quality and believability of your work. It makes it possible to add properly positioned details, stains, graffiti, or what have you to an object. Here are the basic steps:

1. Construct the mesh and apply mapping coordinates (see figure 6.32a).

2. Apply materials to the objects in your scene, adjusting them until the overall color scheme and look fits your needs. Using the non-perspective (orthogonal) viewports, render a close-up of the object on which you want to do additional mapping work, and save the file to disk (see figure 6.32b).

3. Load the render into a paint program and crop it, removing any portions of the image that you don't plan to re-apply to an object. Make the desired alterations and enhancements to the image, such as adding wear, stains, graffiti, text, additional details, altering the color balance, and so forth, then save the file for use as a new map (see figure 6.32c).

4. Back in the 3D program, add the enhanced image to a copy of the original material. Use the modified map as the base for creating any bump, shininess, opacity, or other maps required, and include them in the material as well.

5. If necessary, break the object up by detaching faces, and use planar mapping so that the enhanced image will fit the object perfectly. Render the scene, and make any corrections to the map until you're satisfied with the results (see figure 6.33d).

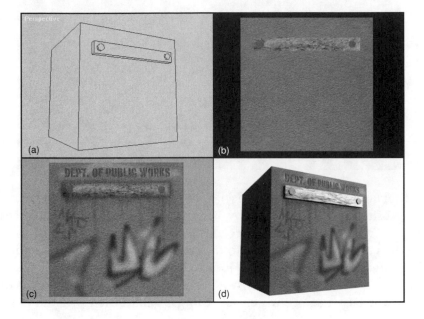

FIGURE 6.32

Using the render/retouch method:
(a) Build the objects and apply mapping coordinates to them.
(b) Apply basic materials and render an orthogonal view.
(c) Crop out anything not needed for the new map, and use a paint program to add additional details.
(d) Re-map the object (detaching faces if necessary) with the enhanced map.

Seamless Tiling

Earlier in the chapter, you saw how small bitmaps can be repeated to create large tiled textures. While many texture libraries offer seamlessly tilable bitmaps, you will probably need to create your own as well. Tiled textures are frequently used for mapping large objects that are made out of a material like brick or steel plates (see figure 6.33).

The main problem with creating a tiled texture is that distracting color and value patterns usually show up when a bitmap is tiled. These patterns or seams are often difficult to anticipate when working on a single tile, so you usually have to either repeat the pattern in the paint program, or apply the texture in the 3D package and render to see the results.

The simplest way to make a seamless tiling texture is to use your paint program to mirror an image horizontally, then mirror the new image vertically. At that point, you can paint extra details and variation in the image, but stay clear of the pixels at the edges. However, you will probably still notice unwanted patterns.

FIGURE 6.33

A custom-painted boilerplate texture map from Critical Path. It was designed to be seamlessly tiled over the surface of a huge furnace.

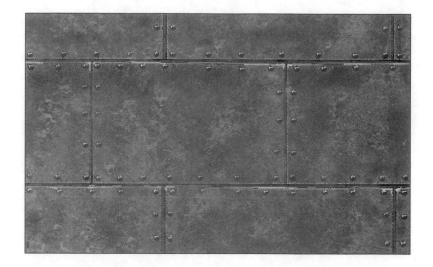

Another method is to use the Offset filter with Wrap Around Edges turned on in Photoshop to shift the image by 50% vertically and horizontally (see figure 6.34). This places what was the corner of the image in the center, and wraps the edges of the image around to meet each other. This enables you to see what the edges of the texture will look like when tiled, and do any retouching necessary to get rid of the seams. When it looks good, just hit Cmd- or Ctrl-F to do the Offset again, which sets things back to their original positions.

FIGURE 6.34

Using the Offset feature of Photoshop is a good way to locate potential seams and fix them without having to apply the texture in a 3D program.

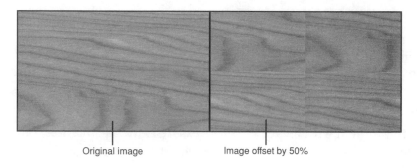

Original image   Image offset by 50%

Another method of creating some incredible tiled textures is with Xaos Tools' Terrazzo, a plug-in for Macintosh Photoshop which performs automatic tiling on selected portions of existing bitmaps.

Flat Poly Tricks

Simple 2D polygons can be used for many objects and effects in a scene, although their very lack of mesh can make it tough to manually locate and select them at times. In addition to using flat polygons for walls and floors where there is no need to see any depth to the surface, they are great for creating the illusion of more complex mesh as well.

By mapping a polygon with an image of a person, tree, or distant structure, you can populate your scene with lots of detail, but almost no increase in mesh. The polygon can either be made in the same shape as the image you plan to map on it, or you can use an opacity map to render the unmapped portions of a rectangular polygon transparent.

Note that many programs take a long time to deal with transparency, so you should try a test to see if you would be better off having the polygon follow the shape of the object rather than using opacity mapping. Remember that you may be able to create a polygon shape quickly by turning the image into a silhouette in a paint program and then using the auto-outlining feature of a draw program to create a polygon or spline outline of it. The outline can be imported into your 3D program as a shape, then mapped with the image.

These tricks can even be used if you're moving the camera around in a scene. Just animate the flat polys so that they're always perpendicular to the camera. This can sometimes be accomplished automatically if your program offers certain kinds of animation behaviors (see Chapter 9, "Animation").

Of course, the effect will look odd if the camera moves a great deal, because the orientation of the objects always remains the same, like the creatures in DOOM-type games. Another technique you can use for some naturalistic imagery is to arrange several polygons with identical images in an array that overlaps in the center of the polygon, such as in the following starfield example.

Creating 3D Star Fields

Several scenes in The Daedalus Encounter called for the view through a cockpit window as a ship traveled through space. The best way to convey a sense of movement in these scenes was to have the stars move toward the ship, then pass out of view, as when looking at the viewscreen in any *Star Trek* episode.

One way to do this is with the starfield generator in Autodesk Animator or using some other utility to create starfields. A drawback to this method is that you're generally limited to a straight-ahead movement, with no turning or variation in speed. Artist Andy Murdock came up with a novel method, creating a cluster of simple stars in 3D Studio through which a camera could be navigated.

Andy started by building a small square polygon and applying an opacity map of a star, basically a filled white circle on a black background to it (see figure 6.35). This "trimmed off" the square edges of the polygon during rendering and left a white dot. The polygon was set to be a two-sided, self-illuminated material, so now the star appeared to shine regardless of lighting. The problem with using a single polygon for a star is that if the camera wasn't positioned perpendicular to the polygon, the circle would be squashed and might even disappear when rendering.

FIGURE 6.35

The star opacity map, applied to a single square polygon. Black areas are transparent, while white ones are opaque.

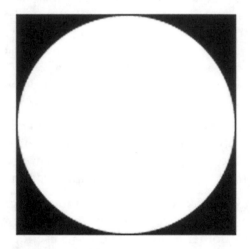

Andy solved this by duplicating the polygon two times and positioned them together, each polygon centered on a different (X, Y, Z) axis (see figure 6.36). The polygons were then attached to form a single object. The result was a simple three-plane object that appeared to be a self-illuminated star when viewed from any angle.

The next problem was distributing the stars. The bare-bones method would have been to manually position a group of stars, scaling them slightly and perhaps adjusting the materials to create some variation. The group would then be duplicated and copied a number of times to create a field of the desired size and density.

Image Gallery

Figure I.1
Frog image created with StudioPaint 3D by David Hornick, courtesy of Alias/Wavefront.

Figure I.2
Wolf image courtesy of Sierra On-line.

Figure I.3
Pixi. Created with LightWave software. Image ©1996
Mike Beals.

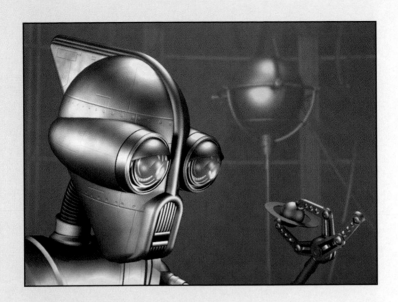

Figure I.4

Robot image created with Kinetix 3D Studio MAX. Image © 1996
Richard Green/Artbot.

Figure I.5

Mechanized warrior image from Wet Corpse. Courtesy of Kronos
Digital Entertainment.

Figure I.6

Boiler Room from Zork:Nemesis. Image by "Goose Ramirez" and Mark Giambruno from a design by Cody Chancellor/Mondo Media. ©1996 Activision.

Figure I.7

Ballroom from Zork:Nemesis. Image by Andy Murdock, with elements by Matt Smiley and Mark Giambruno/Mondo Media. ©1996 Activision.

Figure I.8
Dragon. Created with 3DS R4 and MetaBalls. Image ©1996
Vadim Pietrzynski.

Figure I.9
Capoccia. Image © Alvise Avati/Immagini Interattive.

Figure I.10
Architectural walkthrough created with Alias. Image ©1996 Ruieta DaSilva and Deanan Da Silva/Digital Illusion.

Figure I.11
Flight. Spline model created with Animation Master software. Image ©1995 Stephen C. Chan/Chanime Interactive.

Figure I.12
Watch image created with Alias/Wavefront Studio. Image ©1996
Joan Lindblad.

Figure I.13
Fly3. Image ©1996 Andrew M. Phelps.

Figure I.14

Microcassette Recorder. Created with Caligari trueSpace.
Image ©1995 Oliver Zeller.

Figure I.14

Heritage. Created with Animation Master on a PowerPC-
based Macintosh. Image ©1996 Mike Caputo.

Figure I.15
Koi. Image courtesy of Strata, Inc.

Figure I.16
Lobby from Zork:Nemesis. Image by Marco Bertoldo, with elements
by Peter Herrman and Sebastian Hyde/Mondo Media ©1996 Activision.

Figure I.17
Magic Room. Created with Kinetix 3D Studio R4. Image
© 1996 AniMagicians.

Figure I.18
Map Room. Created in 3DS R4 especially for this book. Image by
Aaron Shi, Ken Lee, and William Bobos/AniMagicians ©1996
AniMagicians.

Figure I.19
Lost at Sea. Created with LightWave 5.0, with post-rendering work done in Photoshop and Fractal Painter. Image ©1996 John P. Roberts.

Figure I.20
Planto. Created with 3D Studio R4, MetaBalls, and BonesPro. Image ©1995 Vadim Pietrzynski.

Figure I.21

Play. Created with Infini-D on the Macintosh. Image ©1996
Marina Luderer.

Figure I.22

Rainbow. Image ©1996 Eric Chadwick.

Figure I.23
Alien restroom image created with 3DS R4 for the CD-ROM game The
Daedalus Encounter. Image by Mechadeus ©1995 Virgin Interactive
Entertainment.

Figure I.24
Sektor 3. Image ©1996 James Mahan.

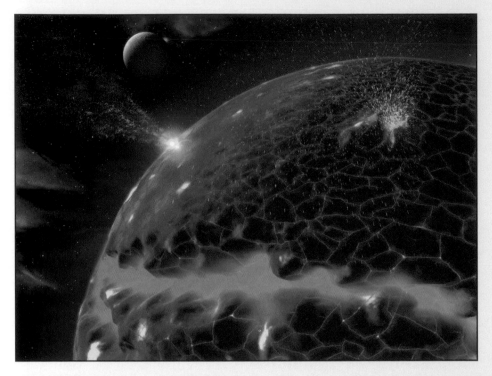

Figure I.25
Solar. Created with Kinetix 3D Studio MAX. Image by Andy Murdock.
©1996 Mechadeus.

Figure I.26
Torture chamber from Zork:Nemesis. Image by David
Horowitz and Mark Giambruno, from designs by Cody
Chancellor/Mondo Media. ©1996 Activision.

Figure I.27

Asylum catwalk area from Zork:Nemesis. Image by Mark Giambruno and Laura Hainke/Mondo Media. ©1996 Activision.

Figure I.28

Factory image from the CD-ROM game Critical Path. Image by Mechadeus. ©1994 Virgin Interactive Entertainment.

Figure I.29
CyberDog fossil image created with 3D Studio R4 and Photoshop. Image ©1996 Laura Hainke.

Figure I.30
Darcron spaceraft/city close-up image from Sinkha. Image by Marco Patrito/Virtual Views. ©1995-96 Mohave.

FIGURE 6.36

Three intersecting opacity-mapped polygons were used make up a single star, which could be viewed from any angle.

Fortunately, the Yost Group's Scatter plug-in for 3D Studio could do this automatically, distributing hundreds of copies of the selected objects (in random sizes, if desired) over the exterior of any object that the artist defined. In this case, Andy applied the star objects to two large spheres, then deleted the spheres, leaving only the starfield. The resulting stars were combined into a single object for convenience.

The next step was to determine the camera path through the starfield, making sure it looked natural and deleting any stars that ended up too close to the camera. The starfield animation was rendered with motion blur activated to enhance the feeling of speed.

Incorporating Video into Materials

The ability to use animated files or video as a texture enables you to integrate live action elements into your materials. One obvious application is in rendering a scene that has control panels filled with flashing lights and video monitors. Animated files also are very useful for special effects like explosions, fire, smoke, and so forth.

Blazing CDs

The *Pyromania!* CD-ROMs from movie effects house VCE, Inc., contain footage of numerous explosions, fire, and smoke effects. All of the footage was photographed against a black background, then digitized and reduced to

640×480 resolution and saved as a series of sequential files on the CD-ROMs. Also included are downsized versions of the files converted to QuickTime movies for quick viewing of the effect.

One way to apply a *Pyromania* effects sequence to your work is to use a digital editing program (Premiere, After Effects, Composer, and so on) to add the effect in post-production. Another method is to convert the files into a format that can be directly used by your 3D animation program and incorporate the effect as a mapped polygon. This is the preferred method for several reasons, but is practically a must if the camera is moving during the effect.

Mapping the effect onto a flat or curved polygon requires the creation of an opacity map because most of the files don't come with an alpha channel.

How this is done will vary with the requirements of your 3D animation system. In some cases, you can simply use the same files or movie in the opacity channel and tweak the controls until the black background becomes transparent. In other cases, the use of a digital editing program or batch processing feature of a graphic file converter (DeBabelizer, Hijack and their ilk) may be used to generate an alpha channel or to palletize the images and replace the black background with your program's "transparent" color. The *Pyromania* CD-ROMs include some information on using Photoshop's Curves feature to remove the background, as well as information on other controls that can smooth out the matte lines.

Video Faces on 3D Mesh

You may find a technique we used in The Daedalus Encounter to place the actor's faces inside 3D spacesuits useful for mixing live video elements into your 3D scenes.

At one point in the game, the story calls for Ari (Tia Carrere) and Zack (Christian Bocher) to don spacesuits and cross over to an alien ship. After our costumer conducted an extensive but unsuccessful search for believable rental suits, we went with my backup plan, which was to create the suits in 3D and use animated texture maps for the character's faces.

Using 3D models had some big advantages anyway, in that we could fly the characters around without having to employ expensive and dangerous flying rigs on the actual set. It also enabled us to design the suits any way we wanted, so they would have a look that matched the other Terran Alliance technology.

Scott Baker designed and built the suits using Alias Animator running on our Silicon Graphics Indigo 2 Extreme system, which has an excellent modeler for this type of work. I took photos of the actors' heads during the shoot and Scott adjusted head models that came with Alias so the models matched the sizes and shapes of Tia's and Christian's heads.

On the set, we had the actors sit down in the cockpit chairs and put pads behind their heads to brace them. The idea was to have the actors say their lines without moving their heads, and then map this live-action video onto the animated 3D heads. It was very difficult for Tia and Christian to remain completely still, as actors instinctively want to move when acting.

When the time came to animate these sequences, the video was cut down to the exact length of the shot and turned into an Autodesk Animator file (called a .FLC file) that 3D Studio could use. The animator had to not only move the arms and legs of the suit, but also turn the 3D heads inside the suits in concert with where the actors were looking at the moment as well as with what they were saying.

Overall, the effect worked very well, and the only downside to our 3D approach was that we couldn't show the real actors taking off the suits without a great deal of very tricky animation that wouldn't be worth the effort. That scene worked around the problem by using live action close-ups and other editing tricks.

General Mapping Tips

The following are some miscellaneous suggestions to help you make professional maps:

◆ Complex objects can be very difficult to map with the usual planar, cylindrical, or spherical mapping systems. If possible, apply the mapping coordinates when you're skinning or lofting the object.

◆ Use dirt and wear to give your objects realism and "a history." Even a clean surface looks more realistic if it has some subtle mottling (after all, no surface is perfect) and remember to vary the specularity maps as well.

◆ Separating (or duplicating and offsetting) the faces on a section of an object enables you to apply custom details to that area while giving the illusion that it's just part of the rest of the surface. This is particularly useful if all of your map layers are used up or your program doesn't have adequate decal support.

◆ If you can't duplicate faces and need to apply another map layer when none is available, try making a simple polygon and positioning it close to the other mesh. Apply the texture to the polygon and use an opacity map to make the unneeded portions transparent.

◆ Give yourself enough time for mapping. It often takes equal amounts of time to model and map objects.

◆ Use a map whenever possible, rather than building geometry. It will speed up your renders and save you time in the modeling stage.

◆ Do test renders at the point where the camera gets closest to the mesh to make sure the resolution of the maps is adequate.

◆ Rendering a scene from a plan or elevation view makes a good starting point for mapping. You also can use a render of a mapped object as a guide for mapping another object to ensure that the maps line up properly.

◆ If you're doing low polygon count modeling, you may want to construct your model and map at a higher resolution first, then render it to create the maps for the low-res version. The subtle shading added to the maps will help make them look smoother on the low poly model.

◆ Be careful that your mapping coordinates are applied relative to the front surface of the object, otherwise the indentations in your bump map will appear to protrude instead of recede.

- Projector lights are a good way to add decal-like textures to a procedurally-mapped object, or one that has used up the map channels.

- The images you create will vary from system to system, mostly due to the monitors. Check your work on a monitor similar to the one the end user is likely to have (usually a low-to-mid range unit). Note that scenes created on Macs often appear darker when ported to PCs, probably due to differences in the gamma of the monitors (see Chapter 10, "Rendering and Output," for more information).

Mapping Tutorials

Topics covered:

> **Using Base Materials**
>
> **Using Procedural Materials**
>
> **Applying Mapping Coordinates**
>
> **Creating Mapped Materials**
>
> **Using Opacity Maps**
>
> **Using the Render/Paint/Map Technique**
>
> **Using Decals**
>
> **Using Animated Maps**

Now that you've constructed most of the blimp, it's time to apply some color and texture to it. This is an excellent opportunity to experiment, so feel free to make your blimp's materials totally different from the ones outlined here.

Like 3D modeling commands, the material editing terminology and features vary from product to product. If the options or settings given in the tutorials are not available in your software, use your manuals and some experimentation to achieve a similar effect.

Using Base Materials

Most of the blimp model will use either mapped or procedural materials, but a few objects will use only the basic surface attribute settings. These objects are the visible searchlight beams, the running lights, and the gondola window.

1. In the material editing section of your software, create a material called RunLite with the following settings: RGB Color: 255, 255, 191. Self-Illumination 100%. Opacity 100%. Additive Transparency. No Falloff. 2-sided. Select all the Run*Xxxnn* objects and apply this material. Do a test render to see if the running lights are now self-illuminated, slightly yellowish objects (see figure 6.37).

2. Create a material called SrcBeam and use these settings: Color: 255, 255, 255. Self-Illumination 100%. Opacity 40%. Additive Transparency. Falloff Outward 100%. 2-sided. Select the SrcBea01 object and apply this material. Do a test render to see if the searchlight is now self-illuminated, and seems brighter in the center.

3. Copy the SrcBeam material and rename the copy Window. Change the Color to 255, 255, 191, and the Opacity to 60%. Select the window in the gondola and apply it. Do a test render to see if the window is now self-illuminated.

FIGURE 6.37

Apply self-illuminated base materials to the running lights, searchlight beam, and gondola window.

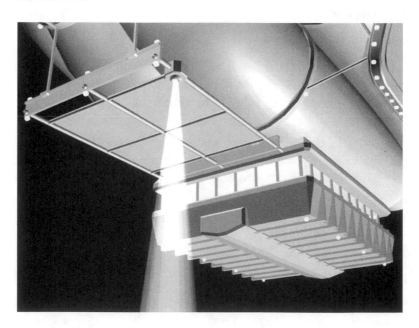

Using Procedural Materials

For ease and reduced rendering times, procedurals will be used for mapping the skin of the ship and most of the other mesh, including the gondola, catwalks, and so forth. Two different procedural materials are needed: a mottled green-gray rubber-like skin for the gasbag, and a procedural rust for most of the metal objects. First, the gas bag material:

1. Create a procedural texture map (using noise or fractals) with the colors 40, 58, 46 and 103, 108, 106 or whatever you like. Set Shininess between 10 and 30. Name the material BagTextr, and apply the material to the GasBag object. Because it's a procedural, no mapping coordinates are required. Render the results, and adjust the noise size to achieve mottling similar to the figure (see figure 6.38).

2. Create another procedural texture with the colors 89, 51, 42 and 143, 121, 110 or similar. Set Shininess to 0. Add some noise to the Bump channel as well, to make the material look pitted. Name the material Rust, and apply the material to the Gondola, except the window. Render the results, and adjust the noise size to achieve mottling similar to the figure.

3. When you're satisfied with the look of the Rust material, apply it to the other metal surfaces on the model, except the thrusters and objects that already have textures applied.

FIGURE 6.38

Apply procedural textures to the blimp skin and metal portions of the model. Procedurals don't require mapping coordinates, which saves a lot of time.

Using Decals

Next, add some banners and signs on the skin of the blimp using decals.

> If your program doesn't offer decals, there's an alternative. You could select a group of faces on the side of the GasBag object and use Detach Faces to turn them into separate objects that you could map individually.

1. Using Photoshop or similar paint program, create a couple of small (128 × 128 pixels or less) signs for your blimp project. Consider using your name or company name, helping to underscore it when a prospective employer looks at your work. You also can use scanned images if desired. In keeping with the overall worn and scruffy feel of the blimp, you may want to fade the colors somewhat and even add some dirt to them (see figure 6.39).

FIGURE 6.39

Create signs and banners in Photoshop to advertise your services, reflect your interests, or just to look interesting. Weather the signs by reducing their saturation and working them over with an airbrush.

2. Following the decal methodology outlined in your software manuals, place the decals on the right side of the ship. Two are shown here, but many more are recommended. Unless your software offers interactive positioning, render the GasBag object and adjust the decal parameters to reduce stretching and tweak the positions (see figure 6.40).

Applying Mapping Coordinates

Objects that use mapped materials require mapping coordinates. This tutorial will cover three of the common ones: planar, cylindrical, and spherical. Make sure you apply appropriate coordinates to other objects requiring image maps.

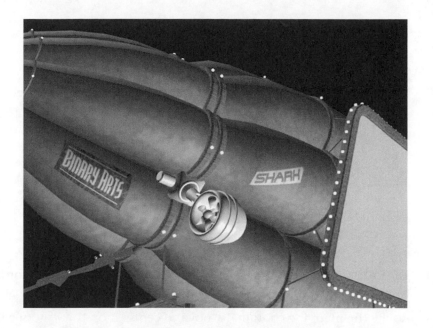

FIGURE 6.40

Add signs and banners
to the GasBag object
using the decal
methods outlined in
your manuals. Many
programs allow 16–32
decals per object.

Normally, you want to apply mapping coordinates as you create each piece of mesh, so that when you duplicate them, all the copies are ready for mapping as well. Because it was impractical to introduce mapping coordinates during the modeling tutorials, add them now to a few objects. In the future, however, make the mapping coordinate application part of your modeling process.

1. Select the object MonPnl01 from the Right viewport. Rotate it into a vertical position to make the application of coordinates easier (see figure 6.41a).

2. Apply planar mapping coordinates, using Fit if available. The mapping coordinate tool should conform to the sides of the MonPnl01 object. Make sure that the planar map is right-side up and that the coordinates are properly oriented so that the left side of the map will be displayed on the left side of the object. Usually there's some kind of indicator that shows this (see figure 6.41b). Return the object to its original position.

It isn't necessary to rotate objects to a horizontal or vertical position when applying mapping coordinates, but it can make it easier. You also can rotate the mapping coordinate tool, as you need to do in order to map the thruster strut, or use an option offered by some programs that aligns to the surface normals.

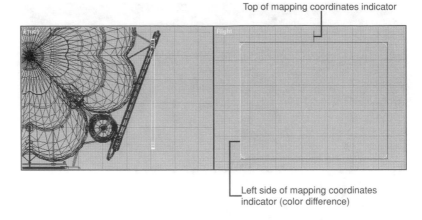

Top of mapping coordinates indicator

Left side of mapping coordinates indicator (color difference)

FIGURE 6.41

Apply planar coordinates to the monitor panel so that an image mapped material can be applied. The mapping coordinate tools often have indicators to show the orientation of the map.

3. Select the object ThrStr01 (see figure 6.42a).

4. Try to apply cylindrical mapping coordinates. Note that the coordinate tool may not be in the correct position (see figure 6.42b).

5. Rotate the mapping coordinate tool and center it on the strut (see figure 6.42c).

6. Scale the coordinate tool to conform to the strut and apply the coordinates to the object (see figure 6.42d).

FIGURE 6.42

Applying cylindrical coordinates: (a) Select the strut object. (b) Activate cylindrical mapping. (c) Rotate the tool to match the angle of the strut. (d) Scale the tool to enclose the strut and apply the coordinates.

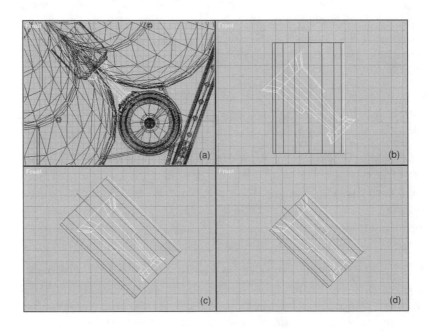

Finally, use spherical mapping coordinates to map individual objects or groups of objects that will have textures applied that don't have to be oriented in any particular manner, such as Aluminum.

> Some programs may not enable you to apply a single type of mapping coordinates to a group of objects. In this case, and in general, the best approach is to apply the most appropriate type of coordinate to each object individually, depending on its shape.

7. Select the rest of the lower portion of the thruster assembly. It will be mapped as a whole (see figure 6.43a).

8. Activate the spherical mapping tool and Fit it to the selected objects. Apply the mapping coordinates to the selected objects as a whole (see figure 6.43b).

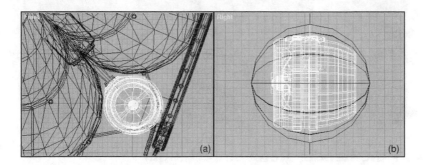

FIGURE 6.43

Applying spherical coordinates to the thruster: (a) Select the lower thruster assembly. (b) Position the spherical mapping tool in the center of the selected objects and apply the coordinates to all selected objects at once.

Adjusting Library Materials

Often, you will find a material in your software's material library that will work as-is for an object. In other cases, you may be able to make slight modifications to turn one material into another. For this example, you create a dirty aluminum finish for the lower thruster nose assembly.

1. Check your material library for a reflective material, such as chrome, that you can use as the starting point. If one isn't available, start with a default material and load REFMAP.GIF from the CD-ROM as a reflection map at 100%. Adjust the material type to Metal shading and set the Shininess between 70–90. Apply the material to the lower thruster assembly you just put coordinates on, and render the results (see figure 6.44a).

2. To make the highly-reflective chrome into a dull aluminum, make the diffuse color a medium gray, then reduce the reflection map setting to about 40%, allowing the gray to show through. Reduce the shininess of the material to about 40 or until it has a dull metallic look. You may want to add some noise to the Bump channel to make the metal look pitted. Reapply the material to the thruster assembly (if required) and render the results (see figure 6.44b). Keep tweaking the material until you're happy with it.

3. You may want to create variations on the dull aluminum, making it darker or lighter, or create some completely different materials (brushed bronze, copper, galvanized steel, etc.) and apply them to individual components of the lower thruster assembly. By using a greater variety of materials, the results are more interesting and realistic.

FIGURE 6.44

Modifying a library material: (a) Apply a typical chrome texture to the lower thruster assembly. (b) Adjust the surface attributes of the material to create a dull, dirty aluminum look.

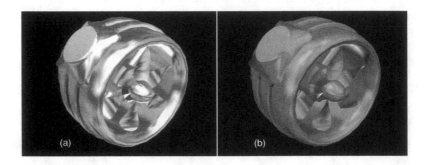

Using the Render/Retouch Technique

Use a variation on the render/retouch technique to create a custom bump map for the strut. This will add additional interest to the object without doing more mesh work.

1. Hide everything in the scene except the ThrStr01 strut object. Rotate it upright and render it in a close-up, then save the render to the hard drive as a 8-bit or 24-bit file (see figure 6.45a).

2. Using Photoshop, load up the render and select the black background (note that you also could render the image with an alpha channel, and then load that channel as a selection when in Photoshop). Invert the selection and fill the object with a medium gray. Crop the image down to the edges of the object outline (see figure 6.45b).

3. Draw some lines and shapes on top of the object, using the outline of the object as a guide to where they will fall when mapped onto the strut. Use different levels of gray to vary the bump amplitude, or height, of the variations (see figure 6.45c).

4. If this were to be a planar map, you could just map the image back on as-is. Because it's a cylindrical map, however, it has to be set up to tile around the perimeter of the object. Do this by selecting a portion of the detail you have created and copying it horizontally across the image, or you could also use the Photoshop tiling filter to accomplish the same thing (see figure 6.45d). Note that another way to do this is to crop the image down to a single tiling section, and use the tiling commands in the mapping coordinate controls to tile the map.

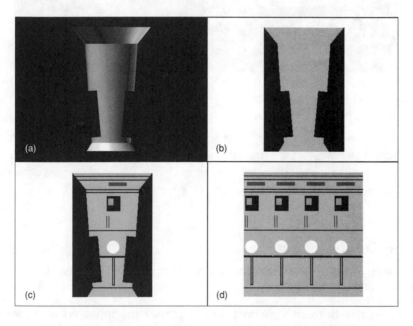

FIGURE 6.45

The render/retouch technique: (a) Render the object. (b) If you need to start clean, fill the object with a solid color. (c) Paint bump details using the object as a guide. (d) Tiling the details for use as a cylindrical map.

5. Back in your 3D program, copy the dull aluminum material and add the custom bump map to it. Set the Bump amplitude to 100%. Map this new material onto the strut and render the results (see figure 6.46).

6. If you need to adjust the position of the map on the object, you can rotate the mapping coordinate tool, or use the UVW mapping settings in the material editor to offset it.

FIGURE 6.46

The thruster strut
textured with the custom
bump map.

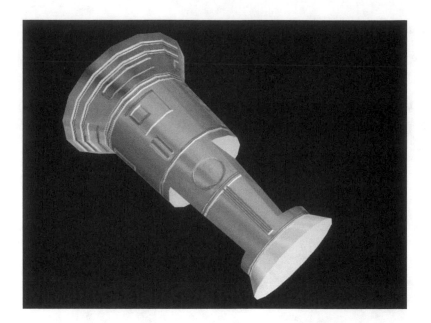

Consider using the render/paint/map technique demonstrated earlier in the chapter to do custom mapping on the gondola. To do this, render the gondola from different orthogonal views and paint on top of the rust texture, but leave it mostly intact. Crop the images down and re-map them onto the gondola objects (you'll have to detach groups of faces to do this).

Using Opacity Maps

Use opacity mapping to turn the flat panel on top of the catwalk into a metal grid.

1. From the Bottom viewport, apply planar mapping coordinates to the object CatGrd01.

2. Copy the Rust material and name the duplicate RustGrid.

3. Create a tilable black and white cross-hatched map to use as an opacity map, or load the map CROSHTC2.TGA from the CD-ROM into the opacity channel of the material and set it to 100% (see figure 6.47a).

4. Apply the RustGrid material to the object CatGrd01.

5. Render the object and adjust the UV tiling settings until the results are similar to the figure (see figure 6.47b).

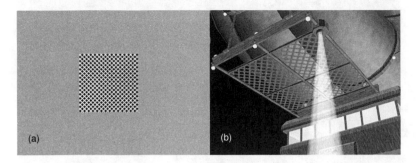

(a)   (b)

FIGURE 6.47

Using opacity mapping: (a) Create a black-and-white tilable cross-hatch. (b) Modify a copy of the Rust material with the opacity map and apply it to the flat panel above the catwalk. The opacity mapping makes the panel look like a wire mesh.

Using Animated Maps

To bring the monitor to life, use an animated map. This could be an earlier render of yours saved as a set of sequentially numbered .TGA files, an .FLC animation, or an AVI or QuickTime file or a clip of digitized video. You also may want to use Premiere to cut together a series of images and animations with wipes and effects for a true advertisement-like feel. Remember that your animation will loop if it's shorter than the animation you're rendering, so make sure that the looping will be seamless if this is the case.

1. Create a material using one of your own animated works as the diffusion map. Set the shininess high if you don't want the image to get washed out when light strikes it in a certain way.

2. Apply the material to the object MonPnl01.

3. Render a still of the scene to check if the mapping coordinates were properly applied. They can sometimes be reversed when dealing with planar mapping (see figure 6.48).

4. To see the full effect, render an animation with the same number of frames as your animated map.

At this point, all objects in the scene should be mapped. If any were missed, select the objects and apply the appropriate material to them.

Note

FIGURE 6.48

Using an animation file for the monitor panel map will add extra movement and life to the scene, even if the blimp is sitting still at the moment.

Summary

In some ways, 3D is becoming more and more like desktop publishing was a few years ago, with the technology coming into everyone's grasp. Now *everyone* is using it. Setting your work apart in this increasingly competitive field will depend not only on your modeling skills, but also on having the ability to create or modify textures that make your mesh sing. To aid you in this task, this chapter took a look at the basics of material creation, then went on to explore mapping coordinate systems and various techniques for obtaining and creating custom maps, including the important render/ retouch method.

The next chapter explores the basics of lighting, and how it can be used to add drama and interesting effects to your 3D objects and scenes.

7

Lighting

Cherubs, an image that makes use of volumetric lighting capabilities of Kinetix 3D Studio
MAX. Image by Jose Maria de Espona of TripleFactor, located in Madrid, Spain.

*T*he storm raged around the keep, assaulting the stonework with sheets of rain as the student labored within on his miniature version of the castle. The modeling was complete, and now he had moved on to setting up the lights. Unfortunately, the scene looked very flat, and the student wished he'd asked some questions of the Master before he had retired for the evening.

As if on cue, a shadow fell across the student and his work, and the lad looked up with a smile. "Master, I..." At that moment, a bolt of lightning stuck just outside the keep, silhouetting the figure in a blinding blue-white aura. The craggy face of the Master gazed down at the student, dramatically underlit by the candle clutched in his aged hands. The old man's eyes were ablaze with orange fire.

"Gaaa!" cried the student, falling back in his chair and sprawling onto the floor.

The old man chuckled. "Sorry for the dramatic entrance, lad." The Master set the candle aside. "But it appears your project could do with a little drama."

"That's for sure." The student dusted himself off and settled in again. "Everything looks so...flat!"

"I'm afraid your choice of the weather conditions and time of day is to blame for that," the old man said. "You've lit the scene with what appears to be hazy mid-morning sun, which is common enough, but none too interesting. Here, let's clear the atmosphere a bit and set the lighting to around sunset." The student nodded as he watched the shadows in the scene darken and grow long. The castle took on a reddish tint from the sunlight peeking over the hilly virtual terrain.

"Ah, what a difference," the young man observed, "just from changing the light."

"Indeed," replied the Master. "Light is as much a tool as the virtual forms themselves. Now, to make the scene even more dramatic, we'll get rid of the sun all together." With that, the sun set completely on the scene, and the castle model was plunged into darkness. "Hmmm. Seems your castle is not a very lively place in the evening, lad."

"I see... I guess I'll make some torches, and light the castle with those. That will be a lot more interesting, with all the different shadows that will be cast."

"Now you've got it." The old man fetched his candle and prepared to rise. "Make sure you make the firelight flicker like this candle, and you might want to add a touch of moonlight to show off the rest of the model. I think you'll find the mixture of warm and cool colors that results quite pleasing." The old man got up and ambled toward the door.

"Thanks, Master," the lad called after him. "That was very illuminating."

"Yeesh," the elder groaned, "don't quit your day job."

Principles of Light

The none-too-subtle moral of the medieval yarn is that lighting has a big impact on the appearance of your final renderings. Flat, shadowless lighting is dull and lifeless, whereas multi-source, shadowy lighting is generally more realistic and much more dramatic. Before you can make lighting work for you, however, you must understand how light itself works.

As you no doubt remember from high-school science class, visible light is composed of a spectrum of colors running from red to violet. When light rays strike an object, some of these colors are absorbed by the material, while others are reflected. The amount and color of the light reflected from objects enable us to see them as red, or lime green, or "that disgusting tooth-gritting purple."

Computer displays, because they're generally viewed by producing light rather then reflecting it, use the additive color model, in which white light consists of equal amounts of red, green, and blue light. If the level of one of these three colors drops slightly below the others, the result is something other than white.

Color temperature is a scale used to differentiate between these near-white spectrums of light. Color temperature is measured in degrees Kelvin, which refers to what temperature a black object must be heated to in order to have it radiate that particular spectrum of colors. This has nothing to do with the operating temperature of light sources, however—it's just a scientific scale of reference.

What color temperature does from a practical standpoint is indicate the warmth or coolness of the light in terms of color. Note that the scale is counter-intuitive, however. For example, cool (meaning bluish) fluorescent lights are rated at 4000 K, while typical warm (yellowish) incandescent lamps are 2900 K. Quantifying color temperature can be helpful at times when you want maximum color accuracy, because our eyes tend to consider the main source of illumination to be *white* regardless of whether it is noon sunlight (5000 K) or a halogen desk lamp (3300 K). However, when the image is output, the color differences may become more noticeable.

Another important element of light is *intensity,* the brightness of the source or reflection. The angle at which a light ray strikes a surface and is reflected into our eyes (called the *angle of incidence*) has an effect on how brightly the object appears to be illuminated from our perspective. For example, if you hold a flashlight in front of your face and point it along your line of sight at a *very* smooth, flat surface, most of the light is reflected back into your eyes, and the surface seems brightly lit. If, however, you stand at a 45 degree angle to the surface, it will appear darker because much of the light is being reflected away from you (see figure 7.1).

FIGURE 7.1

The effect of angle of incidence on apparent brightness: (a)A surface lit and viewed at 90 degree angle. (b)The same surface lit and viewed at 45 degree angle.

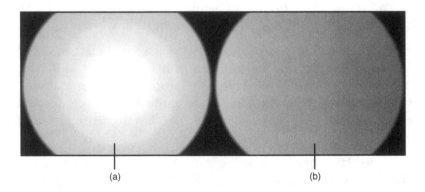

(a)   (b)

Light reflecting off an object goes on to illuminate other objects as well, an effect called *radiosity*. The cumulative effect of all the light bouncing off all the objects in an area is called *ambient light*. This ambient light has no discernible source or direction, but acts to illuminate everything in the scene more or less equally.

Another property of light is that it becomes weaker with distance, which is called *attenuation*. This occurs because the atmosphere is full of tiny particles that block and reflect the light rays. Larger particles like those in smoke and fog dramatically increase the effect, while attenuation occurs to a much lesser extent in space, because there are far fewer particles to block the light rays.

3D Lighting Basics

3D programs seek to duplicate the behavior of light in the real world, in order to make 3D scenes appear as natural and realistic as possible. This also helps to make lighting somewhat instinctive, especially if you have experience with setting up lights for photography work.

Key, Fill, and Ambient Lighting

There are three main types of lighting in photography—key, fill, and ambient—and the principles carry over into 3D programs as well (see figure 7.2). To help understand these lighting types in 3D terms, imagine you modeled a scene of your desk.

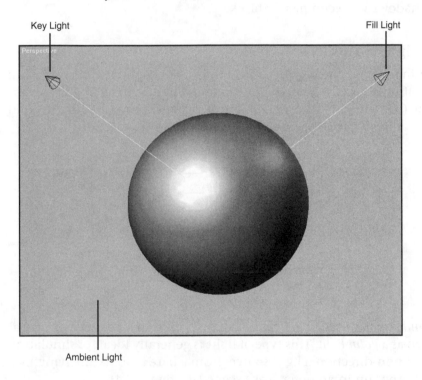

Key Light

Fill Light

Ambient Light

FIGURE 7.2

The three main types of lighting are key light (the main source of illumination), fill light (to bring out details from the shadows), and ambient light (which surrounds the object).

The *key light* is the main source of illumination in the scene, and casts the most apparent shadows. In an outdoor scene, the key light is the sun. Indoors, it's the primary light source, which might be sunlight coming through a window, a nearby lamp, or an electronic flash on a camera. In the imaginary desk scene, you can think of the key light as your bright halogen desk lamp, washing across the keyboard and casting sharp shadows.

The *fill light*, as the name implies, fills in the dark shadows cast by the key light. Fill light in an outdoor scene has to be created artificially, while indoors, it comes from a secondary source of illumination, like distant windows or light fixtures. In our desk example, think of the fill light as the big floor lamp sitting across the room, throwing a soft, even illumination out in all directions.

Ambient light is not really a light source per se, but is actually the light from the key and fill lights bouncing off of walls and objects in reality. However, with the exception of the rare 3D products that use radiosity rendering, ambient light is simulated by lighting all objects in the scene by the same amount. In the desk scene, ambient light would bounce off of everything in the room, illuminating all objects to some degree, and ensuring that none of the shadows were completely black.

3D Light Sources

To mimic these three types of lighting, 3D programs offer several light-generating objects or sources. The four main light sources in 3D programs are Omni (or point) lights, directional (or distant) lights, spotlights, and the global ambient light (see figure 7.3).

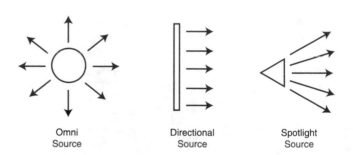

Omni Source   Directional Source   Spotlight Source

An *omni (omni-directional) light* source casts light in all directions, and also is known as a *point light*. This type of light is generally ideal for simulating any kind of non-directional light source, from a bare bulb fixture hanging in an attic to the sun in an outer space scene (see figure 7.4).

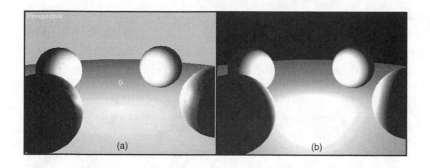

FIGURE 7.4

Omni-directional light source characteristics: (a) An omni light source (white diamond) positioned in center of scene casts light in all directions. (b) Some programs' omni sources cannot cast shadows.

Depending on the program, omni sources may not be capable of casting shadows, which might make them undesirable for use as key lights. In some cases, the light from non-shadow-casting omnis may even pass through objects to light their interiors, or other objects behind them. If this is the case, you may want to limit their use to fill light sources, adjusting them to take the edge off the dark areas in the scene. However, one advantage to this capability is that you can place the light inside a completely enclosed object (a model of a light bulb, for example), and the mesh won't interfere with the light reaching other objects.

Directional lights, also called *distant lights*, project light along one axis only, and all the beams are parallel, not unlike a laser beam. Directional lights are good for simulating sources that are very far away, such as the sun in a terrestrial scene. Because the source is so distant, it causes the light rays to be parallel, so all the shadows cast by this kind of light are parallel as well (see figure 7.5).

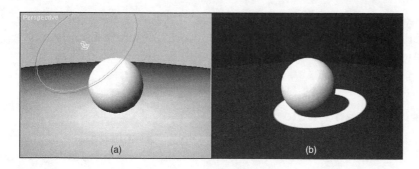

FIGURE 7.5

Directional light characteristics: (a) A directional light source, which casts parallel light rays, aimed down a sphere. (b) The resulting shadows also are parallel.

Spotlights are directional as well, but they radiate light from a single point out into a cone or pyramid the size and shape of which the user can define. As a result, neither the light rays nor shadows are parallel, as they are with a directional light source (see figure 7.6). Generally, spotlights have a target connected to the source that shows where the beam is pointed.

FIGURE 7.6

Spotlight characteristics:
(a) A spotlight source
projects a cone of light
at a sphere. (b)
Shadows created by a
spotlight radiate away
from the source.

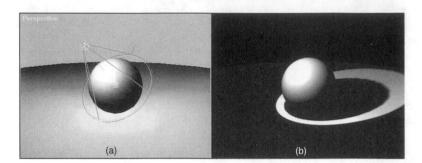

"Spots" can be used in just about any lighting situation, and can even be used to simulate shadow-casting omnis in programs that don't offer them (see the "Lighting Tips" section later in the chapter). You can use them as substitutes for directional lights in 3D programs that lack those sources by setting them far from the objects in the scene. In addition, they're great for adding small highlights and accent lighting, as well as for adding drama and realism to just about any scene.

Lighting Controls and Effects

Nearly all 3D software offers a standard set of controls for light sources, including intensity, color, and shadow settings. Some programs may provide additional controls as well, including include and exclude lists, attenuation, projection mapping, and so forth.

Brightness and Color

Intensity sets the brightness level of the source. While some programs may limit the output to a 255 white, others allow nearly infinite settings by providing a *multiplier* setting to increase the brightness as well.

> Cranking up the multiplier setting is a good way to "blow out" the highlights on an object, or to give a scene the over-exposed appearance of being lit by a blinding light source.

As noted at the beginning of the chapter, *attenuation* is the natural reduction of light intensity over a distance. Your program may offer controls for 3D light sources that enable you to define the amount of attenuation and over what distance it occurs. This control can be very useful in scenes with multiple light sources, because it enables you to limit their influence to the mesh in their vicinity only.

Some programs offer an *invert light* or *dark light* option, which makes a light shine "darkness" onto the target objects. This can help darken corners or other areas without making multiple adjustments to all of the other light sources.

Color is controlled by RGB or HSV sliders in much the same way that material colors are selected, and simulates the use of colored plastic *gels* over photography lights. The use of colored lights can give a scene a theatrical flair, complementing the material colors and adding extra interest to lit surfaces. Colored lights also can be used to create some interesting effects by blending different colored light sources together.

Using complementary colors can add an extra sense of dimension and a dramatic feel to objects, especially if they are somewhat side-lit from opposite angles, so that a shadow runs down the front of the object, keeping the colors separated.

Colored lighting doesn't have to be showy to be effective. By making subtle adjustments to the color balance of a light source, you can simulate the color temperature of an incandescent bulb, a fluorescent tube, or the sun on a hazy day.

Shadows

There are two kinds of shadows available in 3D programs: shadow mapped and ray traced (see figure 7.7).

FIGURE 7.7

Shadow types:
(a) Shadow mapping
produces natural-
looking, soft-edged
shadows. (b) Ray-
traced shadows are
sharper and more
precise.

Shadow Mapped Shadows

Shadow mapping is common in non-ray-traced (scanline) renderers. The technique works by creating a grayscale texture map based on the lighting and mesh in the scene, then applies it to the objects at render time. Mapped shadows are soft-edged and more natural than ray-traced ones, but may be blocky and inaccurate in some situations.

The blockiness can be reduced by increasing the *shadow map size* setting, which adjusts the amount of memory that the system can use to create the map. Increasing the size to 512K or 1MB can go a long way toward smoother shadows, but obviously has an impact on render time as well, especially if there are more than a few shadow maps that need this kind of resolution (see figure 7.8).

FIGURE 7.8

Effects of shadow map
size: (a) Blockiness and
smearing with a 256K
map size. (b) Increasing
the map size to 1024K
reduces the problem but
increases render times.

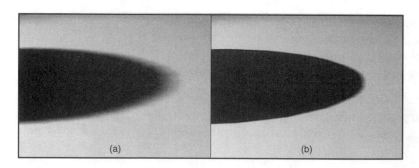

The other problem with shadow maps is that they may not be properly positioned in the scene. This most often occurs at the intersection of two objects, and the shadow of one is being cast on the other. In some cases, the shadow may be offset from the mesh intersection. Adjusting the *map bias* setting moves the shadow closer to or further from the casting object, enabling you to correct this situation.

Ray-Traced Shadows

Ray-traced shadows are defined using ray-tracing renderer techniques, but can be found in some scanline renderer products. Unlike the results of the soft-edged shadow mapping technique, ray-traced shadows have a hard edge, but are very accurate and precise. This is good for sharp, dramatic shadows, like those you would find in space or on airless worlds, such as the moon.

Although ray-traced shadows don't use maps, and therefore don't have blockiness problems, they may occasionally suffer from bias troubles like the shadow-mapped variety. Your program may have a *ray trace bias* adjustment or something similar to adjust the offset of shadows from the casting object.

Hotspot and Falloff

Most spotlights and directional lights have controls that enable you to define the concentration of light in the beam they project. Usually, the adjustments are given in degrees, and represented onscreen by two cones or pyramids that show how wide the beams are set (see figure 7.9).

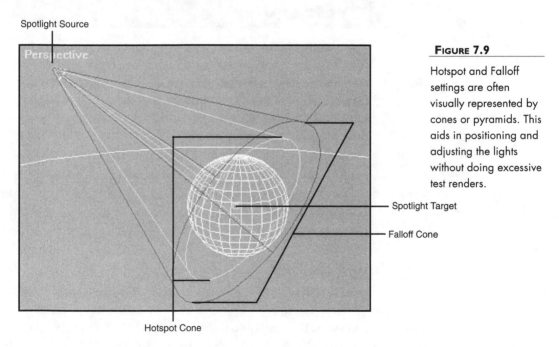

Spotlight Source

Perspective

Spotlight Target

Falloff Cone

Hotspot Cone

FIGURE 7.9

Hotspot and Falloff settings are often visually represented by cones or pyramids. This aids in positioning and adjusting the lights without doing excessive test renders.

The *Hotspot* adjustment defines the angle of the inner portion of the beam of light that is projected at the current intensity setting for that source. The *Falloff* adjustment sets the perimeter of the outer portion of the beam, indicating where the intensity has dropped all the way down to zero.

When the Hotspot and Falloff settings are within a few degrees of each other, the light appears to be sharply focused, with very little transition between full intensity and none at all. When the differences in angles are much larger, the beam looks softer, and tapers off gradually from the bright Hotspot to the edges of the beam (see figure 7.10).

FIGURE 7.10

Effects of Hotspot and Falloff sizes: (a) When Hotspot and Falloff settings are close together, the beam appears focused. (b) Widening the difference between settings makes the beam softer and more diffuse-looking.

Hotspot and Falloff settings enable you to tailor the angle and concentration of the light beams to your needs, enabling you to create the effect of a sharply focused flashlight, or a more diffuse headlight or hanging warehouse-style light.

Some programs offer settings where a selected object either casts no shadows, receives no shadows, or both. This can be useful if you need to position a light inside of an object and other special circumstances.

Include and Exclude

Some programs enable you to set up lights that will affect only certain objects that you identify. There are two ways to do this: *Include* enables you to pick a list of objects that the specified light affects, while *Exclude* is used when you want most of the objects in the scene to be affected, but you want to select a few that should be left out.

Include and Exclude are something of a cheat, because you can't control light that way in the real world. However, because lighting is such a time-consuming process, features like this are great for fine-tuning things, and achieving difficult effects more easily. Case in point: You've set up a spotlight that creates a perfect highlight on one of the objects in your scene. Unfortunately, the spill light from that spot is shining on many other objects that you don't want illuminated in that way. The solution is to add the desired object to the Include list for that light, so that only it is affected.

> Sometimes you may be after a precise mix of highlights and general illumination on a single object, but the highlight sources are washing out the rest of the mesh. One solution is to separate the faces that you want the highlight to appear on, and include only them on the highlight source.

Projection Mapping

Some 3D programs enable you to define a spotlight as a *projector*, meaning you can add a map to the light to change its shape or cause it to throw a pattern onto objects it illuminates.

The idea of controlling the shape of light goes back to photography and film making, where steel cutouts called *gobos* are positioned in front of lights. The Bat Signal searchlight used by Gotham City is a good example of a gobo. Gobos also can be used to pattern the light in natural ways, giving the effect that a scene is being lit by the dappled sunlight filtered through a tree. In 3D terms, gobos are called *projection maps*. Unlike steel photographic gobos, however, these maps can be either grayscale patterns or full-color images (see figure 7.11).

For example, say you create a map consisting of broad horizontal bands of alternating black and white, and then apply that to a projector. When positioned to shine on an object, the map would create the illusion that the light source is being filtered through Venetian blinds. If you used an image of a stained glass window as your projection map, the scene would appear to be illuminated like the interior of a church, without going through the bother of creating a stained glass window object and mapping it, then shining a light source through it.

FIGURE 7.11

Projection map
samples: (a) Star-
shaped gobo,
(b) venetian blinds,
(c) tree branches,
(d) full-color or gray-
scale images can also
be used.

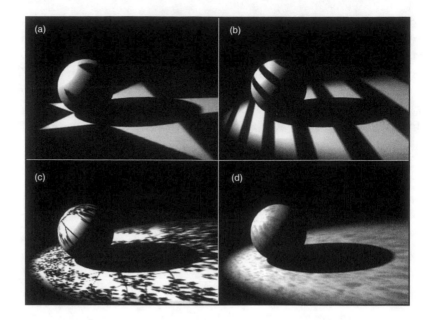

 Projection maps can have some unusual applications, such as acting as another form of texture map. In The Daedalus Encounter, there was a scene where a small ship had smashed into a large alien vessel. We wanted to create skid marks on the alien ship where the craft had slid along the hull, but the procedural texture and the other mapping considerations made that difficult. The problem was solved by making a grayscale map of the skid marks and using a projection light source (set to inverted mode) to "shine" the damage onto the hull.

Lighting Strategies

Your lighting needs and procedures will vary depending on the scene you're working on, but there are a few guidelines that can help. In this section, I'll outline my own general approaches to lighting a scene and dissect an example from the Activision CD-ROM game; Zork: Nemesis.

Default Lighting

Some programs automatically provide *default lighting* in an empty scene, which usually consists of two or three omni or directional lights (shadows off), distributed around the edges of the 3D universe. This enables you to start using shaded modeling modes and doing rendering without having to add a light source (see figure 7.12). Once you do add a light source to the scene, you may want to turn off the default lights (with some programs, the default lighting will automatically be turned off when the user defines a light source).

FIGURE 7.12

Default lighting usually consists of two or three non-shadow-casting omni or directional lights arranged around the 3D universe.

For most of the modeling process, it's a good idea to stick with default lighting, or to set up 1–3 of your own shadowless omni or directional lights to illuminate the scene. At certain points, you may want to set up some shadow-casting lights to check your work, but in general, using a lot of lights (especially with shadows on) just slows you down.

Lighting Arrangements

Before discussing adding finished lighting to a scene, this section looks at some common lighting arrangements and the effects they create on the mood of an image (see figure 7.13).

Figure 7.13

Sample lighting patterns: (a) Frontal, (b) 0° side, (c) overhead, (d) backlight, (e) 45° side, (f) 45° side/front, (g) twin 45° side/front, (h) twin 0° side, (i) underlight.

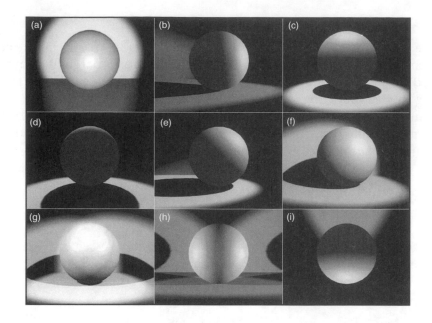

As you can see, the quantity and angle of the light has a great deal of impact, and can aid in giving character to an object. For example, frontal lighting (as in figure 7.13a) gives the impression that the viewer is holding the source of light, such as a flashlight, and the unfortunate sphere has just been caught doing something unsavory. The overhead lighting in figure 7.13c makes the sphere seem like an interrogation suspect. Backlighting an object, as in figure 7.13d, makes the object appear mysterious and potentially dangerous. The dual side lighting in figure 7.13h can be very creepy when applied to a face, and the old horror movie standard, underlighting (figure 7.13i), is always sinister.

Lighting Methodology

In general, try to use as few lights as possible to illuminate a scene. This makes it faster and easier to get the scene lit, because you aren't dealing with a myriad of lights that are all interacting with each other. If you do need to have a lot of additional lights, make sure you get the core lighting scheme worked out completely first, then add the accent lights later on.

In general, ambient light is set to a very dark gray default and is usually left alone. However, if you're working on a space scene, you may find it beneficial to turn ambient light all the way off, and make the ambient setting in your materials black as well. This, along with ray-traced shadows from a single light source, will help to create the hard-edged lighting of realistic spacecraft.

Shadow-casting spotlights generally make the best key lights, and this is often the light that you set up first, adjusting it to kick up highlights on the object surface as well as create interesting, dramatic shadows. The key light should illuminate the main subject in the scene, or even the entire scene (if it's an exterior shot lit by the sun, for example). The key light is the single most important light source, and all of the others will be adjusted to work with it, so take the time to get it just right.

The next step is to add fill light to areas that are too dark at this point, using additional spots or omni fill lights. Because fill lighting is often not represented in the scene by a recognizable light source, you may have to keep the fill light subtle, taking care that it's enhancing the appearance of the scene without drawing attention to itself. You can do this by using attenuation to control the range of the lights, using Include/Exclude, and perhaps turning off shadow-casting features as well. That way, the key light shadows will remain the primary ones in the scene (of course, if the fill light is representative of another light source, like a lamp or window, leave the shadows on). Fill light also can be used to backlight objects, giving them more dimension.

The final step in the lighting process is to add small accent lights as needed, either to represent practical but minor light sources in the scene such as indicator lamps on a control panel. (Note that it is sometimes possible to use a self-illuminated material instead of a light to keep the number of lights in a scene under control.) Another use for accent lights is to highlight secondary and background objects in the scene. Accents can add a substantial kick to an image—don't be afraid to take some artistic license in the way you use them. In other words, don't worry about where the accent light is coming from… if it looks good, no one will question it. Accent lighting also can make good use of Include and Exclude to highlight an object without revealing that there's a light source at work at all, because the surrounding mesh is unaffected.

Lighting Case Study

While working on 3D models for Mondo Media's share of Activision's *Zork: Nemesis* artwork, I was given the task of building the Asylum Catwalk area. The Asylum is a roughly cylindrical structure more than 20 floors high, with an elevator running up along the open central core (see figure 7.14). Because the Asylum was the location where all kinds of sinister research and experiments were conducted, the structure was to have a cold, hard, oppressive feeling.

FIGURE 7.14

The Asylum Catwalk area from Zork: Nemesis. Image by Mark Giambruno and Laura Hainke/Mondo Media ©1996 Activision.

For speed and ease of modification, I built the mesh in a modular fashion, with each of the three modules consisting of a wall section and a floor section. There were three kinds of walls: A plain one, one with a door, and one with an elevator shaft. All the floor sections were the same except for the one with the elevator, and included the circular railing. Each module also had one light fixture.

All the lighting was worked out with only these three modules in the scene, and much of it was refined using only one module to keep test rendering times low. Once the lighting design was completed, the modules and lights were duplicated and positioned as instanced objects, so that they only appeared when the scene was rendered.

My first concern in lighting the scene was to enhance the overall sinister mood of the place by using underlighting. I positioned a large spotlight, pointing up, in the center of the open area below the floor. I adjusted it to cast interesting shadows from the railing onto the walls, which helped break up the otherwise plain mesh. Because ray-traced shadows were too overpowering and hard-edged for the scene, I used shadow mapping. I made the map size fairly large, between 1–2MB, to keep the shadows from being too blocky.

The next step was to set up the lighting for the practical light fixtures that lined the walls. To give the impression that the fixtures were glowing, I placed omni lights with limited ranges just in front of the white tubes to wash out the edges of the fixtures and throw some light on the walls. To complete the effect, I set up spotlights above the railing and pointed them *toward the fixtures* to create a halo of light around them, including the ceiling and floor. Next, I used omni lights to illuminate the areas around the small elevator light fixtures.

The final step in lighting the scene was to set an omni light in the center of the open area, just above the floating sphere. I adjusted this to provide fill light to illuminate the dark portions of the scene so that some detail could be seen.

After completing the mapping, Laura Hainke instanced the mesh and lights from the three modules so that the scene would appear to be of an enclosed, multi-floor structure.

The catwalk scene is a good example of how you can take liberties in designing your lighting. There is no way the practical lights in the scene would create the shadows on the walls the way the key spotlighting does, but because the result looks good, no one worries about that.

Lighting Tips and Tricks

The following sections offer a few of suggestions for achieving certain effects, or working around shortcomings in your software.

Shadowless Omni Workarounds

The problem is as follows: You've got a scene that's supposed to be lit by one or more omnidirectional lights. You want dramatic shadows in the scene, but your program doesn't offer them. The solution is this: Arrange two or more shadow-casting spotlights in the same position where the omni would be located, but facing in opposite directions.

Use pyramids instead of cones to minimize overlapping, and keep the difference between the Hotspot and Falloff as small as possible for maximum evenness in the light distribution. Remember that the shadows may start to look odd if the Hotspots are set too wide, so you may need to use several lights to simulate an omni, not just two.

Visible Lights

Although light source objects are generally invisible in the finished renders, there are times when you may want the light to appear to be visible.

For example, if you were doing a render of a room lit by a bare bulb, you would want the bulb to appear to be glowing. While making the bulb object itself self-illuminated and placing the light source near it (or even inside it) will help, it still may not create the desired effect. To accomplish that, you can take one of three courses of action: First, apply a post-production glow effect to the bulb object (discussed in more detail in Chapter 10, "Rendering and Output"). Second, retouch the finished render by using an airbrush tool to spray white (or the appropriate color) over the vicinity of the bulb, making it appear to glow. Third, if your program offers it, use volumetric lighting.

As the name implies, *volumetric lights* have an adjustable 3D volume associated with them that can be made to simulate the behavior of natural light in an atmosphere. In other words, volumetric lights act as though the enclosed volume were filled with a mist or fog, and diffuse the light inside accordingly. Volumetric lights can be used to create the look of shafts of light in a dusty attic, or the headlights of a car in the fog (see figure 7.15).

Some programs offer visible light cones for spotlights that simulate volumetric lights. In addition, you can simulate visible cones by using translucent mesh. Simply make a cone of the proper diameter to fit the light fixture, then widen it to the desired diameter at the far end. The following are the material setting suggestions:

◆ Color: Adjust to approximate the color temperature of the source

◆ Self-Illumination: Maximum

◆ Transparency Level: 75–95%

◆ Transparency Type: Additive

◆ Transparency Falloff: Inward

FIGURE 7.15

Volumetric lights have an adjustable 3D volume that can simulate the effect of the beam shining through mist or smoke.

If possible, have the cone extend beyond any mesh in the room, so you never see the far end of it. If this isn't feasible, make the cone the maximum desired length and use a opacity map to make it fade out at the far end. This technique was used for the spotlights on the tutorial blimp in Chapter 6, "Texture Mapping."

Lighting Tutorials

Topics covered:

> **Using directional lights**
>
> **Using spotlights**
>
> **Using point lights**

So far, default lighting or work lights have been used for the modeling and mapping processes. While these are good for general illumination, they lack the drama needed for a strong portfolio piece (see figure 7.16).

FIGURE 7.16

Default lighting works
well for construction
purposes, but lacks the
drama that can be
achieved with shadow-
casting lights.

Using Directional Lights

Because this is a night scene, it makes sense to make the key light in the scene shine up from the ground, as though it was coming from floodlights or a city.

1. Create a large, shadow-casting directional light with a radius of about 1600 units or more to encompass the blimp. Make the color a 180, 180, 180 white with a multiplier of 1. The hotspot limits should be as close as possible to the falloff perimeter (see figure 7.17a).

2. Move the light to ground level and rotate it to shine upward at a 15 degree angle, setting it off to the side of the blimp in order to illuminate more of the subject (see figure 7.17b).

3. Mirror the light as an instance, moving the copy to the opposite side of the blimp (see figure 7.17c).

4. Render the scene and adjust the lighting parameters to achieve a satisfactory level of illumination (see figure 7.17d). Note how the suspended mesh casts interesting shadows on the skin of the blimp.

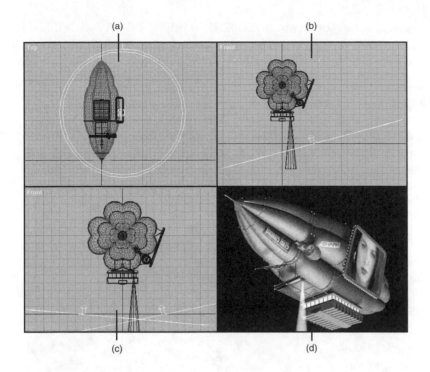

(a) (b) (c) (d)

FIGURE 7.17

Setting the key lighting for the scene: (a) Create a shadow-casting directional light. (b) Move it to ground level and angle it toward the blimp. (c) Mirror copy the light to the opposite side of the blimp. (d) Render the result and adjust the lighting if necessary.

Using Spotlights

In this section you create some rotating beacons (like the ones on police cars) to add some additional light and motion to the ship.

1. Create a simple "bubble gum machine" beacon with a cylinder for the base and a hemisphere for the glass portion located under one of the BagRng objects to which the thruster assembly is attached. Use vertice editing to stretch the base of the hemisphere to meet the base. Set both objects to be non-shadow casting in the object properties section of your software (see figure 7.18a–b).

2. Apply the Rust material to the base and create a new material called YlwLite for the glass part. Make it a 255, 255, 0 bright yellow with Self-Illumination at 100%.

3. Create a free spotlight in the center of the light fixture suspended under the blimp. If your software doesn't offer free spotlights, use a targeted spot with the target a short distance from the source. Adjust the beam to be shadow-casting, and have a hotspot of 65 degrees and a falloff of 80

degrees. Make the beam a 255, 255, 0 bright yellow, with a brightness multiplier of 2. Mirror instance the spotlight and position the copy to face the opposite direction (see figure 7.18c).

4. Render the area around the light and check the results. You may need to experiment a bit to get the results you want (see figure 7.18d).

FIGURE 7.18

Creating the rotating beacons: (a–b) Build and position the beacon mesh. (c) Create two spot-lights facing in opposite directions. (d) Render the result.

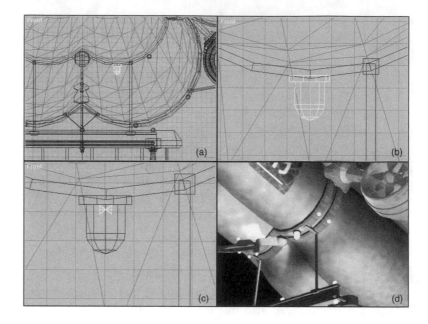

Using Point Lights

Although either point lights or spotlights could be used for the this application, this section shows you how to use a point light with attenuation to try it out.

1. Copy the mesh from the beacon you just built (but not the lights) and position it on the end of the gondola (see figure 7.19a–b).

2. Create a point light in the center of the light fixture. Adjust the light to have a bright red 255, 0, 0 color, with a multiplier of 2. Enable attenuation and set the ranges to 70 units for the hotspot and 160 units for the falloff (see figure 7.19c).

3. Render the result (see figure 7.19d).

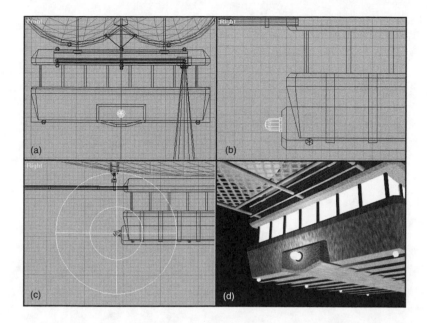

FIGURE 7.19

Using an attenuated point light: (a–b) Copy the beacon mesh and place it on the gondola. (c) Add an attenuated point light to cast a controlled pool of light around the beacon. (d) Render the results.

If your software has non-shadow casting omnis (like 3D Studio), you may see illumination on objects where the light shouldn't be shining, such as the fins under the gondola. In this case, you can use Exclude so those objects will not be affected by the light.

Summary

In the course of this chapter, you've looked at the principles of light in the real world and how they apply to the 3D environment. You've examined the kinds of light sources and controls available in the virtual world, and seen some of the differences (and even advantages) that 3D light sources have, like Include and Exclude. You also saw the different sorts of shadow creation methods and how to adjust them, went over lighting approaches, and got some tips on creating certain effects or simulating real-world lighting as well.

In the next chapter, you will see how the position and focal length settings of the camera can further increase the drama in a 3D scene. You'll also see the use of the camera for storytelling purposes, based on the principles developed by filmmakers over several decades.

The Camera

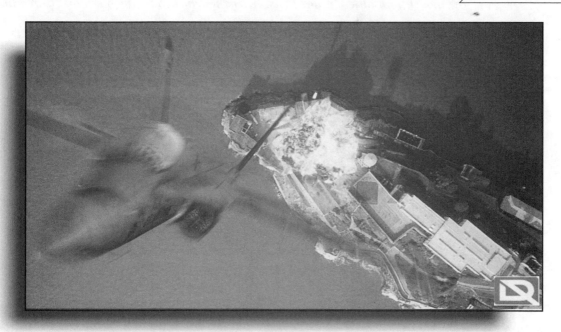

An example of how careful camera positioning helps to tell a story clearly and dramatically. Image created with Alias/Wavefront PowerAnimator. Courtesy of Dream Quest Images.

*T*he old man settled in heavily next to the student, who had been working diligently all afternoon. "You have something to show me?"

"Yes," the student replied. "I've been setting up recording lenses around the castle model to show off the work. Here, take a look at these."

The Master watched as a series of images appeared above the glowing pool, showing the model from different locations. After the tenth slide, the old man cleared his throat and spoke. "Lad, all these views seem to be facing dead center on the subject, and are set so far back that I can see the whole castle."

"Well, yes. I want the viewer to be able to see the whole castle, and I positioned the lenses so they wouldn't cause too much distortion."

"That might be fine if you were taking real estate photos," sighed the conjurer. "But in drama, lad, distortion is an ally."

"Oh."

"Here, allow me to demonstrate." The Master selected a view that faced the front of the castle. "Lowbahl Spiekamm," he muttered, and the eerily floating lens shot down to just above ground level and raced toward the castle drawbridge, coming to a halt near its heavy chain. The Master tweaked the lens slightly, tilting it to face upward a bit.

"Wow," remarked the student, marveling at the way the lens angle made the castle seem to loom above them. "It looks so huge and imposing now."

"Aeroflot Fysheye," intoned the old man, sending the lens soaring high above the virtual landscape. He directed it downward and widened the field of view so that the castle seemed to reach up at them from a broad, peaceful valley.

"A dragon's eye view…" the student said, "Hey, that gives me an idea."

"Good. I've made my point, then." The Master rose. "Don't be afraid to try unique angles, and it isn't necessary to show the whole subject, just what counts."

"Right!" said the lad. "I'm going to do the whole animation in super-wide perspective, from really bizarre angles. It'll be so cool."

"Maylockx Alkiselltzer," groaned the old man, rubbing his stomach and heading for the medicine chest.

Camera Basics

It would seem that our student is either headed for a totally incomprehensible animation, or is laying the foundation for the first medieval music video. Either way, the camera represents the viewer's perspective on the virtual world, and is a key tool in the process of visual storytelling.

This chapter focuses on camera terminology and techniques, and looks at how the storytelling language developed by filmmakers relies on using the right camera locations to get the point across most effectively.

Orthographic versus Perspective Views

Chapter 3, "Delving Into Cyberspace," discussed different viewpoints on the scene, and you've probably been using most of the common default ones (front, back, left, right, top, bottom) for constructing your models. As you recall, these types of viewports are orthographic, meaning that all parallel lines remain parallel regardless of how the viewpoint changes. With camera views, however, the perspective tries to duplicate that of the natural world, where parallel lines eventually converge into vanishing points (see figure 8.1). The photographic term for the contents of a viewport (in other words, the visible portion of the scene) is the *frame*.

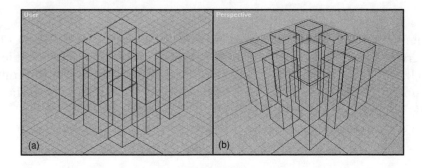

FIGURE 8.1

Orthographic versus perspective views: (a) In isometric viewports, parallel lines remain parallel. (b) In camera or perspective viewports, parallel lines converge, as they do in the real world.

Virtual cameras duplicate the functions and controls of their real-world counterparts, while adding some special features of their own. One of the most common 3D camera controls with a direct relationship to real photo gear is the focal length setting.

Focal Length

In real cameras, *focal length* is the distance from the center of the lens to the image it forms of the subject (assumed to be an infinite distance in front of the lens). The normal focal length of a typical camera is around 50mm, which is similar to that of the human eye. This is why a 50mm lens is also referred to as a *normal lens*.

There is a direct relationship between focal length and *field of view (FOV)*, which is the angle that encompasses everything that can be seen through a lens with a given focal length. The typical FOV for a 50mm lens is 40 degrees (see figure 8.2).

FIGURE 8.2

Focal length has a direct effect on the field of view. As the focal length is reduced, the FOV is widened.

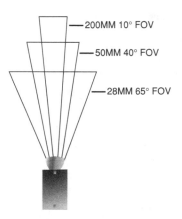

— 200MM 10° FOV

— 50MM 40° FOV

— 28MM 65° FOV

When the focal length of a lens is changed, the field of view changes in an inversely proportional manner. For example, if you reduce the focal length of a lens to 28mm, the FOV widens to 65 degrees. This is why lenses from 20–35mm are commonly called *wide angle lenses*. By the same token, if the focal length is increased to 200mm, the field of view drops to 10 degrees. Lenses with 85mm and longer focal lengths are referred to as *long lenses* or *telephoto lenses*.

Note

With all our discussion of real world cameras and millimeters, bear in mind that film sizes, such as 35mm, are a related but separate subject that has more to do with the final image output settings. This is discussed further in Chapter 10, "Rendering and Output."

At one time, photographers had to have many different lenses available for their cameras to properly shoot a variety of subjects, from a broad vista to a distant animal. As optics became more sophisticated, however, the *zoom lens* was developed, enabling photographers to adjust the lens over a broad range of focal lengths. These days, photographers can usually get by with just two lenses: a 35–80mm zoom and a 80–200mm zoom. These modern lenses often have a *macro lens* setting as well, which enables the user to take extreme close-ups, as though they were using a low-powered microscope.

In the virtual world, focal length is calculated by mathematical formulas, so users can define just about any focal length they want for a given camera. However, real-world cameras are still used as a reference, so many programs offer a standard array of focal lengths in addition to allowing you to type in your own settings (see figure 8.3). Note that there is no need to include the equivalent of a macro setting, because virtual cameras can be placed very close to the subject to achieve that effect.

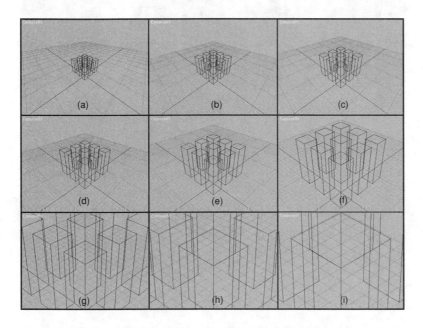

FIGURE 8.3

Sample focal lengths:
(a) 15mm, (b) 20mm,
(c) 24mm, (d) 28mm,
(e) 35mm, (f) 50mm,
(g) 85mm, (h) 135mm,
(i) 200mm.

As you can see, in addition to adjusting the size of the subject, the wide lens settings have a tendency to exaggerate the perspective in a scene, while the longer lenses reduce it. As a result, wide angle lenses often impart a feeling of massiveness to a subject, while telephoto lenses are used to flatten scenes, compressing them so that distant objects seem like they're closer together.

Focus and Aperture

Of course, focal length isn't the only setting on a lens. In fact, the most commonly used control on manual cameras is the focus adjustment. *Focus* adjusts the optics in the camera so that the subject is sharp and clear. However, focus is not object-specific—it is a range, a set of near and far distance figures called *depth of field* (see figure 8.4). Depending on the lens settings, the depth of field may be narrow, with only objects within a few inches of the focus point being clear, or wide (like many fixed-focus cameras), with which everything from a few feet away to infinity is sharp and clear.

FIGURE 8.4

Depth of field effects: (a) Most programs have no depth of field control, so everything is in focus. (b) Variable depth of field enables you to select a portion of the image to be in focus, while everything outside that range is blurred.

(a)　　　　　(b)

The *aperture* of the camera is a variable opening inside the lens that works like your eye's iris. When the aperture is wide open, the maximum amount of light is admitted. When it's closed to a pinpoint, very little light passes through. In camera terms, the different aperture settings are called *f-stops*, and often range from around f1.2 (open) to f16 (nearly closed). While controlling the amount of light reaching the film is one application of the aperture, an aperture also controls the depth of field. To demonstrate, try the following simple experiment.

Close one eye, hold your palm about six inches away from your face, and focus on it. Notice that everything beyond your hand is blurred, because the current depth of field of your eye is fairly narrow. Next, make a circle using the index finger and thumb of your other hand, tightening it so that only a pinpoint of light shines through (something like an over-torqued "OK" gesture). Focus again on your palm six inches from your face, then place your circled finger and thumb directly in front of your eye so that you are looking through the "pinhole." Now both your hand and more of the background are in focus, because you have done the equivalent of closing down the aperture in a camera.

In most 3D programs, there's no equivalent to the focus or depth of field controls, because everything in the scene is equally sharp. While this may be an advantage in most cases, it has the unfortunate side effect of making the imagery look unrealistic as well, because we expect certain things to be blurred. After all, that's how we see the world ourselves. Recently, however, additional features have been added to some programs to allow them to have a focus adjustment, either built into the renderer or as a post-production effect.

Camera Movement

When it comes to movement, virtual cameras hold a massive advantage over their real world counterparts. In 3D space, cameras are free to move anywhere in the scene, even inside objects. In addition, multiple cameras can be defined, allowing the action to be viewed from several angles at the same time.

Clipping Planes and Targets

Another unique capability of virtual cameras is their *clipping plane*, which is a user definable cut-off point that makes everything on the camera's side of it invisible during rendering. Although this isn't normally adjusted, there are instances where extending the clipping plane away from the camera can be useful. For example, this would enable you to create the illusion that objects were being carved away by an unseen force, revealing their interiors, as might be done with an anatomical animation.

Finally, most 3D cameras have a *camera target*, which is a small cube or other object attached to the camera by a line. The target enables you to see exactly where the camera is pointed from any other viewpoint, making it faster and easier to position. In addition, some programs offer cameras that don't have targets, which can be helpful in smoothing out an animation when the camera is being moved along a path.

Camera Moves

In addition to mimicking 35mm cameras, virtual cameras can imitate their motion picture and video counterparts. While most of the following moves require a real camera to be mounted on a tripod or dolly (a wheeled platform), there are no such restrictions for virtual cameras, even though they can behave in the same manner.

Pan and Tilt

Two of the most common moves in film making are pan and tilt. A *pan* is a horizontal rotation of the camera from right to left or vice-versa (see figure 8.5). A pan is often used to move the camera from one subject to another or to see more of a landscape than will fit in the frame.

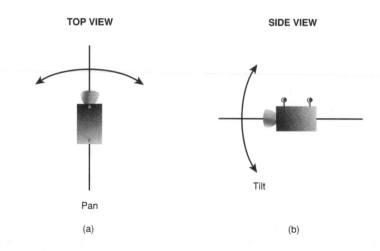

TOP VIEW

SIDE VIEW

Pan

Tilt

(a)

(b)

In motion pictures, a *swish pan* is a type of pan that moves the camera so quickly that it blurs the scene completely. If you try this with the default settings in your 3D program, it probably won't work. You need to use the motion blur option in the software, and you may even need to do some additional post-production work with Photoshop's motion-blur filter to duplicate the effect.

A *tilt* is the vertical equivalent of a pan, rotating the camera up or down. Tilts are often used to showcase tall objects, such as buildings, but also may be used on a character to give the impression that the viewer is sizing them up.

Tracking and Dollying

Dolly and track are two terms that seem to get confused or overlap, depending on which reference or program you use. I'll distinctly separate them to avoid confusion.

A *dolly* is a wheeled platform that a camera is mounted on. The term *dolly* or *truck* also refers to moving the camera around on the floor during the shot to get closer or further from the action, or to view it from a different side (see figure 8.6). In 3D terms, the Dolly command usually moves the virtual camera toward or away from the subject.

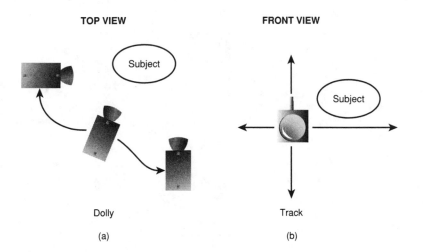

TOP VIEW

Subject

Dolly

(a)

FRONT VIEW

Subject

Track

(b)

FIGURE 8.6

Dolly and track camera movements: (a) Dolly moves the camera around, usually on the same "floor plane" as the subject. (b) Track moves the camera horizontally or vertically.

Occasionally, you'll see an effect in which the room appears to close in around a character, usually to indicate that they feel suddenly claustrophobic or in danger. This effect is created by dollying the camera away from the subject, while simultaneously zooming the lens to keep the subject the same size in the frame. This can be accomplished in 3D programs by using the same technique.

In film making, a dolly is sometimes mounted onto a steel track, allowing the camera to move smoothly along a predefined path. Therefore, *track* usually refers to movement of the camera along a single axis, be it horizontal or vertical. The Track command in 3D programs normally keeps the camera the same distance from the subject, but moves it left or right (along the X-axis) or up and down (along the Y-axis).

Bank and Roll

In the real world, banks and rolls are difficult movements to do unless the camera is hand-held or mounted in a motion control rig, but virtual cameras handle them with ease. *Roll* means to rotate the camera around its viewing axis, making the scene appear to spin (see figure 8.7). *Bank* is simply an automatic roll that some programs do to the camera when it moves through a curve in a path. Creating the illusion that you're flying in a plane or tumbling out of control are two of the most popular uses for roll.

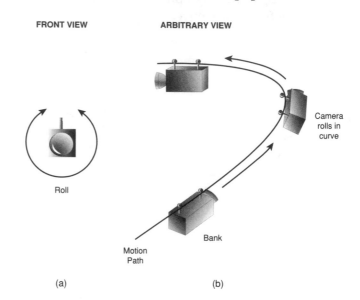

FRONT VIEW   ARBITRARY VIEW

Roll

Camera rolls in curve

Bank

Motion Path

(a)   (b)

Note

There can be a problem when the camera and target become nearly aligned along a certain axis (usually Y), as when you are trying to set up an overhead view of an object. As the alignment comes closer to vertical, the camera may begin to roll dramatically, trying to position itself to be at the opposite angle once it crosses over the axis. One way around this is to simply avoid these situations by keeping your camera target offset from near-vertical.

Directing the Camera

In filmmaking, skillful use of the camera adds as much to a scene's composition and a movie's story as the sets and dialog. Following some basic principles that were developed in the motion picture industry, you can add similar drama to your 3D animations. (Chapter 11, "The Reel," expands on these principles.)

In the early days of filmmaking, movies looked more like stage plays—the camera was locked down, and the actors walked in and out of the frame. The camera was always fairly distant from the action, because directors wanted to be sure the actor's entire body was visible at all times. At the time, it was felt that if only the head were shown, the audience would think it had been chopped off. Tired of this staid look, pioneering director D.W. Griffith (*The Birth of a Nation, Intolerance*) reinvented storytelling for the new medium, providing the basis for the principles and techniques known as *film grammar*.

Viewpoints

One of the precepts of film grammar is that the camera is a (usually unseen) observer, able to move to whatever angle best suits the message or image the director is trying to convey. Although the principles of good composition go back centuries (and are completely applicable to filmmaking), the variety of lenses and newness of the media allowed more experimentation with viewpoints, resulting in unorthodox but effective results.

An example of this is the *bird's-eye* or *high-angle view*, where the subject is seen from an elevated perspective. This type of shot is good for establishing the local environment, because it gives the viewer a commanding view of the surroundings (see figure 8.8). A variation on this is the *overhead view*, where the viewer is directly above the subject. This can be useful in situations where the character feels like a rat trapped in a maze, or creating the feeling that his every movement is being watched.

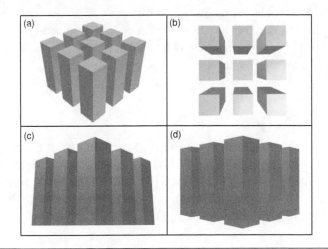

FIGURE 8.8

Camera viewpoint examples: (a) Bird's-eye view, (b) overhead view, (c) worm's-eye view, (d) conventional view.

The *worm's eye* or *low angle view*, in which the camera is positioned just above the ground plane, is popular for giving the subject mass and weight. It is often used to create a sense of foreboding about a location, or to make the subject look more intimidating.

Other angles popular for depicting people are the *head shot*, or *close-up*, where only the head and shoulders of the subject are in view, the *profile* shot, where the subject is shown from the side, the *waist shot*, where the subject is framed from the waist up, and the *knee shot*, where the subject is seen from the knees down, usually to disguise their identity.

A *point-of-view (POV) shot* is one that is seen through the eyes of one of the characters in a film, and commonly used in horror films to represent the killer's actions without revealing their identity. A POV shot isn't limited to a human character, however. Any character can have a POV, and inanimate objects as well, if they're established to be doing something active at the time (like a missile flying through the air, for example).

When two characters are together in the frame, it's called a *two-shot*. One popular framing for the two-shot is the *over-the-shoulder shot*, used when the director wishes to focus on one of the subjects, but still have a shoulder or other portion of the other character in the frame.

Earlier in the chapter, you learned about focal length and its affect on the field of view. It's important to note that a *wide shot* means that you can see all of the subject(s) and a good part of the environment, but doesn't require the use of a wide lens to do this.

> An error I've seen in a lot of student 3D animation is the failure to use the camera to provide drama, usually because it's improperly placed. When setting up the cameras for your work, take the time to experiment with positioning and focal length. Don't be afraid to try an unusual angle, or feel that you have to show the whole subject in every shot.

The Line of Action

This section examines another element of film grammar relating to continuity. During the course of making a film, where scenes may be shot many times from different angles, it's important to maintain *continuity*, so that the action doesn't suddenly reverse from what the viewer expects to see. The *line of action* is an imaginary partition running though the scene, often following the path of the subject, or set up between two characters having an exchange (see figure 8.9).

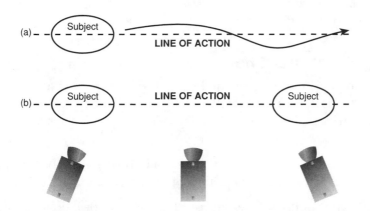

FIGURE 8.9

The line of action: (a) The line may run along a character's path, or (b) connect two characters having an exchange.

The idea behind the line of action is that a character facing to the right in a scene is always facing right, and doesn't suddenly face left because a shot from a camera on the opposite side is inserted. To prevent this sort of jarring switch, the camera should remain on one side of the line, except under certain circumstances.

What if you needed a cut from the other side of the line in order to show something that isn't visible from the current side? In general, if you want a camera to move over the line in anything other than a dolly move, you should bridge the line by having a shot where the camera is pointed in the same direction as the line, and is as close to crossing it as possible. At that point, you can then add shots from the opposite side of the line.

If you take continuity issues into consideration when setting up your cameras and doing the animation, it will help prevent problems in the editing process (see Chapter 11, "The Reel," for more information).

Camera Tutorials

Topics covered:

    Setting the Master Shot

    Camera Positioning Tips

Continuing with the blimp project, this section provides guidance for setting up some cameras for still images and the animation to follow. Use the principles laid down in this chapter and your own sense of cinematic drama to find your own angle on the subject.

Setting the Master Shot

This section is primarily concerned with finding dramatic angles and focal lengths to be used later on for stills or animation. The first camera is set up to provide an overall perspective on the scene, also called a *master shot* in the filmmaking biz.

1. In the Top view, set up a 50mm camera to the right of the blimp, setting the camera target near the center of the ship (see figure 8.10a).

2. In the Front or Right view, adjust the camera to be below the blimp (see figure 8.10b–c).

3. In the Camera view, use the Dolly, Pan, and Track controls so that the blimp nearly touches the edges of the frame. It's fine for the searchlights to extend past, however (see figure 8.10d).

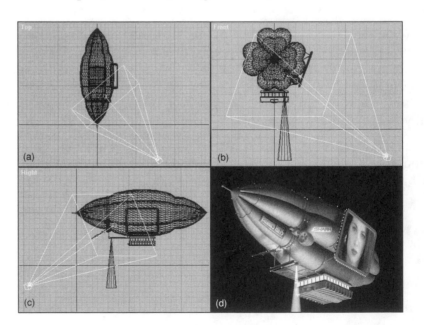

Camera Positioning Tips

Camera positioning is an experimental process, and some surprising results can come from messing around and trying odd angles. In general, set up your camera in the Top or Side views to set the general location, then refine the angle and focal length in the Camera viewport, using the Dolly, Track, and Pan controls.

Four different camera views of the subject follow, with some observations about each. You're encouraged to explore other camera angle possibilities as well.

◆ The first view doesn't work for a still, but has potential for an animation, where the blimp would slide along very close to the camera (see figure 8.11a).

◆ The next shot works for either a still or animation. The camera has a moderately wide 35mm focal length, and is positioned to show most of the elements on the blimp in a dramatic perspective (see figure 8.11b).

◆ This one is a disaster, literally. It looks like the blimp is about to plummet into the ground, and the angle is much too orthogonal, because the camera is positioned almost directly under the blimp. This might still work for an animation, if the camera rolled a bit during the shot (see figure 8.11c).

◆ By changing the angle slightly and rolling the camera around, a good worm's-eye view of the blimp can be achieved. Now that the blimp is pointing more upward, it seems natural (see figure 8.11d).

FIGURE 8.11

Four different angles on the blimp. (a) This shot could be dramatic, but much of the blimp is obscured. (b) A better angle for the approach. (c) The Hindenburg, Pt. II. (d) A better worm's-eye view of the craft.

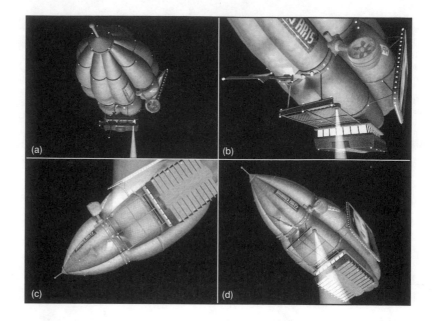

Summary

This chapter began with a look at camera terminology, comparing virtual cameras to their real world counterparts, then applied that to movement as well. It also looked at how the camera influences the storytelling process through angles and continuity devices like the line of action. Proper usage of the camera will assist you in creating dramatic stills and setting up the best viewpoints from which to render your animation.

The next chapter, "Animation," takes the storytelling process a big step forward by turning objects into performers. There, you'll see how the objects, lights, and cameras come together to create the visual message that you want to convey.

9

Animation

Bringing characters to life is the essence of animation. Image created with StudioPaint 3D, courtesy of C. Tappan and A. Graham.

"*Aargh!! This is driving me mad!*" the student exclaimed, jarring the Master out of a sound mid-day nap in his work chair.

"*Ehh? Wha...*" The old man straightened quickly and searched the room with bleary eyes, half-expecting to see the place overrun by stone trolls hunting for a human snack.

"*Oh, please forgive me, Master!*" the student said sheepishly. "*I didn't mean to awaken you.*"

"*Well, I'm WIDE AWAKE now, so tell me what the trouble is.*" The old conjurer struggled out of his chair.

"*Well, it's this soldier. I'm trying to make him march along the ramparts, but his movement looks terrible.*"

"*Yes, well, let's see...*" the old man leaned across the glowing pool and peered at the animated figure.

"*Hmmm. He looks like a robot trying to skate upon ice,*" the Master not so tactfully noted. "*Lad, you have to realize that people and animals aren't mechanical. They move gracefully in arcs, not in rigid angles and straight lines.*"

"*That makes sense,*" replied the student, "*I suppose I need to add more intermediate stages to each movement, then?*"

"*That would be a good approach.*" The old man nodded. "*As for the skating, use some temporary objects to mark the positions of the feet. That will help you to maintain the proper footing.*"

"*Great! Thanks for the advice, Master. I think it'll help a lot.*" The student paused and looked at the old man quizzically. "*Just one thing, though. What's a robot?*"

"*Oh, I saw them whilst flipping channels on the crystal oracle last night,*" the old man replied. "*They're mechanical humans that will someday serve all of mankind's needs.*" He stroked his beard for a moment, then continued wistfully, "*at least, until they unionize.*"

Animation Basics

Technically, *animation* is modifying any kind of object, light, material or camera by moving or changing it over time, but as the conveniently error-prone student discovered in this installment, animation is more than just moving things around. Animation is literally breathing life into something, taking cold, mathematically defined mesh and giving it character and personality.

This chapter looks at the techniques of 3D animation, from basic keyframing to procedural motion. It also delves into the art of character animation, the most challenging (and for some, the most satisfying) part of the 3D experience.

Frame Rates

Although animation is a series of still images (called *frames*), human perception has a characteristic called *persistence of vision*, which is the tendency to continue seeing an image for a split second even after the view has changed. Film and television take advantage of this characteristic to create a sense of fluid motion. Even though film and television display a series of still images, our persistence of vision bridges the gap. The speed at which the images are displayed is called the *frame rate*, and is measured in *frames per second (fps)*.

Generally, the minimum frame rate for acceptable animation is about 15fps, which is slow enough for us to perceive the individual images as being separate (seen as a flickering effect), but is still watchable. The 15fps rate was used extensively in the earlier days of digital video because the single-speed CD-ROM players and slower video cards had a hard time keeping up with anything faster.

The ideal rate for animation is 30fps, which matches video frame rates and is perceived with virtually no flicker. Most multimedia computers are capable of playing back 30fps animation and video now, so consider it the standard for most of your work. If your animation is to be output to film, however, the rate is 24fps, because that's what projection equipment is set to operate at (unless it's a school projector, of course).

Before beginning your animation, you must determine the frame rate at which it will be viewed. Frame rate is the basis of calculating the correct frame numbers to which to move an object over a given length of time. For example, if you decide to go with 15fps, and you want an object to be in motion for 2 seconds, you would start it on frame 0 and stop on frame 29. If you chose 24fps, you would stop on frame 47 instead. Likewise, a 30fps frame rate would have you stopping the movement on frame 59.

Keyframing

To control animation, most programs use a method called keyframing, in which you pose your objects in key positions at specific frames (keyframes). Using a process called tweening, the computer then interpolates the object's positions in the intermediate frames, resulting in smooth motion from one position to the next.

For example, to animate an acorn falling from a tree and bouncing on the ground, you would set at least four keyframes: in the first, the acorn would be just leaving the tree; in the second it would be hitting the ground; in the third, back in the air at mid-bounce, and in the fourth, it would be resting on the ground (see figure 9.1).

FIGURE 9.1

Animating a falling acorn reguires four keyframes to define the acorn's movement. The software uses these keyframes to determine the path for the object to follow.

Setting Keyframes

As discussed earlier, the specific frame numbers for these actions depend on the animation's frame rate and the duration of each action. To generate a keyframe, you select a frame number and then move the object to the desired location. With some programs this is all that's required, but others may force you to confirm the movement by hitting a button.

Here's a step-by-step look at how this keyframing process works in 3D software. To bounce a ball from the top-left corner to the middle of the screen to the top-right corner, you would specify frame 0 and place the ball in the top left corner, thereby setting a keyframe (see figure 9.2). Next, you would change to frame 30 and move the ball to the bottom center of the screen, setting another keyframe at that point. Finally, you would advance the animation again, to frame 60, for example, and move the ball to the upper-right corner, setting the final keyframe. The result is a 61 frame animation (remember, 0 counts as a number).

When the animation is played, the software makes sure the ball is displayed exactly where you placed it in frames 0, 30, and 60, and figures out how to transition the ball between those frames in the smoothest manner possible, based on controls for the keyframe called weighting. This weighting controls the object's path, allowing the object to make a smooth transition into and out of the keyframe.

FIGURE 9.2

Keyframing: (a) At frame 0, the ball is positioned in the upper-left corner. (b) At frame 30, the ball is moved to the bottom center of the screen. Note the line showing the path of the object. (c) At frame 60, the ball is moved again, and the path changes to smooth out the movement.
(d) Between keyframes, the computer positions the ball according to the path it has calculated.

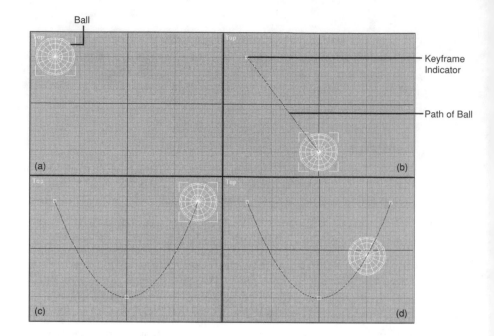

Ball

Keyframe Indicator

Path of Ball

(a)   (b)   (c)   (d)

The results of weighting can be seen in the example as well. Note how the path is straight at frame 30, moving the ball from the first keyframe to the second in a straight line, or linear fashion. When the third keyframe is set at frame 60, however, the preset weighting of the keyframes tries to smooth out the movement by adjusting the path from a straight line into a curve. You'll see how this weighting can be changed in the next section.

Keyframing isn't the only means of controlling the path of an object, however. Another approach is to draw a path with the program's spline creation tools, and then assign an object to move along it.

To manage the information about which objects are moved and when, most programs have adopted a *timeline* animation interface (see figure 9.3). The horizontal axis is broken down into time units and/or frame numbers, and the vertical axis consists of a hierarchical list of objects and lights along with their animatible parameters. Keyframes are indicated by a marker placed on the line that extends out from the parameter's name, and positioned on the appropriate frame number as indicated by the timeline below it. This interface also enables you to add, delete, or move keyframes, in order to adjust the time at which a animation event occurs. To move a keyframe, you simply slide it with the mouse.

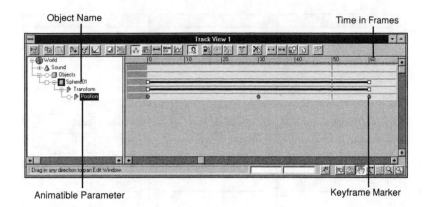

Object Name

Time in Frames

FIGURE 9.3

The animation timeline shows the animatable parameters for each object, with keyframes indicated by a marker placed according to the time (frame number) when the keyframe was created.

Animatible Parameter

Keyframe Marker

In addition to displaying the time in frame numbers, most programs have an option to display it in the *SMPTE (Society of Motion Picture and Television Engineers)* format of minutes, seconds, and frames, which is used extensively in video and film production. For example, a point in the animation designated 57:31:12 would be 57 minutes, 31 seconds, and 12 frames.

Keyframe Weighting

You can alter the keyframe weighting to affect the path of the object around the keyframe. Depending on your program, you may have one or more different keyframe weighting schemes (also called *animation controllers*) to choose from.

The most basic type is a point-to-point *linear weighting*, where the object transitions from keyframe to keyframe in a straight line, with no curvature at all. This is good for mechanical motion but little else.

> ***TCB (Tension/Continuity/Bias) weighting*** is one of the most common means of providing control over the keyframe control points (see figure 9.4).
>
> ***Tension*** varies the amount of curvature that the keyframe allows in the path before and after the keyframe. If the tension is low, the path can be very loose and curved going in and out of the keyframe. If it's tight, the path becomes totally linear between keyframes. Going back to the acorn example, if the tension was set high on the keyframe where the acorn hits the ground, it would seem to ricochet, like a bullet hitting steel.

FIGURE 9.4

TCB weighting is sometimes controlled by a graphical preview dialog, like the one above. The graphics show changes to the curve depending on the TCB settings below it.

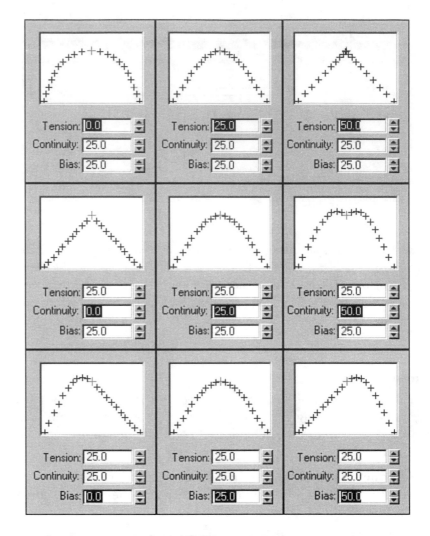

Continuity adjusts how tangent the path is to the control point. The default setting results in a smooth curve, while a low continuity setting tends to have the path overshoot the control point, making the object snap into the curve a bit when it hits the keyframe. High continuity has the opposite effect, and at an extreme appears similar to setting the tension to full, except the move is kept more linear. A low continuity setting on the acorn impact point would cause the acorn to burrow underground, pop back up at the keyframe, dig down again, and then re-emerge for the bounce back up into the air.

Bias adjusts the maximum extreme point, or peak, of the curve. When it's in the default position, the peak occurs at the keyframe (unless the continuity is set high). Low bias causes the curve to peak before the keyframe, and high bias causes it to peak afterward. A high bias setting on acorn ground zero would cause the acorn to pass through the keyframe point and plow into the ground like a meteor, then pop back out for the bounce.

Ease From and **Ease To** control the acceleration of the object into and out of the keyframe. In the default position, there's a certain amount of deceleration coming into the keyframe, and some acceleration coming out, just as though you were driving a car around a curve in the road. By adjusting Ease To, you can vary the amount of acceleration or deceleration prior to the keyframe, while Ease From does the same thing to the far side of the keyframe. Ease controls could have some strange effects on the acorn. For example, if the acorn impact keyframe was adjusted to have a high Ease To setting, the wayward nut would slow down as it got closer to the ground, almost as if it were trying to avoid the impact.

Although weighting is often represented in separate dialogs when the user clicks on a keyframe, the best feedback and control is provided by those systems that enable you to see and edit both the keyframe position and weighting on a Bézier function curve, or on the object's path in the 3D space.

A *function curve* is a graphical way of displaying object transformations. It often consists of three different colored splines, each representing a different axis. If the splines are flat, it means no activity is occurring on that axis. If they curve, however, the amount they are displaced and their position indicates the degree of change on that axis and at what points in time those changes occur. Such *Bézier spline weighting* is very natural, and you may well already be familiar with it from doing 2D spline editing (see figure 9.5). The handles on the control point are capable of controlling the same sorts of parameters that TCB controls do, but in a more intuitive manner. For example, to vary the tension, you shorten the handles, reducing their effect on the spline. To adjust continuity and bias, you position the handles to tweak the curve passing through the keyframe.

FIGURE 9.5

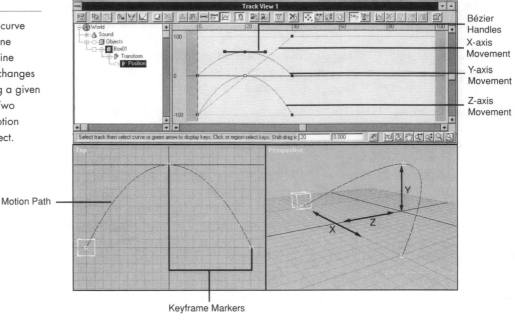

FIGURE 9.5

(top)A function curve with Bézier spline controls. Each line represents the changes occurring along a given axis. (bottom) Two views of the motion path of the object.

Bézier Handles

X-axis Movement

Y-axis Movement

Z-axis Movement

Motion Path

Keyframe Markers

Motion Paths

A useful capability in many 3D programs is the ability to work directly with the *motion path* of an object, which is a graphical representation of its movement, shown by a spline with small markers at each keyframe (see figure 9.6). You also may be able to edit the motion path directly, which can make it a lot easier to establish a complicated movement quickly and get fluid results. If your program offers this capability, you can grab the spline at any keyframe point and move it around, with the path adjusting automatically to show you the revised movement. You also may be able to add, delete, and adjust the weighting of each keyframe with instant feedback.

In some cases, these motion paths can be imported or exported, enabling you to generate them from object shape information or to use them in other animation work. For example, you could modify the complex helical path created to sweep an object, turning it into a motion path for an object or camera, which would allow it to accurately follow the original form's contours.

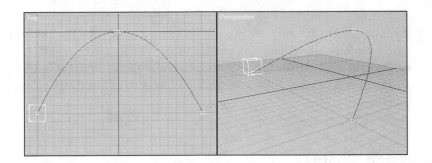

FIGURE 9.6

Motion paths show the trajectories of objects and may incorporate keyframe markers, individual frame markers, and direct Bézier or TCB manipulation.

Pivot Points and Axes

Just as in the modeling process discussed In Chapter 3, "Delving Into Cyberspace," in animation an object may be transformed around one of several axes or points of rotation, or *pivot points*. Often, the desired pivot point won't be in the default location, which is the center of the object. In the case of a jointed character, for example, the pivot point for the lower arm is the elbow, located at the *end* of the arm. You also may need to relocate the pivot point in order to have objects spin around a remote axis, located on another object or out in 3D space (see the "Nulls" section later in the chapter for more tips on this).

In most cases, the pivot point for an object can be relocated by choosing the Pivot Point or Center of Rotation command and selecting the new point by clicking in one or more viewports. The axis of rotation is often set by the general axes constraints setting or by using a hot key or mouse key to choose the desired axis.

It should be noted, however, that many programs don't allow the repositioning of the pivot point during an animation. Therefore, it's nearly always best to define pivot points for objects before the animation process is started.

Preview

At some point in the animation process, you will want to see a representation of how things are moving. In most cases, there will be some kind of *preview* mode that will either display a simplified version of the scene in real time, or output a fast-rendering version as an animation. Be aware, however, that previews can be misleading, and you have to rely on properly rendered tests in order to be sure everything is working properly.

Tip

If you need more accuracy or the program's real-time preview can't keep up with the complexity of the scene, you can usually render a low resolution flat or Gouraud shaded animation with mapping and shadows turned off in a fairly short amount of time. Hide unnecessary objects to speed things up even more.

Links and Chains

In order to create jointed characters, machines, or other objects that have multiple parts that move each other, connections have to be established between the component objects. This is accomplished through the use of links. A *link* is a connection between two objects, so that animation affecting one also influences the other. When a link is established, one object is called the *parent*, and movement applied to it is transferred to the second object, the *child*.

A *chain* is a series of linked objects, using the same parent and child relationship, but extending it by additional generations to grandchild, great-grandchild, and so forth. So, if the parent is moved, the child is moved, and because the child is the parent of the grandchild, the grandchild is moved as well.

If it weren't for links and chains, jointed objects would fall apart as soon as you started to animate them. By joining objects together with linking, you create a hierarchical tree in which moving the trunk (parent) affects all the branches (offspring), and moving a single large branch affects the smaller branches (later generation offspring) attached to it (see figure 9.7). In fact, the tree model is often used to display the link relationship between objects when working with the animation.

Linking objects is not necessarily like welding the objects together, however. There are different kinds of links that can be established that affect the behavior of the chain. One link, sometimes called a *ball joint*, enables the two objects to rotate around a full six axes (see figure 9.8). If you don't want the link to be that free, you can set up *constraints* by turning off some of the axes of rotation. The amount of rotation also can be constrained by angle limits, so that the joint can't fold in one direction or back on itself. This would result in the joint becoming more like a hinge or elbow.

HIERARCHICAL TREE STRUCTURE

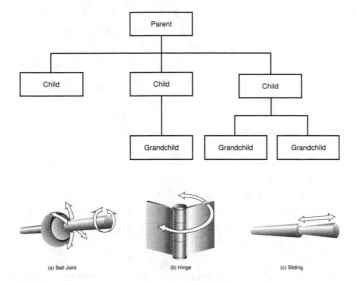

FIGURE 9.7

Graphical representation of the hierarchical tree structure of potential links. This information is often presented in text outline format in 3D software.

FIGURE 9.8

A physical representation of some of the types of links and constraints available in a typical 3D program.

Other links may not enable rotation at all, but set up a sliding relationship between the objects, like segments of a collapsing telescope. In this case, the link is constrained to a single axis of movement which is along the length of the two objects. The allowable distance of movement also can be constrained, so that the sections don't come apart.

The method of establishing links and chains varies among programs, but generally you select the Link command or icon, then select the child object followed by the parent object or vice-versa. At that point, you can establish additional links or edit the link to add constraints. You can test the performance of the link by moving the objects around in the interactive animation environment. Naturally, you also can *unlink* an object from the chain, removing it from the influence of other objects.

In programs that have separate modeling and editing modes (like 3D Studio R4), establishing links in the animation module can generate strange results if the objects are edited later in the modeling mode. In cases like this, you should unlink the object before editing it, then re-link it later on.

Nulls

Nulls or *dummy objects* are used as invisible components of a chain or as reference points for establishing remote axes of rotation. They usually appear as cubes or other simple objects when you're editing the animation, but do not render, which is why they are considered invisible. Nulls or dummies may be part of the standard set of object creation tools, but they're more likely to be found in the animation toolbox instead. For example, in modular 3D programs like 3DS R4, they can only be created in the Keyframer mode. Other than that, they can be scaled, rotated, and moved like any other 3D object.

Nulls are frequently made large enough to enclose a complex linked object, then assigned as the parent to the enclosed objects in order to more easily move them around as a unit. This makes it less likely to affect a child object when trying to locate the parent of the chain, which in the case of a humanoid figure, would be the relatively small and frequently obscured pelvis (see figure 9.9).

FIGURE 9.9

Establishing a null (the box surrounding the human figure mesh) or dummy object as the parent in a complex chain makes it easier to select and move the linked objects.

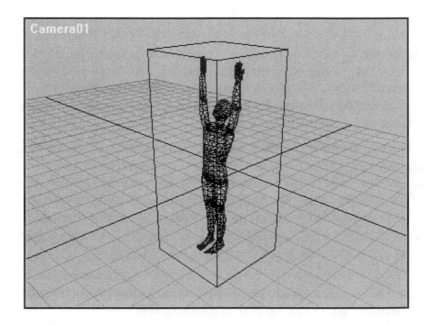

Another use for nulls is to establish a rotational axis some distance from an object, because it can be hard to accurately select the right spot in open 3D space. In this case, the null serves as a visual marker containing the correct center of rotation. On top of that, it can move, so that the center of rotation can change over time.

Nulls also are good for marking waypoints or providing other reference marks for animation. In the opening story, the Master suggested using temporary objects to mark the footprints of the soldier. Null objects are perfect for this.

Forward and Inverse Kinematics

Forward kinematics is the default method of animating linked objects, in which the movement of the parent object affects all the offspring on down the chain. If you move the parent, the children move too. If you rotate the parent, you rotate the children, and so forth. Of course, because there's no backward link from the child to the parent, the child also can be moved independently, which can mean a break in the mesh if you move the child away.

This method of animation makes a lot of sense for mechanical devices, because they usually operate in the "this moves that" mode that forward kinematics duplicates. It's not so good for character animation such as a walking action, however, because it requires you to move the body first, then adjust all the limbs to be in the proper places. This usually results in *skating*, a problem where the position of a character's feet slide around on the ground instead of remaining firmly planted.

Inverse kinematics (IK) is a method of controlling linked objects by moving the end of the chain and having the rest of it conform, a bit like the tail wagging the dog. For example, with forward kinematics, if you were animating an arm and wanted to touch the finger to an object, you would start by adjusting the root object (the upper arm), then the forearm, the wrist, and finally, the finger. This is very laborious and inaccurate, and requires a number of corrections and fine adjustments to come out right. With IK, you move the finger directly to the object, and the wrist, arms (and even the rest of the body) will bend and adjust smoothly and automatically to make it work (see figure 9.10).

IK makes it much easier to animate characters, because you can concentrate on the final position of hands and feet, rather than on the full-body adjustments you have to make to ensure that the limbs can reach their targets. Also, because the movement of the limbs in response to the changes is fairly natural, and tends to affect much of the body, you get a lot of "free" animation with IK, meaning that you don't have to go in and make as many adjustments to keep the form looking loose and natural. This is also one of the downsides to IK, because you don't have precise control over how the body is responding to your demands. Therefore, you may often have to use a combination of forward and inverse kinematics in your animation.

FIGURE 9.10

(a–d) Forward
kinematics requires
individual adjustment of
each object in order of
hierarchy to reach the
goal. (e–f) Inverse
kinematics
automatically adjusts
the tree so that the user
can move the end of the
chain to the goal
directly.

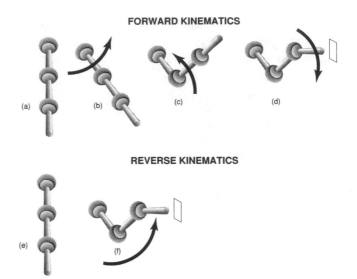

FORWARD KINEMATICS

(a) (b) (c) (d)

REVERSE KINEMATICS

(e) (f)

Inverse kinematics can be used with any sort of properly linked object, including jointed characters and skeletons (discussed in the next section). Generally, IK offers six axes of rotation, allowing full freedom of movement, but you should constrain some of the axes so that a character's joints move in a natural manner only (in other words, the elbows don't bend backward).

Bones Deformation

Bones deformation is the technique of animating an object (usually a character) by defining and animating an internal skeleton that automatically deforms the surrounding mesh. In the case of humanoid characters, the *skeleton* is a much simplified version of our own, with bones for the arms, hands, fingers, legs, spine, and so forth. You can animate the skeleton by forward or inverse kinematics, and the pre-defined areas of the surrounding mesh (the skin, if you will) will be smoothly animated along with it (see figure 9.11).

Not only is bones deformation one of the best ways to animate the broad motions of an un-jointed (seamless) mesh character, but the bones also can create subtle distortions of the mesh as well, allowing muscles to bulge, the chest to heave, and so on. Even facial expressions can be created with bones deformation.

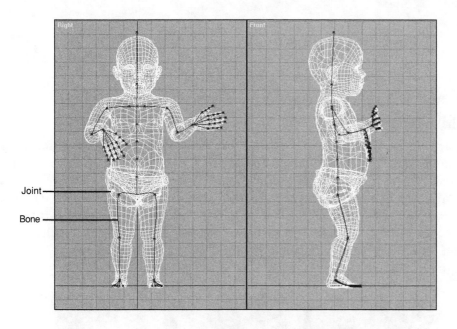

Joint

Bone

FIGURE 9.11

A seamless mesh of a baby attached to a bone deformation skeleton. By moving the bones with forward or inverse kinematics, the mesh will move as well.

If bones deformation is not part of your standard 3D package, there's a good chance that someone offers it as a plug-in routine. Naturally, bones deformation processes vary from product to product, but here's a general outline of the procedure:

1. Create the mesh skin by standard modeling techniques or by using a digitized character. It's generally set in a neutral pose, preferably with any body joints at least partially open.

2. Create a skeleton, either by defining bones one-by-one, or by using a standardized skeleton and adjusting it to fit. The skeleton should be completely enclosed by the mesh.

3. Define those areas of the mesh that fall under the influence of a given bone. Although the mesh around most of the bone will probably be automatically included, there will probably be some fine tuning required in the joint areas (such as the shoulder) to prevent, say, a portion of the rib cage being affected by the upper arm bone.

4. Reassign portions of the mesh. Testing the effects of the bone deformations will probably result in creases showing at various undesirable points. Further refinement of the mesh assignments may be needed, or you may need to add additional elements to correct this. In some cases, you may be able to define *tendons* that pull on certain areas of the mesh according to other deformations in the skin.

5. Define the subtle stretching and bulging of the skin when a joint or bone is moved in a certain way. This may be controlled by a path deformation technique similar to those used in sweeping an object, or you may have to do it manually to the mesh.

Morphing

Morphing as it relates to 3D animation is a technique that allows smooth changes to occur to an object's shape by defining beginning, end, and possibly intermediate forms as guides or *targets*. Good examples of what morphing is capable of are the transformations of the liquid metal T-1000 in *Terminator 2: Judgement Day*. Morphs can turn just about any form into another, but they also can be used to animate organic forms realistically, such as a snake's slithering motion or a sneezing man's facial contortions (see figure 9.12).

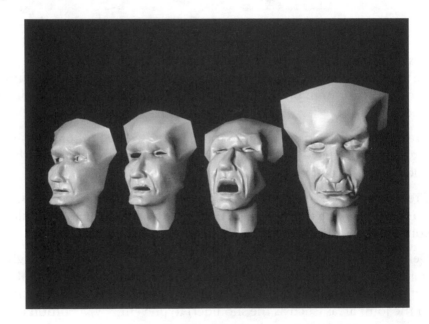

Before bones deformation became popular, morphing was one of the few ways to animate an un-jointed character. It still remains one of the only ways to transform one (non-parametric) polygonal object into another, but it's no small task.

In most software, the shapes you morph from and to (the morph targets) must have the same number and orientation of vertices, so that the program knows exactly where each vertice being animated starts and ends. This can be difficult to accomplish if you build the targets as two separate objects, so users often construct one of the target objects, then copy and transform it vertice-by-vertice into the next target. Also, because the software uses a straight line approach to moving the vertices from their starting to ending positions, intermediate targets are often needed to prevent parts of the mesh from collapsing or distorting in some undesirable way during the animation.

Once the targets are created, you set a keyframe for each form of the object, telling the animation program that it's supposed to transform the object completely by this time. The software then handles the movement of the vertices automatically, adjusting them frame-by-frame to make a smooth transition.

Deformation Grids

Deformation grids or *space warps* are a means of defining an area in 3D space that has an automatic effect on objects passing through its influence. Depending on the type of deformation selected, the object may respond to gravity effects, become wavelike, disintegrate, or change its path (see figure 9.13).

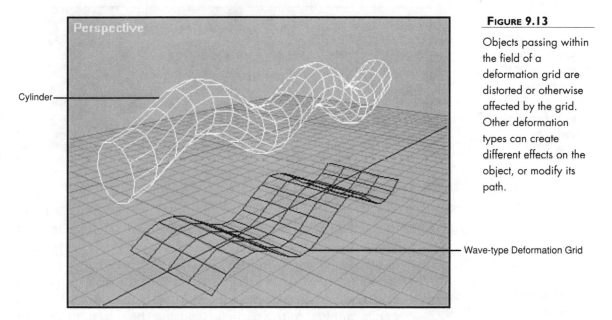

FIGURE 9.13

Objects passing within the field of a deformation grid are distorted or otherwise affected by the grid. Other deformation types can create different effects on the object, or modify its path.

Deformation grids make it easier to cause certain effects to occur on cue, such as having an object shatter as it strikes a floor, or to create motion that would be a chore to do by hand, such as animating a boat on a storm-tossed sea.

Using deformation grids is pretty straightforward. Depending on the program, you usually just set the object in position and adjust its parameters to the desired settings (you may have to set parameters on any objects you want to be influenced as well). After that, any objects that move over or through the grid area are automatically deformed.

Particle Systems

Some software packages offer built-in or add-on particle systems. *Particle systems* are 3D animation modules that enable you to generate and control the behavior of a vast number of tiny objects, which can simulate such natural effects as water, fire, sparks, or bubbles. A couple of good examples of particle systems at work are the solar flare and luminous gas cloud in the opening of *Star Trek: Voyager*. The individual objects are usually very simple, consisting of only a few faces, but when the proper material is applied to them and they are massed together, they act like the individual molecules making up a larger organism, taking on a form that belies their simplicity (see figure 9.14).

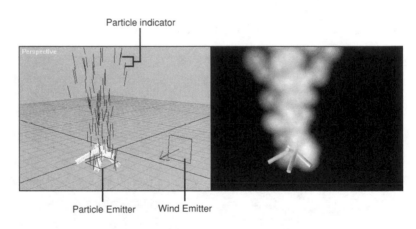

Particle indicator

Particle Emitter   Wind Emitter

FIGURE 9.14

Particle systems can create controlled fluid or vaporous effects (in this case, smoke). The appearance of the particles depends on the type of material applied to them.

The value of particle systems is that they bring a natural vaporous or liquid element into the normally hard-edged and well-defined 3D environment. Unlike such post-production fire effects as VCE's *Pyromania* (featured in the February 1996 issue of *InterActivity*) offers, however, they can be animated as part of the rest of the scene and made to interact with other 3D objects. Real-world physics can be applied to the particles, causing them to bounce naturally off other objects. You also can apply user-defined levels of gravity, wind, and other forms of turbulence as well. For example, you could design a particle system to act like water and cascade automatically off of 3D obstacles to make a virtual waterfall (see figure 9.15).

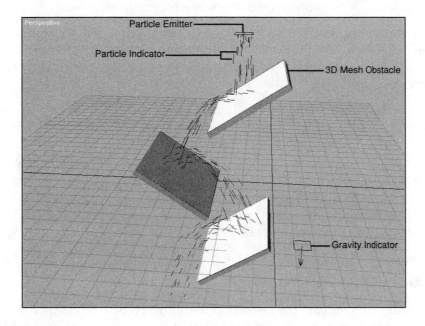

FIGURE 9.15

A particle system waterfall. Particle systems can interact with mesh in the scene and can be affected by forces like wind, turbulence, or gravity.

In general, particle systems work by enabling you to define an *emitter*, which is usually a simple polygonal shape that acts as a point of origin for the particles. The emitter is often scaleable, allowing the effect to be generated across a large area. There may be some sort of *boundary object*, perhaps part of the emitter itself, that limits the effect to its interior. The user defines the approximate number of particles to be active at any given time, then applies a material to them. If wind, turbulence, or gravity effects are needed, those parameters are set next. Because rendering particle animation is time consuming, some programs offer an interactive preview mode that enables the user to examine the general effect before rendering.

Procedural Motion

Because the actions of deformation grids and particle systems are set by formulas and parameters and not accomplished through direct user keyframing, the movement of particle systems is sometimes referred to as *procedural motion*, but there are other techniques that carry this title as well. For example, a *noise controller* is a type of animation controller that uses randomly generated noise to vary the size or position of an object. This would be useful to portray a piece of equipment vibrating out of control. Another is the *audio controller*, which uses the amplitude of a digital audio file to control motion. This would be useful for synching actions to a prerecorded soundtrack, or possibly even doing some rough lip synching.

An *expression controller* is another source of animation data—it uses formulas you input to control the action of objects in the scene. This can be very useful for accurate mechanical simulations, or to illustrate a scientific principle using 3D animation.

Behaviors are object-level controllers (Look At, Bounce, Spin, and so on) that simplify certain animation work. You assign a behavior to a given object, and it does what you tell it automatically, freeing you to build on that action to make a more complex movement. For example, if you were animating a scene in which an eye were watching a rolling ball, you could assign a Look At or Point Toward behavior to the eye and make the ball the target object. From then on, no matter how you move the eye or the ball, the eye would always be looking in the right direction.

Character Animation

Character animation is the process of imbuing objects not just with simple movement, but with *personality*. Note that the last sentence said "objects," not "characters." That's because any 3D object, including a simple cube, can have personality, depending on how the animator makes it move. By the same token, even the most detailed and accurate human model can come off as being lifeless if its motions are dull or mechanical. The key to compelling characters is making them act naturally, and there are several techniques that can help you—from the low-tech watching the mirror approach to using high-tech motion capture equipment.

Body Language

If you're planning to be a character animator, you'd better become an avid people watcher as well. Consciously or not, humans and many animals use *body language* to communicate their states of mind. Folded arms or fidgeting, for example, may indicate boredom or impatience depending on the situation. When people are at ease, their posture relaxes, and if they're sitting down, they may seem to sprawl out a bit. This is just the opposite if the person is tense—they will be rigid and withdrawn.

Animators rely heavily on body language like this to communicate the emotional states of their characters, and to give them a natural and realistic feeling. This is a lot of work, because the default mode for objects in 3D graphics programs is utterly still and rigid. The use of body language is particularly important for characters that have no other way to communicate, such as the lamps in John Lasseter's *Luxo Jr.* animation (see figure 9.16).

FIGURE 9.16

The desk lamps in the short film *Light Entertainment* (a.k.a. *Luxo, Jr.*) rely on human-like body language to communicate their emotions. Image ©1989 Pixar.

Generally, animators rely on their own body language instincts as a guide for moving their characters. In a sense, they become actors, portraying the roles of their virtual counterparts and noting their own actions and mannerisms, which they then re-create in the program. This isn't limited to human body language either—you can take on just about any role, from cautious mouse to city-trampling monster. Just make sure the door is closed when you start getting into your Godzilla suit. People might talk.

When doing character animation, try to keep your subject standing or moving in an asymmetrical way. For example, people generally don't stand with their weight evenly on both feet, or their shoulders perfectly level all the time. They shift their weight, dip one shoulder or the other, put a hand in a pocket, and so on. Injecting such subtle shifts in position when a character is standing "still" keeps him natural looking. Also, when doing speech or lip synching animation, remember that more than a person's mouth moves when she's talking—her eyebrows raise, her hands gesture, her whole body gets into the act.

If you're doing character animation, it's a good idea to have both a full-length and hand-held mirror available. You can act out broad body motions in the full-length mirror, and use the hand-held one for facial expressions. You also can face away from the full mirror and use the hand-held mirror to see what your motions look like from the rear.

Timing also plays a role in conveying emotions. How long characters maintain positions, how long they pause before reacting to something, and the speed at which they move can speak volumes about their state of mind. Having an easy-to-reset stopwatch is a useful tool for timing these gestures as you act them out.

Rotoscoping

If you need more help than a mirror can offer, *rotoscoping* enables you to copy from or add to reality easily. Rotoscoping is the process of adding film or video to animation, either as a finished element or for use as a reference for the animated characters. Using a video program such as Adobe Premiere and a video capture card, you can digitize video or film and load the frames into the background of a 3D package. This provides you with a very accurate frame-by-frame reference of a motion. By positioning the model beside or on top of the images, you can duplicate the activity very accurately. In this way, you can think of rotoscoping as the "poor man's motion capture system." Most 3D programs support rotoscoping, drawing the reference images from a series of numbered still images, or from an animation or digital video file. The image sequence is set to begin at a given frame number, and automatically changes whenever you advance to a different frame.

Motion Capture

The popularity of 3D character animation for games, television, and movies is partially the result of advances in generating realistic motion in an economical manner. *Motion capture* is any one of several processes that enable a performer's actions to be digitized and used to drive 3D characters. There are several types of motion capture technologies, each with its pros and cons.

One of the most popular motion capture methods uses a battery of wired RF (radio frequency) transmitters that are strapped onto the performer's body near the main joints. They emit a radio signal to a central receiver, and the software calculates the position of the transmitters relative to the receiver, in essence capturing the figure's position at any given moment. Recently, completely wireless motion capture systems have been introduced, allowing the performer much more freedom of movement (see figure 9.17).

Another motion capture system uses *optical tracking*, where the performer is covered with little targets (usually white disks or balls), and a video camera is used to digitize his actions. Here, the software tracks the position of the targets and uses that to determine the figure's positions. Prior to the introduction of the wireless radio systems, optical motion capture was the only way to record high-action sequences over a large area.

Optical or mechanical tracking is also used for *facial motion capture*, so that a character can speak and have expressions on top of their overall body movement. This is still done separately from the body motion capture, but at some point, an integrated solution will probably be developed.

The use of motion capture allows the creation of vast amounts of character animation that would take far longer to create with keyframe methods, but it does have its drawbacks. First of all, it's still a fairly expensive proposition, although there are service bureaus popping up, so you can satisfy your needs without having to purchase the gear. Second, the capture methods are still far from perfect, so animators often have to adjust the movement manually to take out glitches, or add motion that wasn't properly captured.

Motion Libraries

With a custom motion capture session being uneconomical for many projects, companies like Viewpoint have started to offer motion libraries for sale, just as they offer libraries of mesh. In addition to things like walk and run cycles, *motion libraries* offer action like reaching, bending, stretching, eating, dancing, and so forth. There are also martial arts moves and sports motions like swinging a baseball bat or throwing a football.

Although it's unlikely that you would be able to do an entire animation using only these canned sequences, they do give you a head start on creating custom animation that includes libraries as a component. They're also useful for adding motion quickly to background subjects to inject more activity into a scene without a lot of extra work.

The motion library data is used just like any motion capture information— by applying it to the bones of your character. Of course, the motions are all derived from humans, so if you're applying them to a character that has additional joints or some other alien characteristics, some modification is bound to be needed.

Animation Tutorials

Topics covered:

> **Creating Nulls and Links**
>
> **Duplicating the Mesh with Links**
>
> **Creating Looping Rotation**
>
> **Creating Blinking Lights**
>
> **Adjusting Motion Paths and Controls**
>
> **Using Inverse Kinematics**

Creating Nulls and Links

This tutorial will guide you through the creation of nulls and links for thrusters to make it move properly when animated.

1. Create a null object in the center of the thruster, extending beyond the shroud to make it easier to select. Name it ThrNUL01. Use Align to center the null around the shroud, then rotate it 45 degrees (see figure 9.18a).

2. Use Axis Move to slide the null's local axis forward until it's in the center of the mounting bracket. This will ensure that the thruster pivots around the mounting bracket, not the center of the shroud (see figure 9.18b).

3. Link the blades and other parts of the prop to the thruster nose cone, ThrNos. Try rotating the nose around its central axis to see if the blades spin properly (see figure 9.18c).

4. Link all of the thruster components, including the strut, to the null object ThrNUL01. Try rotating the null around the local axis that points toward the center of the mounting bracket to see if it turns properly, then return it to its original position (see figure 9.18d).

Use the same techniques to link the mirrored spotlights for the rotating beacon to a null object.

1. Create a null object in the center of the glass dome on the beacon object, extending beyond the glass to make it easier to select. Name it BeaNUL01. Use Align to center the null around the glass (see figure 9.19).

2. Link the two spotlights (and their targets, if any) to the null object. Try rotating the null around the beacon's central axis to see if the lights spin properly.

FIGURE 9.18

Linking thruster
components:
(a) Positioning the null
object. (b) Adjusting
the local axis of the
null for proper rotation.
(c) Linking the blades
to the nose cone.
(d) Testing the links by
rotating the null object.

Null Object

Local Axis Indicator

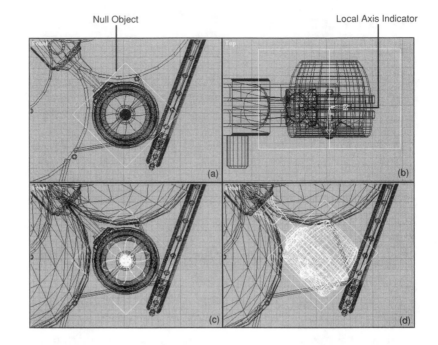

FIGURE 9.19

Prepare the beacon for
animation by creating a
null object centered over
the beacon and linking
the spotlights to it.

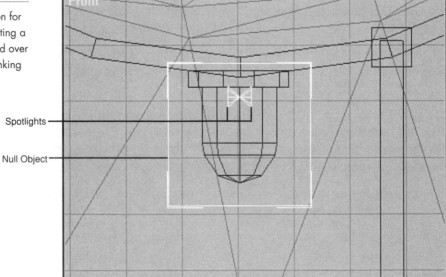

Spotlights

Null Object

Creating Looping Rotation

Looping rotation can be achieved in several ways, depending on the capabilities of the software. For example, you may be able to assign a behavior that does it automatically. Here, a keyframed loop is created that can be varied in length and number of rotations to do the job. The steps describe the process for the blimp thruster, but you should create a similar movement for the rotating beacons as well.

1. Activate the animation module or mode for your software. Go to frame 30 (see figure 9.20).

2. Rotate ThrNos01 around its central axis a full 360 degrees, making the linked blades rotate. Move the animation slider back and forth from frame 0 to frame 30 to make sure the rotation is working properly. You may need to assign a linear rotation controller to the motion, or adjust the continuity on the TCB controller for both keyframes to 0 in order to eliminate variations in speed or direction.

Current Frame Indicator   Frame 30 Keyframe   Time (in Frames)

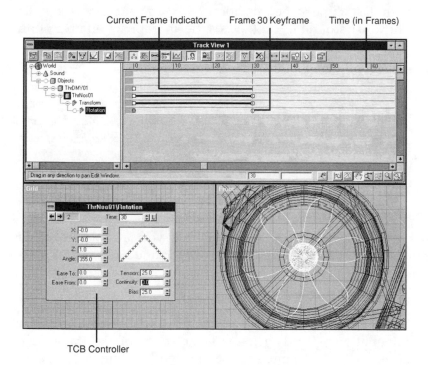

TCB Controller

FIGURE 9.20

Creating a rotational loop: By activating animation mode, going to frame 30, and rotating the thruster nose cone 360 degrees (along with the blades, because they're linked), a rotational keyframe is created.

At this point, if you were to render frames 0–29 and play them back in a continuous loop, the propeller would rotate smoothly. The reason you would not include frame 30 is because you would then have two frames (30 and 0) that were identical, and the loop would have a momentary hitch in it at that point.

3. Use the same technique to rotate the dummy object attached to the rotating beacon light. Have it spin at the same rate, 360 degrees, over the course of 30 frames.

If you want this rotation to repeat over a longer period, either use a rotation behavior, or use the following method.

1. Determine the total length of the animation and calculate the number of times the blades would have to rotate for that period of time.

2. With the first keyframe at frame 0, activate the animation mode and go to the last frame of the animation, based on your calculations. Rotate the ThrNos01 around its central axis the appropriate number of times.

Note that some 3D packages ignore rotations of more than 360 degrees between keyframes. For example, if you rotated an object 380 degrees, the program may only consider it to have been rotated 20 degrees, ignoring the full rotation completely. In these cases, there may be special settings you can use (see your manual) or you may have to set a series of keyframes, rotating the object 360 degrees or less each time.

Creating Blinking Lights

To create the effect of a blinking strobe light, you can animate the brightness setting of the point light on the end of the gondola.

1. Activate the animation module or mode for your software. Select the point light next to the gondola (see figure 9.21a).

2. The light's color was set to 255, 0, 0 red when it was created, and this information is held in frame 0. Refer to this keyframe as the "ON keyframe." Go to frame 1 and set the light's output level to 0, or its color to 0, 0, 0 black. This one is referred to as the "OFF keyframe" (see figure 9.21b).

3. Copy the ON keyframe in frame 0 to frame 5. If you were to render the animation now, the light would be on in frame 0, off in frame 1, and gradually increase in intensity from frames 2 to 5 (see figure 9.21c).

4. While some programs offer controllers that simply turn things on or off, assume that this feature is unavailable. Therefore, copy the OFF keyframe for the light from frame 1 to frames 4 and 6. The light remains off between frames 1 and 4 because both keyframes are OFF types (see figure 9.21d).

5. Render frames 0–6 as an animation. The light should blink twice, once at frame 0, and again at frame 5. You can then copy frames 4 through 6 as needed to continue the blinking sequence.

6. Use a similar process to animate the color of the beacon object itself, from a bright red material to a very dark red to reflect the changes in the light levels.

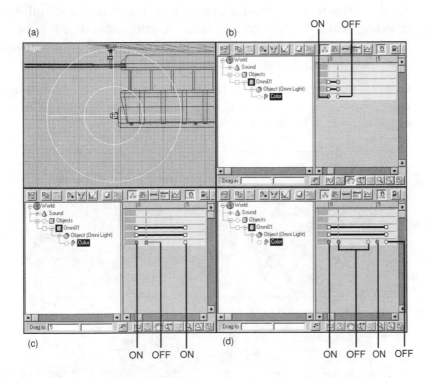

FIGURE 9.21

Creating a blinking light: (a) Select the point light next to the gondola. (b) Frame 0 is already ON, because the light was set to a bright red. Go to frame 1 and change the color of the light to black, turning it OFF. (c) Copy the ON keyframe to frame 5. (d) Copy the OFF keyframe to frames 4 and 6.

Duplicating the Mesh with Links

The last step in the general modeling process is the mirroring of portions of the mesh that have links and materials applied to fill out the rest of the model.

1. Select the spire assembly and Rotate-copy it around the center of the GasBag, so that there are four of them at 90 degree angles (see figure 9.22a).

2. Copy the beacons, searchlights, and other elements that need to be duplicated on the other side of the blimp into position. Rotate the copied beacon 90 degrees so that the beams from the two beacons won't be pointed at each other. Place a second copy of the searchlight assembly near the front of the blimp, facing forward to act as a headlight. The monitor assembly doesn't need to be duplicated, because it won't be seen in the shots you are doing (see figure 9.22b).

3. Select the thruster assembly, including the strut and base objects. Mirror-copy them and move the copies into position on the opposite side of the blimp (see figure 9.22c).

4. Hide or Freeze the GasBag, monitor and gondola assemblies, front searchlight and the ball and cylinder extending from the nose cone of the blimp. Use Mirror-copy to create a reversed copy, and position the mesh, using the GasBag as a reference (see figure 9.22d).

5. Create a large null object in the center of the GasBag, extending out a comfortable distance. Name it BmpNUL01. Unhide and/or Unfreeze all objects and link them to the null object.

FIGURE 9.22

Finishing off the mesh:
(a) Duplicating the spires. (b) Mirroring the thruster assembly. (c) Copying the searchlight and beacon. (d) Mirroring most of the mesh on the front half of the blimp.

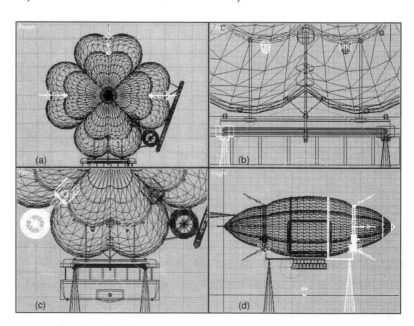

Adjusting Motion Paths and Controls

At this point, it's time to move the airship around a little. The basic plan is to have the blimp come into the frame, slow down, and stop. On your own, you can have it dock at this point with a tower that you'll be using in the next tutorial. Because the cameras and lights are already set up, make the current position of the blimp the ending point for the animation, and move backward. This is actually a pretty common practice in animating, because it enables you to set things up precisely in the modeling phase.

1. Activate the main camera view that was set up in the Chapter 8, "The Camera," tutorials. The blimp was linked to the large null object earlier, so the blimp will be moved by moving the BmpNUL01 null object (see figure 9.23a).

2. To speed things up during animation and test renders, turn off all mesh except for the GasBag object and null. If your software offers a fast viewport mode, switch to it so that the screen updates even faster (see figure 9.23b).

3. Activate animation mode and set the total length of the animation to 121 frames (meaning that it ends on frame 120, because there is a frame 0). This is much too short for the move you are going to do, but is more practical for this type of tutorial. You can extend the overall length of the animation later. In the top view, note the present position of the blimp (see figure 9.23c).

4. Go to frame 120 and rotate the null object 90 degrees clockwise. Move the null diagonally until the GasBag object is just off the edge of the Camera view (see figure 9.23d).

5. Select the movement (translation) keyframe at frame 0 and examine the TCB controller. The blimp should settle into or out of position, rather than start or stop abruptly, so set the Ease From control to about 35 (see figure 9.24a).

6. The move is too linear right now, so go to frame 60 and move the null object to create a little curvature to the path (see figure 9.24b).

7. Keep an eye on the animation timeline to make sure that the keyframes are properly located, and that other object parameters haven't been inadvertently altered (see figure 9.24c).

8. Make a preview or quick render of the move from the camera viewport and make any adjustments to the path or controller settings. Try to avoid extreme settings, because they tend to cause trouble in adjacent keyframes as well.

FIGURE 9.23

Moving the blimp:
(a) Select the camera viewport. (b) Hide unnecessary mesh.
(c) Switch to the Top view and activate animation mode.
(d) Rotate the null that the blimp is linked to and move it diagonally until it disappears from the camera viewport.

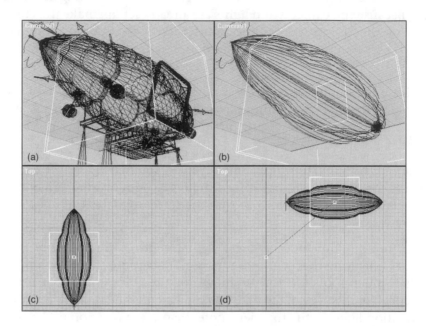

FIGURE 9.24

Completing the blimp move: (a) Set the TCB controller for the starting frame to Ease From frame 0. (b) Add a keyframe in the middle of the path to make it curve a bit.
(c) Check your work in the animation timeline periodically, and use it for any time or weighting adjustment of keyframes.

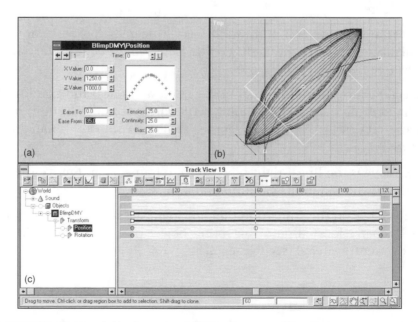

This is just the beginning of setting up an animation move like this. Once the movement is solid, go in and add additional elements, such as subtle rocking, drifting, and elevation changes, as if a breeze were affecting the blimp. You also can rotate the thrusters and have the blimp's attitude change in response. Don't forget to continue the looping animation of the lights and props throughout the length of the animation.

Using Inverse Kinematics

Located on the CD-ROM is an additional model of a docking structure constructed by the book's Technical Editor, Simon Knights. You may either import the model when needed, or build a docking tower of your own design as another component of your exercises. Because the tower and blimp are both large projects that could bog down your system if loaded simultaneously, only the key portions of the tower and blimp will be used in this tutorial.

In this tutorial, set up movement constraints on the pre-built tower, then experiment with Inverse Kinematics to see how the tower equipment can be moved to grab hold of the docking point of the blimp.

1. Load the exercise file IKTUT.3DS or IKTUT.DXF from the CD-ROM. This file contains portions of the tower and blimp project (see figure 9.25a).

2. The key portions of the tower relating to IK are the gear-like platform and the docking machinery mounted on it (see figure 9.25b).

The purpose of the exercise is to link and constrain the docking equipment (see figure 9.25c), so that it can be swung around and latch onto the end of the blimp nose cone (see figure 9.25d).

3. Identify the components of the base assembly, which will rotate around the geared platform. These components will be linked to the Base object, which will have constraints applied to it (see figure 9.26a).

4. It's nearly always best to adjust the pivot point of objects before linking. Make sure that the Base object's pivot is at the center of the geared platform.

5. When linking, make sure that you understand the order in which your software asks you to link objects. Start at the Base object, making this the

parent of the base assembly objects above it. When all the base assembly objects are linked, continue the process by linking the Rack object to the chain. Continue on, linking the other members of the rack assembly to the Rack object. Finally, link the Rod object, and then the plunger, onto the chain. At this point, you should have linked everything between the Base object and the plunger at the end of the rod assembly.

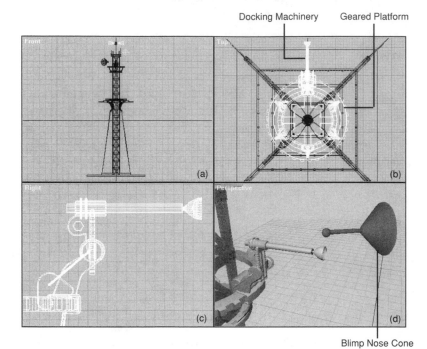

Docking Machinery   Geared Platform

Blimp Nose Cone

6. To confirm that you have linked everything correctly, rotate the Base object around the pivot point, which you already set to the center of the geared platform. All of the pieces should move with the Base as it circles the platform. Many software packages also have a Show Hierarchy or Show Tree command that enable you to visually check that the links in the model are correct.

7. Next, all of the joints of the mechanism have to be defined. This involves choosing whether a joint rotates or slides, then determining in what ways it needs to be constrained.

8. Using the method described by your manuals, set the Base object to be a rotational joint constrained to rotate around the vertical axis, so that it can freely traverse the perimeter of the geared platform, but cannot rotate in any other direction (see figure 9.26b).

9. Set the rack to be a sliding joint, and constrain it so that it can move up and down along the vertical axis only. Set the constraints so that it will not smash down into the base assembly when lowered, or come apart from it when raised (see figure 9.26c).

10. The plunger-like rod assembly also needs sliding constraints, allowing it to extend outward and retract while remaining inside the sleeve at the top of the rack assembly. As with the last step, make sure it doesn't slide too far in or out (see figure 9.26d).

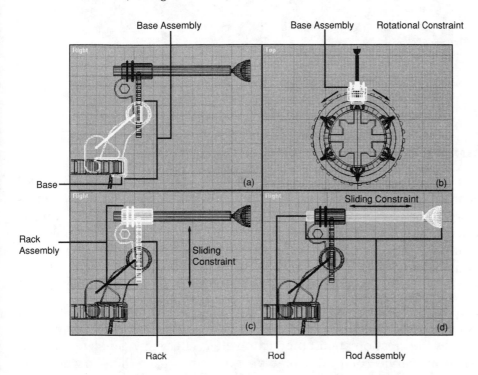

FIGURE 9.26

Setting the constraints: (a) Link the various components of the docking machinery from the Base to the plunger at the end of the Rod. (b) Constrain the base to rotate around the platform only. (c) Set the rack assembly to slide up and down. (d) Set the rod assembly to slide back and forth.

11. Once all the constraints are set, make sure that IK is active and prepare to test the docking machinery movement (see figure 9.27a).

12. Select the end of the plunger and simply move it to the nose cone. If everything is set properly, the docking machinery will rotate and slide as needed to make the two objects meet (see figure 9.27b).

FIGURE 9.27

Test the constraints by selecting the end of the plunger and simply move it to the nose cone. If everything is set properly, the docking machinery will rotate and slide as needed.

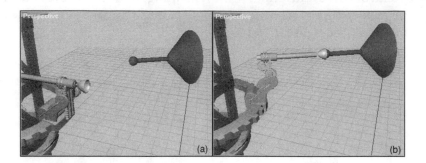

Summary

This chapter started out with a look at basic animation terminology and techniques, from the timeline to motion paths, and discussed the differences between forward and inverse kinematics. It discussed how bones can be added to mesh to animate and distort it, and touched on the tools and techniques of character animation. Although this was just an overview, you should now have an understanding of the basic techniques, and be able to build your skill and understanding through practice and experimentation.

Chapter 10, "Rendering and Output," explores render time issues like resolution, aspect ratios, color depth, palettes, and atmosphere. You will see the uses and creation of post production effects like glows and lens flares, as well as an overview of the different types of output, from slides to videotape.

Rendering and Output

This inhospitable planetoid, featuring particle system eruption effects, was created with Kinetix 3D Studio MAX.
Image by Andy Murdock ©1996 Mechadeus.

*T*he Master rose slowly from his chair and stretched. "I'm thinking of retiring early, lad," he said to the student, who was mulling over a scene floating above his glowing pool.

The youth shook himself out of his reverie. "Oh, can I ask a couple quick questions before you leave?"

"Certainly. Let's see what you have." The Master walked over to consider the student's scene, set near a pond with the castle a short distance away. Tiny fireflies circled the pond, zipping into and out of the image. "Nice job on the lighting," the old man said, "and the composition is good too. Needs a little atmosphere, though."

"That was my first question!" chirped the student. "How do I summon a bit of mist?"

"Fawghorne Vaeporrub," intoned the Master, causing a gentle vapor to rise from the pond. The fog took the edge off the castle in the background and made the scene much more realistic.

"That's great," commented the lad. "Now, about the fireflies. They just look like little white dots floating around."

"Indeglow Luciferase," replied the old man, causing the white specks to generate tiny halos of light. "You see, they just needed a bit of a glow to them, like the real thing."

"Wonderful!" exclaimed the student. "But there's still something funny about the way they move."

"Hmmm." The old man settled into a chair to rest his weary bones. He studied the movement of the fireflies for a short while, then said, "Yes, you see the ones that zip in and out of the image, close to our viewpoint? They're too sharp."

"Too sharp?" asked the lad.

"Yes, they should blur a bit when they move, like so. Dizipaace Shinkansen," the Master chanted, making a swirling gesture with his hand. Now, the fast moving fireflies left short and subtle but realistic trails of light as they darted about.

"Excellent! That did it!" cried the lad. The Master smiled and got halfway up before the student bade him to wait. "Just one more thing. How would I make the fireflies swarm together and transform into a fairy princess in a swirl of color and light?"

The old man groaned and fell heavily into his chair once more. It was going to be a late night.

Rendering

As the Dark Ages Master demonstrated, some effects can be applied to 3D imagery at rendering time to take the hard edge off and make it appear more natural and realistic. Before you're ready to attempt these digital sleights of hand, however, you must review some render time basics, such as resolution, alpha channels, palettes, and so on.

Resolution

After you decide on the type of rendering to use—Flat, Phong, Ray Tracing, or any of the others detailed in Chapter 3, "Delving Into Cyberspace"—you must tackle the question of resolution. As you no doubt recall, resolution refers to the number of vertical and horizontal pixels in an image. Resolution is defined by a set of two numbers, such as 640 × 480, which means that the image is 640 pixels wide (horizontal), and 480 pixels high (vertical).

The relationship between the height and width of the image is called the *aspect ratio*, and is calculated by dividing the horizontal resolution by the vertical resolution. In the 640 × 480 example, the aspect ratio would be 640 divided by 480, which equals 1.33:1 (or 4:3). This is a common aspect ratio for computer monitors and 35mm photography. However, if you were doing film special effects work, the aspect ratio would be between 1.33:1 and 2.35:1, depending on the type of film and projection system, because movie screens are much wider in relation to their height.

The following is a list of common resolutions and aspect ratios:

512 × 482, 1.06:1—Video resolution

640 × 480, 1.33:1—Base level computer monitor resolution

800 × 600, 1.33:1—Moderate level computer monitor resolution

1,024 × 768, 1.33:1—High level computer monitor resolution, low print resolution

2,048 × 1,536, 1.33:1—Moderate print resolution

4,096 × 3,072, 1.33:1—High print resolution

3,072 × 2,048, 1.5:1—High 35mm slide/film resolution

> QuickTime VR and similar formats enable the user to navigate around a 360 degree still image view of a space or object (See Chapter 1, "The Virtual Path"). To create this kind of "surround" rendering, you can set up a camera to rotate a total of 360 degrees over a space of 120 frames. Render your images at the vertical resolution desired, but make them only three pixels wide. When the rendering is done, assemble the first 190 three-pixel-wide renderings into a single panoramic image.

Another value related to resolution may be more familiar to you as a printer specification: *dots per inch* or *DPI*. This DPI measurement means exactly what it says—the number of dots that the medium can display (or print) in one inch. With computer monitors, a dot is a pixel, and the setting varies according to the size of the monitor and the resolution. However, you can usually adjust the monitor to yield 72–75 dpi, which translates to a 1,027 × 768 resolution on a 17" monitor. This dpi setting works out nicely for desktop publishing work, because common printer resolutions are usually a multiple of 75, such as 150, 300, 600, or 1,200 dpi.

To see how pixels and dpi interrelate when printing, consider the 640 × 480 image as an example. If you print the image at a low-quality 75 dpi, the resulting image is 8.53" × 6.4". To calculate this, you simply divide the resolution by the dpi value. At a moderate 150 dpi, it would yield an image 4.27" × 3.2". At 300 dpi (the typical laser printer maximum), it would only be 2.13" × 1.6" and so forth. By the same token, suppose you wanted to create an image that would print at 8.0" × 10.5" at 150 dpi. By multiplying the size of the final image by the desired dpi, you get a required image resolution of 1200 × 1575.

Color Depth

The *color depth* of an image is how many colors each pixel is capable of displaying. The value is usually expressed in terms of how many bits (a computerese term for a single binary number) an image contains. In an 8-bit image (such as a .GIF file), for example, each pixel is represented by 8 bits (called a *byte*), which allows the pixel to be any one of 256 different colors. To understand how the eight turns into 256 you must take a side trip into some math.

As you know, computers use binary numbers, also called Base 2. A single binary number (a bit) can only be one of two things: either 0 or 1. Therefore, to represent larger numbers, a series of bits are strung together, like 1011. The position of each binary number within the series (from right to left) becomes an exponent of 2, and then they are added together. For example, binary 0001 = 1, binary 0010 = 2, binary 0100 = 4, and so on. In this way, 8 bits = binary $11111111 = 2^7+2^6+2^5+2^4+2^3+2^2+2^1+2^0 = 128+64+32+16+8+4+2+1 = 255$. Because zero counts as a number, a total of 256 numbers can be represented.

By the same token, a 4-bit image has a maximum of 16 color possibilities (8+4+2+1 = 16, when 0 is counted), a 16-bit image has 65,536 potential colors per pixel, and a 24-bit image has a whopping 16,777,216 color options. The latter palette is nearly the full range of colors that are visible to humans, and enables you to work with smooth, accurate color images.

In color images, the total number of bits per pixel is divided by three, and assigned to each of the three primary colors that make up light: red, green, and blue. In other words, in a 24-bit image, there are 8 bits of red information, 8 bits of green, and 8 bits of blue. Each R, G, or B *channel*, being 8-bit, can display that color in any one of 256 levels of brightness, with 0 being no brightness and 255 being full brightness. That's why RGB colors are specified by three sets of numbers, such as 0,0,0 (black), 255,255,255 (white), 255,0,0 (red), 255,0,255 (violet), and so forth.

Alpha Channel

Just when you've got bit counts figured out, along come alpha channels. An *alpha channel* is an optional layer of image data that provides an additional eight bits of information about transparency. This information is simply tacked onto the RGB data that defines the image, so a 24-bit image with an alpha channel becomes a 32-bit image. The alpha channel, like each of the R, G, or B channels, is capable of 256 levels of intensity, but instead of being interpreted as a color, the information is used to vary the transparency of the associated image against a background (see figure 10.1). In this way, the alpha channel functions as a *mask* or *matte*, allowing portions of an image to be seen, while the rest is replaced with the background image.

FIGURE 10.1

Alpha channel
example:
(a) Foreground (FG)
image with opaque and
translucent objects.
(b) Alpha Channel from
FG image.
(c) Background (BG)
image. (d) Composite
of FG image over BG
image using alpha
channel to control
transparency.

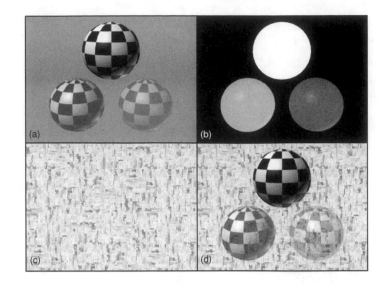

In most programs, 0 (black) is fully transparent, so pixels of that color in the alpha channel would not allow the foreground image pixel in the same position to show up at all, meaning that the background pixel color would be unaffected. A 255 (white) pixel would be completely opaque, making the foreground image pixel completely obscure the background pixel. All other levels of gray would blend the foreground and background pixel colors to some degree.

Because alpha channels allow for transparency effects, multiple images with alpha channels can be composited together into a single image. Using alpha channels is a convenient method for compositing 3D images over still photographs or video, because you can render the model with the alpha channel setting activated, and any objects that appear automatically mask out the background image, enabling you to combine the images in a paint or editing program.

Alpha channels also are convenient when working entirely in 3D, because render-intensive scenes can be broken into layers and rendered with alpha channels, then composited together later. This is particularly useful when dealing with elements that can be used in multiple scenes, because you have to render them only once, then can combine them with other elements later on. This also gives you the opportunity to use image processing on the layers to adjust contrast, change the color balance, or add effects. In addition, digital video can be inserted into 3D scenes by filming the subjects against a blue or green background, then dropping the solid color background out by converting it to an alpha channel.

> The multi-layer 3D approach was used extensively in the Artemis cockpit scenes of *The Daedalus Encounter*. The scenes consisted of five layers, starting with a looping render showing POV movement through a starfield. Next came a still image of the ship's hull, which was repositioned to make more of the stars visible. On top of that was the interior of the cockpit, with control panels and displays. Next came the actors in their chairs, the only live element in the composite. Finally, the foreground layer was a console that was located between the two actors.

In most programs, activating the alpha channel is easy. It's usually located in the render options dialog, and is either on or off. Compositing can then be done in the 3D program's video post system (if it has one) or in Photoshop or a digital video editing program like Premiere.

Palettes

A *palette* is the full set of colors used or available for use in an image. It is generally limited to 256 colors or less, but any digital image could be considered to have a palette, although palettes larger than 8-bits get too ungainly to modify (see figure 10.2).

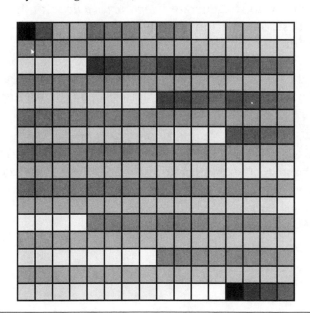

FIGURE 10.2

A 256-color (okay, grayscale) palette. Each individual color location is called a color register.

Not so long ago, palette management was a major consideration in the multimedia industry. Presentation designs had to be carefully planned to ensure that all the graphics would work with a single palette or that the switching of palettes was carefully disguised. Still, despite all the planning, the last few hours before the deadline were often devoted to tracking down *palette flashes,* the bizarre color shifts that can occur when a palette is changed.

Now, with most newer systems offering 32K–1.6M colors, the painful memories of having to deal with 256-color graphics are steadily fading. Still, there are many situations that still demand the speed or other special capabilities of 8-bit graphics, particularly games and products or presentations designed for the broadest possible market.

When developing a product or application designed to be used with an 8-bit graphics display, you will probably have to force the image to a pre-defined palette to avoid flashes. If you have to do this, there is a lot to be said for using the native palette of the target system (the Windows or Apple *system palettes*). Because these palettes are already pre-loaded and all of the desktop graphics and most other applications use them, the problem of the screen flashing is eliminated, because you never switch to a custom palette. Unfortunately, the system palettes are ill-suited to most photographic images, and usually result in smooth gradients becoming banded or other strange patches of color.

If your 24-bit image needs to be reduced to 8-bit or less, you can use the 3D program or Photoshop to generate an *optimized palette* for the image, one that includes the best combination of colors to keep it as faithful as possible to the original. Unfortunately, the palette that works best for one image rarely works well for another, unless they have a very similar color scheme. If you have multiple images that need a single palette, try grouping them all together into a single image and extracting a palette from that.

There was an article in *Morph's Outpost* a few years ago in which someone came up with a universal palette that they had developed (if I recall correctly) based on a study of how the human eye perceives color. I tried to locate some additional information about this palette and its creator on the Web, but couldn't find any mention of it. However, it is included on the CD-ROM as UNIVPAL.GIF so you can give it a try.

Using the *dither* setting can help a lot as well, because it allows the program to break gradients up into patterns of variously colored pixels that work like the printing process to simulate a wider range of colors. The best type of pattern to use for most images is a *diffusion dither*, because the positions of the pixels are randomized, and look more natural and unobtrusive.

While Photoshop with a diffusion dither does a fine job of palletizing images, the best program I ever came across for converting 24-bit photographic imagery to 8-bit was a Mac product called Fast Eddie, from Paradigm Concepts, Inc.

One interesting offshoot of the 8-bit palette is the ability to perform color cycling animation. This type of animation works not by altering the image itself, but by changing the colors in it through direct manipulation of the *color registers* (the individual "paint pots" in the palette). This method is often used to create the illusion of water flowing in 8-bit images.

The most impressive application of palette animation I've seen was in a daily organizer product called Seize the Day, created by one of LucasArts' animators. It featured 12 fantasy landscape scenes with effects like rippling water and reflections. Interestingly, the scene would change in keeping with the time of day, causing the lighting and colors to change as the sun rose and set. On random days, even the weather would change, at times appearing to be foggy or overcast, or even raining.

Antialiasing

Because digital images are basically made up of a matrix of dots, lines that aren't perfectly horizontal or vertical take abrupt "drops" when they enter a new row or column of dots (an effect called *stairstepping*). The resulting lines look jagged, which is why images containing them are described as "having the *jaggies*" (see figure 10.3).

Antialiasing is a method of reducing jagginess by filling in pixels at the stairstepping points with colors that are midway between the line color and the background color. The result softens the stairstepping and makes the line look more fluid.

FIGURE 10.3

Line types: (a) Non-anti-
aliased line showing
stairstepping effect.
(b) Antialiasing inserts
middle tones that blend
the line into the
background, reducing
the jaggies.

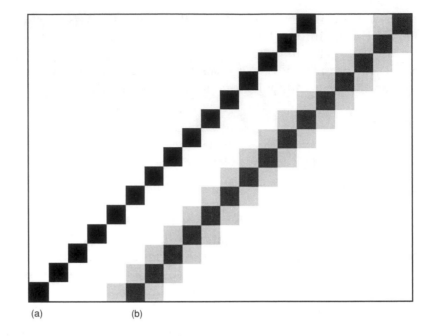

(a)   (b)

Most programs enable you to adjust the amount of anti-aliasing in an image
or at least turn it on and off. Because anti-aliasing does increase render times,
you may want to leave it off for most of your test renders, then turn it back
on for final testing and output.

Atmosphere

Adding *atmosphere* settings to a model causes it to render with a user-defined
level of diffusion, creating the effect of objects being seen from great
distances or through a mist.

Fog is the most common atmospheric effect, and is just what it sounds like,
a mist effect. It can, however, have colors assigned to it, so it's really more like
smoke (see figure 10.4). Fog is usually defined with a set of ranges that
delineate where the effect begins and ends, as well as a pair of percentages
indicating minimum and maximum concentration.

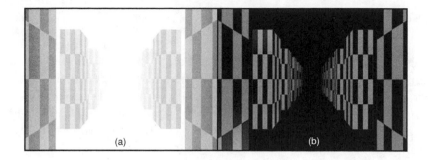

FIGURE 10.4

Atmosphere samples:
(a) Fog effect using
white for the
atmosphere color.
(b) Depth cueing
created by using black
for the atmosphere
color.

(a) (b)

If the fog color is more or less white, you get an effect similar to real fog. If the color is black, distant objects become dark or totally black, which can be convenient for downplaying a background without having to fiddle with the lighting too much.

> It's a good idea to use fog for most exterior scenes. Keep the color on the blue side and the concentration low for "clear days" so that distant objects have a realistic haze to them.

Some programs have the capability to use bitmaps to define fog color, or even volumetric fog, which is similar to the volumetric lighting discussed in Chapter 7, "Lighting." *Volumetric fog* can often be animated, so that realistic variations in the mist concentration drift through the scene.

Geometry Channel

Although a rare feature, the Geometry Channel is an interesting item that bears mentioning. *G-buffer* or *geometry channel* support means that the program is capable of outputting additional image channels that use grayscale images to describe the *geometry* in the model. G-buffer channels include: Distance, Normals, XYZ position, UV coordinates, and others.

With the right kind of image editing or post processing software, this feature could enable you to do such seemingly impossible things as replacing the texture map on a object *after the image is rendered*. This would be particularly useful in applications where the structure of something has been decided upon, but the material is still under consideration. One use would be in the kitchen cabinet design business, where a 3D model of the kitchen with the new cabinets has been built, but the clients want to look through different wood types and finishes without waiting for the scene to be re-rendered.

Post-Production Effects

There are effects that are difficult to achieve in the animation or rendering phases of production, so some 3D products offer *post-production effects*, which include transitions, color manipulation, and a host of special effects. If your program doesn't offer this capability, you can use the video painting techniques discussed later in this section, or rely on digital video editing software (see Chapter 11, "The Reel") for most of the effects mentioned in this section.

One of the most common capabilities of built-in post effects is compositing images and animation using alpha channels or chroma keys, as discussed earlier. Other functions include generating lens flares, glows, and motion blur.

Lens Flares

A *lens flare* is the pattern of bright circles and rays that is seen when you point a camera lens at the sun or other bright light source (see figure 10.5). Lens flares add realism to scenes with bright lights, helping to create the illusion that a real camera was used for the shot. Interestingly, although the human eye never experiences this kind of effect, we're so used to seeing it in films and television that it "looks right" to us.

FIGURE 10.5

Lens flares are caused by bright sources of light interacting with camera lens elements. Their appearance varies significantly, depending on the lens type and brightness of the light source.

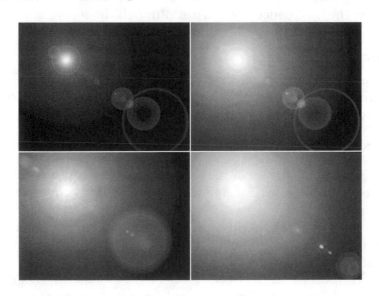

Depending on the program, the lens flare control may be built-in, or added on as a plug-in. Controls range from a basic brightness control to extensive choices of real-world lens effects. Some products, such as LightWave, can use any source of light to generate a lens flare. Other programs may have invisible "generator objects" or emitters that are the focus of the effect. In this case, you would place the generator near the apparent light source.

Lens flares are particularly dynamic and effective when either the camera or the light source causing the flare are in motion. Another nice touch is to have the subject block the light source momentarily as it moves across the screen.

Glows

Chapter 7, "Lighting," talked about ways to add a realistic halo of light, or *glow,* to an exposed light source (such as a bare bulb). The glow effect is a commonly needed one for 3D graphics, and many products incorporate this capability (see figure 10.6).

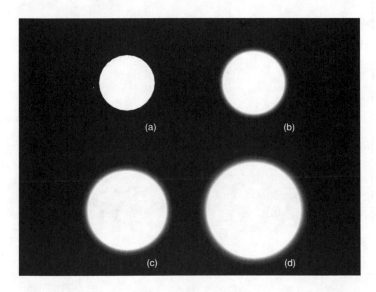

(a)

(b)

(c)

(d)

FIGURE 10.6

Glow effect samples: (a) Self-illuminated object without glow. (b–d) Various amounts of glow applied to the object.

In most cases, glows are applied by the software after the image is rendered as part of the video post process. Glows are usually either assigned to objects (using a G-buffer), a particular color in the scene, or a material. Using a particular color to trigger the glow effect can be troublesome, because there may be other objects in the scene that are of a similar color, but aren't intended to glow.

Another problem is that glows may not work if there is a translucent object between the glowing material and the camera. This might occur if you built a typical light fixture where the bulb is protected by a glass cover of some kind. If you applied the glow to the bulb, the glow may not appear, because the glass is in the way. There are two workarounds for this. First, you could make the glass cover itself glow instead. Second, you could render a foreground layer for the scene that would just have the exposed portion of the glass against an alpha channel, then composite the images together.

Motion Blur

Motion Blur is the smearing of an image when the subject or camera is in motion (see figure 10.7). Motion blur is a natural occurrence, and fast-moving objects look unnaturally sharp if the effect isn't present. It also works well in still images to convey a sense of movement and speed.

FIGURE 10.7

Motion Blur effects:
(a) Unaffected object.
(b) 20-pixel Motion Blur applied with Photoshop.
(c) 5-step motion blur created by 3D renderer.

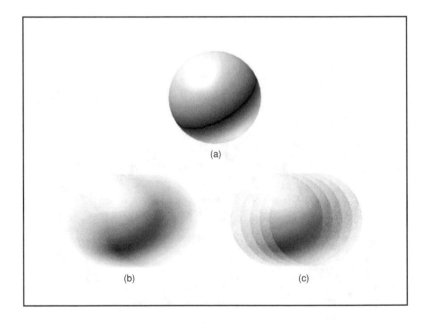

(a)

(b)   (c)

Motion blur occurs in photography because the shutter on the camera is open long enough for a significant movement to occur. Because virtual cameras have no shutter and freeze all action perfectly, this effect has to be added through special rendering techniques or post-production image processing.

One of the common techniques used by programs to create motion blur is rendering the scene a number of times while advancing the animation slightly. The multiple images are then composited together into a single, motion-blurred image. Of course, this means a 4–5 fold increase in rendering time. Another way to create the effect is to apply a directional blurring filter in post production, which produces a more realistic result.

> If you opt to do motion blurs with Photoshop (discussed in the next section), you can reduce your workload by rendering the object to be blurred against an alpha channel and by restricting the blur effect to objects that pass close to the camera. Motion blur is most apparent in this situation, but falls off quickly once the object is advancing through the frame more slowly.

Video Painting

Despite the capabilities of built-in video post features or digital video editing products like Premiere, there may be some times when even more control or capabilities are needed to pull off an effect. For this kind of work, you can turn to your good old 2D paint program, or one that features *video painting* capabilities (the ability to paint on a digital video file, either frame-by-frame or over a series of frames). It can be more time consuming, but these methods enable you to do compositing, create lens flares, and apply glows and motion blurs with a great deal of control over the final result.

While Photoshop doesn't currently offer video painting, you can export frames from the video editing software, paint on them, or add selection-controlled effects, and then re-import them into the DVE software.

Fractal Painter, on the other hand, has frame painting controls built-in, enabling you to preview your work much more easily than with Photoshop. Fractal also offers a wide range of interesting effects brushes and filters. The downside is that many artists find Fractal's interface clumsy to use and lacking in the solid, basic brush controls that are Photoshop's strength.

Autodesk Animator has been around a long time as an animation tool, but it used to be limited to 256 colors, making it a poor choice for video work. That changed with the release of Animator Studio, a whole new animal that can work with 24-bit Video for Windows files. On top of the 2D animation tools that made Autodesk Animator so popular, the new version has added audio importation and synching capabilities.

Dedicated video paint programs, like Strata, Inc.'s Media Paint and Special Effects Pack #1, also enable you to add paint-style effects or touch up problem areas in digital video. But in addition to typical paint tools like brushes, lines, selections, fills, and polygons, Media Paint offers animated procedural effects that can be applied over time. One set of tools enables you to animate points across the screen, following parameters such as Speed, Gravity, Size, Friction, and so forth. Using these tools enables the user to create spark effects without having to animate them individually, as they would with most other products. Other tools provide effects like squiggling lines and electrical arcs (see figure 10.8).

FIGURE 10.8

Strata's Media Paint and Special Effects Packages enable users to create procedural 2D post effects, like these electrical arcs.

We made good use of both Premiere and Photoshop post effects in Daedalus. Premiere allowed us to composite the bluescreen video over the 3D backgrounds, adjust color balance to get rid of the bluish cast, create complex multi-layer mattes and composites, and do some easy but effective static and video roll effects. Photoshop was used to add sparks and debris coming off two colliding ships, as well as to cause some real spherical props held by the actors to be absorbed and disintegrated into a receptacle created with 3D graphics. For details on how these effects were accomplished, see *The Official Guide to the Daedalus Encounter* and the July 1996 issue of *Inter-Activity* magazine.

Output

Once you've decided what to render and how to render it, that just leaves *where* to render it. This section discusses the various output destinations, examines common file formats and compression methods, and explains the special requirements of videotape.

Output Options

The typical output media for animation includes computer files, photographic slides, and videotape. Take a look at what each of these has to offer.

Files

The primary destination for your rendering is most likely a file or files stored on the hard drive, even when your project will ultimately be output to a 35mm slide or videotape. Because outputting to a file is an integral part of your 3D software, there's not a lot to be said about it, short of considering the file formats and compression methods available, which is discussed later.

Of course, an important part of the disk output process is file naming and management. For information on these subjects, and how to develop a file naming convention, refer back to Chapter 4, "3D Modeling." Information on mass storage options to hold all those files can be found in Chapter 2, "Nuts and Bolts."

The biggest problem you're likely to experience with disk output is running out of hard drive space. Remember that rendering often consumes a great deal of virtual memory provided by the hard drive, so the amount available when you start the render may drop by tens of megabytes or more later in

continues

Videotape

Before desktop video became so popular, animation was often output directly to videotape using expensive single-frame VCRs. In some cases, special interface gear also was required, such as VTR controllers that would sense when the frame was rendered and activate the VCR. Besides being expensive, frame-by-frame animation takes a heavy toll on the video recorder, and forces you to put a great deal of trust into a single $30.00 tape cassette.

With today's mass storage being so fast and reasonably priced, it has become a lot more common to save the files to disk first, then lay the animation off to tape using desktop digital video gear, a commercial framestore (high speed digital playback system), or off-line frame-by-frame recording. There are, however, a number of restrictions related to video output, which are discussed in more depth later in this section.

Slides

35mm slides are another popular output method for still imagery. Although just about any resolution will work for slides, for the best results, create high-resolution images at around 3,072×2,048 pixels or higher, keeping the aspect ratio at 1.5:1 (3:2). You can have the slides made by a service bureau (unless you have a film recorder).

Prints

Print is also a popular output destination, but the subject of matching the image onscreen to the final press result could fill a book by itself. The main things to keep in mind are that screen and print color gamut are quite different, so there are a lot of RGB colors you can have in your rendering that won't reproduce properly in a CMYK print. *CMYK (Cyan Magenta Yellow blacK)* refers to the different colors of ink in the 4-color process that are applied as tiny dot patterns to form the gamut of printing colors. Photoshop has many features that are geared toward making the transition from digital file to print output, including a CMYK viewing mode as well as filters and alerts that flag or correct unprintable colors.

Calibration

Computer monitors suffer from several big drawbacks. First, they're very non-standard, varying tremendously from manufacturer to manufacturer and model to model. Second, they have easily changed brightness and contrast settings. As a result, if you look at the same image using different monitors, you will almost certainly see differences in hue, saturation, and brightness.

This lack of standardization is an endless source of wasted time and frustration in computer graphics. Different artists working on different systems see different results, and make corrections based on false information. As a result, when scenes from these artists are assembled into one project, the inconsistencies become glaringly obvious.

The best way to correct this problem is to use a quality monitor, and to adjust it regularly with a *color calibrator*, a device that is held up to the screen and adjusts the monitor using a special reference image that is displayed at the time. Unfortunately, these devices are still fairly uncommon outside of companies that work with digital imagery bound for print.

One adjustment that you can easily make is *gamma*, which refers to the overall brightness of the screen. Photoshop has a built-in gamma adjustment, as do some 3D programs. This enables you to adjust the screen gamma by using an onscreen pattern of dots as a guide. Gamma varies by display, platform and output type, so adjusting it in this manner enables you to see how your monitor image (gamma 1.6–2.0) will look when output to a CMYK print (gamma 1.8) or on videotape (gamma 2.2).

Some programs may offer several gamma adjustments, one for the screen, one for file output, and perhaps one for file input as well. Leave the file gamma settings at the default setting unless you're certain that you need to change them. Altering the output gamma can cause big problems if your work is being integrated with other work that has a different gamma setting.

Compression

To reduce image and animation or digital video file sizes, various methods have been devised to compress the data in the file. There are two general categories into which this compression falls: lossy and lossless.

Lossless compression reduces file size without impacting the image quality by finding strings of identical information and using an algorithm to encode the color and location of repeated data. For example, if you were compressing a file that had a 100 pixel long block of solid white, the compression software would use a shorthand method like "255×100" instead of repeating the number 255 one hundred times in the file. Because the data isn't really lost, just recorded in a more efficient way, the image quality remains unchanged. Lossless compression capability is built into many of the image formats, including .GIF, .TGA, .TIF, and others.

Lossy compression reduces file sizes by changing the data or throwing some of it away. The most popular types of lossy compression are reducing the color depth or using compression algorithms to eliminate small differences in pixel colors. While lossy compression usually has a negative impact on the image quality, the degradation can be reduced by generating a custom palette, or using only a moderate amount of compression.

Digital video file formats like .AVI and QuickTime are designed to accept plug-in compression methods called *codecs (COmpressor/DECompressorS)*. Some of the popular ones are MS Video, Indeo, and Cinepak. Each has its own strengths and weaknesses, and the correct selection depends on the application, target platform, and storage medium. MPEG compression seems to be the winner for picture quality and compression, but often requires some special hardware for compression and playback.

File Formats

There are quite a number of image formats in use, ranging from proprietary formats used by only one or two programs or platforms to those that span virtually all systems. Unless otherwise noted, all of the following are 24-bit or 32-bit formats that can handle lower bit depths as well:

◆ *AVI (Audio Video Interlaced)* was developed by Microsoft as the digital video standard for PCs. It can accept many different types of compression methods.

◆ *BMP (BitMaP)* was developed by Microsoft as the native format for icons and images in the Windows environment. It is interchangeable with *DIB (Device Independent Bitmap)*.

◆ *FLC (FLiCk)* is an 8-bit animation format developed for Autodesk multimedia products. It features lossless compression in several resolutions. An older format, *FLI*, was limited to a 320 × 200 maximum resolution.

◆ *GIF (Graphics Interchange Format)* is an 8-bit lossless compression format owned by CompuServe but used extensively by commercial and shareware products. Recently, the popularity of animation on the Web has led to the use of GIF as an animation format, a capability it always had, but that was rarely used until now.

◆ *IFF (Interchange File Format)* is popular on the Amiga system, and has made its way onto other platforms through products like LightWave.

◆ *JPG, JPEG (Joint Photographic Experts Group)* was developed as a lossy way to radically compress photographic images by eliminating minor differences in pixel colors. This method achieves one of the highest compression rates, but can cause undesirable artifacting if pushed too far, or compressed more than once. If you use this method, it's a good idea to have a lossless version saved as well. JPEG also can be used to compress digital video files.

◆ *LBM* is an 8-bit format popularized by Deluxe Paint, a rather old program that's still popular for creating game graphics and other 256-color imagery.

◆ *MPG, MPEG (Motion Picture Experts Group)* is a lossy video compression method that's considered to be the best currently available. There are two implementations, MPEG 1, which is currently in use for CD-ROM-based video, and MPEG 2, which is used by the new DVD players.

◆ *PCT, PICT (PICTure)* is the native still image format popular on the Macintosh. A unique feature of this format is that it can contain both bitmap and vector information (from a drawing program). A variation on this format, *PICS (PICTure Sequence)* is used for storing animation.

◆ *PCX* is an 8-bit format used mostly on the PC platform. It originated with Z-soft's PC Painter software.

◆ *QT (QuickTime)* was developed by Apple as the first commercial digital video format for the Macintosh. It can be applied to both still and video files, and can accept a variety of different compression methods. A variation called *QTW (QuickTime for Windows)* was developed for the PC.

◆ *TGA (TarGA)* is a still image format developed by TrueVision for use with their Targa line of videographics boards, designed for capturing video and outputting computer graphics or digital video to tape. It features lossless compression.

◆ *TIF, TIFF (Tagged Image File Format)* is a still image format that has slightly different implementations depending on whether you're using a PC or Macintosh, but many programs are now equipped to accept either variation. TIFF has several different lossless compression options.

The question of which format is most appropriate to use will depend on the type of image and your application. For images with a limited number of flat, solid colors, any of the 8-bit formats (GIF, PCX) will work fine. Images with smooth gradations or photographs are better off with the 24-bit formats (TGA, TIFF). If file size is a concern, your best bet is JPEG. For video files, AVI or QuickTime are normally used, unless you have the gear and software to do MPEG compression.

Video Considerations

If you plan to record your animation for playback with video equipment, there are some restrictions to take into consideration.

Video Standards

First of all, there are three video standards in common use around the world. Each of these standards uses its own set of signal configuration, frame rate, and resolution standards:

> **NTSC (National Television Standards Committee)** is used in the Americas and Japan. It is characterized by 525 scan lines at 60Hz.

> **PAL (Phase Alternating Line)** is used throughout most of Western Europe. It uses 625 scan lines at 50Hz.

> **SECAM (Systeme Electronique Couleur Avec Memoire)** is used by France, Russia, and other Eastern European nations. Like PAL, it uses 625 scan lines at 50Hz, but other aspects about the signal make them incompatible with each other.

NTSC televisions have 525 scan lines, meaning that the electron beam paints the image with a total of 525 horizontal passes every 1/30th of a second (called a *frame*). However, the lines aren't scanned in sequence, because the beam scans only every other line during the first 1/60th of a second (called a *field*), then goes back and paints the ones it skipped the first time (a process called *interlacing*). It then starts all over for the next image in the sequence.

The reason these time periods are in 60ths of a second is related to the American household power system, which is 120 volts AC (Alternating Current) at 60Hz (60 cycles per second). That's why other countries have

50Hz television standards—because they use 50Hz power systems. In any case, the method used to display television signals has two impacts on computer graphics:

First, horizontal lines only one pixel high tend to flicker, because they're only being painted once per frame, instead of twice like the rest of the image *appears* to be. This is very distracting and undesirable, so make sure that your horizontal lines are at least two pixels high.

The second is that movement should occur every 1/60th of a second to be as smooth as possible. If you render your animation normally (*frame rendering*), it will only be updated every 1/30th of a second, or after a full frame has been displayed. To get the best quality, you need to use the *field rendering* option of your 3D software, which causes it to render the images in the same way the television displays them: as two images, the first with every odd scan line rendered, the second with every even line. Using this method takes twice as long, but makes fast-moving objects look much smoother, because the image is being altered just as fast as the television can display it.

If you're rendering an animation to fields on multiple machines, ensure that the field rendering settings are identical. Otherwise, one machine may be generating the even lines first, while the other is doing the odd. This must be kept consistent, or your video will appear to shake up and down at times.

In addition, if you plan to have your work viewable in countries that use standards other than your own, check your software to see if it has options for outputting that type of signal (remember you still need a recorder capable of handling that format). If not, you can save the video in the local standard format and have the tapes converted at a video post facility. The other possibility is that some companies abroad may have multi-format VCRs that can accept any VHS tape.

Visible Area

One problem common to all video formats is that much of the recorded image is never seen, because part of the television screen is covered up by the case and bezel holding the tube in place. This condition, where the picture tube is not revealing the entire image, is called *overscan*. To make matters worse, the amount of overscan on a television varies from model to model, and even from set to set. In order to take this into account when videotaping subjects, the television industry established two guidelines: *video safe* and *title safe*. These are actually boxes displayed on the monitors of broadcast video cameras, which graphically delineate the portions of the image that are likely to show up on any television. The outer guideline, called *video safe*, is considered the edge of the typical television set's screen, so anything outside of that may not be visible (see figure 10.9). The inner guideline, *title safe*, is the reliable limit for any text that will be displayed on the screen, such as titles or credits.

Title Safe Perimeter
Video Safe Perimeter
Image Perimeter

Your 3D program also may offer video safe and title safe guidelines, possibly as one of the options for a viewport (particularly a camera viewport). If you plan to output to video, use these guidelines in framing your subject to ensure that your work will be seen on any television.

Color Smear and Moiré

Another consideration is that certain colors will smear on a television screen. This is a particular problem with reds, but can happen with any saturated color. To avoid this, you must stay within the gamut called *video safe colors*. Some programs may offer filtering or alerts that warn you when a material or background color falls outside this range. If yours doesn't offer such a feature, then keep your luminance levels below 80 percent of maximum, and do a video test to check for smearing.

The FCC (Federal Communications Commission) strictly prohibits the broadcast of colors outside the NTSC standards. If your animation is intended for broadcast, you should have someone use video test equipment like a waveform monitor and vectorscope to check your work. Otherwise, the broadcasters will crank down the signal until everything meets standards, which may result in much of the image being illegibly dark.

As if this isn't enough, patterns in the materials applied to your 3D objects can cause moiré patterns when recorded to video. This is very common with black-and-white striped patterns, but can show up with just about any sort of non-solid-color texture. Your program may offer map filtering controls to reduce or eliminate this problem.

Rendering and Output Tutorials

Topics covered:

> **Adding Glow Effects**
>
> **Creating Fog**
>
> **Alpha Channel Compositing**
>
> **Rendering Animation**

The rendering and output phase of a project gives you the opportunity to add special effects or produce multi-layered composites from different animations. For the blimp tutorial, the focus will be on glow and fog effects, as well as using an alpha channel to composite a still image.

Adding Glow Effects

Adding effects such as glows to the running lights makes the lights much more realistic. In some programs this is a post-production effect, while in other programs it's part of the rendering process, so the instructions here are very general.

1. The glow effect may be triggered by a setting assigned to the light objects themselves, or in the material applied to the object. Determine the

correct parameters and set them so that all the spherical running lights on the ship will glow.

2. In some programs, you may have to set up a post-production effects task list to create the effect. Consult your manual on how to accomplish this.

3. Render the image as a straight still or through the video post module of your software, depending on the requirements of the glow effect (see figure 10.10).

FIGURE 10.10

Glow effect applied to the point light material. Glows are often added as post-rendering effects or as part of the rendering if volumetric lighting is used.

If your program doesn't offer glow effects, consider creating the glows with translucent spheres that enclose the point lights. Use material settings similar to those on the visible searchlights to create the illusion of a glow.

Creating Fog

By adding atmosphere effects to the scene, the ship appears to come out of the fog. This adds an element of mystery and realism, but would require some lighting adjustments to simulate a daytime setting. Here, just try it out as an opportunity to play with the effect.

1. Depending on your program, set the render setup parameters or environment to allow Fog. Set the minimum level to 0 percent and the maximum to 100 percent, and the fog color to white.

2. Set the ranges on the camera to define the beginning and end of the fog effects. In the example, the circles surrounding the camera indicate the minimum and maximum ranges. Set the minimum range at the point where you want the blimp to be completely clear, and the far range to the point where you want the blimp completely occluded (see figure 10.11a).

3. Render test stills to check the effect, and adjust the ranges as needed (see figure 10.11b).

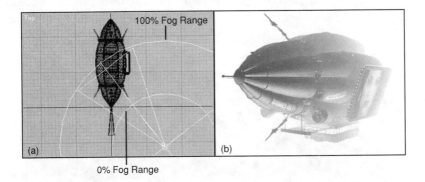

FIGURE 10.11

Controlling fog effects: (a) Set the ranges on the camera to delineate the distance or range over which the fog effects operate. (b) Render the result and adjust the ranges or density percentages to suit your needs.

Alpha Channel Compositing

This exercise composites a still image with an alpha channel against a background, then uses retouching to add additional interest.

1. Select a background image for the blimp. It might be a cityscape or other landscape image, or something entirely abstract. A file called HONGKONG.JPG is provided on the CD-ROM if you don't have anything else available.

2. Set a camera at the proper location and focal length to match the background. If your software supports it, loading the image into the background is helpful for establishing this (see figure 10.12a).

3. Although some products enable background images to be automatically composited during the rendering process, they would become a single image, making it difficult to adjust the foreground and background separately. Therefore, render the image with no background, but with the alpha channel turned on. Use an image resolution that's the same as the background image (see figure 10.12b–c).

4. Load the background image into Photoshop. Load the blimp render with alpha channel in as a separate document. In the blimp document, Choose

the Selection:Load Selection menu option, and set the dialog to use Channel #4 (the alpha channel) as the new selection. Click OK and the blimp should appear with a selection lasso around it. Choose Edit:Copy to place the selection into the clipboard, then choose the background document. Create a new layer, then use Edit:Paste to paste the blimp into the new layer (see figure 10.12d).

5. Make any desired adjustments to the color balance, levels, or positions of the two layers. You also can paint additional details onto the blimp, or add lens flare effects and airbrushed glows to the lighting, if desired.

FIGURE 10.12

Compositing an image: (a) Load in the background image, and adjust the position and focal length of the camera to match the scene. (b) Render the foreground with an alpha channel. (c) The alpha channel, shown for reference. (d) Composite the foreground and background in Photoshop or video post. HONKONG.JPG background image by Brent Blackett.

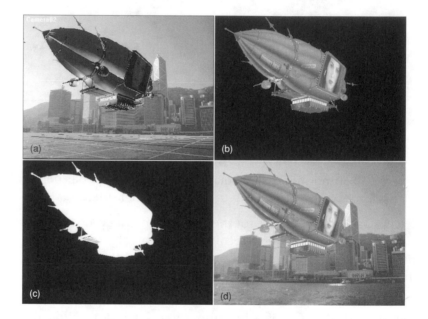

Rendering Animation

The final stage of the formal tutorials is to render the animation from the Chapter 9 tutorials off to AVI or QT files.

1. Check your hard drive for adequate space. You may want to de-fragment it first if the rendering will consume a lot of virtual memory.

2. Choose your camera viewpoint and set up the rendering parameters as follows: 640 × 480 resolution, using an animation or Cinepak-type codec,

Alpha channels off (unless you plan to composite it over a background later), frames set to the total length of the animation.

3. Render the animation. Make sure the images have rendered properly before leaving the system alone to proceed. If your software doesn't have a render time estimator, use the time it takes a typical frame to render and multiply that by the number of frames in the animation.

Chapter 11, "The Reel," discusses the techniques of editing different camera viewpoints together to tell the story in an interesting and effective manner. It is recommended that you use the information presented in that chapter to help cut together the different clips you can generate from this scene.

Summary

This chapter looked at the render time issues you're likely to be faced with when outputting your animation. These considerations include resolution, aspect ratios, color depth, palettes, and atmosphere. Post production effects and their creation were also examined, including glows, lens flares, motion blurs, and other custom effects that you can add with paint software or digital editing programs. Finally, it looked at common types of output, from digital files to 35mm slides to print output, as well as many of the problems involved in laying off animation to videotape.

Chapter 11, "The Reel," delves into the process of creating a reel, from brainstorming for ideas to script writing and direction issues to doing the sound and editing. This is where your work moves from a collection of animation clips into a finished work.

The Reel

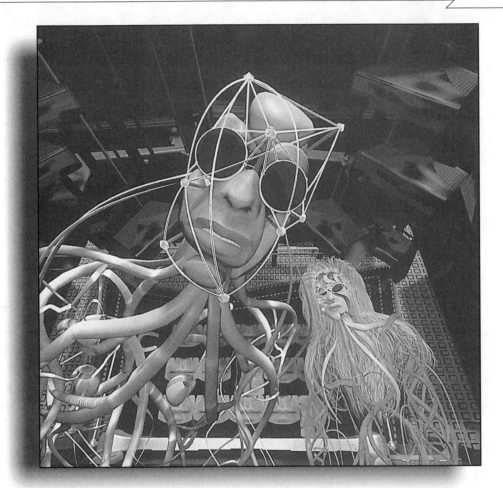

A pair of virtual thespians confront their creator in The End, an Academy Award winning animation by Chris Landreth. Courtesy of Alias/Wavefront.

"*G*ads, but you're up early," grumbled the Master as he stumbled into the workroom, half-asleep and clutching a steaming tankard of Blackthorne tea. He padded slowly across the cold stone floor over to where the student was hard at work, pouring over a table filled to overflowing with all manner of notes and sketches.

"I'm working on my demo," explained the young man, altogether too buoyant given the early hour. "Wanna see?" Taking the Master's grunt as an enthusiastic yes, the student began to spin his tale.

"It opens with a young conjurer standing on the ramparts of a mighty keep at dawn. Gazing into the sky, he sees a small dragon soar down towards him. With a cry, it lights upon his shoulder, and he gives it a friendly pat. In a nearby tower, a princess smiles at the scene, her eyes full of wonder for the handsome and mysterious young man. Suddenly, the hills are blackened by hordes of approaching barbarians..."

Some time later, the lad concluded with, "...then, once the king and princess have been rescued from the dark tower of the evil sorcerer, and his barbarian hordes have been repelled from the keep, the powerful young conjurer calls forth the grown-up dragon to carry the princess and himself toward the setting sun."

"So, what do you think?" asked the young man, beaming. The Master put down his now stone-cold tea and placed both hands on the lad's shoulder. He leaned close to the young man's face, gazing at him intently. The Master got so close, in fact, that the student could see every tiny crease in the old man's weathered skin, and could count the capillaries in the aged, bloodshot eyes.

"Is it your intention, lad, to look like ME before you finish your project?" rumbled the Master.

"I...er...uhhh, well, n-no..." came the stuttering reply.

"Well, then," whispered the old man, "you may just have to cut a scene, then."

"S-sure," the student babbled out. "W-what should I cut?"

"Oh, everything from 'Suddenly, the hills were blackened by hordes of barbarian soldiers' onward should do it," growled the Master. He released the lad, then *snatched up his chilly tankard. The only sound in the chamber was his bones creaking as he made his way back toward the door.*

"I-I'm sorry, Master," said the student, realizing his folly.

"Ah, 'tis not your fault, and I'm the one to apologize for being upset," replied the old man, stopping to turn back and smile reassuringly. "I should have known better than to suggest you get some ideas by going to see that Dragonheart, Princess Bride, and Excalibur triple-feature at the drive-in last night."

Telling Your Story

One of the first decisions you have to make about your demo reel is whether you will simply be showcasing your abilities, or trying to tell a story. While a showcase contains a number of different models, animation fragments, and so forth strung together in a visual collage, a story, even a simple one, is more likely to be memorable, and demonstrates skills other than your 3D talents.

What it comes down to is this: if you only have the time and resources to compile your existing work (and perhaps add a few transitions to bridge the pieces together), that's fine, and most reels are just like that. However, if you want your work to stand out from the others, and particularly if you want to get into the character animation field, a good story-based reel can take you a long way.

Most people drawn to the animation field, be it traditional or CG, have a story they want to tell (or re-tell). These stories range from short, often humorous bits running only a few seconds to feature-length efforts of epic proportions, rather like the student's ambitious concept.

Whatever your tale, be it short or long, funny or poignant, complex or minimalistic, doing your reel is your opportunity to share your vision and talent with others. It's your opportunity to be a Steven Spielberg or a James Cameron, a Tim Burton or even an Ed Wood. On the other hand, because we're talking animation here, perhaps a better goal would be a Chuck Jones, a John Lasseter, or a Mamoru Oshii.

Developing a Concept

Few things are more mysterious than the creative process. When working on a project, sometimes the ideas seem to spring forth immediately, needing only the details worked out. Other times, you rack your brain for days or weeks. Help is available, however, when those dark moments strike. Inspiration is everywhere—in films, books, museums, comics, music, conversations, and nature. All you have to do is look for it.

What If...

A good technique is to free yourself from everyday experience, and allow your mind to explore things from unique perspectives, without concern for whether they're accurate or even possible. For example: What would it be like to live in a drop of pond water? What if inanimate objects could talk? What if everything was made of ice? What if the world was inside out? What if *we* were inside out?

Ewww.

The point is, 3D animation allows you the freedom to explore the impossible (or at least, the extremely unlikely), so you may want to take advantage of that.

Ideas based on personal experience can be very powerful, especially if you can imbue your 3D characters with the emotions that experience brought forth. Creating an animation based on something that you feel strongly about may result in some very potent imagery, and viewers who connect with your story will appreciate you for more than your ability to make a good-looking model or a nice camera move.

Academy Award winning animator Nick Park gets the inspiration for some of his work from conversations with ordinary folks. For the short film *Creature Comforts*, Park recorded interviews with people, asking them what it was like to live in a big city. A typical response was something like, "It's too crowded, there isn't enough space, and it's too noisy. I was a lot happier where I was before." He then used the recordings as the dialogue for claymation animals being interviewed about life in a zoo.

How the Other Half Does It

For a fresh perspective, look at foreign films and books. You'll find a wealth of folklore, imagery, and concepts that may lead you in directions you would never have gone if you relied strictly on American culture and ideas. The Japanese, for example, produce a vast amount of *anime* (animated films), television series, and OAVs. *OAVs (Original Animation Videos)*, which are also called *OVAs (Original Video Animation)*, are animations that are produced for the direct-to-video market. While much of this animation focuses on space battles, giant robots, and high school romance, there are a lot of unique and interesting story concepts, effects, and editing tricks from which to learn.

> One of the most visually stunning examples of anime is Masamune Shirow's *Ghost in the Shell*, which is available on video. The film combines traditional cel animation with 3D graphics, and features some impressive mechanical designs and interesting ideas. Directed by Mamoru Oshii (*Urusei Yatsura*, *Patlabor*), the film will probably be pretty difficult to follow unless you're familiar with the original *manga* (Japanese term for comics).

Note

Another route is to look through stock photo catalogs and art books. These two sources may work because they're filled with hundreds of widely varying images. I haven't seen it, but I've heard that the film *Koyaanisquatsi: Life out of Balance* is like looking at hundreds of stock video clips strung together.

The Software Route

Say you've puzzled and puzzled 'til your puzzler is sore, but you still haven't come up with anything? Well, if you're *thoroughly* stuck or want an idea that's totally off the wall, you might consider an "idea generator" software program, such as IdeaFisher. It works by assembling random sets of words from categories you select. It sounds kind of hokey, but I guess it comes down to what you would create out of a seeming jumble of words, such as "pizza, turtle, samurai."

Group Brainstorming

Need a little help with your concept? Bouncing ideas off another person can pay off in a big way with unexpected and interesting thoughts. It's also a good way to do a reality check on what you have in mind, to make sure it doesn't get the dreaded, "That sounds just like that movie/animation/TV show I saw last week," response.

Back when I was taking Crystal 3D/Topas classes at CAI, our class was unusually small—only three people. So, when the time came to do our final class project, a group animation piece, we had to make sure that we took on something that was possible given our limited human resources. Classmate Kevin Byall and I kicked ideas around while we made the six hour drive to

Los Angeles to attend the NCGA show. The concept we came up with was *Meter Madness*, a humorous look at what happens to a coin when it's deposited into a parking meter. By the time we reached LA, we had dozens of different ideas for goofy things to happen to the penny, including laser scanning, a thorough washing, mug shots, and so on (see figure 11.1).

FIGURE 11.1

The penny washer, an example of the goofy (and low res) devices located inside the parking meter. Created with Crystal 3D software on a 286 PC. Image ©1990 Mark Giambruno.

A few years after finishing my classes, I visited the school to give a talk during their open house. While I was there, the head of the faculty told me that their videotape of *Meter Madness* had been so popular for demonstrations that it had completely worn out. I attribute its popularity to the fact that it told a simple story, making it more compelling than cool visuals alone.

Brainstorming on the commercial projects I've been involved with usually included the entire art staff, the producers, programmers, and sometimes client representatives. The sessions produced a lot of ideas, but seldom a consensus. Most of the time, it fell upon the creative or project director to weed out all but two or three of the ideas for further development. Sometimes, two seemingly disparate ideas were combined to create a unique approach. In other cases, the brainstorming led to nothing at all, and the ultimate idea was inspired by an offhand comment, an image from a film or magazine, or the stirrings of a half-asleep mind as its owner slapped the snooze bar for the third time.

Writing the Script

Unless you plan to make your work a "stream of consciousness" animation, you should put your ideas on paper and formulate a script. Although your story is likely to be a very short one, here are some guidelines for story design that can help.

The Three-Act Structure

Most stories can be broken down into what is called the *three-act structure*. Such stories have—not surprisingly—a beginning, a middle, and an end, which are also referred to as the setup, development, and resolution phases.

Setup

Act I, the story's setup phase, introduces the characters, the environment, and the situations. Keep this act fairly short, setting up a clear direction and style for the story. You don't want the viewer getting lost and wondering what's going on, instead of enjoying the piece. At the end of Act I, the viewer should have a clear idea of the characters, the key situations, and especially the central question of the story. Typical central questions are: Will the cop catch the bad guy? Will the aliens take over the Earth? Will the lovers be reunited? Act I often ends with a turning point in the story, an event that turns the story around or forces the main character to make a major decision, such as choosing to embark on a quest.

Development

In-depth story development occurs in Act II. The longest act, it contains the meat of the story and is the part when characters become more deeply involved with each other, new information comes to light, and previously unclear intentions start to become known. It is also one of the most difficult portions to figure out, because it can easily bog down and lose your viewer's attention. Act II also ends with a turning point, very often taking the form of a *dark moment*, during which all seems lost. This is usually followed by a change in the direction of the story, and an acceleration of the action.

Resolution

Usually the shortest and most exciting of the three, Act III is the resolution of the story. In Act III, the central question of the story, set down in Act I, is finally answered, in what is called the *climax*. Following the climax is usually a brief *aftermath* or *epilogue* that reassures the viewer that everything is okay again. In many films, the aftermath often sets the stage for a sequel as well.

Balls and Blocks

Don't worry that the three-act structure seems too complex and involved for your portfolio pieces. Even very simple and brief stories can follow this structure. For example, consider Alan Coulter's *Balls and Blocks,* which is a short piece from the Hash Inc. Animation Master demo reel.

During the introduction and title sequence voice-over, the artist's son asks his dad to look at something that he has set up. The kid's little demo turns out to be balls rolling down a makeshift ramp and onto a seesaw-like arrangement of toy blocks, which form the title of the piece. The segment serves as both a title sequence and acknowledgment of his son as providing the inspiration for this piece.

The first act opens with a yellow Hot Wheels-like track arranged in roller coaster fashion, floating in the sky. The sounds of children playing can be heard, and then you see variously colored balls rolling along the track. They come off the biggest hill and roll through a stone arch that straddles the track at the bottom. Next, the main character is introduced, but he is a *block*, not a ball. He hesitates for a moment, then slides down the hill and smacks into the arch. Because he has corners, he's too big to fit through the arch. A turning point in the story has been reached, and Act I closes.

At this point, you know the setting, and the main character. You also know the central question of the story—how will the block get through the arch, if at all? The core of this story could be considered "the odd man out" or "the fish out of water."

During the second act, a crowd of balls gathers at the top of the hill to taunt the outsider and watch as he strains to force himself through the opening. At one point, he tries to pound his own corners flat, rounding himself off, but he still can't fit. It looks hopeless, and he gives up. This is the dark moment, and the second turning point that marks the end of Act II.

In the final act, one of the balls gets upset at the others, rolls down the hill to comfort the block, and offers to help push. Seeing the good Samaritan ball and the block are trying hard, other balls join in to help, and the climax is reached when part of the arch is knocked out of the way, and the block makes it through. The aftermath shows both balls and blocks playing happily now that the obstruction is gone.

Of course, not all animations follow this structure, and some have been made famous through their rejection of it. Probably one of the best known is *Bambi Meets Godzilla*, an old black-and-white hand-animated piece. Over half the piece is an opening credit sequence, showing a Disney-style deer peacefully grazing in a meadow. In the credits, creator Marv Newland fills every role, from Executive Producer to Writer, Director, Cameraman, you name it. The credits end, and a huge Godzilla foot crushes Bambi in an instant. Again, the lengthy and ludicrous credits roll. Godzilla's toes curl, and the scene fades to black.

Scriptwriting Tips

The following are some suggestions to help you organize your thoughts and generate a script for your animation:

◆ Try to keep things loose at first, putting ideas down in outline form, shuffling them around, and adding or deleting pieces until you're happy with the story as a whole. Getting too far along with one portion of the story without having the rest figured out leads to problems and wasted time.

◆ Make character notes and use them to help define the personalities and actions of your virtual actors. In some cases, you may find it helpful to create a little history for certain characters, using this to guide you in determining how they might respond to a situation.

◆ Even though you're using high-tech tools, rely on traditional techniques to tell your story. The grammar of filmmaking is well-established and accepted, so take advantage of it.

◆ Set the mood early in the story, possibly with an establishing shot that evokes an emotional response from the viewer. If it's a dark or sad tale, for example, opening with a rainstorm would be the obvious (albeit cliché) choice.

Designing the Look

Sketches come next, developing and adapting the various idea fragments into a form that suits your needs. Drawing simultaneously enables you to explore the possibilities while it forces you to make your inspiration concrete. Sketches also are vital when you're in a group development effort. When you talk about your concepts, you never know how others are envisioning them, but when you put a sketch on the table, everyone tunes to the same wavelength.

In the design process, both style and substance come to the fore. Should the project imagery be in a classical style? Contemporary? Retro, perhaps? Is the emotion you want the viewer to experience upon viewing this work awe, humor, or sadness? Of course, the execution of the work has just as much bearing on the viewer's reaction as the design does, so ensure that everyone understands the intent of your design.

Characters should be sketched out in detail, because they're difficult to execute in 3D, and a little extra prep work results in a faster and more satisfying modeling experience. It also may be worthwhile to create a model sheet, showing the character exhibiting a range of different expressions and body language. By knowing how you want to exaggerate the character's form in advance, you can more easily plan proper mesh density and bone locations in the model.

Planning out anything but the simplest environment pays off as well. At the very least, you should have a map of where the main objects in the scene are located to plan out the actions and camera angles. This also can help you determine which portions of the environment can be flat polys or other low- res objects, as well as which objects will need to be executed in high resolution.

Finally, creating at least thumbnail sketches of key scenes will help you work out overall compositional issues and give you a head start on storyboarding.

Storyboarding the Action

Storyboarding is the process of visualizing an animation by breaking it down into a sequence of sketches that illustrate the key points in the scene. They are often left as pencil sketches, but may be inked and colored with markers if they're intended for presentations. The boards often include arrows indicating the movement of various objects in the shot. Usually, there is a description of the scene and dialogue or voice-over excerpts in a box below the image.

Storyboarding requires you to interpret the script, making the words into a visual experience. Whether an action or visuals will be boring or dramatic often depends on the camera position and focal length of the lens. Where the script might say, "A group of Terran fighters fly LEFT across frame," the storyboard shows the size of the planet, the position of the ships, and the camera angle. Although they are seldom as dramatic as the finished sequence, storyboards serve as an excellent starting point for an artist setting up a shot. This is important, because the same action that looks terrific from one angle may be totally disorienting or dull if viewed from another.

The storyboards also are used to indicate camera movements, like pans and tilts, in addition to the movement or actions of objects or characters in the frame. Such movement is usually represented by arrows drawn in perspective along the path of an action.

Often, you can come up with modeling shortcuts during the design and storyboarding process. If you plan your action carefully, you may not need to build large portions of some of the models if they won't be seen. You also may be able to design certain models to be flat, mapped polygons by considering how close the camera gets to them and how long they will remain on screen. Filmmakers get away with all kinds of things because they know just how long they can show something on screen before the viewer realizes that it's fake.

Storyboarding styles range from glorified stick figures to comic book-quality artwork, but whatever the style, the boards should at least suggest the composition, lighting, and movement within a scene. The best way to budget your storyboarding time is to figure out how many panels are required to tell the story succinctly, then divide the number of hours you have available by that amount. Unless your boards are of the stick-figure variety, you'll probably need at least 5 minutes per frame.

Storyboarding an animation is no small task, and it can be one of your greatest assets or a complete waste of time depending on the circumstances. If you're working on personal pieces (like your reel), you may already have visualized the action, or prefer to experiment in 3D. In a larger project that involves several other animators, or if you have a client that has to sign off on the animation concept, you may not have a choice. On the other hand, if the concept or movements are fairly straightforward, or if the scene would be difficult to sketch out, you might be better off doing a 3D animatic instead.

Animatics are simple recreations of a scene made with anything from paper cut-outs to G.I. Joe's to 3D primitives. They serve a dual purpose in film productions, enabling the effects people to work out movement and timing issues, as well as providing stand-in footage until the real shots are completed. In the case of 3D animatics, they enable the animators on a group project to get a head start before the final models are ready, easing the inevitable crunch at render time. They also can demonstrate the feel of an animation far better than a static storyboard.

For more information on storyboarding techniques, I recommend a book like *Comps, Storyboards, and Animatics*. Another reference with many cinematic storyboard examples is *Film Directing: Shot by Shot*. While this book deals mainly with conventional "live" cinematography, it's important to remember that the techniques work just as well with 3D animation. Remember, just because you have a virtual camera capable of flying anywhere in a continuous shot doesn't mean that you should use it that way.

Producing the Animation

With the script completed, some design sketches in hand, and perhaps some storyboards as well, it's time to launch into the production process. *Production* is the bulk of what you do as a 3D artist—the creation, mapping, animation, and rendering of scenes.

Because most of this book has focused on the production aspects of 3D, there isn't much more to be said here, except that when setting up your animations, be sure to over-render the scenes a bit. *Over-rendering* means that you render between a few more frames and a second or two of animation at the beginning and ending of a sequence than you think you'll need. This will give you some leeway in adjusting the length of the scene during the editing process.

Editing Your Scenes

Editing is one of the key elements in the post-production phase of the project. *Editing* is the process of assembling the various scenes created and rendered during production and turning them into a cohesive whole. To this end, good editing results in a well-paced, understandable, and enjoyable viewing experience. Bad editing results in confused, disoriented, or just plain bored viewers (the agonizingly long effects shots in *Star Trek: The Motion Picture* come to mind).

> Editing is an art form in and of itself, and I can't hope to cover even a fraction of it in this short section. For more information and guidelines, get a good book, like *Edward Dmytryk on Film: Editing*, or assistance from someone experienced in editing techniques, when you assemble your reel.

Editing Definitions

Film editing has its own vocabulary. Most of the terms are applicable to animation editing, as well, so I've adapted their definitions to reflect this.

Cut (or *shot*): The smallest individual piece of an animation. It may be a single frame or an entire sequence. A cut also refers to the edited version of the entire project.

Sequence: A segment of the story. It usually has a beginning, middle, and end.

Scene: A sequence or collection of sequences that takes place at a single location.

L-Cut: A cut during which the sound from Cut A overlaps the image from Cut B.

Insert: In filmmaking, a shot of an inanimate object, used to bridge sequences or establish a new location.

Rough Cut: A version of the animation in which all the pieces are in place, but the timing hasn't been fine-tuned.

First Cut: The editor's first complete cut. In filmmaking, this cut is then reviewed by the director.

Director's Cut: The result of the director's revisions to the First Cut.

Final Cut: Producers often retain the right to revise the film after the Director's Cut, so this is the release version of the film.

Editing Concepts

Editing uses some fairly straightforward precepts to determine where and when to make a cut. It is not, however, a formula-based process, it is just as much an art form as building a model or animating a character.

Probably the most important thing to bear in mind is that you never make a cut without a reason. Just because something looks cool from a certain angle is no reason to throw it in (unless, of course, you're doing something like a music video, where the style is to use disjointed sequences).

Basically, a cut should always show the viewer one of three things:

1. What the viewer wants to see, whether the he or she realizes it or not. This means you may have to anticipate what the viewer expects to see, and when they expect to see it, and place the cut there. An example would be a scene in which one character is lecturing another. Rather than focusing only on the speaker, there should be cuts to the listener from time to time, because the viewer wants to see the other character's reaction to what is being said.

2. What the viewer *should* see, whether the viewer wants to or not. This includes sequences that the viewer must be aware of in order to make sense of the story later on.

3. What the director or editor *manipulates* the viewer into thinking that he or she *wants* to see. This is where the filmmaker creates misleading impressions on the viewer, allowing them to follow one train of thought while setting it up to be derailed later on.

Editing Tips

Although editing is three parts black arts for each part learned mechanics, here are some tips to help you "choose what to lose."

◆ The viewers should remain immersed in the story, rather than be allowed the opportunity to remember that they are watching animation.

◆ Cuts should never draw attention to themselves. They should remain unnoticed and not disrupt the viewer's concentration.

◆ Never show the viewer something unimportant, unless you're using it as a short bridging device, such as an insert.

◆ Once a cut has delivered its punch, don't linger on it.

◆ Never make a cut without a positive reason. In other words, never cut "just to change things."

◆ Whenever possible, cut *during* action. Don't have everything come to a complete stop before the cut. For example, if a character is leaving the screen, cut at the point his eyes leave the frame, instead of waiting for him to clear the frame completely.

◆ Viewers notice rhythm changes, so cutting at the moment a character's foot hits the ground helps smooth the transition.

◆ Except at the beginning or end of a sequence, always use the L-Cut, which allows the audio from Cut A to overlap the image from Cut B. With animation, the entire soundtrack is often added after the picture is complete, so this principle can be used at that stage.

◆ Make sure that your edits don't have the camera crossing the line of action in a scene. This should be avoided if the principles laid down in Chapter 8, "The Camera," are followed, but keep an eye out for it here as well.

◆ Don't try to use fancy transitions just because the program can do them. Most of your cuts should have no transition at all, but those at the beginning or end of a scene may use a fade or wipe.

◆ If you have to repeat the same shot during a scene for some reason, make sure the later cuts are kept brief, because the viewer is already familiar with the subject.

◆ If you need to linger on something, do it at the beginning of the cut, while the shot is still fresh to the viewer's eye.

- By using a loud sound, or forcing the viewer to re-focus their attention, you may be able to mask a "problem" cut.

- POVs (such as an insert of a letter being read from the point of view of one of the characters) are difficult to time properly. Make sure you give the viewer plenty of time to read things.

Editing Tools

Editing can be accomplished using either video recording gear or computers equipped with video editing hardware.

Video-based editing is best done with SVHS, Hi8, 3/4" or Beta SP decks so that the image degeneration inherent in the editing and duplication of videotape will go unnoticed in the final result. In addition to needing two of these video decks to make a master tape, you also may require an editing controller to synchronize and operate the decks. Some professional and *prosumer* (professional/consumer) level gear may have editing capabilities built into the deck's controls and remotes. When the editing is completed, the master tape is duplicated, usually onto VHS tape, for distribution.

Unless you have access to video editing gear, getting the work done can be an expensive proposition. Video editing suites are usually quite pricey, especially because many require that you pay an operator to run the equipment. Facilities like BAVC (Bay Area Video Coalition) in San Francisco, which are set up to enable students and other non-professionals low-cost access to video gear and editing suites, are an economical alternative.

While still fairly expensive, adding quality *digital video editing* capabilities to your computer can cost you less than half of even an SVHS or Hi8 editing setup. Some of the most popular systems include Radius VideoVision Studio cards for Mac-based products, and the TrueVision Targa series for PCs. Hard drive space gets eaten up fast with digital editing, so you also need *at least* 1–2GB of AV-compatible hard drive space.

The most popular editing software for desktop digital video is Adobe Premiere (see figure 11.3). Premiere allows *nonlinear editing*, which means you can do the editing in any sequence you desire, as opposed to most tape-based systems, which require that you start at the beginning and work through until the end.

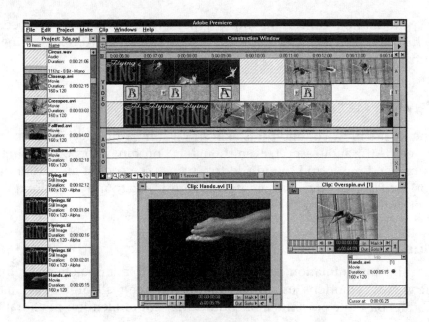

FIGURE 11.3

Adobe Premiere is a popular digital video software package that offers non-linear editing of image and sound. It can be readily used for animation editing and the addition of basic special effects as well.

Adding Post-Production Effects

Performing video or digital video editing on your work also gives you the option to do *post-production effects*, which include unusual transitions, color manipulation, and a host of special effects. In some cases, these effects would be difficult to achieve in the animation or rendering phases of production, so post work gives you the opportunity to apply them as part of the editing process.

Video Effects

While the basic video editing systems frequently offer *ADO (Ampex Digital Opticals)* -style effects like seizing a frame of video and spinning it around, duplicating it, stretching it, and so forth (think cheesy used car commercials), the digital editing software provides more sophisticated possibilities. Products like Premiere and Adobe After Effects can do all the ADO effects, plus Photoshop-style filter effects like Spherize distortions, Find Edges, Blurs, Emboss, and the like.

Post-production effects also enable you to combine live video and animation together, by using alpha channels or chroma keys to drop out the background and enable you to composite the different elements together. After Effects, in particular, excels at such compositing effects.

For information concerning other types of post-production effects and techniques such as video painting, refer to Chapter 10, "Rendering and Output."

Paying Attention to the Sound

One of the most common mistakes in creating a first reel is to ignore or underrate the audio aspect, even though it's nothing short of amazing how much good music and sound add to a scene. The coolest animation in the world still comes off feeling empty until music and sound add the emotional undertones that bring the imagery to life.

Music

For films and animation, music provides a way to manipulate and reinforce the viewer's emotions, usually without them even realizing it. This makes a production more powerful and compelling, not to mention memorable.

Of course, most people (artists included), know little more about music than what is needed to work their CD players. What they *do* know is what sounds good, at least to them, and this is the key factor in selecting music to go with the visuals you have prepared.

Just as there are all kinds of animation styles and looks, there are all kinds of music to choose from. Although the high-tech feel of 3D animation often encourages a contemporary, techno sound to go with it, something funky or nostalgic can be used to great effect. Classical music is another popular choice, as it has a timeless quality that can be just as appropriate for a space battle as for a character animation piece.

Music Sources

Of course, the ideal source for your reel's music is a professional score composed especially for your work. Given most artist's limited budgets, this is probably not an option. However, you may find a local band that will license an original piece to you for a reasonable fee. You may even be able to work out a mutual trade where you can use the music and they can use your animation for a video or stage effects.

Another option is *buy-out music*, which is a little like getting an image from a stock photography outfit. You get a demo CD of different music, pick out the score you want, and pay a flat fee. Other CDs may enable you to use any of the music for the purchase price of the CD, more like the texture libraries discussed in Chapter 6, "Texture Mapping." Unfortunately, you're unlikely to find anything really exciting on these CDs, as most are created with the multimedia presentation market in mind, and tend to be somewhat lifeless.

What if you want to use music from professional recording stars? Well, because the music is protected by copyright, you will have to obtain permission from them to use it in your reel. (Good luck!) Another point to consider with popular music or songs is that it may trigger thoughts or feelings about the musicians or singer, rather than the emotions you want to evoke with your animation. You don't want someone musing about Michael Jackson's weirdness when they should be concentrating on your animation.

Sound Effects

Like music, sound effects add extra mood and impact to your visuals and help to make the action more clear. Using the right sounds can make your work seem more realistic, bizarre, or humorous. The trick is getting the right sound and putting it in the right place. However, the perfect moment to insert a sound effect is not necessarily the instant at which the picture would indicate. Experiment with the position of effects to see if they work better when leading or trailing the picture. Also, remember that a sound effect that occurs just before a cut should usually extend into the next shot.

Royalty-free sound effects are a lot easier to come by than royalty-free music. *Sound effects CDs* can be found in any music store, and contain hundreds of different sounds, from raindrops to explosions. In addition, you can use them as-is, or modify them to suit your needs.

Most Hollywood film sound effects are created specifically for the movie, using what is called a foley stage. A *foley stage* is a soundproof room filled with all manner of different flooring types, tools, building materials, musical instruments, and even fresh vegetables. Sound designers use these materials to create the sound by pounding or stepping on them, rubbing them together, breaking them in half, and so on. Recording the sounds this way gives them much more control over the type and duration of the effect, and produces effects that don't sound "canned," the way effects CDs might.

You can create your own simple foley stage with a good microphone, tape recorder, and some typical household items. You also can record direct to your hard drive using your computer's sound card, but you may have trouble masking the sound of your computer's cooling fan. Whatever you do, don't block the airflow going into or out of the machine to try and muffle the noise.

Bear in mind that the sounds don't have to be literal, meaning that you don't have to set off a firecracker to get an explosion sound. You may find that popcorn popping works very well when tweaked a bit. Also, breaking fresh celery or tearing apart a head of lettuce can produce some interesting effects. For mechanical sounds, try running thin objects like pencils or pens across rough surfaces. To create the sound of lava bubbling, use an immersion heater in a cup of milk, and so forth.

To further enhance your pre-recorded or foley sounds, use some audio manipulation software like SoundEdit for the Mac or Sonic Screwdriver for the PC. Try dropping a steam locomotive sound by three octaves or slowing down tropical bird calls to get an idea of how much sounds can be changed by this kind of software. Premiere also enables you to do some effects, in addition to providing fade controls and other basic audio editing capabilities.

Summary

This chapter began exploring the creative process a bit, and looked at some ways to generate and develop ideas. It discussed the value of adding story elements to a reel, and went through the pre-production processes of scriptwriting, designing, and storyboarding a piece. It also talked about post-production, the editing, visual effects, and audio aspects of doing a reel. Your demo reel is vital ammunition in your most important battle: getting a job.

The next and final chapter explores the business aspects of 3D animation, discussing the pros and cons of being an employee or contractor, how to assemble a resume and portfolio, and how to secure the job you want.

12

Getting the Job

Getting a job in 3D graphics won't guarantee you a Monopoly, but you probably won't be starving, either. Image courtesy of Kinetix ©1995 Westwood Studios. MONOPOLY ©1935, 1995 Parker Brothers.

*S*weat dripped from the student's brow into the glowing pool, distorting the ethereal castle image over which he labored.

The Master settled into a chair across from his feverishly-working pupil. "What's the matter, lad?"

"I've got a meeting today with KeepCo Castle Construction," the student replied. "I'm trying to get hired as a visualizer."

"Ah! An interview, then? No wonder you're so nervous." The old man nodded with understanding. "After all, you're putting yourself and your labors on the selling block, and have to accept the opinion of others as to your worth."

The student stopped cold and gazed at the Master with saucer-like eyes. "I…I hadn't thought of it like that." The droplets of sweat cascading from his forehead had turned into rivulets.

The old man chuckled and handed the student a handkerchief. "Relax. Why don't we try a dry run together? Perhaps that will put you more at ease."

The lad finished dabbing his brow and smiled. "Yes! That would be great!"

Once the student had taken several deep breaths, the Master fell to questioning him, asking about his education and skill while the young man struggled to give the right answers and remain well-composed.

After a time, the Master stood up. "Well, I'm ready to see your work now."

"But it's right here," the confused student replied, "in my glowing pool."

"Ah, but you won't be interviewed here. Bring your spells along and conjure them on my pool instead."

The student swallowed hard and followed the Master over to his glowing pool. Settling in, the student began to conjure his castle imagery, but little things started going wrong. Portions of the model didn't appear, and the animation was jerky. The rivers of sweat returned to his brow, and suddenly the entire visual crumbled into sparkling dust.

"Hmmm. Not too impressive, eh?" the old man muttered, unsuccessfully trying to hide a wry smile.

"What went wrong? I don't understand!"

"Spellware incompatibilities." The Master sighed. "I'm running a different MOS* on my glowing pool right now. You see, lad, you can't rely on others to have the correct equipment to make your presentation work properly. And bringing your own pool to an interview would be awkward, hmmm?"

"I see. So I should use a spell format that any glowing pool could use?"

"A step in the right direction," replied the Master. "But what if they don't have a glowing pool available? What of your presentation then?"

The student thought for a moment, then nodded. "Always bring hard copy," he replied.

"Good plan, lad." The Master patted the young man's shoulder. "But you might just want to lay the whole thing off to tape as well. After all, everybody's got a VCR."

---

*Magical Operating System

Choosing Your Path

Whether you're looking for a position as a medieval visualizer or a modern 3D animator, job interviews can be very stressful, especially when you're new to the field or meeting with a company for which you desperately want to work. You are putting yourself under scrutiny, your work under a magnifying glass, and your future on the line. Being prepared and anticipating questions, however, can take the some of the pressure off and improve your chances.

The first and, perhaps, most important question is one you must ask yourself: Do you want to work as a contractor, or as an employee? There are pluses and minuses to both paths.

Employee

Working for a company is the path that most people choose to follow, at least at first. Consider the pro side of the equation:

◆ *Less (or no) experience may be required.* Many outfits seek raw talent and train or develop it to suit their needs.

◆ *On the job training.* This goes hand-in-hand with the previous statement, and means that you may get training without having to pay for it. In fact, you may get paid yourself.

◆ *No big expenditures required.* You don't have to buy any gear or software; it's all provided for you.

◆ *Social atmosphere.* You get to work with others in a (hopefully) pleasant environment, making new friends and learning from your 3D peers.

◆ *Assistance is close by.* If you have a problem or question, you will probably be able to find the answer quickly.

◆ *Benefits.* Most companies offer some mix of health plans, retirement plans, stock options, and other bonuses. Don't count on that 20-year retirement pension, however. People change jobs an average of every seven years.

◆ *Paid vacations and holidays.* It's hard to beat getting paid for doing nothing!

◆ *Job security.* In general, you're pretty secure in this field if you're a good employee. The field is still growing, and although there have been layoffs and closures, there are always new opportunities as well.

Balancing out this rosy picture of full-time employment are the following problems:

◆ *Bosses.* You may end up working for or with people who are overly picky, indecisive, or otherwise unpleasant.

◆ *Less control.* When you work for someone, you generally have to do whatever job comes down the pipe. Sooner or later, this will probably lead to a Project from Hell, which may leave you praying for a quick and easy death.

◆ *Less flexible free time.* As an employee, you get sick days, vacation, holidays, and so forth. However, your vacation schedule may be subject to approval based on company needs, not your own. And, if you suddenly decide that you want to take a month off, you may not have a job when you get back.

◆ *Lower pay.* This will vary, of course, but in general an employee will make substantially less than an active contractor.

◆ *Commuting.* Although some companies may offer some flexibility in your schedule, you may still find yourself in traffic or crowds day-in and day-out.

◆ *Potential relocation.* To work somewhere, you have to live within commuting distance. That means that many people will have to move in order to take a job. This can be a plus or minus depending on your situation.

Contractor

As a contractor, you may work for certain firms on a regular basis, or just move from company to company as jobs come along. Contracting requires a stronger portfolio than full-time employment and some capital as well, not to mention intestinal fortitude. Here are the pluses:

◆ *More control.* If you're skilled and fortunate, you will have your choice of jobs to pick and choose from. In many cases, you also will have much greater creative control over what you're doing, especially if it's for a company without its own art staff.

◆ *More flexible free time.* Schedules permitting, you can take time off whenever you feel like it. Work a four-day week, or a six-day week. Take off in the middle of the day for a movie or a two-hour lunch. Want a six-week vacation? You got it (assuming you can pay for it). If you work from home, you also may save yourself a few hours of commute time each day.

◆ *Set your own hours.* Depending on the nature of the work, you can set the schedule that you want, be it nine in the morning to five at night, or five at night to nine in the morning.

◆ *Tax write-offs.* Taxes are also a downside (the following page), but you can write off quite a few things when you're a contractor. This includes equipment and software, travel expenses, food, and lodging when you're out of town, and so forth. If you work at home, you also can write off part of your rent or house payment, telephone bill, and other utilities.

- *Travel opportunities.* You may be able to secure jobs that are located in other cities or even other countries, enabling you to travel on someone else's nickel. The tax-deductible nature of business trips also makes it more likely that you will attend out-of-town conferences.

- *Work variety.* You'll probably experience a lot more variety in the kind of work you do as a contractor. Being self-employed also gives you the opportunity to explore different kinds of work, outside of creating computer graphics.

- *Higher pay.* Contractor rates are often two to three times higher than employee wages. Therefore, even if you don't work full-time, you may make as much or more than someone else who does.

Before you spend all that higher pay on a fast car and a big screen TV, factor in the top two drawbacks of contracting:

- *More overhead.* You have to deal with the equipment and time overhead involved in running your own business. Not only do you have to buy your own computer, peripherals, and software, but also you have to pay for your own health insurance, pay higher taxes, look for work, handle invoices and books, and so forth.

- *Higher taxes.* Self-employed people pay 15% of their gross income to Social Security, which is twice as much as an employee pays out. In addition, you may have other expenses to pay that an employee wouldn't have to deal with, such as business license fees, equipment insurance, and so on.

- *Less security.* Contracting is a sink or swim affair. You have to have the resources to be able to get through slow periods, some of which may last a few months. You can't always rely on clients paying you on time, and some may not pay you at all.

- *Isolation.* If you do most of your work off-site, especially if it is at your home, you may suffer from a sense of isolation. If you don't feel comfortable working alone for long periods, this could be a major downside.

- *Pressure.* This is a fact of life for employees as well, but contractors may feel it more because they stand to lose a client or funds if they don't deliver on time. However, this may be offset depending on how much control the contractor has over the project.

◆ *Separation of work and leisure.* A common problem among contractors is that they have a hard time quitting work when they should, especially when they work at home. For some, work is always gnawing at them, and it is all too easy to spend the evening hours working on a project instead of relaxing. For others, the work is very enjoyable, so it becomes a kind of leisure activity as well, which may or may not be a good thing.

A Personal Choice

Whether you decide to become an employee or a contractor will depend on your mental attitude and personal needs as much or more than your skills. In most cases, you'll have to work in both capacities before you can decide which one you prefer, and even then you may find that your needs change over time.

Know Your Market

In considering how and where you want to work, it's vital to research the field you are interested in, so that you can find out the current conditions, potential growth, and the types of jobs available. To find out what's hot and what's not in your field of endeavor, read the trade magazines, talk with people working in the industry, and search the Web and Usenet for information and messages concerning the field. Search for trends, and make conservative predictions about where the most growth or demand might exist a few years down the road. In this way, you may be able to position yourself in a high-growth segment of the industry, which will offer many more possibilities for advancement and income.

In addition to watching industry trends, try to identify the companies that are dominating your market, as well as the ones that seem to be floundering. Select the ones that are of greatest interest to you and research them in depth.

Researching Companies

One of the biggest mistakes you can make going into a job interview is not knowing much about the company you are approaching. Companies doing 3D graphics often actively seek attention and press, so there's no excuse for not finding out what they're up to. By doing this, you can integrate your strengths and interests into what the company is focusing on, and tune your portfolio and interview answers accordingly.

For example, say you want to work for Virtual Carnage, a company that makes a popular real-time 3D game called *DeathBots*. By visiting their Web site, you find out *DeathBots II* is in the works. With a little preparation, you can say in the interview, "I know you're doing a sequel to *DeathBots*, which I loved playing, by the way, so I built some low-polygon DeathBots of my own design just to show you." Assuming that you're sincere and create good designs and models, you may cinch the job. Of course, if you botched the work, you've probably just blown it, so make absolutely sure your models meet or exceed the company's standard of work.

Company Web sites are excellent places to start your research, and often have information about projects in development, job opportunities, and so forth (see figure 12.1). They also tend to provide a lot of useful background information about the firm as well as its future plans.

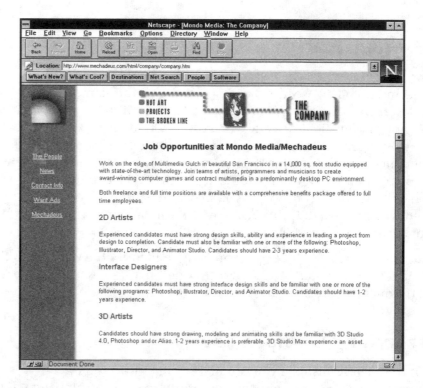

If the company doesn't have a Web site or you want additional information, you may be able to get a publicity package or copies of press releases from them. Contact the company's marketing or public relations departments and see what they have available.

Magazines are a very good source of information, but bear in mind that they have 2–3 month production schedules, so sometimes the news items may be a bit dated in a fast-moving industry like CG. Online versions and online-only magazines and message boards may be more current, so check them out as well (see figure 12.2). See Appendix B, "Recommended Reference," for a list of print publications.

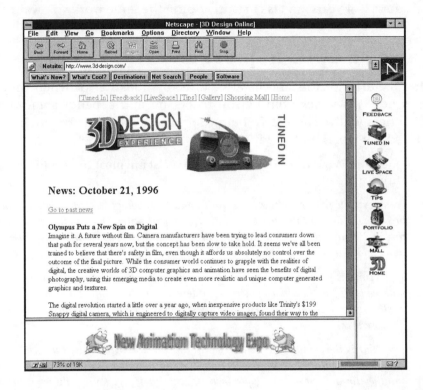

FIGURE 12.2

3D Design is a print magazine that also maintains a Web site with news, files, and resources. Contents ©1996 Miller Freeman, Inc.

If you're interested in the gaming field, go to software stores and see which developers are turning out the coolest games. Companies with successful products are often looking to expand, but competition for those jobs will be greater as well.

Conferences are an excellent way to see the products of many companies, talk with their representatives, get tons of literature, and discover trade publications that aren't sold on newsstands. There also may be job fairs or recruitment drives going on—good opportunities to get interviews with distant firms without having to fly there at your own expense. If there is a conference coming up that you plan to attend, call the companies you're interested in and see if you can schedule a meeting with them.

Finally, talking to people who work or have worked at a company is the best way to find out what the conditions are like, but remember the potential for bias in their opinions. Someone who left the company disgruntled is likely to give you a negative impression of it, while someone who was only recently hired on may still have a rosy view, unaware of the problems that may lie ahead. The most balanced opinions are likely to come from someone who has been there 2–4 years, and is currently doing the same work you want to do.

Making a Good Impression

What are art directors and creative directors looking for when they hire someone? This varies from person to person and depends somewhat on which field you've chosen. To help you make a good impression, however, I turned the tables on some interviewers, including myself.

Question: What three things about an artist are most important to an Art Director?

Answer: *The first is probably the traditional (non-computer-generated) art portfolio, which shows off the artist's innate ability and skills. Design often plays a big role in 3D graphics, so studying this portfolio is a good opportunity to appraise an individual's ability to communicate ideas in visual form.*

The second is the personality of the individual. Will the artist fit into the company and the team? Is the artist upbeat and interested in the company's projects? Does he or she seem alert and intelligent, quickly grasping the ideas and concepts being discussed?

The third is the computer-generated portfolio. What programs are they using, and how skilled have they become with them? Will additional training be needed, or can they jump right in and be productive? Does their style and ability suit the company's needs?

Q: What kinds of things instantly turn you off to an artist?

A: *Being late for an interview. A poor or incompatible attitude, such as being surly, distracted, or overconfident. Talking too much or slamming others is definitely annoying. Being dishonest, such as having pieces in their portfolio that they either didn't do themselves or haven't credited others with assisting on. Wearing a potent cologne or perfume.*

Q: How important is education in choosing one candidate over another?

A: *In the arts, education is much less important than ability. In general, it's nice to see an art degree on the resume, because it means the artist has been trained in all the core theory and techniques of art, but it's definitely not required. As far as* *schools go, unlike many fields, art schools or programs tend to be very indiscriminate in who they accept, so you get a broad range of student quality out of most institutions. One notable exception is the Art Center in Pasadena, CA, that seems to turn out consistently high-caliber graduates, and there are some other good schools as well.*

Q: How big a role does an artist's experience play in the decision?

A: *Naturally, it's very desirable to get an artist with the skills and experience to make an immediate impact on the quality of the team. The reality of the situation, however, is that most people like this are happy where they are, have started their own companies, or have gone into contracting. Most of the people interviewing are fresh out of school, and therefore hiring decisions are based on who seems to have the greatest potential.*

Q: Is the personal appearance of the artist a factor?

A: *Not really. People are hired on their personality and portfolios, not what they look like. People with really unusual appearances (bizarre hair, lots of piercings, etc.) can be distracting in the interview, but their appearance wouldn't prevent an art director from hiring them, assuming it isn't for a position where they would be interfacing with an incompatible client. Never show up dirty or smelly, however.*

Q: What kind of attitude do employers like to see in an interview?

A: *Definitely upbeat. Employers want people who are awake and excited about what the company is doing and how they can be involved. The interview should try to stay positive throughout—if an artist starts complaining about the last job they had, that sends up a red flag.*

Q: How do you like to see a portfolio presented?

A: *The artist should be prepared to speak about each piece without hesitation, but not dwell on any one too long unless asked questions about it. A clever or neatly organized portfolio is a plus, but the contents far outweigh the packaging. The most important thing is that the portfolio can be viewed with a minimum of fuss. VHS tape is great for animation, but still images are best in printed or slide form, because the detail is easier to see.*

Building an Identity

Now that you know some of the factors that influence a potential employer's decision, you need to build an "interview identity" for yourself that is compatible and desirable to companies. Your interview identity consists of your resume, your portfolio, and how you present and conduct yourself at the interview.

Resume Tips

Your *resume* is a one- or two-page summation of who you are and why you are the right person for a company to hire. Many books have been dedicated to the art of creating a resume, and it would be well worth the effort to read one before starting on your own. The following, however, are a few helpful tips:

Be creative, but make sure it's legible. A cool design or spin on the traditional resume can be an eye-catcher, but don't let difficult-to-read fonts or an overly bizarre layout get in the way of the information.

Use high-quality paper. You probably won't send out more than a few dozen resumes, so you might as well use good paper. If the paper has a visible watermark, make sure it's right-side up. These are small things that may go unnoticed, but they can make an unconscious impression about quality.

Keep it short and to the point. If at all possible, keep your resume down to one page. Sum up your education and experience in a neat, logical manner. Consult an up-to-date resume book for different formats you can use. Don't include references, but indicate that they are available on request.

Include a cover letter. Address a one-page cover letter to the person directly responsible for reviewing applicants (if you can find out the person's name). The cover letter is an excellent opportunity to point out your unique qualifications for that company's particular job. Use a warm (but not overly familiar), conversational tone in your letter.

Check your spelling. Your word processor probably has spelling and grammar checkers, so make use of them. Poor grammar and spelling make a very bad impression on some people. Whatever you do, make sure you properly spell the recipient's name.

Have someone read it before you send it out. A second pair of eyes will help to ensure that your resume is clear and easy to read, and that you haven't overlooked anything.

If you're uncomfortable about creating such an important document yourself, consider getting help from a good resume outfit. They will make sure the information is formatted properly and that the document looks professional and reads well.

Some people like to send *disk-based resumes*, which use an authoring program like Macromedia Director to turn them into multimedia presentations. If you choose to do this, make sure you include a player program or make the file self-running, and always include a printed version of your resume as well. This ensures that it won't be overlooked in a file or simply ignored as being too much trouble to look at.

Business Cards

You probably think of business cards as being something that only a contractor would need, but they're very useful to artists looking for employment as well. First of all, business cards are very convenient and professional, and make the statement that you mean business. They're useful at conferences and other functions where people meet as a way to get your contact information to someone quickly and unobtrusively. Naturally, contacts respond by giving you their business card, and you end up with the contact information you need to get in touch with them later.

For artists, the design of your business card acts as a mini-portfolio, making a statement about your design and 3D skills. Boring black text on white business cards get stuffed in a pocket and forgotten. Let's take my own first business card, ordered from a generic set of samples at an office supply store, as an example (see figure 12.3). Yuck. It's got all the basic contact information, but it really doesn't say a thing about my abilities as an artist, does it?

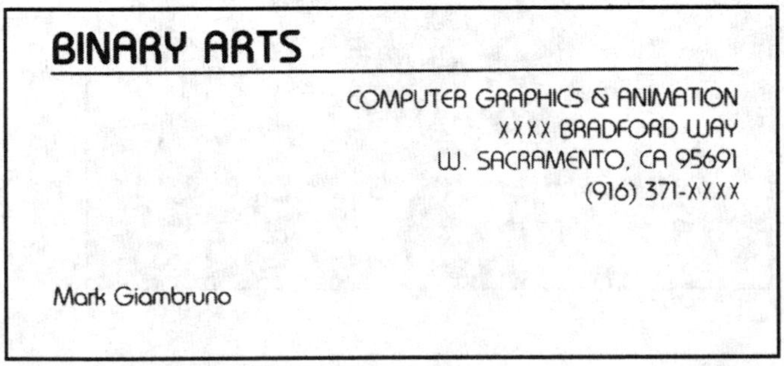

BINARY ARTS

COMPUTER GRAPHICS & ANIMATION
XXXX BRADFORD WAY
W. SACRAMENTO, CA 95691
(916) 371-XXXX

Mark Giambruno

FIGURE 12.3

My old Binary Arts business card came from an office supply outfit. Doesn't exactly scream "I'm a 3D-artist" does it?

Contrast that with the look of the full-color business cards I now use (see figure 12.4). Unlike the old ones, these get comments from nearly everyone who receives them. They give the recipient a visual example of my abilities, and people are more likely to keep them.

FIGURE 12.4

My new CyberDog
Studios business cards
make a visual pun on
the Terminator films.
They are much better at
communicating what I
do, and act as a mini-
portfolio sample. Image
©1996 Mark
Giambruno.

NoNeg Press in Sacramento prints inexpensive business cards in full color
and at 200 lpi. A minimum order is 750 at $69, with additional sets of 750
available at $39. You can transmit your artwork to their BBS, and they will
ship the cards to you in 10 days or so. Visit http://www.business-card.com
for more information.

No matter what the design, your business card should contain your name, daytime telephone number, fax number, and e-mail address, as well as your Web site if it's related to your 3D graphics skills. Whether you list your physical address is up to you. It clearly needs to be available if you're expecting someone to send you mail or packages, but if you work out of your home, it also means you might get unexpected visits or be put on mailing lists that you don't want. One solution is to stamp your address on the back of some cards, and keep both versions with you.

Choosing Portfolio Pieces

Choosing the *right* works to include in your portfolio is rarely an easy decision. Naturally, it's important to showcase your best work, but you also want to show your range, and you don't want to include too many pieces or the presentation will drag. When selecting traditional works to include, try to avoid using too much art school work, because all student work has a tendency to look alike.

In all cases, remember this: *a portfolio is only as strong as its weakest piece*. Weed out anything that's sub-par, any item that isn't among, say, the best 10 to 15% of your work. It's better to have a portfolio with only five good pieces in it than one with fifteen that includes a bunch of mediocre items.

Try to show a good range of unique and individual works, rather than variations on a theme. In other words, it would be best to have some mechanical designs, some organic works, some straight 2D paint pieces and so on, instead of showing only mechanical designs, even if that's what you do most. Sending in too many similar works can make you look like a one-trick pony, no matter how good your stuff is. This holds true for your traditional work as well—show a good range of subjects and media, from pencil to pen & ink to painting. If you made some nice hand-built ceramics or sculpture, enclose photos of them as well.

Make sure that each piece shows that a lot of time and care went into its preparation. Don't include anything that you just knocked out in a few hours, because it will look it. Don't include any pieces based on tutorials from software manuals unless you have taken them well beyond the book's stopping point.

Without a doubt the worst portfolio samples I ever received were color inkjet prints of some squares and ovals in different colors. It looked like someone had just been playing around with a drawing program for about 20 minutes, and decided they were now a CG artist. At first I thought it was a joke, but then I noticed that they had included full contact information. The only thing that rescued it from the trash was the fact it was *so lame* it was worth saving.

Format Options

When dealing with computer-generated work or photographs of traditional work, you have several different formats to choose from, including color prints, slides, and electronic media. Some of these options are good for mailing samples, while the rest are better for interview presentations.

Prints and Slides

Color prints, especially 8.5" x 11" or larger, look great and are easy to present in an interview situation. For CG work, use a service bureau with photographic or dye sublimation printing for best results (see Chapter 10, "Rendering and Output," for more information). Color prints are expensive, however, so you probably don't want to send them out in the mail, especially because they may not come back (at least for a while).

35mm slides are a good alternative to prints, especially if you're sending out samples. The main problem with them is their size, because you can't rely on the recipient having a magnifying viewer or loupe at hand. Therefore, make sure that the image "pops" even in the small dimensions, or it may end up looking weak or unclear. If you're taking slides to an interview, keep them in a clear plastic binder-style storage page, so that they can be easily held up to the light or plunked down on a light table. Of course, you also could bring a magnifying viewer of some kind so that they will be sure to see the detail in your imagery.

You also may want to consider larger format transparencies, like 2.25" x 2.25" (called two-and-a-quarter square) or larger. These cost significantly more to have made, but they're much easier to view, and make a quality impression.

Tape

For showing animation, a VHS tape is your safest bet. Nearly all companies have a VCR these days, and you don't have to worry about software incompatibilities or system availability. VHS quality is not the best, but if you use good tape and make first generation copies from a 3/4" or Beta SP Master, the tape will still look pretty good. While it's a good idea to have a Beta SP copy available, don't rely on companies having one of those expensive decks around—unless you're applying at a video production house or other outfit that's heavily into video.

If you do a tape presentation, be sure to give due consideration to music and sound. Both have a tremendous effect on the impact that an animation makes. See Chapter 11, "The Reel," for more details.

Electronic Media

Sending files on electronic media is convenient and inexpensive, but it does expose your work to easy copying, so be sure to electronically stamp your images with your name and copyright information (using a paint program) to protect your rights.

Some companies are primarily PC-based, while others may use Macs or SGIs exclusively, so consider that when deciding which media format to use. In general, a 3.5" HD PC-formatted disk with images in JPEG format is the safest route, but you may want to include a Mac disk with JPEG or PICT images just to cover yourself, and to provide a backup.

The highly popular ZIP disk and its older SyQuest cousins are other alternatives, but they are still a little expensive if you're sending out a lot of them. You will want them returned because of the cost but that means your work won't remain in the company's files. If you go this route, be sure to send a self-addressed and prepaid padded mailer for the media's return.

Now that Recordable CD-ROM drives are becoming commonplace, a lot of people are starting to use CD-R media as a way to deliver samples and presentations. If possible, burn your CD-ROM with a cross-platform format so that it can be read on both Macs and PCs.

If you decide to distribute samples or make a presentation with electronic media, keep the following things in mind:

◆ *Check your disks*. Make sure that your disks are working properly, are virus-free, and that the files haven't been corrupted. Art directors receiving corrupt—or, worse, virus-infested—disks are unlikely to ask for a replacement, or consider your application further. Be sure to bring a back-up disk with you to the interview.

◆ *Keep file sizes under control*. Don't use the high capacity of the media as an excuse to use uncompressed file formats. Nobody wants to wait around while you load up a bunch of five-megabyte images. Use a JPEG compression level that allows the file to load quickly, but doesn't significantly impact the image quality.

◆ *Have an alternative format ready*. If you're going to use electronic media for an interview, make sure you have your own laptop to show it on, or that the company is set up with a readily available system that definitely suits your needs. Arrive early and get the system prepped, and if there's any sort of problem at all, have your samples with you in print or slide form so that you don't waste any time, or make a bad impression.

A relatively new idea in portfolios is not sending samples at all, but simply directing the company to your *Web portfolio*, a Web site where a neatly formatted multimedia presentation awaits (see figure 12.5). Of course, this requires that you have the skill (or assistance of someone who has) to assemble, debug, and maintain a Web site. In addition, there are some potential drawbacks, the biggest of which is the possibility that the art director doesn't have the time or inclination to go look at your site. Therefore, be sure to include at least a printed resume with your letter. Including a few slides or images on disk would be a good ideas as well.

If you opt for the Web approach, do some research on your Internet provider first by conducting speed and reliability tests with a dummied-up Web site. The following are some important tips:

◆ Make sure the pages and images load up quickly *during business hours*, when art directors are likely to be checking it out. Many small pages are better than a few long ones for fast load times.

◆ Code the HTML for the page to look good with Netscape or Internet Explorer, because you probably have no idea which one they're using. Use a "safe" version of each (one that has been out for a while and just about everyone has adopted), not necessarily the latest release, and never a beta version.

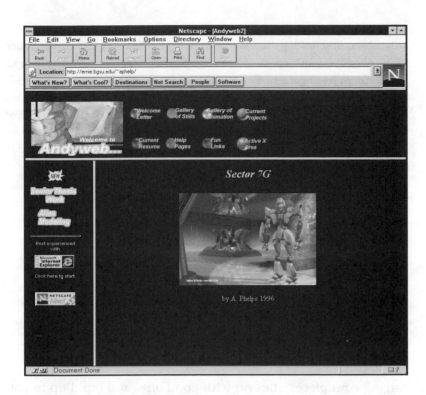

FIGURE 12.5

A Web portfolio places your work within easy reach of potential employers. This one is by artist Andy Phelps at http://www.bgsu.edu/ ~aphelp. Contents ©1996 Andrew Phelps.

◆ Lots of animated GIFs and Javascript gimmicks can get in the way, so put the extra effort into improving the images instead.

◆ Keep the thumbnail versions of the images compact enough to load quickly, but allow the viewer to download larger images as well.

Portfolio Presentation

Showing your portfolio is just like making a sales presentation. You're trying to sell yourself and your talents to a skeptical buyer (in this case, a potential employer). Like many business people, they've seen all the sales pitches and gimmicks before, so you have to do your best to make yourself stand out from the crowd. Your portfolio should be neatly packaged, designed to start smoothly and proceed without a hitch. It should close up quickly and easily. If you're using prints, a nicely bound ring-style portfolio enables you to quickly tune the samples to match your potential employer's needs. It also enables you to flip through the images one at a time with one or two interviewers, or remove and spread them out if you're showing them to a larger group.

When I was first making the rounds at the beginning of my CG career, much of my portfolio work consisted of large-format drawings, airbrush works, and paintings (see figure 12.6). To carry it, I got a relatively massive 30" x 40" portfolio. On a couple of occasions, the first words out of the interviewer's mouth were something like, "My God, that's the *biggest* portfolio I've ever seen!" Often, the size of the portfolio heightened curiosity when I showed up for interviews, which is never a bad thing. I can't say I'd recommend it, though—it's just too bulky.

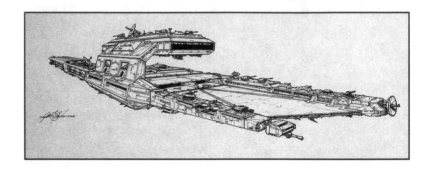

In arranging your pieces, start off with good ones and build up to your best works, with the last image being the *kicker*, your show-stopping image. Leave that one out as you continue the interview. This arrangement holds true for sending out samples as well. If you're using electronic media, name the files so that the kicker is the last one in the directory.

The most important thing about making a presentation is to think it through, instead of trying to wing it. Know in advance what you're going to say about each piece, being sure to leave a little time for questions or comments. Doing practice runs with other artists acting as the interviewers can help prepare you for unexpected questions, and weed out work that might be best left at home.

Interviews

So you've researched the companies you want to approach, written your resume, gotten your portfolio together, run through your presentation, and now you're ready to be interviewed. Before you fire off your letters and hope for the best, you need to consider some techniques for increasing your chances of getting an interview.

Getting In

First off, you've got to remember that the vast majority of places you send your resume and samples to will either not respond, or will send a form letter or postcard saying, "Thanks for your interest, we'll keep your resume on file." Well-known companies get inquiries day-in and day-out, and there simply aren't enough positions available to be filled with even a fraction of the applicants. So, if you're shipping your resume and samples off to companies like Industrial Light and Magic, don't hang around the house waiting for a phone call.

Unless you're approaching a large company that has a *Human Resources Department* responsible for filtering all of the applications, you may improve your chances by finding out the name of the person responsible for reviewing new applicants, and address your package to them. That way, your resume is less likely to end up on the wrong desk.

The best way to increase your chances of getting a meeting at a company that's tough to crack is to meet an employee, such as an artist or producer. Ask around and see if any of your friends or acquaintances know someone who works there. Have your mutual friend introduce you, and maybe the insider will be willing to help you out with advice or contact information, if nothing else. If you hit it off, maybe you can set up a visit to the facility, which will give you a chance to meet your contact's coworkers and employers.

Even if nothing comes of it at the time, maintaining contacts with people is a great way to find out about opportunities early on, because project directors often ask their artists for suggestions first when trying to locate additional talent.

In the book *The Art of the Brothers Hildebrandt*, Ian Summers recounts how identical twin artists Greg and Tim Hildebrandt showed up at Ballantine Books without an appointment. They were underdressed, soaking wet, and carried two garbage bags filled with torn, crumpled, and coffee-stained sketches, which they spread out on the reception area floor. Their work was so incredible, however, that they were commissioned on the spot, and went on to do the famous Lord of the Rings calendar artwork and many book covers for the company. While it's true that your art is far more important than your appearance, if you show up like this, your work had better be *stellar*.

It can be a double-edged sword, but sometimes persistence can pay off. Contacting someone every few weeks may seem pretty annoying (and it certainly can be), but you might wear them down and get yourself a chance if they admire persistence. On the other hand, they may also tell you to never bother them again, so use this only as a last resort.

Dressing

Clearly, what to wear at an interview will vary depending on whether you're meeting some guys from a small video game development house or applying for a position at a major architectural firm. A rule of thumb to apply is to dress as least as well as the people who work at the company, if not a little nicer. A T-shirt would probably be the low-end for a visit to the game company, while a long-sleeve shirt and tie would be fairly dressy. Wear a suit, and they'll probably wonder if you know what kind of company you're trying to work for. On the other hand, a shirt and tie would be a minimum for the architectural firm, with a business suit being more appropriate for a job applicant.

Of course, artists are expected to be a little out of the mainstream, so you probably have a little more leeway than you think. Just make sure you don't try to come off as *too* cool, with your all-black designer suit, white high-tops and $300 shades.

From the Too Hip For Their Own Good File:

One applicant I interviewed was a pudgy fellow wearing what looked like Captain Kirk's leisure wear from *The Wrath of Khan*. I've long since forgotten what his work looked like, but I'll never forget how weird he looked in that bulging high-tech pleated shirt.

Surviving Your Interview

Without a doubt, a job interview can be a very stressful experience, especially if you have never been through one before. While it's natural to be nervous about it, you don't want that to impair your interview. Try to relax and be yourself. If you think you will be overly nervous, practice with your peers (tell them to be tough on you) or try to set up your interviews with the companies you are least interested in working for first, in order to get some practice and hopefully relax a bit for when the interview really counts.

If you're in an interview and feel yourself getting stressed, tell the interviewer about it, and he or she will probably help put you at ease. It's better to admit that you're very nervous than to come off looking rigid.

Remember that a handshake is a social exchange, and a way to define hierarchies. In an interview, you're the subordinate, so don't try to impress the interviewer with your Kung-Fu grip. Also, make sure your hands are warm and dry. Cold, moist, and limp handshakes are probably worse than bone-crushers. If you have a business card, give it to the interviewer after shaking hands and introducing yourself.

The first order of business is often a short tour of the facility. The interviewer shows you around, gives you a look at the kind of work the company's doing, introduces you to a few people, and so forth. During this tour, ask a few good questions, be friendly, and compliment impressive work.

Throughout the interview, be *alert*, paying attention to every word said to you. Usually, the interviewer will tell you what kind of people and skills they're looking for, and give you the opportunity to address their needs. If they don't bring this up, be sure you ask what they're looking for, and when they plan to add the new resources. Then, *shut up and listen*. When you're asked a question, make your answers accurate and concise, neither too clipped or too verbose. Definitely don't jabber on endlessly, even if the interviewer doesn't seem to mind. They may simply be acting polite, even as they mentally shred your application. Remember, however, that people who hardly say a word during an interview are just as likely to be rejected.

Don't expect the interviewer to offer you a job on the spot, but be prepared for the possibility. If this is the job you really want, that would be an ideal time to discuss the particulars. If you still have other positions you want to investigate, see if you can get them to give you an offer (in writing, or write it down during the discussion) and tell them that you're very interested, but want to give their offer some thought. Chances are, they'll understand and appreciate that. Give the interviewer a date (preferably within a week) that you will be ready to make a decision, and stick to it.

Following Up

A day or so after the meeting, send a letter to the interviewer, thanking them for taking the time to get together with you. Make any comments you think will help your case, like pointing out anything important that you forgot (or didn't have a chance) to mention.

At that point, the best thing to do is cross your fingers and wait a while. You should know from the questions you asked at the interview when your potential employer is planning to make a hiring decision. Consider calling a few days before they plan to decide if you really want the position, but it's best to have a good excuse to do so, like offering to send along some additional work that fits with their style or plans.

Negotiating

It's difficult to know what a company is willing to offer if they're interested in hiring you, unless you're responding to a classified advertisement that lists the wage. In general, the interviewer won't even mention the monetary aspect of the job unless they think you're a good candidate, so take it as a good sign if the subject comes up during the interview.

If the subject *doesn't* come up, you should probably ask, because the interviewer may find it odd that you aren't even interested in the pay or benefits. You shouldn't bring it up until the interviewer has had an opportunity to tell you about the company and has asked you if you have any further questions. Whatever you do, *don't* ask about salary when there are other people present who aren't directly responsible for hiring you, such as other artists or producers. Wait for an opportunity to speak with the interviewer alone. If you don't get the opportunity, the company is probably still looking.

Salaries

If you do get an offer, remember the hard, cold fact that nearly every company will try to pay you less than you're worth. This is typical and understandable when you're first starting out, because companies have the excuse of wanting to try you out, or that you need experience or training. However, some companies will cheerfully let you remain at a starting wage for as long as possible. In fact, unless they have a regular performance review schedule, you may work for years without a raise, unless, of course, you *ask* for one.

In any case, while your initial salary may be a bit low if you don't have much experience, make sure that your salary always remains commensurate with your abilities. If you feel underpaid, you probably are, and companies would usually rather give you an increase than have to go through the process of hiring someone new.

There's an unwritten law that says that people should never discuss what they make. At some firms, your salary may even be considered confidential under the conditions of your employment contract. So how do you know if you're getting a fair rate or not? Well, here are some round numbers, depending on experience. These figures are rough estimates for the 1996 video game industry.

◆ **$0–$15/hr.** Interns and others with little or no experience, usually working part-time and trying to break in.

◆ **$15–$25/hr.** Artists with 1—3 years of experience in the field, working in a production capacity.

◆ **$25–$35/hr.** Senior artists with 3—5 years experience, often handling teams of artists.

◆ **$35–$50/hr.** Contractors with over 3 years experience.

Benefits

Most companies with more than a few employees will offer some sort of benefits. In some cases, the benefits may be available only after the employee passes a probationary period running from several weeks to a year. Benefits may include health insurance, 401K or other retirement plans, royalties, profit sharing, stock options, increased vacation or free days, bonuses, and so on.

Health insurance is normally offered as an HMO plan, like Kaiser or Blue Cross, where the recipient may have to pay a small visit charge of $5–$15 if he or she needs medical assistance. This benefit would cost you about $100–$200 or more per month if you had to pay for it yourself.

Retirement plans are a means of saving and investing part of your salary, building it up until you retire. Common plans include Keogh and 401K. Because the overwhelming majority of people will change jobs several times in the 20–40 years it takes them to reach age 65, the plans can often be switched over when you leave. The best deal for the employee is when the company provides some sort of contribution to the plan, above and beyond paying the cost of administration. In this case, the company kicks in everything from small change to a buck for every dollar you contribute to your own fund. Obviously, this can make your investment grow much faster. Contractors often use individual IRAs or Mutual Funds as their retirement or investment plans.

Royalties are usually reserved for senior artists and producers, but some companies pay royalties to everyone on the team. Royalties are a percentage of the company's profits on a product or service, calculated after expenses. Royalties may range from anywhere between a small fraction of one percent to ten percent or more, depending on the situation.

Profit sharing is a distribution of a percentage of the company's profits for a fiscal quarter or year. As with royalties, the percentage you get will depend on your position, responsibilities, and length of time with the firm. Your share of the profit probably won't exceed more than a few percent, however, and will usually be much smaller.

Stock options are an opportunity to purchase company stock at a discount. You can choose to hold onto the stock, or sell it at a profit. Of course, a company has to be publicly traded on the stock exchange to truly offer stock. Sometimes, however, startups may offer the promise of stock, which only becomes tangible if the company is successful and eventually goes public.

Finally, the rule to live by when arriving at a salary/benefit package is: *Get it in writing*.

Contract Issues

Most companies will require you to sign an employment agreement or contract when you're hired. The contract usually states that anything you do for the company is considered a *work for hire*, and you don't hold any rights to that work. In other words, everything you do belongs to the company.

The contract also may limit your ability to do work outside the company for others, or to develop your own products and services. If, for example, you develop a game on your own time while working for a game company, you run the risk of having them claim it as their own unless you can show that it was developed without any of their equipment, materials, resources, or technology.

While most of this is pretty standard, there are a couple of issues that artists should be concerned with. First, because you have no ownership of the work you create, you often need written permission to include these works in your portfolio. If possible, you should ensure that the contract enables you to do so automatically, assuming that the company is free to use the images for self-promotional purposes. In some cases, the company may be doing the work for a third party that doesn't allow this, at least for a period of time, and this would restrict you as well.

Second, given the situation with salary increases discussed earlier, it would be nice to see a guaranteed timetable for performance reviews to give you a shot at a raise.

Advancing Your Career

Years ago, once you took a position at a company, you could expect to remain there for a long time, possibly even retiring after 20 years to a gold watch and pension. Since this is becoming a rarity in today's volatile business environment, it's a good idea to keep an eye out for new opportunities and signs of potential trouble in your company or market.

Switching companies can be a good way to get a substantial salary increase or move to a higher position. You may not even have to leave to accomplish this, because if you're offered an attractive position or pay increase by another company, you can speak to your own employers about it. If they value your continued presence, they will be quick to close the gap between what you're currently making and what you've been offered.

If you do quit, try to part on good terms. It may be tempting to blast deserving parties as you walk out the door for the last time, but the small sense of satisfaction you might feel will be overshadowed by the bad reputation that you may develop.

Also, be careful about switching ships too often, because it can look very bad on your resume. No one wants to hire someone who shows a pattern of leaving companies after a year or two. It's just too expensive to train someone, and the fact that they don't stay around may indicate that they are a problem employee.

Making and maintaining contacts in the industry is key to positioning yourself with an eye toward the future. If something comes up and you decide to switch jobs, or your company starts floundering, you have people to talk to that may be eager to hire you on, or point you in the right direction.

Reading and acquainting yourself with new technologies helps to keep you aware of the trends and future of your industry. You should regard learning as a lifelong endeavor. If you don't keep up, eventually you'll get left behind, or someone who's more on top of things will get the position that you want.

Summary

Computer Graphics is a very exciting and rewarding field, with a lot of growth potential. All it takes to succeed is a commitment to quality, some perseverance, and an eye for art. At this point, I've given you just about every piece of advice I can think of for starting a successful new career or moving ahead in your present CG job. The rest is up to you. *Gambatte yo!* (Do your best!)

Appendix A

Glossary of Terms

Alphabetically Challenged

3D acceleration Video hardware enhancements that dramatically speed up the display of 3D scenes (if the software is written to take advantage of this capability).

3D digitizer A mechanical arm with sensors that determines the physical position of key points on an object and creates a 3D version based on that data.

3D object library Stock 3D objects sold in a variety of different formats and resolutions as an alternative to modeling.

3D paint software A software program or plug-in that enables the user to paint texture maps directly on a 3D model.

3D scanner A device that uses optical and/or laser technology to scan a physical object, to generate a wireframe mesh (and sometimes a full-color map) of the object. This technology is often used to create highly accurate models of complex objects or people.

A

angle of incidence The angle at which a light ray strikes a surface and is reflected into the viewer's eyes.

anti-aliasing A method of softening rough edges in an image by adding or modifying pixels near the stair stepping points. These create a blend between the object and background colors.

additive color model The way in which colors are created with light, as opposed to pigment. In the additive model, red, green, and blue are the primary colors, and mixing them together creates white.

ADO Ampex Digital Opticals. Basic video effects named after a company that made the dedicated video gear to create them. ADO-style effects include changing the scale of a segment of video, stretching it, spinning it around, reversing it, and so forth.

align A command that brings object surfaces flush with each other or centers multiple objects along one or more axes.

alpha channel An optional layer of image data that provides an additional 8 bits of information about transparency. The alpha channel is used as a mask for compositing one image over another.

ambient color The hue an object reflects if it isn't directly illuminated by a light source. It is intended to be representative of the color of the light reflecting off of the objects in a scene, but only radiosity rendering can truly accomplish this.

ambient light In theory, the cumulative effect of all the light bouncing off all the objects in an area. Generally set as a global value that illuminates all objects in the scene equally.

animated texture A video or animation file used instead of still images as a texture map, causing the texture on an object to change over time when the scene is rendered.

animatic A rough animation intended to work out timing and composition issues. Often inserted in the working cut of a film as a placeholder for effects sequences that aren't yet completed.

animation controller Any of a number of different methods for creating or modifying animation keyframes or object behavior. Controllers include TCB, Bézier, audio, noise, and expression.

animation In 3D graphics, the modification of any kind of object, light, material, or camera by moving or changing it over time. The creation of action or movement with inanimate objects.

anime Japanese loan-word (word adapted from a foreign language) for animated films, television programs, or other works. Pronounced ANNIE-MAY.

array A matrix or pattern of objects extrapolated from a single object or group of objects. Common types include linear arrays (which follow a straight line) and radial arrays (which form all or part of a circular path).

aspect ratio The relationship between the height and width of an image, expressed as a decimal ratio. It is calculated by dividing width by height. For example, an image 4" wide and 3" high would have an aspect ratio of 1:1.333…

atmosphere A user-defined level of aerial occlusion (such as fog) applied to a scene, creating the effect of objects being seen from great distances or through a mist.

attach A command that allows two separate elements to be joined into one object. The opposite of *detach*.

attenuation The gradual reduction in the intensity of light as it gets further from the source, which is caused by light being occluded by particles in the atmosphere. In 3D programs, attenuation is a light source option controlled by range settings.

axis An imaginary line in 3D space that defines a direction. The standard axes used in 3D programs are called X, Y, and Z. The plural form of axis is axes, pronounced AXE-EASE.

B

B-spline A type of spline that has control points with equal weights that adjust its shape. Control points rarely reside on the resulting curve in this type of spline.

ball joint A type of constrained link that allows two joined objects to have an axis of rotation

bank The rotation (or *roll*) that an object or camera may perform when it moves through a curve in a path. This simulates the results of centrifugal force on a real-world object as it executes a turn.

behavior Object-level controller (Look At, Bounce, Spin, and so on) that simplifies some animation work by having the computer reorient the objects according to the set behavior.

bend A transform that deforms an object by applying torsion around the selected axis.

bevel A flat transitional plane located between two other planes, usually set at an angle that is half the difference between the two. Also called a *chamfer*.

Bézier splines A type of spline in which the control points always reside on the resulting curve.

Extending out from the control points are tangent points, which allow the curve to be modified without moving the control points.

bias In a TCB (Tension, Continuity, and Bias) animation controller, bias adjusts the location of maximum extreme point (or peak) of the motion path or control curve in relation to the keyframe.

bluescreen A blue background that serves as a stage for actors. The blue can be removed after filming and replaced with a different background. Costumes and props shot on a bluescreen stage cannot contain blue or purple pigments, because the compositing process would cause any blue or purple elements to become transparent. An alternative is greenscreen, which allows blue and purple objects, but no green ones.

bones deformation A technique of animating an object (usually a character) by defining and animating an internal skeleton that automatically deforms the surrounding mesh.

Boolean operation A set of commands that adds or subtracts one object from another. They are commonly used to re-shape or "drill holes" in objects.

bounding box A stand-in in the shape of a box that has the same overall dimensions as the object. Bounding boxes replace mesh-intensive objects during movement or other translations, so that the system won't be bogged down redrawing a large amount of mesh.

box coordinates A type of mapping coordinate system well suited to rectangular objects. It applies the image coordinates from six different directions, one for each surface on the object.

bump map A grayscale image that varies the apparent surface roughness of an object by manipulating the normals.

buy-out music Stock music that can be used commercially for a set fee, as opposed to paying a royalty. The music samples are available on CD, and work much the same way as stock photography purchases.

C

CAD/CAM Computer Aided Design/Computer Aided Manufacturing. CAD is the use of the computer and a drawing program to design a wide range of industrial products, ranging from machine parts to homes. CAM uses CAD drawings to control the equipment that manufactures the final object.

camera target A small cube or other object attached to a virtual camera that indicates the center of the camera's field of vision (in other words, where the camera is pointed).

CD-R drive CD-ROM Recordable drive. A CD-ROM drive capable of recording most CD-ROM formats on special CD-R media. These recorders are used to "burn" CD-ROMs during the development process so the program can be checked from its destination format, and can even be used to create music CDs.

chain A series of linked objects, using the hierarchical parent-child relationship, but extending it by additional generations to grandchild, great-grandchild, and so forth.

chamfer See *bevel*.

channel An individual attribute of a material that can accept images, or be set to affect the appearance of the object to which they are applied. Typical channels include Diffuse, Bump, Opacity, Shininess, and Self-Illumination.

character animation The process of imbuing objects not only with movement, but with personality. Virtually any object can take on personality if character animation techniques are applied to it.

cheap mesh A slang term for an object that has a low polygon count, or is very efficient and quick to render.

child An object linked to another that is closer to the beginning of the hierarchical tree (its parent).

chroma The color of an object, determined by the frequency of the light emitted from or reflected by the object.

chroma key A process that electronically removes a solid color (usually blue or green) and allows it to be replaced with another image. Often used to composite actors into virtual environments. In some cases, a video "super black" signal is used instead of a visible color.

clipping plane Also known as the *viewing plane*. A user-definable cut-off point that makes everything on the camera's side of it invisible during rendering.

closed shape A shape that has an inside and an outside, separated from each other by an edge.

CMYK Cyan Magenta Yellow blacK. The different colors of ink in the 4-color printing process that are applied as tiny dot patterns to form full-color images.

codec COmpressor DECompressor. Any one of a number of different methods for compressing video and playing it back. Digital video file formats like .AVI and QuickTime are designed to accept plug-in compression technologies in the form of codecs.

color The hue of an object, determined by the frequency of the light emitted from or reflected by the object. In computer graphics, color is determined by the combination of Hue, Saturation, and Value in the HSV color model, or Red, Green, and Blue color levels in the RGB model.

color calibrator A device that is held up to the screen and adjusts the settings of the monitor using a reference image.

color depth The amount of data used to display a single pixel in an image, expressed in bits. For example, an 8-bit image contains 256 colors or levels of gray.

color temperature A value, in degrees Kelvin, that is used to differentiate between near-white spectrums of light.

component software A software architecture in which the core program and add-on features are all modular and interconnected, allowing them to work together as if they were a single product.

compositing The process of combining different elements into a single scene. This may refer to combining still photos or bluescreen video with computer graphics backgrounds, or be applied to any process in which separate images are combined together.

compression rate The speed at which digital video data is encoded for playback, defined in kilobytes per second (KB/s). For the movies to play back properly, the target system must be capable of pulling the movie data off the storage medium and displaying it at that speed.

constraint A restriction placed on the movement of an object in IK, in order to force it to behave like a physical joint.

continuity In a TCB controller, continuity adjusts how tangent the path is to the control point. In filmmaking, it is the process of maintaining a smooth flow of consistency in props, costumes, action, and direction from shot to shot in a scene.

control vertices (CVs) Control points that exert a magnet-like influence on the flexible surface of a patch, stretching and tugging it in one direction or another.

coordinates Two or three sets of numbers that use a grid-based system to identify a given point in space.

cubic coordinates See *box coordinates*.

cut Also referred to as a shot, it is the smallest individual piece of an animation or film. It may be a single frame, or an entire sequence. Also refers to the edited version of the entire film.

cut scene In computer gaming, a pre-determined video or animated sequence that's played to show story progression or the results of a user action.

cyberspace In 3D graphics, the coordinate-based virtual space inside the computer's memory where 3D scenes are constructed and animated.

cylindrical coordinates A mapping coordinate system that wraps the image around one of the object's axes until it meets itself, like a label on a soup can.

D

dataset A collection of information that describes a 3D object. A dataset may contain 3D coordinates, material attributes, textures, and even animation.

decal An image that can be scaled and moved around on an object independently of any other texture mapping.

default lighting The startup lighting in a 3D program, which enables the user to begin rendering without having to define a light source.

deform fit A type of deform modifier that enables you to define the shape of an object using an X-axis outline, a Y-axis outline, and one or more cross-sections.

deform modifier A means of applying transform settings to change the outline of a cross-sectional object as it's swept along a path.

deformation grid Also known as a space warp. An object that defines an area in 3D space that has an automatic effect on objects passing through its influence. Deforms include Wave, Ripple, Explode, Gravity, and so forth.

deformation map See *displacement map*.

depth of field That portion of an image that is properly focused. In photography, depth of field is controlled by the aperture setting. In 3D graphics, depth of field is normally infinite, but some products offer control over it as part of the camera settings.

desktop video Digital video editing and effects capability added to a computer with special video cards and software.

detach An operation that disconnects an element of a larger object, separating it into two objects. The opposite of *attach*.

diffuse color The hue assigned to an object. This is the color that is reflected when the object is illuminated by a direct lighting source.

diffuse map A mapping channel used to alter the object's color away from that defined by the color setting, usually into a pattern or image.

diffusion dither A type of dithering where the differently colored pixels are randomized to an extent, smoothing the blend.

digital camera An electronic camera that records images onto built-in memory or tiny diskettes that can be downloaded into a computer.

digital retouching The process of using 2D paint programs to modify photographic stills or movies.

digital sound Audio that has been converted to a binary format, allowing it to be manipulated by and played back on a computer. Music CDs use digital sound recorded in 16 bits at a 44.1KHz data rate, and better sound cards can provide this level as well.

DVD Digital Versatile Disc. A new optical disc format for both video and computer files that features much higher data capacity than CD-ROM.

digitizing The process of transforming images, objects, or sounds into a digital form that a computer can manipulate.

directional light Also called a distant light. A virtual illumination source for simulating far away light sources like the sun. It projects light along one axis only, and all the light rays (and hence, the shadows) are parallel.

displacement map Also known as a deformation map. A

grayscale image applied to an object that actually distorts the mesh, deforming it according to the gray value. Often used to create terrain models.

distant light See *directional light*.

dither An image process that breaks gradients up into patterns of variously colored pixels. These work like the four-color printing process to simulate a wider range of colors.

dolly In filmmaking, a wheeled platform that a camera is mounted on, and the process of moving the camera around on the floor during the shot. In 3D software, it usually means a camera movement made toward, away from, or around a subject as though the camera were mounted on a wheeled tripod.

dongle A hardware key, which is a physical device plugged into the serial port of a computer or attached in line with the keyboard that unlocks high-end software for use.

double-sided object An object with normals on both sides of the object's faces, allowing it to be seen from any viewpoint, even inside.

DPI Dots Per Inch. Resolution expressed as the number of dots or pixels that the medium can display in one inch. Most computer displays are based on 72dpi, and 300dpi is a common laser printer output resolution.

Duke Nukem 3D An insidious and addictive program, created by 3D Realms in order to ensure that all other game software developers' efforts grind to a halt.

dummy object See *null*.

DVE Digital Video Editing. The use of a desktop video system to edit and add special effects to video.

E

ease from A keyframe parameter that controls the acceleration of the object or event as it leaves the keyframe.

ease to A keyframe parameter that decelerates an object or event as it approaches the keyframe.

editing The process of assembling the various scenes created and rendered during production, turning them into a cohesive whole.

emitter A simple polygonal shape that acts as a point of origin for particles in a particle system.

engine The portion of a software program that manages and updates the real time 3D graphics.

exclude A feature that allows listed objects to be unaffected by the selected light source.

export Saving a file in a cross-program or cross-platform format, like DXF.

extrude/extrusion The process of pushing a 2D shape into the third dimension by giving it a Z-axis depth.

F

face The area enclosed by the edges of the polygon.

face extrusion A process that takes a selected face or faces and extrudes them in or out from their current positions.

face mapping An image mapping type that tries to conform the image to pairs of faces that share an invisible edge.

facial motion capture A motion capture system designed to record facial expressions and lip movements.

falloff The portion or range of a light source that is at a reduced or 0 intensity setting. Also, a transparency option that sets how much more or less transparent an object is at its edges.

field of view (FOV) The angle, in degrees, that encompasses everything that can be seen through a lens or virtual camera viewport.

field rendering Output option that renders images in the same way that a television displays them: in two alternating passes, one with every odd scan line rendered, the other with every even line. Compare with *frame rendering*.

file format The manner in which data is organized in a computer file. Common image file formats include BMP, PICT, and TGA. Popular 3D file formats include 3DS, DXF, and OBJ.

fillet Also called a radius edge. An arcing transition between two planes or lines.

fill light Light source used to fill in a dark area of a scene, such as a shadow cast by the key light.

film grammar The storytelling methodology developed by director D. W. Griffith and others to make the best use of the film medium.

first vertice The vertice in a shape that is used for orientation during skinning operations.

Usually the one that was created first, but any vertice can be assigned as such.

flat shading A display or rendering mode that shows off the surface and color of the object in a faceted manner, because the polygons aren't smoothed.

focal length The distance in millimeters from the center of the lens to the image it forms of the subject (assumed to be an infinite distance in front of the lens). Short focal lengths produce wide angle images, while long ones are used for telephoto shots.

foley stage A soundproof room filled with numerous objects and materials used to create sound effects.

forensic animation An animated re-creation of an accident or event using whatever data (or speculation) is available. Popular for demonstrating a complex series of events in courtroom situations.

forward kinematics The default method of animating linked objects, in which the movement of the parent object affects all the offspring on down the chain.

frame In filmmaking or animation, a single still image that is part of a sequence. Also, the visible portion of a scene when viewed through a camera or viewport.

frame rate The speed at which film, video, or animated images are displayed, in frames per second (fps).

frame rendering The default output option that renders the entire image. Compare with *field rendering*.

freeze Also called ghost. A command that leaves an object visible in a scene, but prevents it from being selected or changed.

function curve A graphical way of displaying object transformations or other animatible parameters.

G

G-buffer Also called a geometry channel. Additional image channels that use grayscale images to describe the geometry, normals, textures, and other information in the model.

gamma In a computer display, refers to the overall brightness of the screen. Also, a measure of brightness for all output technologies as a way of predicting their appearance when the image is viewed on a computer display.

gamut The color range that can be represented by a particular display or printing technology.

gel In filmmaking, celluloid filters placed over spotlights to change their color. Sometimes used as another term for *projection map*.

geometry channel See *G-buffer*.

geometry General term for 3D objects. Also, incredibly boring subject in high school.

glow A light source setting or post-production effect that creates a soft halo of light around selected objects or materials.

gobo In filmmaking, steel cutouts that change the shape of quality of a spotlight. See *projection map*.

Gouraud shading Also called smooth shading. A display or rendering mode that produces smoothly blended object surfaces that are much more realistic than flat renderings.

greenscreen Similar to *bluescreen*, but allows the costumes or props to contain blue or purple pigments. Of course, with a greenscreen the subject can't have any green pigment.

grid Cross-hatched lines visible in the viewport, and used like graph paper for determining scale when creating objects.

group A command that enables the user to select a related collection of objects, then temporarily combines them into a whole.

H

hidden line A display or rendering mode that draws the edges of an object as in a wireframe display, but only ones that would be visible if the object were opaque.

hide A command that makes an object invisible.

hotspot The portion or range of a light source that is at the full intensity setting.

HSV Hue-Saturation-Value. A color selection interface used in computer graphics that enables the user to adjust hue (chroma), saturation (intensity), and value (brightness) to select a color.

hue See *color*.

I

image library A collection of royalty-free or stock images, often on CD-ROM, that are professionally photographed and scanned.

import Loading a file saved in a cross-program or cross-platform format, like DXF.

include A light source option that enables the user to select a list of objects that the specified light will affect. All other objects in the scene are ignored.

instance A type of duplicate of an object or light source in which changes to one are adopted by all.

intensity A measure of the brightness of a light source. Also, another term for *saturation*.

inverse kinematics (IK) A method of controlling linked objects by moving the far end of a hierarchical chain, which then causes the rest of the chain to conform.

inverted light Also known as a negative or dark light. Makes a light source work in the opposite way, by lowering the illumination level of whatever is in range.

J

jaggies Slang term for lines or areas of an image that are not anti-aliased.

K

key light The main source of illumination in the scene, usually casting the most apparent shadows.

keyframe In 3D graphics, a user-defined point where an animation event takes place. The computer then tweens the events from keyframe to keyframe. In a digital video file, it is a frame that contains the entire image, instead of only changes from the previous frame.

keyframing The process of defining keyframes for animation.

L

lathe The process of spinning a 2D shape around an axis, extruding it in small steps as it is rotated.

lens flare The pattern of bright circles and rays that is seen when you point a camera lens at the sun or other bright light source.

linear array A series of objects duplicated from the original along a straight line trajectory.

linear weighting Animation control type in which tweening is done in a continuous, even manner, with no variation in speed or direction.

link A hierarchical connection between two objects.

local coordinates Coordinate system that uses the object itself as the basis for the axes.

luminosity See *self-illumination*.

M

magnet tool A tool designed to make 3D sculpting easier by attracting or repelling vertices when it's brought close to the object.

map channel See *channel*.

map A bitmapped image, either scanned or painted, that gives a material unique qualities that aren't available by simply varying surface attributes.

mapping Also called texture mapping. The process of developing and assigning material attributes to an object.

mapping coordinates A set of coordinates that specify the location, orientation, and scale of any textures applied to an object.

maquette A small, often highly detailed sculpture that is used to visualize a character in three dimensions.

mask A black and white or grayscale element that is used to prevent certain areas of an image from being affected by a process. Called a matte in filmmaking.

material The encompassing term for all of the different images and settings that are assigned to an object's surface.

matte See *mask*.

mesh optimization The process of reducing the density of a mesh object by combining closely aligned faces.

mesh Slang term for a 3D object or scene, called that because it resembles a wire mesh sculpture.

metaballs A form of modeling where the user builds forms out of spheres, and the software blends them together into a single mass.

mirror A transform that reverses an object or copies a reversed version of it along the selected axis.

moiré A pattern that appears in video images that contain small repetitive textures, or in scans when the scanning resolution doesn't match the printing resolution. Pronounced MOR-AY.

morph Animated 2D and/or 3D technique that makes one image or form smoothly transform into another.

motion blur The smearing of an image when the subject or camera are in motion.

motion capture Any one of several processes that enable a performer's actions to be digitized and used to drive a bones deformation system for 3D character animation.

motion library A stock collection of animated movements for bones deformation systems (usually motion captured) that offer actions like reaching, bending, stretching, eating, dancing, and so forth.

motion path A spline that represents the path of an object, used for reference when making adjustments to the animation.

multiplier A light source setting that increases the intensity of the light past the RGB setting limits.

non sequitur Nonsensical words or actions, or statements that are absurd or meaningless. Also called political platforms.

non-linear editing Editing system that enables the user to edit scenes in any desired sequence, as opposed to starting at the beginning and working through to the end.

non-planar polygon A polygon in which one or more of the vertices are on a different plane from the others, which can result in a rendering bug.

normal An imaginary marker (usually represented by a little line or arrow) which protrudes from a polygon face and indicates which side of the polygon is visible, and what direction it's facing.

null Also called a dummy object. An object that does not render, so it can be used as an invisible component of a chain or as a reference point for establishing remote axes of rotation.

NURBS Non-Uniform Rational B-Splines. A type of spline that has control points that reside away from the resulting curve, and has weights to control the curve. It uses knots that define the number of control points on a given portion of the curve.

point light Also known as an omni (omnidirectional) light. A light source that casts light in all directions.

opacity The degree to which light rays cannot penetrate an object. Defines the same quality as transparency, but from the opposite end of the scale.

opacity map A grayscale image loaded into a material's opacity channel that makes the object's surface appear to vary from opaque to transparent.

operand An object or shape being used in a Boolean operation.

optical tracking Motion capture method where the performer is covered with little targets (usually white disks or balls), and a video camera is used to digitize their movements.

optimized palette A palette that features the best range of colors to display a given image.

optimize In 3D graphics, to reduce the density of a mesh object by combining closely aligned faces. Also used to refer to reorganization of a hard drive to place all data in contiguous sectors.

origin point The center point of the cyberspace universe, where the central axes meet. Identified by the coordinates 0, 0, 0.

orthographic projection In 3D graphics, a display mode in which the viewer's location is infinitely distant from the scene, so that all lines along the same axis are parallel. Viewports like top, side, front, and user usually display orthographic views.

output Stage in 3D production where a file, photographic slide, section of videotape, or other media is used to store the image or animation.

palette The full set of colors used or available for use in an image. Usually refers to images with 256 colors or less.

palette flash A flashing or color shift that occurs when an image's palette is altered abruptly.

pan A side-to-side rotation of a camera around its vertical axis.

parametric coordinates Semi-automatic mapping coordinates that can be applied during the creation of any parametric object.

parametric modeling A 3D modeling system in which objects retain their base geometry information and can be modified at almost any point by varying the parameters that define them.

parent In a chain of linked objects, the object that is closer to the base of the hierarchy than the other object attached to it (its child).

partial lathe A lathe operation in which the cross-sectional shape is not revolved a full 360 degrees.

particle system An animation module that enables the user to generate and control the behavior of a vast number of tiny objects. Used to simulate natural effects like water, fire, sparks, or bubbles.

patch modeler A 3D modeling system that uses a network of control points to define and modify the shape of the patch, which is usually a lattice of either splines or polygons.

persistence of vision The tendency of the human eye to

continue seeing an image for a split second after the view has changed.

Phong rendering A rendering method that retains the smoothness of Gouraud shading, but adds specular highlights for more realism.

pivot point The user-defined rotational center of an object, often the same as the point where the three local axes meet.

pixel PI(X)cture ELement. The smallest unit of graphics that a video adapter generates, usually about the size of a pinpoint. Pixels can be of nearly any color, depending on the capabilities of the adapter.

planar coordinates A type of mapping coordinate system well-suited to flat objects. It applies a set of rectangular image coordinates from a single direction.

plug-in An add-on feature that works within a software program. Plug-ins are popular for adding new capabilities to products without generating a new version of the software.

point In 3D space, the smallest area that it is possible to "occupy" is called a point. Each point is defined by a unique set of three numbers, called coordinates.

polygonal modeling The basic type of 3D modeling, in which all objects are defined as groups of polygons.

polygon A closed shape with three or more sides.

polyline A line with more than one segment (at least three vertices).

post production effects Also called video post effects. In 3D graphics, this refers to transitions, color manipulation, or special effects applied to an animation after it has been rendered.

pre-rendered animation Term used in computer game production that refers to animation that is generated at an earlier time, then stored in a form that allows playback on demand.

preview In 3D graphics, an output mode that creates a fast-rendering test animation, or a display mode that generates a simplified version of the scene in real time.

primitive Any of a number of basic 3D geometric forms, including cubes, spheres, cones, cylinders, and so forth.

procedural texture A type of texture that is mathematically defined. It can be used to simulate wood, marble, and other materials, but usually doesn't look as realistic as scanned textures.

projection map Also called a gobo. An image added to a light source that changes the light's shape or causes it to throw a pattern onto objects it illuminates.

projection Another term for a mapping coordinate method (cylindrical mapping is the same as cylindrical projection).

projector A light source that uses a projection map or gobo.

pulling points Slang term for *vertice-level editing*.

Q

quad A four-sided polygon commonly used in 3D programs.

R

radial array A series of objects duplicated from the original along a rotation-based trajectory.

radiosity The property that states that light reflecting off an object goes on to illuminate other objects as well. Also, a rendering method that takes into account the color and shape of all surfaces in the scene when calculating illumination levels,

and produces images of near-photographic realism.

radius edge See *fillet*.

ray tracing A rendering method where the color and value of each pixel on the screen is calculated by casting an imaginary ray backward from the viewer's perspective into the model, to determine what light and surface factors are influencing it.

real time The immediate processing of input data and graphics, so that any changes result in near-instantaneous adjustments to the image.

reflection map An image or process used to create an environment for a reflective object, in order to roughly simulate the effects of ray tracing on reflective objects.

refraction The bending of light waves that occurs when they move through different types of materials.

refraction mapping A material option used as a means of simulating the effects of light refraction in programs that don't offer ray tracing.

refresh rate The number of times per second that the screen image is repainted on the monitor, measured in cycles per second, or Hertz (Hz).

rendering The process wherein the computer interprets all the object and light data and creates a finished image from the viewport you have selected. The resulting image may be either a still, or a frame in an animation sequence.

RGB Red-Green-Blue. The three primary colors in the additive (direct light) color model. Computer monitors vary the brightness levels of red, green, and blue pixels in order to create the gamut of displayable colors.

roll To rotate a camera around its viewing axis, making the scene appear to spin.

rotate A transform that spins an object around the selected axis.

rotoscoping The process of adding film or video to animation, either as a finished element or for use as a reference for the animated characters.

S

saturation Also called intensity. The measure of how concentrated a color appears to be. A fully saturated red, for example, cannot be any more red than it is, whereas a red with low saturation begins to turn gray.

scale A transform that adjusts the size of an object. Also, the mathematical relationship between the size of a subject in reality and the size of its representation on paper or in 3D. A typical architectural scale, for example, is 1/4"=1'0".

scanline rendering Typical rendering method used by non-ray-tracing programs. Renders the image as a series of horizontal lines.

segment A step or division in an object, similar to the way a building is divided up into floors.

self-illumination A material channel or control that adjusts the degree to which an object appears to be lit from within.

self-illumination map A grayscale image loaded into the material's self-illumination channel that creates the impression that some portions of the object are lit from within.

shadow map size A setting that adjusts the amount of memory that the system can use to create a given shadow map. The larger the map, the more refined and detailed it will be.

shadow mapping A method of creating shadows in scanline renderers that works by creating a grayscale texture map based on the lighting and mesh in the scene, then applies it to the objects at render time.

shininess The overall reflective nature of the object—in other words, its glossiness.

shininess map A grayscale image loaded into the material's shininess channel that varies the reflectivity of the surface. Used for making portions of an object dull or shiny.

single-sided polygon The default type of polygons, which can only be "seen" from the side with the normal. For example, if you create a sphere with single-sided polygons and move the viewpoint inside the object to render an image, the sphere won't be visible.

skating A common problem in character animation created with forward kinematics or cheapo motion capture, in which the position of a character's feet slide around on the ground instead of remaining firmly planted.

skeleton The linked internal bone structure that can be used to deform the surrounding mesh when using a bones deformation system. In humanoid 3D characters, the skeleton is a very simple version of our own.

skew A transform that forces one side of an object in one direction along the selected axis, and the other side in the opposite direction.

skinning A method of creating 3D objects by generating a "skin" over a group of (usually different) cross-sections.

smooth shading See *Gouraud shading*.

SMPTE Society of Motion Picture and Television Engineers. In video and 3D graphics, a time format consisting of minutes, seconds, and frames (57:31:12 would be 57 minutes, 31 seconds, and 12 frames).

snap A feature that causes the cursor to snap from one position to another according to a user-defined grid spacing, or in reaction to object edges and vertices.

solid modeling A special form of 3D for engineering applications that adds information about the weight, density, tensile strength, and other real-world facts about the material to the model's dataset.

specular color The hue of any highlights that appear on an object at Phong rendering levels or higher. Specular color is also affected by the Specularity setting or mapping, and by the color of lights.

specular highlight The bright reflections of light seen on glossy objects in Phong rendering levels or higher.

specularity A material channel or control that adjusts the color and intensity of the object's highlight, if it has one.

specularity map An image loaded into the material's specularity channel that varies the color and intensity of the specular highlights of the surface. Useful for creating the effect of prismatic or metal flake surfaces.

spherical coordinates A mapping coordinate system that wraps the image around the object in a cylindrical manner, then pinches the top and bottom closed to surround it.

spline A line, usually curved, that's defined by control points. Bézier, B-spline, and NURBS are common types of splines.

spotlight A directional light source that radiates light from a single point out into a user-defined cone or pyramid.

squash and stretch Modified scale operations that treat the object as though it had volume.

Squashing an object makes it spread out around the edges, while stretching it makes the object get thin in the middle.

stairstepping The stair-like jaggedness of a computer-drawn line or object that isn't anti-aliased.

steps The number of additional vertices generated between control points on a spline or pre-defined vertices on a poly.

storyboarding The process of visualizing a film or animation by breaking it down into a sequence of sketches that illustrate the key movements in the scene.

subtractive color model The reflected light color model in which red, yellow, and blue are the primary colors, and mixing the three together results in a muddy brown.

surface attribute A basic material setting, such as color, shininess, or transparency, that affects all parts of an object equally.

sweep The process of creating a 3D object by extruding a single 2D cross-section along a path.

system palette The pre-defined range of colors defined by the computer's operating system software.

T

tangent point Also called a weight. The portion of a spline control system that acts like a magnet to attract the spline in its direction.

taper A transform that compresses and/or expands an object along the selected axis.

target A positioning aid that enables the user to see where a camera or light is pointed from any viewport.

TCB controller Tension/Continuity/Bias controller. One of the most common methods of providing control over the keyframe control points.

teeter A type of deformation modifier that allows the cross-section to be rotated around the X and/or Y axes perpendicular to the path.

tension In a TCB controller, the amount of curvature that the keyframe allows in the path before and after the keyframe.

terrain model A 3D representation of a landscape, often generated by using a grayscale topographical map to apply displacement mapping to a grid object.

texture map A bitmapped image, either scanned or painted, that gives a material unique qualities that aren't available by simply varying surface attributes.

tiling The technique of repeating an image to cover a larger area.

tilt The vertical equivalent of a pan, created by rotating the camera up or down around its horizontal axis.

timeline A graph-like interface for viewing and manipulating animation events. Time is usually reflected along the X-axis, while animatible parameters are located on the Y-axis. At the intersection of the two axes are keyframes or other markers to indicate the type of animation event.

title safe The portion of the screen in which text should be contained if the image were output to video. Title safe is defined by an inner perimeter that can be superimposed on the viewport.

track Usage varies, but this usually refers to movement of the camera along a single axis, be it horizontal or vertical.

transform A general term for an operation that alters the position, size, or shape of a object. Typical transforms include move, scale, rotate, bend, twist, skew, taper, and stretch.

transparency A measure of the amount of light that can pass through an object. Some programs use the similar but opposing term, opacity.

triangle A three-sided polygon, the basic polygonal shape used in 3D software. Has the advantage that it cannot become non-planar.

tweening Process in which the software takes control of how the object is transformed or blended between keyframes.

twist A transform that wrings an object around the selected axis.

U

user axis An axis that the user can define independently. A user axis can be at any angle, or it can be aligned to an existing axis.

UV or UVW coordinate system UV or UVW coordinates look similar to the XY image coordinate system, but they conform to the mesh no matter how it twists or bends. UVW coordinates are used for mesh objects, and shifting them allows very precise repositioning of maps on an object.

V

vacation What I'm taking after this book is finished.

value The lightness or darkness of a color (tinting or shading).

vertice-level editing The manipulation of the individual vertices of an object to change its shape.

video acceleration Hardware enhancements to the video card that make it more effective for displaying digital video.

video capture The process of digitizing a video signal coming from a camera, VCR, laserdisc, or other source and saving it into RAM or as a file. Often the first step in digital video editing.

video safe (boundary) The portion of the screen that should appear on the average television if the image were output to video. Video safe is defined by an outer perimeter that can be superimposed on the viewport.

video safe colors Colors that fit into the luminance and saturation limits set for television broadcast. Colors outside this range blur and distort the video signal.

view coordinates A coordinate system that uses the viewport as the basis for the X, Y, and Z axes. These axes remain the same no matter how the user's perspective on the 3D scene changes.

viewing plane A plane surrounding the viewpoint at a perpendicular angle. It is an imaginary flat panel that defines the limits of the user's field of view.

viewpoint A position in or around cyberspace that represents the viewer's current location.

viewport In 3D software, a window that looks into 3D space.

virtual Something that doesn't exist in real life but that the computer can visualize and manipulate. A 3D object is a good example. It doesn't really exist outside of the computer's memory, but the user can manipulate the object as though it did exist.

virtual memory The use of hard drive space as temporary storage when the computer system runs low on RAM.

virtual reality (VR) A computer system that can immerse the user in the illusion of a computer generated world and enable the user to navigate through this world at will. Typically, the user wears a head-mounted display (HMD) that displays a stereoscopic image, and wears a sensor glove, which permits the user to manipulate "objects" in the virtual environment.

volumetric light A type of light source with an adjustable 3D volume that can simulate the behavior of natural light in an atmosphere.

VRML Virtual Reality Markup Language. A Web browser technology that enables the user to explore simple 3D environments online.

W

weight See *tangent point*.

weld An operation that combines the overlapping vertices of shapes or objects together.

wireframe A display or rendering mode that draws objects using lines to represent the polygon edges, which makes the object resemble a sculpture made of wire mesh.

world coordinates The fundamental coordinate system of 3D space, which is unchanged by the user's viewpoint.

X, Y, and Z

X-axis Typically the horizontal or width axis, running left and right.

XY coordinates The normal coordinate system for 2D images and shapes. The X axis runs horizontally, and the Y axis vertically.

Y-axis Usually the vertical or height axis, extending up and down.

Z-axis The axis normally associated with depth. It runs forward and back.

Appendix B

Recommended Reference

This appendix contains a list of books and publications that you may find useful for additional information, reference, or inspiration. Some of these titles may be out of print, but there are probably revised editions or similar volumes available.

Titles marked with an asterisk (*) indicate that the text in is Japanese only, so unless *anata wa Nihon-go ga yomimasu* (you can read Japanese), these publications are included here for their images. By the way, because I can't read much of it either, some of the Japanese titles don't have the publisher's name listed. Still, as long as you have the title, you can get hold of them. Although some of these import titles may be found at a bookstore, you will probably have more luck at comic book stores or from Japanese bookstores and importers such as Nikaku Animart (408) 971-2822, http://www.nikaku.com. Note that the Japanese authors' first and last names have been reversed to read in the Western style.

Animated Filmmaking

The Analysis of Ghost in the Shell*
ISBN# 4-06-319640-2

This is Animation: Patlabor the Movie and Original Animation Series*
Shogakukan (publisher)
ISBN# 4-09-101577-8

Chuck Amuck: The Life and Times of an Animated Artist
By Chuck Jones
Avon Books
New York, NY
ISBN# 0-380-71214-8

Disney's Art of Animation: From Mickey Mouse to Beauty and the Beast
By Bob Thomas
Hyperion
114 - 5th Avenue
New York, NY 10011
ISBN# 1-56282-899-1

Toy Story: The Art and Making of the Animated Film
By Steve Daly and John Lasseter
Hyperion
114 - 5th Avenue
New York, NY 10011
ISBN# 0-7868-6180-0

Art Books

The Art of The Brothers Hildebrandt
By Ian Summers
Ballantine Books
New York, NY
ISBN# 0-345-27830-5 (hardback)
ISBN# —345-27396-6 (paperback)

A Closer Look: The Art Techniques of Patrick Woodroffe
By Patrick Woodroffe
Harmony Books
225 Park Avenue South
New York, NY 10003
ISBN#0-517-56506-4

The Graphic Works of M.C. Escher
Hawthorne Books Inc.
70 - 5th Ave.
New York, NY 10016

Horripilations: The Art of J.K. Potter
By Nigel Suckling
Paper Tiger
An Imprint of Dragon's World Ltd.
Limpsfield
Surrey, Great Britain RH8 0DY
ISBN# 1-85028-255-2

H.R. Giger's Biomechanics
By H.R. Giger
Morpheus International
200 N. Robertson Blvd., Suite 312
Beverly Hills, CA 90211
ISBN# 0-9623447-1-0

H.R. Giger's Necronomicon and Necronomicon II
By H.R. Giger
Morpheus International
200 N. Robertson Blvd., Suite 312
Beverly Hills, CA 90211
ISBN# 0-962-34472-9
ISBN# 0-962-34476-1

Intron Depot 1
By Masamune Shirow
Harumichi Aoki Seishinsha Co., Ltd.
Shinkosan Bldg. 710
1-13-38 Nishi Honmachi, Nishi-ku
Osaka 550, Japan
ISBN# 4-87892-011-4

Michael Whelan's Works of Wonder
By Michael Whelan
Ballantine Books
New York, NY 10022
ISBN# 0-345-32679-2

Mindfields: The Art of Jacek Yerka, The Fiction of Harlan Ellison
Morpheus International
200 N. Robertson Blvd., Suite 326
Beverly Hills, CA 90211
(310) 859-2557
ISBN# 0-9623447-9-6 (paperback)
ISBN# 1-883398-03-7 (hardcover)

Parallel Lines
By Peter Elson and Chris Moore
Quick Fox
33 West 60th Street
New York, NY 10023
(212) 246-0325
ISBN# 0-8256-9569-4

Sinkha
By Marco Patrito and Virtual Views
Movave
2 West St. George Blvd, Ancestor Square
St. George, UT 84770
(801) 652-5300
http://www.sinkha.com
ISBN# Available 1st Quarter 1997
(Available as a printed volume or on CD-ROM)

Spectrum: the Best in Contemporary Fantastic Art
By Cathy Burnett and Arnie Fenner
Underwood Books
P.O. Box 1607
Grass Valley, CA 95945
ISBN# 0-88733-188-2 (softcover)
ISBN# 0-88733-189-0 (hardcover)

Spectrum 2: The Best in Contemporary Fantastic Art
By Cathy Burnett and Arnie Fenner
Underwood Books
P.O. Box 1607
Grass Valley, CA 95945
ISBN# 1-88742401-6 (softcover)
ISBN# 1-887424-02-4 (hardcover)

Sorayama: Hyper Illustrations
By Hajime Sorayama
Bijutsu Shuppan-Sha, Ltd.
2-36 Kanda Jinbo-cho
Inaoka Building, Chiyoda-ku
Tokyo, Japan
ISBN# 4-568-50102-4

Sorayama Hyper Illustrations Part 2
By Hajime Sorayama
Bijitsu Shuppan-Sha Ltd.
Tokyo, Japan
ISBN# 4-568-50129-6

Comics and Manga

Battle Angel Alita (Manga/ trade paperback series)
By Yukito Kishiro
Viz Comics
San Francisco, CA 94107
ISBN# 1-56931-003-3 (Volume 1)
(There are currently six volumes of translated BAA manga available)

Hard Boiled (trade paperback)
By Geof Darrow and Frank Miller
Dell Publishing
666 - 5th Avenue
New York, NY 10103
ISBN# 0-440-50450-3

Computer Graphics

The Art of 3-D Computer Animation and Imaging
By Isaac Victor Kerlow
Van Nostrand Reinhold
115 5th Avenue
New York, NY 10003
ISBN# 0-442-01896-7

Becoming a Computer Animator
By Mike Morrison
SAMS Publishing
An Imprint of Macmillan Publishing
201 West 103rd Street
Indianapolis, Indiana 46290
ISBN# 0-672-30463-5

The Computer Animation Dictionary
By Robi Roncarelli
Springer-Verlag
New York, NY
ISBN# 0-387-97022-3
ISBN # 3-540-97022-3

Painting With Computers
By Mario Henri Chakkout
Rockport Publishers
146 Granite Street
Rockport, MA 01966-1299
(508) 546-9590
ISBN# 1-56496-212-1

The Photoshop 3 Wow! Book
By Linnea Dayton and Jack Davis
Peachpit Press
2414 Sixth Street
Berkeley, CA 94710
(510) 548-4393
(510) 548-5991
ISBN # 1-56609-178-0

Fiction (Novels)

Neuromancer
By William Gibson
Ace Books
Berkeley Publishing Group
200 Madison Avenue
New York, NY 10016
ISBN# 0-441-56959-5

Snow Crash
By Neal Stephenson
Bantam Publishing
414 East Golf Rd.
Des Plains, IL 90016
(312) 827-1111
(800) 223-6834
ISBN# 0-553-56261-4

Filmmaking and Special Effects

The Art of the Empire Strikes Back
By Vic Bulluck and Valerie Hoffman
Ballantine Books
New York, NY
ISBN# 0-345-29335-5 (hardcover)
ISBN# 0-345-28833-5pbk (paperback)

The Art of Return of the Jedi
Ballantine Books
New York, NY
ISBN# 0-345-31254-6 (hardcover)
ISBN# 0-345-30957-X (pbk)

The Art of Star Trek
By Judith & Garfield Reeves-Stevens
Pocket Books
1230 Avenue of the Americas
New York, NY 10020
ISBN# 0-671-89804-3

The Art of Star Wars
By Carol Titelman
Ballantine Books
New York, NY
ISBN# 0-345-28273-6
ISBN# 0-345-29565-X (pbk)

How Did They Do It? Computer Illusion in Film & TV
By Christopher W. Baker
Alpha Books
An Imprint of Macmillan
Publishing
201 West 103rd Street
Indianapolis, Indiana 46290
ISBN# 1-56761-422-1

Industrial Light and Magic: The Art of Special Effects
Thomas G. Smith
Ballantine Books
New York, NY
ISBN# 0-345-32263-0

Film Directing Shot by Shot
by Steven D. Katz
Michael Wiese Productions
3960 Laurel Canyon Blvd., #331
Studio City, CA 91604
(818) 905-6367

From Star Wars to Indiana Jones: The Best of the Lucasfilm Archives
By Mark Cotta Vaz and Shinji Hata
Chronicle Books
275 Fifth Street
San Francisco, CA 94103
ISBN# 0-8118-0997-8 (hardback)
ISBN# 0-8118-0972-2 (paperback)

The Official Guide to The Daedalus Encounter
By Mark Giambruno
Brady Publishing
An Imprint of Macmillan Publishing
201 West 103rd Street
Indianapolis, Indiana 46290
ISBN# 1-566-86-295-7

On Film Editing
By Edward Dmytryk
Focal Press
An Imprint of Butterworth-Heinemann
313 Washington Street
Newton, MA 02158-1626
(617) 928-2500
ISBN# 0-24-051738-5

Lighting Secrets
By Alan Brown, Joe Braun and Tim Grondin
Writer's Digest Books
1502 Dana Avenue
Cincinnati, OH 45207
ISBN# 0-89879-412-9

Special Effects: Creating Movie Magic
By Christopher Finch
Abbeville Press
505 Park Avenue
New York, NY 10022
ISBN# 0-89659-452-1

Graphics Production

Comps Storyboards and Animatics
by James Fogle and Mary E. Forsell
Watson-Guptill Publications
1515 Broadway
New York, NY 10036-8986
(212) 764-7300

How To Prepare Your Portfolio
By Ed Marquand
Art Direction Book Company
10 East 39th D Street
New York, NY 10016.
ISBN#0-910158-69-X (cloth)
ISBN#0-910158-70-3 (paper)

Industrial Design

Oblagon
By Syd Mead
Kodansha
Japan
ISBN# 4-06-201525-0

Sentinel
By Syd Mead
Big O Publishing
P.O. Box 6186
Charlottesville, VA 22906
ISBN# 90-6332-591-6

Sentinel II
By Syd Mead
Kodansha
Japan
ISBN# 06-203452-2

Periodicals

3D Artist Magazine
3D ARTIST Magazine /
Columbine, Inc.
P.O. Box 4787
Santa Fe, NM 87502
(505) 982-3532
http://www.3dartist.com

3D Design Magazine
Miller Freeman, Inc.
600 Harrison Street
San Francisco, CA 94107
(415) 905-2200
http://www.3ddesign.com

Animation Magazine
Thoren Publications
28024 Dorothy Drive, Suite 200
Agoura Hills, CA 91301
(818) 991-2884
Animag@aol.com
http://www.imall.com/stores/
Deer_Run_Greenery/stores/
foobar1/stores/animag

Car Styling Magazine
San'ei Shobo Publishing Co., Ltd.
1 Suwacho, Shinjuku-ku
Tokyo, Japan

Cinefex: The Journal of Cinematic Illusions
P.O. Box 20027
Riverside, CA 92516

Computer Graphics World
PennWell Publishing Company
10 Tara Boulevard, 5th floor
Nashua, NH 03062-280
(918) 835-3161

Computer Shopper
One Park Avenue
New York, NY 10016
(212) 503-3900

Heavy Metal
584 Broadway, Suite 608
New York, NY 10012

Hobby Japan*
Hobby Japan Co., Ltd.
5-26-5 Sendagaya, Shibuya-ku
Tokyo, Japan

**Interactivity: The How-To
Multimedia Magazine**
Miller Freeman, Inc.
411 Borel Ave., Suite 100
San Mateo, CA 94402
(415) 905-2200

**New Media: The Magazine
for Creators of the Digital
Future**
Hypermedia Communications
Inc.
P.O. Box 3039
Northbrook, IL 60065
(800) 253-6641

**Next Generation: Leading
Edge Computer and Video
Games**
Image Publishing Inc.
1350 Old Bayshore Highway,
Suite 210

Burlingame, CA 94010
(415) 696-1661

**Planet Studio: The
Professional's Guide to
Autodesk® Multimedia**
Tech Media Publishing
80 Elm Street, Box 802
Peterborough, NH 03458
(603) 924-0100

Step-By-Step Graphics
Dynamic Graphics, Inc.
6000 N. Forest Park Drive
Peoria, IL 61614-3592

**Videogame Advisor: The
Interactive Gaming Industry
Guide**
Cyberactive Publishing Inc.
64 Danbury Road, Suite 500
Wilton, CT 06897
(203) 761-6150
(Provided free of charge to
qualified professional buyers
within the interactive gaming
industry)

Wired Magazine
P.O. Box 191826
San Francisco, CA 94119-1826
(800) SO-WIRED
http://www.wired.com

Reference

Eyewitness Books (series)
Alfred A. Knopf, Inc.
201 E. 50th Street
New York, NY 10022
(212) 751-2600

**The Complete Book of Rocks
and Minerals**
By Chris Pellant and Helen
Pellant
Dorling Kindersley, Inc.
95 Madison Avenue
New York, NY 10016
ISBN# 0-7894-0619-X

Gemstones of the World
By Walter Schumann
Sterling Publishing Co. Inc.
New York, NY 10016
ISBN# 0-8069-3089-6

**The Macmillan Visual
Dictionary**
By Ariane Archambault, Jean
Claude Corbeil
Macmillan Publishing Company
201 W. 103rd Street
Indianapolis, IN 46290-1097
(800) 545-5914
(800) 428-5331 orders
ISBN# 0-02-578115-4
ISBN# 0-02-528160-7 (hardcover)

Scriptwriting

Making A Good Script Great
By Linda Seger
Samuel French Trade
7623 Sunset Boulevard
Hollywood, CA 90046
ISBN # 0-573-69921-6

**The Writer's Journey:
Mythic Structure for Story-
tellers and Screenwriters**
By Christopher Vogler
Michael Wise Productions
4354 Laurel Canyon Boulevard,
Suite #234
Studio City, CA 91604
(818) 379-8799
ISBN # 0-941188-13-2

Appendix C

Resources

Organizations

ACM SIGGRAPH Professional Directory
http://siggraph.org/gen-info/prochap/chapters.html

American Film Institute Online
http://www.afionline.org/home.html

Association for Computing Machinery (ACM)
http://info.acm.org

European Association for Computer Graphics
http://www.eg.org

Graphic Arts Technical Foundation
http://www.gatf.lm.com

Graphic Communications Association
http://www.gca.org

IEEE Computer Society
http://www.computer.org

Schools

Advanced Computing Center for the Arts and Design
http://www.cgrg.ohio-state.edu

American Institute of Graphic Arts
http://www.dol.com/AIGA

Art Center College of Design
http://www.artcenter.edu

ASIFA's List of Animation Schools

http://samson.hivolda.no:8000/asifa/additional_schools.html

Computer Animation Lab at Calarts

http://emsh.calarts.edu

Computer Arts Institute

http://www.sirius.com/%7Ecai

Cornell University Program of Computer Graphics

http://www.graphics.cornell.edu

DigiPen Applied Computer Graphics School

http://www.digipen.com

Graphics and Visualization Center

http://www.cs.brown.edu:80/stc/STC_Overview.html

Rhode Island School of Design

http://www.risd.edu

School of Communication Arts

http://www.digiweb.com/~accia

Stanford Computer Graphics Laboratory

http://www-graphics.stanford.edu

CG and Animation-Related Web Sites

3DSite—Links to 3D Software Web Sites and Information

http://www.lightside.com/~dani/cgi/software-packages-index.html

Computer Graphics

http://mambo.ucs.edu/psl.cg.html

Computer Graphics and Visualization

http://www.dataspace.com/WWW/vlib/comp-graphics.html

Computer Graphics on the Net

http://ls7-www.informatik.uni-dortmund.de/html/englisch/servers.html

Computer Graphics Techniques and Related Links

http://mvassist.pair.com/Graphics.html

Computer Graphics World Online

http://www.cgw.com/

Digimation

http://www.digimation.com

Digital Creativity

http://www.mediacentral.com

GraphicLinx
http://www.graphiclinx.com

Siggraph Artist's Connection
http://siggraph.org/artdesign/
sigartists.html

That's Animation Index
http://mambo.ucsc.edu/psl/
thant/thant.html

**USENET Computer Graphics
FAQs**
http://www.cis.ohio-state.edu/
hypertext/faq/bngusenet/comp/
graphics/top.html

Virtual Designs Group
http://www.vdg3d.com

**Walt Disney Feature
Animation**
http://www.disney.com/
DisneyPictures

Appendix D

Software Products and Publisher List

This appendix provides contact information for most of the popular 3D software products. It also contains notes and capsule reviews of those products that I have experience using (as of June, 1996). However, things move quickly in the software world, and you should rely on the most recent information in magazine reviews and product literature when making your decision.

All of the following reviews are for PC products, although many of the products are available for the Macintosh or SGI/Unix platforms as well. Contact information for all publishers follows the review section.

Portions of the following material dealing with 3D software information and reviews originally appeared in an article I wrote for *InterActivity* magazine (Copyright 1996 Miller Freeman, Inc.), and is used with permission.

3D Studio Release 4 (Kinetix)

Recently, Autodesk created a new division, called Kinetix, which is responsible for the company's various multimedia, entertainment, and Internet-oriented products. One of these products is the hugely successful 3D Studio product, which is the most popular visualization package in the world. In 1996, it held 30% of the overall market (over two times its nearest competitor) and 45% of the PC market, with 70,000 registered copies.

3D Studio does a broad variety of tasks very well, making it a favorite among multimedia and game developers who need that kind of flexibility. Although overshadowed by other products in the film and broadcast market, it was used for the effects in the movie *Johnny Mnemonic*.

3D Studio R4 is the only DOS-based product listed, but has the advantage of being a well-supported, proven production tool that performs well even on 486 machines.

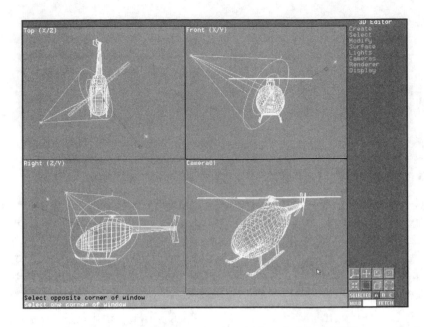

With the release of 3D Studio MAX, it's unclear what will become of the original 3D Studio, with its DOS-based architecture dooming the product to extinction at some point. Still, the sheer popularity of the product and its much lower system requirements are almost certain to keep it in the mainstream for years to come.

System Requirements and Features

3DS R4 requires a 386 or faster PC, MS-DOS 3.3 or later, 8MB RAM, 20MB free hard drive space, SVGA video, and a CD-ROM drive. Like some of the other high-end programs, it has a hardware "dongle," a copy protection device that plugs into the parallel port.

R4 is primarily a polygonal modeler, but patch and NURBS modeling are available via IPAS plug-ins. It has a good complement of deform tools, including, Twist, Teeter, Bevel, Fit, and Bend, as well as tools for vertice, face, and edge-level work. The program also features 2D and 3D Boolean operations.

The IPAS plug-in system allows the addition of new modeling tools, particle systems, post-production effects, and so forth, and is well supported by third party developers.

The program has eight shader channels: Diffuse (2), Opacity, Bump, Specular, Shininess, Self-Illumination, and Reflection. Each channel can have its own texture map, and procedural textures are also available. Plus, animated files can be used as textures, backgrounds, and light gels.

Lights types include Omni (point) and spotlight. Omni lights don't cast shadows, however. Lights have range settings and Include/Exclude lists, and the spotlights have variable hotspot and falloff settings.

R4 has an animation timeline, and features IK with constraints, a keyframe scripting language, and particle systems. Rendering types include Wire, Flat, Gouraud, Phong, and Metal. Alpha Channel Support is provided, as well as field, batch, and network rendering. A Video Post feature allows compositing and effects to be performed automatically.

The product comes on 3.5" floppies, and includes a "World Creating Toolkit" CD-ROM filled with models, maps and sample animations. Suggested retail price is $2,995, but substantial discounts are sometimes available to students.

Conclusions

3D Studio R4 is an extremely popular and proven production tool with a lot of great features, including strong polygonal modeling, a good material editor, and a solid animation system. Although some of the newer features are a bit disjointed from the main program due to the nature of the IPAS plug-ins, the program has strong support from third party developers.

Still, unless the price of R4 drops, MAX offers far more capabilities and potential for growth for an additional $500. Therefore, if you're shopping for a product in the $3K range, I can only recommend R4 if you have a system (such as a 486 or slow Pentium) that won't handle MAX.

3D Studio MAX 1.0 (Kinetix)

One of the key points of the new 3D Studio MAX is that it's the first visualization tool designed specifically for Windows NT, taking full advantage of the multiprocessor/multitasking capabilities of the platform. The program is heavily *multithreaded*, meaning that if you add a second processor, you nearly double the performance of the product. This is not the case with most of the other 3D packages that will run on NT, because they tend to be ports from other platforms and don't have the necessary multiprocessor support.

FIGURE D.2

3D Studio MAX was designed from the ground up for Windows NT, and offers parametric modeling, a powerful materials editor, and high-end animation capabilities.

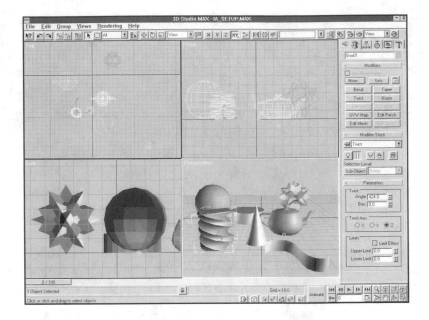

MAX also is the first commercially available object-oriented *component software*, which means that it can accept third-party modeling tools, animation controllers, renderers, and other features. These add-ons share the same interface and work seamlessly with everything else in the program. This is a big advance over the IPAS plug-in structure of Release 4, in which many of the add-ons had their own interface and way of doing things.

The other two major advances of MAX over R4 are its spline-based, parametric modeling design and the fact that nearly everything is easily animatible, from the object creation process itself to deformations and Booleans to… well, you name it.

This product seems to embrace the bastions of its predecessor's success, namely the serious multimedia and game developer. It also is turning an eye toward stealing some of the high visibility television and motion picture work that Lightwave, Alias|Wavefront, and SoftImage currently dominate.

System Requirements and Features

MAX has fairly high system requirements, needing a P5/90 or faster PC (Intel-based processors only at this time), Windows NT 3.51, 32MB RAM (64–128MB Recommended), and 100MB free hard drive swap space (200–300MB or more recommended, depending on scene complexity). It also requires an

800 × 600 × 256 display (1024 × 768 × 256 PCI/VLB recommended, 1280 × 1024 × 16.7M Heidi compatible double-buffered 3D accelerator ideal) and a CD-ROM drive. Like R4, it too has a hardware dongle for copy protection.

The product features a modeless design, and has *object oriented extensibility*, meaning that add-ons integrate seamlessly into the software architecture and work with everything else in the program. It also has a user-definable undo/redo depth with separate streams for scene and viewport actions.

Modeling types include parametric, spline, polygonal mesh, and Bézier patch. There are a standard set of deform operations, and nearly every operation remains editable in a *stack*, which is a history of modifications made to an object. Boolean operations are interactive, non-destructive, and animatable. MAX also features "space warps," which are invisible objects that affect the mesh or particles that pass nearby. Effect types include: explosion, ripple, wave, gravity, wind, deflector, and mesh displacement.

MAX features a very powerful material editor, with shader channels for Ambient, Diffuse, Specular, Shininess, Shininess Strength, Self-Illumination, Opacity, Filter Color, Bump, Reflection, and Refraction control. Shaders can be composed of bitmap and procedural material hierarchies of unlimited depth. It also supports animated textures, backgrounds, and light gels.

Light types include Ambient, Omni, Free Spot, Target spot, and Directional, and some of these feature Include/Exclude lists and highlight placement features. In addition, volumetric lighting supports animated smoke, glow, and haze effects, with volumetric shadows for lights.

The program has an animation timeline with multiple controllers, including linear, Bézier, TCB, noise, and expression (mathematical formula). These controllers can be layered, blended, copied, and instanced. Plus, virtually all functions are animatible, and graphable operations have function curve control. The program also has IK with constraints, plus all-purpose spray-like and snow-like particle systems that are constrainable by gravity, deflection, and displacement space warps.

MAX provides multiple rendering modes up to Metal shading with Alpha channel support, cropped or enlarged region rendering, object and scene motion blur, and network rendering (even across the Internet). Of special interest to those doing video work are the field rendering and NTSC/PAL color correction features.

The product ships on a CD-ROM with an excellent set of full-color manuals, and registered users receive the full SDK (Software Development Kit) free. The Suggested Retail Price of MAX is $3,495.

Conclusions

MAX is very powerful, and it will rapidly become even more so as wave after wave of plug-ins hits the market, adding cool new features and (hopefully) correcting some oversights, such as the relatively cumbersome 2D spline functions. On the whole, however, the program has a strong modeler with excellent material editing and animation capabilities as well as quality rendering.

This product's price range and hefty system requirements generally limit it to multimedia and broadcast production shops, but Kinetix has promised very substantial discounts for students and educators.

Animation Master v3.18 (Hash, Inc.)

FIGURE D.3

Animation Master is a character animation program as opposed to a generalized 3D visualization product. One of its custom capabilities is a stride length animation controller that reduces skating in walk cycles.

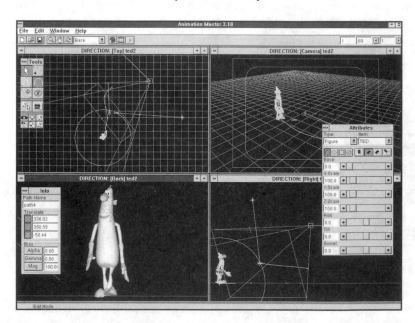

This product, formerly called Playmation, is careful to bill itself as a character animation system as opposed to a general purpose 3D package. This is underscored by the video demo reel that comes with the product, showcasing a number of character animation pieces that show off the capabilities (and flaws) of the product. Among these is one of the best manually created human head models around, a real show-stopper.

System Requirements and Features

Animation Master's requirements are fairly light, needing a 486DX/33 or faster PC, Microsoft Windows 3.1 or Windows NT, 8MB RAM (16MB recommended), VGA graphics, and a CD-ROM drive. In addition, the product also is available for the Mac and SGI platforms.

Modeling capabilities are very basic, limited to patch-based splines, with polygonal output support. Very few of the tools common to most 3D modeling programs are provided.

The program has a standard set of Shader Channels, including Ambience, Roughness, Specularity, Reflectivity, Transparency, Refraction, and Cookie Cutter. It also features decaling, plus animated textures and backgrounds.

Light types include: Distant, Bulb (point), Spot (hard edge), and Klieg (soft edge), all shadow-casting.

For animation, the program uses a spline-based editable motion graph. Actions are treated as behaviors, and can be loaded on top of each other to produce complex combinations. Besides IK animation with constraints, there is a Stride Length feature that reduces character *skating* (where a character's feet appear to slide around when walking).

Rendering quality ranges from flat to ray tracing, with alpha channel support.

Animation Master ships on a CD-ROM, and does not have a printed manual. Instead, a video tutorial is provided on VHS tape. It retails for $699.

Conclusions

Animation Master is designed to be a character animation system, not a general-purpose 3D visualization package. The modeler, while handling organic forms much better than some of the competition, is not well-suited to doing other types of modeling. The program uses many non-standard conventions, and combined with the lack of a printed manual, hinders the learning process.

I was disappointed to see that despite the product's many custom character animation features, some of the demos (including those that Hash itself was involved with) showed numerous animation flaws. This included skating, and objects "held" in character's hands that were continuously jumping around. The program also includes libraries of actors and motions, but even here the skating runs rampant.

One thing I can say for sure about Animation Master is that it's *different*. Whether that is "freed from suffocating constraints of traditional 3D animation methodologies" different or "un-intuitive, awkward and lacking in some basic and important features" different is your call. If you're doing character animation on a tight budget, this may be your tool. Still, you'll probably want to consider other competitively priced products that feature good animation features as well.

Extreme 3D v1.0 (Macromedia)

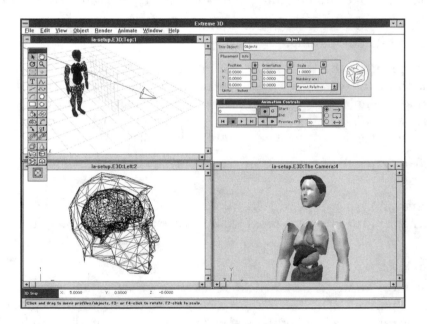

Extreme 3D is the successor to Macromodel, adding much better material editing to the product along with animation capabilities. E3D seems to be oriented toward the artist making the transition from 2D drawing programs, with both the toolset and the tutorials reinforcing that position. The program's low cost ($329 street), also makes it attractive to those who are more accustomed to 2D software prices.

System Requirements and Features

Extreme 3D requires a 486/50 or faster PC (Pentium recommended), Windows 3.1 32s, Windows 95 or Windows NT, 16MB RAM (24MB recommended) and 20MB free hard drive space. SVGA color (24-bit recommended) and a CD-ROM drive is also needed. It has identical implementations on Mac and PC (even to the point of allowing mixed platform distributed rendering), a plus for those using both platforms or making a transition.

The program uses conventions from popular 2D illustration, animation, and rendering programs, making it feel a bit more familiar than some other programs to those coming from a 2D background.

Modeling types include spline, patch, and polygon, with a standard set of deforms. The program has a useful 2D Fillet tool that makes automatic radius corners. It also does 2D and 3D trims, which are similar to Boolean operations.

The shader channels are basic, limited to Diffuse, Bump, Reflection, Specular, and Roughness.

Lights include Distant, Omni, and Spot, plus an unusual visible spotlight cone feature that looks something like a basic volumetric light.

The hierarchical timeline gives access to all animation parameters, and supports time or frame-based increments. The Bézier motion paths can be directly modified within the 3D viewport, and all editable parameters are animatible. It also features a Look At behavior.

Rendering is limited to Phong only, but features alpha channel support.

The product ships on CD-ROM, and includes a second CD-ROM with a collection of Wraptures texture maps. The retail price is $499.

Conclusions

E3D is well-suited to organic modeling, and bears consideration as an adjunct to a polygonal modeler like 3DS R4. As a sole package for the student, graphic artist (especially one familiar with 2D drawing applications), or multimedia house with a need for its modeling abilities, Extreme 3D warrants a good look.

Animation-wise, it has an awkward way of doing some things, but it's usable. If the somewhat lackluster rendering is adequate for your purposes, the speed and network rendering capability should make it appropriate for small production projects.

The texture map-related material editing is not as powerful as some of the other similarly priced products, but is fine for most work. While the program exhibited some reproducible bugs, remember that this is version 1.0.0, and that sort of thing is to be expected, unfortunately.

form◆Z RenderZone v2.8 (auto◆des◆sys)

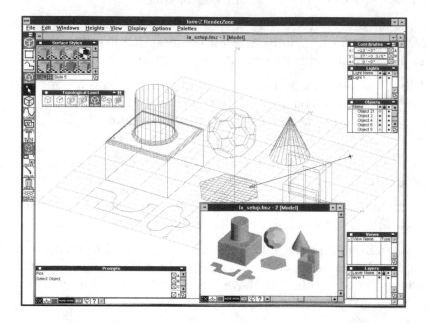

form◆Z RenderZone is an enhanced version of the original CAD-oriented form◆Z modeling package available for both the Mac and Windows platforms. As its name implies, RenderZone brings expanded material and ray trace rendering capabilities to the party. Other than that, the two packages (and for that matter, their implementation on each platform) are nearly identical.

Note that unlike all the other products in this roundup, form◆Z RenderZone has no animation capabilities at all. Therefore, if you need a product that can do animation, you either have to obtain some additional software, like RenderMan (which then makes many of the advantages of the RenderZone version of form◆Z redundant), or select a different product.

System Requirements and Features

RenderZone requires a 386DX or faster PC (486 or Pentium recommended), Windows 3.1 (with Win32s), Windows 95, or Windows NT 3.5 or later, 20MB RAM (32MB+ recommended), and 20MB free hard drive space. Also required are a 24-bit color video card and a CD-ROM drive.

form◆Z features CAD-Accurate modeling, with virtually unlimited Undo/Redo depth. Modeling types include parametric spline, patch, and polygonal, with a robust set of deform tools. The advanced rounding feature creates automatic fillets and radius corners on 3D forms, and the unique Query tool provides info on objects, including surface area and volume. 2D and 3D Boolean operations and trims are supported, and transform sequences can be saved as macros. In addition, the program has an integrated 2D drafting module for standard CAD work.

The shader channels are limited to Color, Reflection, Transparency, and Bump, but the program does support up to 32 overlapping decals per object, as well as procedural textures.

All lights are shadow casting, and you can choose from distant, omni, and spotlight types. There is a visible spotlight cone option that resembles volumetric lighting as well.

The program has no animation features at this time.

There are multiple levels of rendering up to full ray trace with alpha channel support.

RenderZone comes on a CD-ROM with a very extensive set of manuals. The MSRP is $1,995.

Conclusions

form◆Z is, first and foremost, a modeling program. Some of its features in this regard are normally reserved for products costing thousands of dollars more, so at $1,495, it seems well worth the price for the 3D-oriented production or multimedia house.

Whether the RenderZone option is worth the additional $500 to you probably depends on if you need to do animation or just still images. RenderZone provides average to good shaders and rendering in a fully integrated manner, but the dedicated renderers (such as RenderMan and

Electric Image) have much more advanced shader capabilities. The drawback is that the models have to be imported into a second application to render them off.

In any case, form◆Z deserves due consideration as an adjunct to an integrated package with a less capable modeler, or as the primary modeler when used in conjunction with a dedicated rendering product. However, lack of an animation system may force some users to look elsewhere or buy an additional software package for that purpose.

Lightwave 5.0

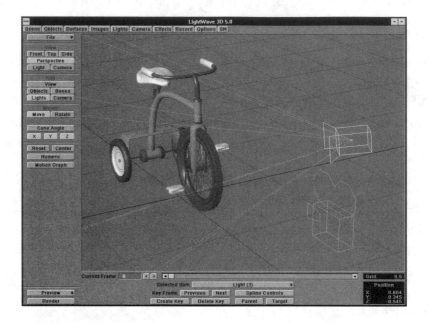

Lightwave originally began as the modeling program for the famous Video Toaster product, an add-on for the Amiga that was designed to do production quality videographics and editing. Eventually, the program was ported to other systems, including SGI, several flavors of NT processors, and Windows 95.

The product's capabilities are among the best known to the general populace due to its use on the television shows *Babylon 5, SeaQuest, Hypernauts,* and others. This speaks well for Lightwave's image quality and suitability as a production tool. It also is popular with multimedia designers doing high-res 3D environment projects.

System Requirements

For the PC platform, Lightwave requires a minimum of a 486 or faster PC (Pentium recommended), Windows 95 (with 16MB RAM) or Windows NT (with 32MB RAM) and 10MB free hard drive space. A 24-bit color video card and a CD-ROM drive also are needed.

Lightwave is a cross-platform package that is available for Win95, WinNT, SGI, DEC Alpha, MIPS, and the Amiga. It has a polygonal modeler with a large range of deform tools, plus 2D and 3D trims and Booleans. One of its most interesting features is its ability to subdivide a polygonal object in three ways: faceted, smooth, or Metaform. Think of this as the ability to take a low-res sphere and increase its resolution until it is smooth. Metaform takes great advantage of this ability and is very impressive, enabling you to create rather clunky-looking low-res objects (or groups of objects joined together) and then pump up the resolution to smooth out the jagginess and blend the forms together.

MetaNURBS is a new feature that enables you to convert 4-sided polygons into NURBS splines. The splines can be modified with the main tools, but must then be frozen and the object reconverted into polygons before importing it into Layout.

The program has a good range of shader channels and material editing features, including an expanded range of procedural textures that can be auto-animated.

Light types include point, spot, and distant, all of which are shadow casting. In addition, the program is well known for its advanced lens flare capabilities and options.

Editable Motion Graphs and onscreen paths aid the animation process, but the program lacks a complete timeline. Along with the IK constraints, there are bones deformation features, and the cameras have an unusually large number of controls and options. Plus, nearly all attributes can be animated by keyframe or envelope.

Rendering is excellent, due to the fast ray trace capabilities of the product. Alpha channel support is also provided.

Lightwave comes on CD-ROM for $1,495, an increase of $500 over the previous version.

Conclusions

Lightwave is hindered by its outdated user-interface design and reliance on separate Modeling and Layout modules. Experienced users who are used to having an integrated modeling/rendering environment will probably find the product frustrating in that respect. The animation capabilities also are impeded by the absence of a proper timeline.

On the plus side, powerful and unique modeling features, impressive shaders, and drop-dead beautiful renders are your reward for putting up with the product's unusual workflow scheme. Oh, and don't forget all those lens flare options.

Overall, Lightwave packs some impressive features into an under-$1,500 production-quality package. Users with a need to do broadcast or high-end multimedia environments and character animation (and who don't mind the idiosyncrasies of the product) should seriously consider it.

Ray Dream Studio (Fractal Design)

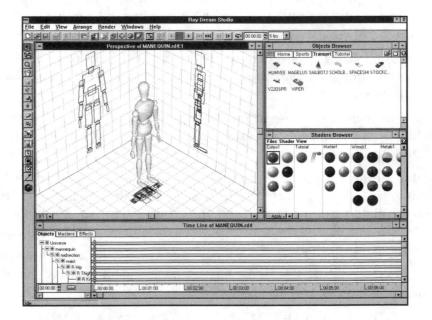

Ray Dream Studio was recently acquired by Fractal Design, makers of the popular Fractal Design Painter software. It's a bundle containing four integrated packages: Ray Dream Designer 4, Ray Dream Animator, Extensions Portfolio (plug-in SDK), and Dream Models (3D clip art). The company touts Designer as the leader in 3D illustration, and to be sure, there is some nice looking stuff in print that was done with this product. Ray Dream's roots started on the Mac, but the product looks like it has made a good transition to the Windows environment.

In keeping with the company's philosophy of offering 3D tools at 2D prices, Studio has a very low price, and can be obtained for about $299 street. This makes it one of the few 3D packages that just about anyone can afford.

System Requirements and Features

Studio has light minimum system requirements, calling for a 486 or faster PC, Windows 3.1, Windows 95, or Windows NT, 12MB RAM (16 MB Recommended), and 40MB free hard drive space. However, in practice the program is rather sluggish even on a P6/200, so be forewarned. 256 color graphics are a minimum (although accelerated 16- or 24-bit video is recommended), and a CD-ROM drive also is required.

The product features an unusual Bézier spline modeler with a standard complement of deforms. Drag-and-drop features are present throughout, along with numerical entry, 3D alignment tools, and unique modeling and scene Wizards.

The material library comes with 350 pre-built shaders, a good selection of shader channels, and an advanced Shader Editor. Animated textures, backgrounds, and light gels are supported. The product has a slow but useful 3D paint utility.

Studio has an animation timeline, IK with constraints, and behaviors such as bounce, spin, point at, and track.

The program sports ray tracing and Phong Z-buffer renderers, with alpha channel and an unusual array of G-buffer output options. In addition, the render area can be moved and resized directly on-screen. A render time estimator also is provided.

Ray Dream Studio comes on CD-ROM, with 500 rather low-res textured models and an Extensions Toolkit for creating Plug-Ins. The Suggested Retail Price is only $499.

Conclusions

As you might expect from such a low-cost program, there are some weak points, speed being one of the most obvious. The unusual modeler is something you will have to try for yourself, but intermediate or advanced users will probably find it too restricted.

The animation timeline is certainly usable and better than many, but suffers from a few significant flaws. The Shader controls are one of the bright spots, and combined with the acceptable rendering quality, make it suitable for light to moderate 3D illustration work. In addition, the low cost makes it a very good option for those who want to learn or use 3D, but have a very tight budget.

trueSpace[2] v2.0 (Caligari)

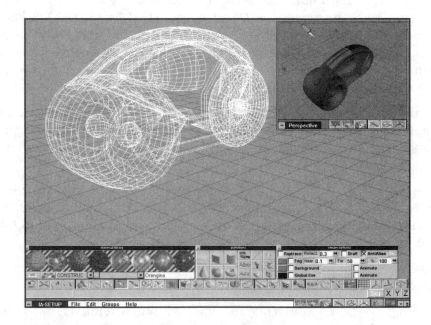

Like several other products in the roundup, trueSpace[2] has its roots in the Amiga world, a situation that usually means a down-to-earth MSRP for the end-user. It also often means a sort of "We're gonna prove that we're just as good as the big boys" attitude in the design, leading to a feature-rich toolset along with an over-optimistic view of what the hardware can deliver in terms of graphics speed. To be fair, this approach is pretty common in Mac-based products as well, and is increasing on PC products.

trueSpace² retails for a reasonable $795 ($499 street) and $149 for trueSpace² SE, an entry level package with a street price of only $95. This review focuses strictly on the full version, but you may want to look into the SE feature set if you only need a basic product.

System Requirements and Features

trueSpace² has suspiciously light system requirements: a 386 or faster PC (Pentium recommended), Windows 3.1, Win95, Windows NT, 8MB RAM (16MB Recommended), and 8MB of free hard drive space. VGA graphics (3D accelerator card recommended) are needed, along with CD-ROM drive (for the utilities and libraries, because the program itself comes on 3.5" floppies).

The user interface is icon-based, with floating panels (called palettes), and nearly all of the functions can be mouse-driven. In addition, the UI has a full-screen viewport with auxiliary floating windows, with real-time shading available using built-in Intel 3DR technology.

Modeling types include spline, patch, and polygon (with direct object deformation and surface sculpting). The deforms don't fall into normal categories due to the nature of the modeler, but space warps are available in object, plane, and pipe configurations. The program also supports Boolean operations.

trueSpace² has a healthy range of shader channels, including Color, High-light, Shininess, Bump, Reflection, Transparency, Refraction, and Glow. Procedural materials also are available, as is rotoscoping, a 3D paint utility, and support for Photoshop-compatible plug-in filters.

Spot, point, and distant lights are provided, and they are all shadow casting.

The program has a very basic animation timeline, IK with constraints and Look At behavior.

Renderers include flat & Phong Z-buffer, plus ray tracing and alpha channel support. Motion blur, depth of field, and field rendering options also are available.

The program ships on 3.5" floppies, with 600 3D objects, hundreds of textures, and materials on the trueClips CD-ROM. It retails for $795.

Conclusions

trueSpace² features accurate real-time shaded feedback with small scenes, some nice sculpting tools, and an acceptable set of mapping options with good rendering, but has some serious drawbacks. Poor animation capabilities, lack of control and feedback in some fundamental modeling tools, and limited shader capabilities, to mention a few.

Due to the product's weaknesses, artists needing a moderately priced tool for 3D illustration work should weigh it alongside others at or below its price point. Those needing good animation tools should look elsewhere for the moment.

Other Products

The preceding products are by no means the only ones worth consideration. Following are notes about some of the other popular programs that weren't included in these reviews.

Strata Studio Pro is a highly regarded Mac product that features some very good shader libraries and an excellent ray tracing renderer. They should have a Windows version of the product out by the time you read this.

Electric Image is a high-end rendering package for the Mac that is used in production environments. It requires the use of a separate modeling package, such as form◆Z, however.

Rhino is a promising new NURBS modeler that has been described by some as rivaling Alias|Wavefront's. However, the price is expected to be less than $1,000.

Amapi is a multiplatform modeler from France that sports an unusual interface design.

Infini-D is a popular, low-cost 3D program for the Macintosh.

I covered TriSpectives Professional 1.0 in the *InterActivity* review, but I was so displeased with its slowness and poor rendering quality that I left it out of these capsule reviews. It may be worth a look if you're a product designer with a very fast system, however.

On the SGI platform, Alias|Wavefront Studio software is still considered to have the ultimate modeler, and offers some excellent special effects shaders and particle systems. SoftImage is still the king for animation, and the new release for the Windows NT platform is sure to increase its popularity.

Recommendations

Here are some recommendations based on the PC versions of the software that I reviewed in the preceding sections.

All the $1,495+ packages deliver good to excellent modeling capability, with Extreme 3D and trueSpace² being good bets for organic modeling on a budget.

Only the mid to high-end products can really deliver for those in the production multimedia and broadcast arenas. If you can afford them, it's tough to go wrong with SoftImage, 3D Studio R4 or 3D Studio MAX, with SoftImage having a big advantage in character animation. Lightwave offers an excellent price-performance ratio and deserves strong consideration.

For animators, all the production-quality packages noted above are good, and all the rest have significant flaws. Animation Master may be worth a look if you're doing character animation but can't afford Lightwave or one of the others.

If you're an illustrator who is more interested in simpler, designer images, a package with more shader options and nicer rendering may be in order. Artists needing a moderately priced tool for 3D illustration work should weigh trueSpace² alongside others at or below its price point. For students, hobbyists, or those with light 3D needs, Ray Dream has a lot to offer (especially for the price), but the modeler is fairly lightweight.

3D Software Publishers

Contact information for 3D software publishers is provided in the following list, organized by product name. Be sure to check out their Web sites for the latest information, samples, and demo versions.

3D Studio R4, 3D Studio MAX

Kinetix (A Division of Autodesk, Inc.)
642 Harrison Street
San Francisco, CA 94107
(800) 879-4233
(415) 507-5000
http://www.ktx.com

Alias|Wavefront Studio

Alias|Wavefront
530 East Montecito Street
Santa Barbara, CA
(805) 962-8117
http://www.alias.com

-or-

110 Richmond Street East
Toronto, ON CANADA M5C 1P1
(416) 362-9181
http://www.alias.com

Amapi

Yonowat Inc.
333 Kearny Street, Suite 617
San Francisco, CA 94108
(415) 788-1652
http://www.yonowat.com

Animation Master, Martin Hash's 3D Animation

HASH, Inc.
2800 E. Evergreen Blvd.
Vancouver, WA 98661
(360) 750-0042
http://www.hash.com

Electric Image

Electric Image Inc.
117 East Colorado Boulevard, Suite 300
Pasadena, CA 91105
(818) 577-1627
http://www.electricimg.com

Extreme 3D

Macromedia
600 Townsend Street
San Francisco, CA 94103
(800) 326-2128
(415) 252-2000
http://www.macromedia.com

form◆Z, form◆Z RenderZone

auto◆des◆sys inc.
2011 Riverside Drive
Columbus, Ohio 43221
(614) 488-9777
http://www.formz.com

Infini-D

Specular International
7 Pomeroy Lane
Amherst, MA 01002
(800) 433-SPEC
(413) 253-3100
http://www.specular.com

Lightwave

NewTek
1200 SW Executive Drive
Topeka, KS 66615
(800) TOASTER
http://www.newtek.com

Ray Dream Studio

Fractal Design
5550 Scotts Valley Drive
Scotts Valley, CA 95066
(408) 688-5300
http://www.rahul.net/raydream

RenderMan

Pixar Animation Studios
1001 West Cutting Blvd.
Richmond, CA 94804
(510) 236-4000
http://www.pixar.com

Rhinoceros (Rhino)

Robert McNeel & Associates
3670 Woodland Park Avenue North
Seattle, WA 98103
(206) 545-7000

SoftImage

Microsoft Corp.
One Microsoft Way
Redmond, WA 98052
(800) 576-3846
(206) 365-1359
http://www.softimage.com
or http://www.microsoft.com

trueSpace^2

Caligari Corp.
1935 Landings Drive
Mountain View, CA 94043
(415) 390-9600
http://www.caligari.com

TriSpectives Professional

3D/EYE, Inc.
(800) WIN95-3D x2665
(716) 871-6675 x2665
http://www.eye.com

2D Software and Utilities Publishers

Contact information for 2D software and utilities publishers is provided in the following list, organized by product name. This list also includes 3D paint utilities, because they're generally not standalone 3D applications, but add-on utilities. Be sure to check out their Web sites for the latest information, samples, and demo versions.

AfterEffects

Adobe Systems
P.O. Box 6458
Salinas, CA 93912-6458
(800) 833-6687
http://www.adobe.com

Amazon Paint

Interactive Effects
102 Nighthawk
Irvine, CA 92714
(714) 551-1448
ben@ifx.com

Animator Studio

Autodesk Inc.
111 McInnis Parkway
San Rafael, California 94903 USA
(415) 507-5000
http://www.autodesk.com

Black Box

Alien Skin Software
800 St. Mary's St., Suite 100
Raleigh, NC 27605-1457
(919) 832-4124
http://www3.catalogue.com/alienskin

DeBabelizer

Equilibrium
3 Harbor Drive, Ste. 111
Sausalito, CA 94965
(415) 332-4343
http://www.equilibrium.com

Fast Eddie (Mac shareware)

LizardTech
(206) 320-9969
http://www.lizardtech.com

Fractal Design Painter

Fractal Design Corporation
P.O. Box 66959
Scotts Valley, CA 95067-6959
(408) 430-4000
(800) 846-0111
http://www.fractal.com

Hijaak Pro

Quarterdeck Corp.
13160 Mindanao Way, Suite 300
Marina Del Rey, CA 90292
(310) 309-3700
(800) 683-6696
http://www.quarterdeck.com

Kai's Power Tools

MetaTools Inc.
6303 Carpinteria Avenue
Carpinteria, CA 93013
(805) 566-6200
http://www.metatools.com/kpt
MetaSales@aol.com

MeshPaint 3D

Positron Publishing
http://www.3dgraphics.com/meshpaint.html
positron@radiks.net

Photoshop Premiere

Adobe Systems
P.O. Box 6458
Salinas, CA 93912-6458
(800) 833-6687
http://www.adobe.com

Pyromania! and Pyromania2

Visual Concept Entertainment (VCE)
PO Box 921226
Sylmar, CA 91392-1226
(800) 242-9627
(818) 367-9187

StudioPaint 3D

Alias/Wavefront An SGI Company
555 Twin Dolphin Drive, Suite 160
Redwood City, CA 94065
(415) 596-7000
http://www.alias.com

Taarna 3D Paint (renamed Flesh)

Discreet Logic
5505, boul. St-Laurent
Montreal, Quebec, Canada H2T 1S6
(514) 272-0525
http://www.discreet.com
product_info@discreet.com

Terrazzo

XAOS Software
55 Hawthorn, Suite 1000
San Francisco, CA 94105
(800) BUY-XAOS
http://www.xaostools.com

IPAS Boutique plug-ins

The Yost Group
(Contact an authorized Autodesk reseller)

Image and Mesh Library Publishers

Contact information for image and mesh library publishers is provided in the following list, organized by product name. Be sure to check out their Web sites for the latest information, samples, and demo versions.

Acuris

931 Hamilton Avenue
Menlo Park, CA 94025
(415) 329-1920
3dmodels@acuris.com

ArtBeats

ArtBeats Software
PO Box 79
Myrtle Creek, OR 97457
(503) 863-4429
Applelink: ARTBEATS

Imagetects

7 West 41st Avenue, Suite 415
San Mateo, CA 94403
(408) 252-5487
http://www.techexpo.com/firms/imagtect.html
imagetects@aol.com

Viewpoint Datasets

Viewpoint DataLabs Intl.
625 South State Street
Orem, UT 84058
(800) DATASET
http://www.viewpoint.com

Wraptures

Thought I Could
107 University Place, Suite 4D
New York, NY 10003
(212) 673-9724
75056.1733@compuserve.com

Zygote

Zygote Media Group
3344 Oak Cliff Drive
Salt Lake City, UT 84124
(801) 278-5934
dan@zygote.com

Other Software Products

A short list of other software products mentioned in the text.

Seize the Day

(No information available)

Sinkha

Mohave
2 West St. George Blvd, Ancestor Square
St. George, UT 84770
(801) 652-5300
http://www.sinkha.com

Hardware Manufacturers

Contact information for selected hardware manufacturers is provided in the following list, organized by product name. Be sure to check out their Web sites for the latest information.

Ascension Technology Corp.

P.O. Box 527
Burlington, VT 05402
(802) 860-6440
http://www.ascension-tech.com

Logitech Mice/Trackballs

Logitech Inc.
6505 Kaiser Drive
Fremont, CA 94555
(510) 795-8500
http://www.logitech.com

Microtek Scanners

Microtek
(800) 654-4160
(310) 297-5000
http://www.mteklab.com

SCSI Sentry

APS Technologies
6131 Deramus
PO Box 4987
Kansas City, MO 64120-0087
(800) 862-6805
(816) 483-1600
http://www.apstech.com
sales@apstech.com

SupraModems

Supra (now merged into Diamond Multimedia)
Diamond Communications Division
312 SE Stonemill Drive, Suite 150
Vancouver, WA 98684
(800) 4-MULTIMEDIA
(360) 604-1400
http://www.diamondmm.com

Powercell Backup Power Systems

American Power Conversion (APC)
132 Fairgrounds Road
PO Box 278
West Kingston, RI 02892
(800) 800-4272
(401) 789-5735
http://www.apcc.com

Spaceballs

Spacetec IMC Corporation
The Boot Mills
100 Foot of John St.
Lowell, MA 01852
(508) 970-0330
http://web.spacetec.com

Speakers

Yamaha Electronics Corp.
6600 Orangethorpe Avenue
Buena Park, CA 90620
(800) 4-YAMAHA
(714) 522-9105
http://www.yamaha.com
info@yamaha.com

Wacom Graphics Tablets

Wacom Technology Corp.
501 SE Columbia Shores Blvd., Suite 300
Vancouver, WA 98661
(206)750-8882
http://www.wacom.com
sales@wacom.com

ZIP and JAZ Drives

Iomega Corporation
1821 West Iomega Way
Roy, UT 84067
(800) MY STUFF
http://www.iomega.com

Appendix E

Image Contributors

Activision
11601 Wilshire Blvd.
Los Angeles, CA 90025
(310) 473-9200
http://www.activision.com

Alias|Wavefront
530 East Montecito Street
Santa Barbara, CA
(805) 962-8117
http://www.alias.com
-or-
110 Richmond Street East
Toronto, ON CANADA M5C 1P1
(416) 362-9181
http://www.alias.com

AniMagicians
Aaron Shi
asamagic@aol.com
http://www.amagic-inc.com
Artists: 3D Studio R4/MAX

Alvise Avati
Senior Animator,
Immagini Interactive
Rome, Italy
mc1827@mclink.it
http://www.alvise.com

Mike Beals
bacasino@earthlink.net
http://home.earthlink.net/
~bacasino
Artist: LightWave

Mike Caputo
(718) 356-5380
mcaputo@panix.com
http://www.panix.com/
~mcaputo
Artist: Animation Master,
cel animator

Stephen Chan
Chanime Interactive
10381 Alpine Drive, Suite B
Cupertino, CA 95014
(408) 732-9728
schan@chanime.com
http://www.chanime.com
Artist: Animation Master

Digital Illusion
Ruieta Da Silva and
Deanan Da Silva
(510) 547-0286
delusion@delusion.com
http://www.delusion.com
Artists: Alias/Wavefront,
CyberWare scanning services

Foundation Imaging
(805) 257-0292

Richard Green
ArtBot
green@artbot.com
Artist: 3D Studio R4/MAX

Laura Hainke
CyberDog Studios
(415) 522-1735
cyberdogst@aol.com
Artist: 3D Studio R4, Photoshop,
Fractal Painter

James C. Hill
Cactus Valley Software
80 West Bowery Street,
Suite 300B
Akron, OH 44308
asitter831@aol.com

Kinetix
642 Harrison Street
San Francisco, CA 94107
(415) 547-2000
http://www.kinetix.com

Simon Knights
SK Computer Graphics
San Francisco, CA
(415) 695-0506
76535.1775 @compuserve.com
Artist: 3D Studio R4/MAX, Com-
puter graphics instruction

Joan Lindblad
Bio Gärdet
Hangövägen 25
S-115 74 Stockholm, Sweden
+46 8 562 090 80

joan.l@biogardet.se
Artist: Alias/Wavefront Studio

LucasArts
PO Box 10307
San Rafael, CA 94912
(415) 721-3300
lucasarts3@aol.com
http://www.lucasarts.com

Marina Luderer
473-1/2 Sanchez
San Francisco, CA 94114
(415) 487-9114
Artist: 3D Studio R4, Infini-D,
Photoshop

James Mahan
San Francisco, CA
mayhem@sirius.com
www.sirius.com/~mayhem
Digital painting specialist,
instructor for 3D/multimedia

Andrew McNab
Great Britain
amcnab@ibm.net

Mohave
2 West St. George Blvd,
Ancestor Square
St. George, UT 84770
(801) 652-5300
http://www.mogames.com

Mondo Media/Mechadeus
135 Mississippi, 3rd Floor
San Francisco, CA 94107
(415) 865-2700
http://www.mechadeus.com

Mplayer (Mpath Interactive)
10455-A Bandley Drive
Cupertino, CA 95014
(408) 342-9932
http://www.mpath.com

**National Center for
Atmospheric Research**
P.O. Box 3000
1850 Table Mesa Drive
Boulder, CO 80307-3000
(303) 497-1000
http://www.ncar.ucar.edu

OnLive! Technologies
10131 Bubb Road
Cupertino, California 95014
http://www.onlive.com

Andrew M. Phelps
aphelp@bgnet.bgsu.edu
http://www.bgsu.edu/~aphelp
*Artist: Alias/Wavefront,
3D Studio R4/MAX*

Vadim Pietrzynski
Schillerstr. 102
72458 Albstadt
Germany
+49-(0)7431-590057 v
+49-(0)7431-52837 f
100605.1207@compuserve.com
Artist: 3D Studio R4/MAX

Pixar
1001 W. Cutting Blvd.
Richmond, CA 94804 USA
(510) 236-4000
http://www.pixar.com

John P. Roberts
302 Montrose Court
Franklin, TN 37069
(615) 790-4232
jphillipr@aol.com
http://members.aol.com/
JPRcgrafx/jport.htm
*Artist: LightWave, Photoshop,
Fractal Painter*

Sense8
100 Shoreline Highway, Suite 282
Mill Valley, CA 94941
(415) 289-2960
http://www.sense8.com

Sierra On-line
3380 - 146th Place SE, Suite 300
Bellevue, WA, 98007
http://www.sierra.com

Strata, Inc.
2 West St. George Blvd.
St. George, Utah 84770
(800) STRATAFX
(801) 628-5218
Applelink: D2022
http://www.strata3d.com

TruFlite
Martin D. Adamiker
Kapellenweg 14
A-5082 Groedig, Austria
martin.adamiker@siemens.at
-or-
100703.1773@compuserve.com
(Tony Kehlhofer)
http://www.truflite.com

Virgin Interactive Entertainment
18061 Fitch Ave
Irvine, CA 92714
(714) 833-8710
http://www.vie.com

Virtual Views
Turin, Italy
http://www.sinkha.com

Westwood Studios
2400 N. Tenaya Way
Las Vegas, NV 89128
http://www.westwood.com

Oliver Zeller
PCROliver@aol.com
http://users.aol.com/pcroliver
Artist: trueSpace, Photopaint, Photoshop

Index

Symbols

A

O

OAVs (Original Animation
Videos), 401
objects
  3D graphics, 102-103
    cameras, 112-113
    converting 2D shapes, 143-149
  animation
    bones deformation, 344-346
    deformation grids, 347-348
    forward and inverse kinematics,
      343-344
    morphing, 346-347
    particle systems, 348-349
    procedural motion, 349-350
  chaining, 340
  character animation, 350-354
    body language, 350-352
    motion capture, 352-354
    motion libraries, 354
    rotoscoping, 352
  duplicating, 158-160
    arrays, 159-160
    copying and instancing, 158-159
  grouping, 132-133
  instanced, adjusting, 180
  linking, 340
  naming, modeling, 121-123
  sculpting (face extrusions), 201-202
occupations, 26-31
  animators, 29
  career paths, 419-423
    building interview identities,
      427-436
    independent contract work, 421-423
    interviews, 426-427, 436-440
    job markets, 423
    negotiating, 440-443
    researching companies, 423-426
    working for companies, 420-421
  designers, 27
  gathering more information, 32-36
    books and periodicals, 36

    internships, 33
    learning on your own, 32-33
    schools, 33-34
    seminars, shows, and organizations,
      34-35
  mappers, 28
  modelers, 27
  producer/director, 26
  production assistants, 30
  programmers, 30-31
  working conditions, 31-32
omni (omni-directional) lighting
  sources, 112, 292
OnLive! Technologies (Web site), 513
opacity
  defined, 459
  map channels, 242
  mapping tutorial, 284-285
  surface attributes, 235-237
open lathes, creating, 167
open sweeps, 146, 170-171
operands, 459
  Boolean operations, 198
optical media, 63-64
  CD-ROM Recordable (CD-R)
    drives, 63
  Digital Versatile Disc (DVD), 64
  magneto-optical drives (MO), 63
optical tracking (defined), 459
optimization, 85-90
  memory and bootup, 86
optimized palette (defined), 460
organic forms (modeling), 203-207
  mesh blending, 206-207
  Metaballs, 205
  skinning, 204-205
organizations, 479
Original Animation Videos, *see* OAVs
Original Video Animation, *see* OVAs
orthographic projection (defined), 460
orthographic views (cameras), 315-316
output (rendering), 383-391
  calibration, 385

primitive (defined), 461

primitives, 149-150

printers, 74-75

prints
portfolio formats, 432
rendering output options, 384

procedural materials mapping
tutorial, 277

procedural motion (animation),
349-350

procedural texture (defined), 461

procedurals (texture mapping),
244-245

producer/director (occupations), 26

production assistants (occupations), 30

programmers (occupations), 30-31

projection mapping
(lighting controls), 299-300

publishers (software)
2D software, 504-507
3D software, 501-504
3D/EYE, Inc., 504
Acuris, 507-508
Adobe Systems, 504-507
Alias|Wavefront, 502, 506-507
Alien Skin Software, 505-507
ArtBeats Software, 507-508
Autodesk Inc., 505-507
auto◆des◆sys inc., 503-504
Caligari Corp., 504
Discreet Logic, 506-507
Equilibrium, 505-507
Fractal Design Corporation,
505-507
HASH, Inc., 502-504
image and mesh libraries, 507-508
Imagetects, 507-508
Interactive Effects, 504-507
Kinetix (A Division of Autodesk,
Inc.), 501-504
LizardTech, 505-507
Macromedia, 502-504
MetaTools Inc., 506-507
Microsoft Corp., 504

NewTek, 503-504
Pixar Animation Studios, 503-504
Positron Publishing, 506-507
Quarterdeck Corp., 505-507
Robert McNeel & Associates,
503-504
Specular International, 503-504
Viewpoint Datasets, 507-508
Visual Concept Entertainment
(VCE), 506-507
Wraptures, 508
XAOS Software, 507
Yonowat Inc., 502-504
Zygote, 508

Pyromania! CD-ROMs, adding video
(texture mapping), 271-272

Q

QIC (Quarter Inch Tape), 64

QT (QuickTime) image file format, 387

quad (defined), 462

Quarterdeck Corp. (Web site), 505

R

radiosity (defined), 462

radius edges (meshes), 192-193

RAID (Redundant Array of Inexpensive
Disks) (hard drives), 61

Ray Dream Designer, 255

Ray Dream Studio (Fractal Design),
497-498

ray tracing
defined, 462
rendering, 48-49

ray-traced shadows, 297

read/write heads (hard drives), 59

recordable CD-ROM drives, 433

Reduced Instruction Set Computer, *see*
RISC

Redundant Array of Inexpensive Disks,
see RAID

references
books
animated filmmaking, 471-472

X-Z

MACMILLAN COMPUTER PUBLISHING USA

A VIACOM COMPANY

Support:

If you cannot get the CD/Disk to install properly, or you need assistance with a particular situation in the book, please feel free to check out the Knowledge Base on our Web site at **http://www.superlibrary.com/general/support**. We have answers to our most Frequently Asked Questions listed there. If you do not find your specific question answered, please contact Macmillan Technical Support at **(317) 581-3833**. We can also be reached by email at **support@mcp.com**.